GACE

EARLY CHILDHOOD EDUCATION
001, 002

By: Sharon Wynne, M.S.

XAMonline, INC.
Boston

To obtain permission(s) to use the material from this work for any purpose including workshops or seminars, please submit a written request to:

XAMonline, Inc.
25 First Street, Suite 106
Cambridge, MA 02141
Toll Free 1-800-509-4128
Email: info@xamonline.com
Web: www.xamonline.com
Fax: 1-617-583-5552

Library of Congress Cataloging-in-Publication Data

Wynne, Sharon A.
   GACE Early Childhood Education 001, 002 / Sharon A. Wynne. 3rd ed
   ISBN 978-1-60787-064-7
   1. Early Childhood Education 001, 002
   2. Study Guides
   3. GACE
   4. Teachers' Certification & Licensure
   5. Careers

Disclaimer:

The opinions expressed in this publication are the sole works of XAMonline and were created independently from the National Education Association, Educational Testing Service, or any State Department of Education, National Evaluation Systems or other testing affiliates.

Between the time of publication and printing, state specific standards as well as testing formats and Web site information may change and therefore would not be included in part or in whole within this product. Sample test questions are developed by XAMonline and reflect content similar to that on real tests; however, they are not former test questions. XAMonline assembles content that aligns with state standards but makes no claims nor guarantees teacher candidates a passing score. Numerical scores are determined by testing companies such as NES or ETS and then are compared with individual state standards. A passing score varies from state to state.

Printed in the United States of America   œ-1

GACE Early Childhood Education 001, 002
ISBN: 978-1-60787-064-7

Table of Contents

COMPETENCY 4
UNDERSTAND READING FLUENCY AND COMPREHENSION ACROSS THE CURRICULUM

COMPETENCY 5
UNDERSTAND COMPREHENSION STRATEGIES FOR LITERARY AND INFORMATIONAL TEXTS ACROSS THE CURRICULUM

COMPETENCY 6
UNDERSTAND SKILLS AND STRATEGIES INVOLVED IN WRITING FOR VARIOUS PURPOSES ACROSS THE CURRICULUM

DOMAIN III

COMPETENCY 23
UNDERSTAND BASIC PHYSICAL EDUCATION PRINCIPLES, PRACTICES, AND ACTIVITIES...................... 416

COMPETENCY 24
UNDERSTAND BASIC ELEMENTS, CONCEPTS, AND TECHNIQUES ASSOCIATED WITH THE ARTS 437

SAMPLE TEST

GACE
EARLY CHILDHOOD
EDUCATION 001, 002

SECTION 1
ABOUT XAMONLINE

XAMonline—A Specialty Teacher Certification Company

Created in 1996, XAMonline was the first company to publish study guides for state-specific teacher certification examinations. Founder Sharon Wynne found it frustrating that materials were not available for teacher certification preparation and decided to create the first single, state-specific guide. XAMonline has grown into a company of over 1,800 contributors and writers and offers over 300 titles for the entire PRAXIS series and every state examination. No matter what state you plan on teaching in, XAMonline has a unique teacher certification study guide just for you.

XAMonline—Value and Innovation

We are committed to providing value and innovation. Our print-on-demand technology allows us to be the first in the market to reflect changes in test standards and user feedback as they occur. Our guides are written by experienced teachers who are experts in their fields. And our content reflects the highest standards of quality. Comprehensive practice tests with varied levels of rigor means that your study experience will closely match the actual in-test experience.

To date, XAMonline has helped nearly 600,000 teachers pass their certification or licensing exams. Our commitment to preparation exceeds simply providing the proper material for study—it extends to helping teachers **gain mastery** of the subject matter, giving them the **tools** to become the most effective classroom leaders possible, and ushering today's students toward a **successful future**.

SECTION 2
ABOUT THIS STUDY GUIDE

Purpose of This Guide

Is there a little voice inside of you saying, "Am I ready?" Our goal is to replace that little voice and remove all doubt with a new voice that says, "I AM READY. **Bring it on!**" by offering the highest quality of teacher certification study guides.

Organization of Content

You will see that while every test may start with overlapping general topics, each is very unique in the skills they wish to test. Only XAMonline presents custom content that analyzes deeper than a title, a subarea, or an objective. Only XAMonline presents content and sample test assessments along with **focus statements**, the deepest-level rationale and interpretation of the skills that are unique to the exam.

Title and field number of test

→Each exam has its own name and number. XAMonline's guides are written to give you the content you need to know for the specific exam you are taking. You can be confident when you buy our guide that it contains the information you need to study for the specific test you are taking.

Subareas

→These are the major content categories found on the exam. XAMonline's guides are written to cover all of the subareas found in the test frameworks developed for the exam.

Objectives

→These are standards that are unique to the exam and represent the main subcategories of the subareas/content categories. XAMonline's guides are written to address every specific objective required to pass the exam.

Focus statements

→These are examples and interpretations of the objectives. You find them in parenthesis directly following the objective. They provide detailed examples of the range, type, and level of content that appear on the test questions. **Only XAMonline's guides drill down to this level.**

How Do We Compare with Our Competitors?

XAMonline—drills down to the focus statement level.
CliffsNotes and REA—organized at the objective level
Kaplan—provides only links to content
MoMedia—content not specific to the state test

Each subarea is divided into manageable sections that cover the specific skill areas. Explanations are easy to understand and thorough. You'll find that every test answer contains a rejoinder so if you need a refresher or further review after taking the test, you'll know exactly to which section you must return.

How to Use This Book

Our informal polls show that most people begin studying up to eight weeks prior to the test date, so start early. Then ask yourself some questions: How much do you really know? Are you coming to the test straight from your teacher-education program or are you having to review subjects you haven't considered in ten years? Either way, take a **diagnostic or assessment test** first. Also, spend time on sample tests so that you become accustomed to the way the actual test will appear.

This guide comes with an online diagnostic test of 30 questions found online at *www.XAMonline.com*. It is a little boot camp to get you up for the task and reveal things about your compendium of knowledge in general. Although this guide is structured to follow the order of the test, you are not required to study in that order. By finding a time-management and study plan that fits your life you will be more effective. The results of your diagnostic or self-assessment test can be a guide for how to manage your time and point you toward an area that needs more attention.

After taking the diagnostic exam, fill out the **Personalized Study Plan** page at the beginning of each chapter. Review the competencies and skills covered in that chapter and check the boxes that apply to your study needs. If there are sections you already know you can skip, check the "skip it" box. Taking this step will give you a study plan for each chapter.

Week	Activity
8 weeks prior to test	Take a diagnostic test found at www.XAMonline.com
7 weeks prior to test	Build your Personalized Study Plan for each chapter. Check the "skip it" box for sections you feel you are already strong in. ✗ SKIP IT ☐
6-3 weeks prior to test	For each of these four weeks, choose a content area to study. You don't have to go in the order of the book. It may be that you start with the content that needs the most review. Alternately, you may want to ease yourself into plan by starting with the most familiar material.
2 weeks prior to test	Take the sample test, score it, and create a review plan for the final week before the test.
1 week prior to test	Following your plan (which will likely be aligned with the areas that need the most review) go back and study the sections that align with the questions you may have gotten wrong. Then go back and study the sections related to the questions you answered correctly. If need be, create flashcards and drill yourself on any area that makes you anxious.

SECTION 3
ABOUT THE GACE EXAMS

What Is GACE?

GACE (Georgia Assessments for the Certification of Educators) tests measure the knowledge of specific content areas in K-12 education. The tests are a way of insuring that educators are prepared to not only teach in a particular subject area, but also have the necessary teaching skills to be effective. The Evaluation Systems group of Pearson Education, Inc. administers the tests and has worked with the Georgia Professional Standards Commission to develop the material so that it is appropriate for Georgia standards.

The most reliable source of information regarding GACE tests is either the Georgia state Department of Education or *www.gace.nesinc.com*. Either resource should also have a complete list of testing centers and dates. Test dates vary by subject area and not all test dates necessarily include your particular test, so be sure to check carefully.

If you are in a teacher-education program, check with the Education Department or the Certification Officer for specific information for testing and testing time-lines. The Certification Office should have most of the information you need.

If you choose an alternative route to certification you can either rely on our website at *www.XAMonline.com* or on the resources provided by an alternative certification program. Many states now have specific agencies devoted to alternative certification and there are some national organizations as well:

National Center for Education Information

http://www.ncei.com/Alt-Teacher-Cert.htm

National Associate for Alternative Certification

http://www.alt-teachercert.org/index.asp

Interpreting Test Results

The results of all GACE tests are reported as scaled scores rather than raw scores. The number of scorable questions that are answered correctly in the selected-response section are combined with the scores from the constructed-response section and the total is converted to a scale of 100-300 with 220 representing a passing score. Follow the guidelines provided by Pearson for interpreting your score.

What's on the Test?

GACE tests vary from subject to subject and sometimes even within subject area. For GACE Early Childhood Education (001, 002), the assessment consists of two tests with a combined total of approximately 120 multiple-choice questions and 4 constructed-response questions. The breakdown of the questions is as follows:

Category	Approximate Number of Selected-Response Questions	Approximate Number of Constructed-Response Questions
001:		
I: Reading and English Language Arts	40	1
II: Social Studies	20	1
002:		
III: Mathematics	25	1
IV: Science	20	1
V: Health, Physical Education, and the Arts	15	0

Question Types

You're probably thinking, enough already, I want to study! Indulge us a little longer while we explain that there is actually more than one type of multiple-choice question. You can thank us later after you realize how well prepared you are for your exam.

1. **Complete the Statement.** The name says it all. In this question type you'll be asked to choose the correct completion of a given statement. For example:

> **The Dolch Basic Sight Words consist of a relatively short list of words that children should be able to:**
>
> A. Sound out
>
> B. Know the meaning of
>
> C. Recognize on sight
>
> D. Use in a sentence

The correct answer is C. In order to check your answer, test out the statement by adding the choices to the end of it.

Which of the Following. One way to test your answer choice for this type of question is to replace the phrase "which of the following" with your selection. Use this example:

> **Which of the following words is one of the twelve most frequently used in children's reading texts:**
>
> A. There
>
> B. This
>
> C. The
>
> D. An

Don't look! Test your answer. _____ is one of the twelve most frequently used in children's reading texts. Did you guess C? Then you guessed correctly.

5. Roman Numeral Choices. This question type is used when there is more than one possible correct answer. For example:

> **Which of the following two arguments accurately supports the use of cooperative learning as an effective method of instruction?**
>
> I. Cooperative learning groups facilitate healthy competition between individuals in the group.
>
> II. Cooperative learning groups allow academic achievers to carry or cover for academic underachievers.
>
> III. Cooperative learning groups make each student in the group accountable for the success of the group.
>
> IV. Cooperative learning groups make it possible for students to reward other group members for achieving.
>
> A. I and II
>
> B. II and III
>
> C. I and III
>
> D. III and IV

Notice that the question states there are **two** possible answers. It's best to read all the possibilities first before looking at the answer choices. In this case, the correct answer is D.

3. **Negative Questions.** This type of question contains words such as "not," "least," and "except." Each correct answer will be the statement that does **not** fit the situation described in the question. Such as:

> **Multicultural education is not**
>
> A. An idea or concept
>
> B. A "tack-on" to the school curriculum
>
> C. An educational reform movement
>
> D. A process

Think to yourself that the statement could be anything but the correct answer. This question form is more open to interpretation than other types, so read carefully and don't forget that you're answering a negative statement.

4. **Questions that Include Graphs, Tables, or Reading Passages.** As always, read the question carefully. It likely asks for a very specific answer and not a broad interpretation of the visual. Here is a simple (though not statistically accurate) example of a graph question:

> **In the following graph in how many years did more men take the NYSTCE exam than women?**
>
>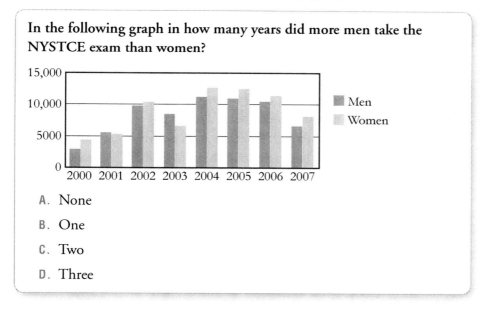
>
> A. None
>
> B. One
>
> C. Two
>
> D. Three

It may help you to simply circle the two years that answer the question. Make sure you've read the question thoroughly and once you've made your determination, double check your work. The correct answer is C.

SECTION 4
HELPFUL HINTS

Study Tips

1. You are what you eat. Certain foods aid the learning process by releasing natural memory enhancers called CCKs (cholecystokinin) composed of tryptophan, choline, and phenylalanine. All of these chemicals enhance the neurotransmitters associated with memory and certain foods release memory enhancing chemicals. A light meal or snacks of one of the following foods fall into this category:

   - Milk
   - Rice
   - Eggs
   - Fish
   - Nuts and seeds
   - Oats
   - Turkey

   The better the connections, the more you comprehend!

2. See the forest for the trees. In other words, get the concept before you look at the details. One way to do this is to take notes as you read, paraphrasing or summarizing in your own words. Putting the concept in terms that are comfortable and familiar may increase retention.

3. Question authority. Ask why, why, why? Pull apart written material paragraph by paragraph and don't forget the captions under the illustrations. For example, if a heading reads *Stream Erosion* put it in the form of a question (Why do streams erode? What is stream erosion?) then find the answer within the material. If you train your mind to think in this manner you will learn more and prepare yourself for answering test questions.

4. Play mind games. Using your brain for reading or puzzles keeps it flexible. Even with a limited amount of time your brain can take in data (much like a computer) and store it for later use. In ten minutes you can: read two paragraphs (at least), quiz yourself with flash cards, or review notes. Even if you don't fully understand something on the first pass, your mind stores it for recall, which is why frequent reading or review increases chances of retention and comprehension.

5. **The pen is mightier than the sword.** Learn to take great notes. A by-product of our modern culture is that we have grown accustomed to getting our information in short doses. We've subconsciously trained ourselves to assimilate information into neat little packages. Messy notes fragment the flow of information. Your notes can be much clearer with proper formatting. *The Cornell Method* is one such format. This method was popularized in *How to Study in College*, Ninth Edition, by Walter Pauk. You can benefit from the method without purchasing an additional book by simply looking up the method online. Below is a sample of how *The Cornell Method* can be adapted for use with this guide.

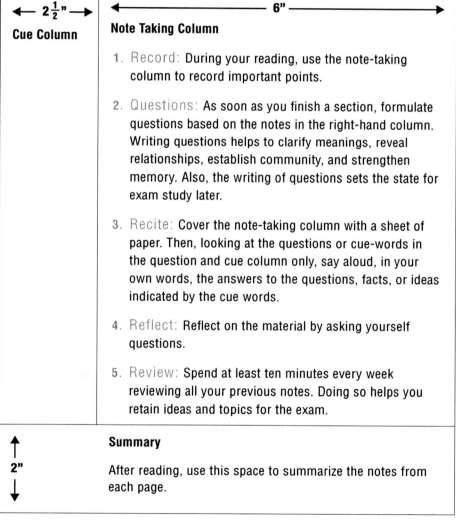

← 2½" →	← 6" →
Cue Column	**Note Taking Column**
	1. Record: During your reading, use the note-taking column to record important points.
	2. Questions: As soon as you finish a section, formulate questions based on the notes in the right-hand column. Writing questions helps to clarify meanings, reveal relationships, establish community, and strengthen memory. Also, the writing of questions sets the state for exam study later.
	3. Recite: Cover the note-taking column with a sheet of paper. Then, looking at the questions or cue-words in the question and cue column only, say aloud, in your own words, the answers to the questions, facts, or ideas indicated by the cue words.
	4. Reflect: Reflect on the material by asking yourself questions.
	5. Review: Spend at least ten minutes every week reviewing all your previous notes. Doing so helps you retain ideas and topics for the exam.
↑ 2" ↓	**Summary** After reading, use this space to summarize the notes from each page.

Adapted from How to Study in College, Ninth Edition, by Walter Pauk, ©2008 Wadsworth

6. Place yourself in exile and set the mood. Set aside a particular place and time to study that best suits your personal needs and biorhythms. If you're a night person, burn the midnight oil. If you're a morning person set yourself up with some coffee and get to it. Make your study time and place as free from distraction as possible and surround yourself with what you need, be it silence or music. Studies have shown that music can aid in concentration, absorption, and retrieval of information. Not all music, though. Classical music is said to work best

7. Get pointed in the right direction. Use arrows to point to important passages or pieces of information. It's easier to read than a page full of yellow highlights. Highlighting can be used sparingly, but add an arrow to the margin to call attention to it.

8. Check your budget. You should at least review all the content material before your test, but allocate the most amount of time to the areas that need the most refreshing. It sounds obvious, but it's easy to forget. You can use the study rubric above to balance your study budget.

> The proctor will write the start time where it can be seen and then, later, provide the time remaining, typically fifteen minutes before the end of the test.

Testing Tips

1. Get smart, play dumb. Sometimes a question is just a question. No one is out to trick you, so don't assume that the test writer is looking for something other than what was asked. Stick to the question as written and don't overanalyze.

2. Do a double take. Read test questions and answer choices at least twice because it's easy to miss something, to transpose a word or some letters. If you have no idea what the correct answer is, skip it and come back later if there's time. If you're still clueless, it's okay to guess. Remember, you're scored on the number of questions you answer correctly and you're not penalized for wrong answers. The worst case scenario is that you miss a point from a good guess.

3. Turn it on its ear. The syntax of a question can often provide a clue, so make things interesting and turn the question into a statement to see if it changes the meaning or relates better (or worse) to the answer choices.

4. Get out your magnifying glass. Look for hidden clues in the questions because it's difficult to write a multiple-choice question without giving away part of the answer in the options presented. In most questions you can readily eliminate one or two potential answers, increasing your chances of answering correctly to 50/50, which will help out if you've skipped a question and gone back to it (see tip #2).

5. Call it intuition. Often your first instinct is correct. If you've been study-ing the content you've likely absorbed something and have subconsciously retained the knowledge. On questions you're not sure about trust your instincts because a first impression is usually correct.

6. Graffiti. Sometimes it's a good idea to mark your answers directly on the test booklet and go back to fill in the optical scan sheet later. You don't get extra points for perfectly blackened ovals. If you choose to manage your test this way, be sure not to mismark your answers when you transcribe to the scan sheet.

7. Become a clock-watcher. You have a set amount of time to answer the questions. Don't get bogged down laboring over a question you're not sure about when there are ten others you could answer more readily. If you choose to follow the advice of tip #6, be sure you leave time near the end to go back and fill in the scan sheet.

Do the Drill

No matter how prepared you feel it's sometimes a good idea to apply Murphy's Law. So the following tips might seem silly, mundane, or obvious, but we're including them anyway.

1. Remember, you are what you eat, so bring a snack. Choose from the list of energizing foods that appear earlier in the introduction.

2. You're not too sexy for your test. Wear comfortable clothes. You'll be distracted if your belt is too tight or if you're too cold or too hot.

3. Lie to yourself. Even if you think you're a prompt person, pretend you're not and leave plenty of time to get to the testing center. Map it out ahead of time and do a dry run if you have to. There's no need to add road rage to your list of anxieties.

4. Bring sharp, number 2 pencils. It may seem impossible to forget this need from your school days, but you might. And make sure the erasers are intact, too.

5. No ticket, no test. Bring your admission ticket as well as **two** forms of identification, including one with a picture and signature. You will not be admitted to the test without these things.

6. You can't take it with you. Leave any study aids, dictionaries, note-books, computers, and the like at home. Certain tests **do** allow a scientific or four-function calculator, so check ahead of time to see if your test does.

7. Prepare for the desert. Any time spent on a bathroom break **cannot** be made up later, so use your judgment on the amount you eat or drink.

8. Quiet, Please! Keeping your own time is a good idea, but not with a timepiece that has a loud ticker. If you use a watch, take it off and place it nearby but not so that it distracts you. And **silence your cell phone**.

To the best of our ability, we have compiled the content you need to know in this book and in the accompanying online resources. The rest is up to you. You can use the study and testing tips or you can follow your own methods. Either way, you can be confident that there aren't any missing pieces of information and there shouldn't be any surprises in the content on the test.

If you have questions about test fees, registration, electronic testing, or other content verification issues please visit *www.gace.nesinc.com*.

Good luck!

Sharon Wynne
Founder, XAMonline

DOMAIN I
READING AND ENGLISH LANGUAGE ARTS

PERSONALIZED STUDY PLAN

PERSONALIZED STUDY PLAN

KNOWN MATERIAL/ SKIP IT

PAGE	COMPETENCY AND SKILL	
60	**5: Understand Comprehension Strategies for Literary and Informational Texts Across the Curriculum**	☐
	5.1: Recognizing types of literary and informational texts	☐
	5.2: Identifying characteristics and functions of literary elements and devices	☐
	5.3: Applying strategies for developing students' literary response skills	☐
	5.4: Demonstrating knowledge of genres, themes, authors, and works of literature written for children	☐
	5.5: Recognizing common patterns of organization in informational texts	☐
	5.6: Applying knowledge of strategies for promoting comprehension of informational texts	☐
79	**6: Understand Skills and Strategies Involved In Writing for Various Purposes Across the Curriculum**	☐
	6.1: Recognizing developmental stages of writing	☐
	6.2: Analyzing factors to consider in writing for various audiences and purposes	☐
	6.3: Demonstrating knowledge of the writing process	☐
	6.4: Applying revision strategies to improve the effectiveness of written materials	☐
	6.5: Recognizing common patterns of organization in informational texts	☐
	6.6: Demonstrating knowledge of the use of research skills and computer technology to support writing	☐
96	**7: Understand the Conventions of Standard English Grammar, Usage, and Mechanics**	☐
	7.1: Demonstrating knowledge of the parts of speech	☐
	7.2: Demonstrating knowledge of elements of appropriate grammar and usage	☐
	7.3: Demonstrating knowledge of appropriate mechanics in writing	☐
	7.4: Identifyinging appropriate corrections of errors in sentence structure	☐
	7.5: Demonstrating knowledge of various types of sentence structures	☐
116	**8: Understand Skills and Strategies Involved in Speaking, Listening, and Viewing Across the Curriculum**	☐
	8.1: Applying knowledge of conventions of one-on-one and group verbal interactions	☐
	8.2: Analyzing ways in which verbal cues and nonverbal cues affect communication	☐
	8.3: Demonstrating knowledge of strategies for promoting effective listening skills	☐
	8.4: Recognizing types, characteristics, and roles of visual and oral media	☐
	8.5: Demonstrating knowledge of oral, visual, and multimedia presentations	☐

COMPETENCY 1
UNDERSTAND CONCEPTS OF PRINT AND PHONOLOGICAL AWARENESS

SKILL 1.1 Recognizing developmental stages in learning to write and read

In 2000, the National Reading Panel released its now well-known report on teaching children to read. In a way, this report slightly put to rest the debate between phonics and whole language. It argued, essentially, that word-letter recognition was as important as understanding what the text means. The report's "big 5" critical areas of reading instruction are as follows:

- **Phonemic Awareness:** This is the acknowledgment of sounds and words (for example, a child's realization that some words rhyme). Onset and rhyme are two of the skills that might help students learn that the sound of the first letter "b" in the word *bad* can be changed with the sound "d" to make it *dad*. The key in phonemic awareness is that when you teach it to children, it can be taught with the students' eyes closed. In other words, it's all about sounds, not about ascribing written letters to sounds.

- **Phonics:** As opposed to phonemic awareness, the study of phonics must be done with the eyes open. It is the connection between the sounds and letters on a page. In other words, students who are learning phonics might see the word *bad* and sound each letter out slowly until they recognize that they just said the word.

- **Comprehension:** Comprehension simply means that the reader can ascribe meaning to text. Even though students may be good with phonics and even know what many words on a page mean, some of them are not good with comprehension because they do not know the strategies that would help them to comprehend. For example, students should know that stories often have structures (beginning, middle, and end). They should also know that when they are reading something and it does not make sense, they will need to employ "fix-up" strategies in which they reread the text look for clues. Teachers can use many strategies to teach comprehension, including questioning, asking students to paraphrase or summarize, utilizing graphic organizers, and focusing on mental images.

> In 2000, the National Reading Panel report on teaching children to read stated that word-letter recognition was as important as understanding what the text means.

- Fluency: Fluency is the ability to read in much the same manner as speaking: with fluidity and smoothness. Students who are fluent readers are more likely to be successful with comprehension, since they are less focused on individual words and more focused on what is actually being read.

- Vocabulary: Vocabulary demonstrates the strong ties between oral and written language. Students who are learning to read are just beginning to realize the link between the words they say and the words they read. Increasing vocabulary—whether by listening to others, reading to themselves, or being read to—will help students with both comprehension and fluency.

Methods used to teach these skills are often featured in a "balanced literacy" curriculum that focuses on the use of skills in various instructional contexts. For example, with independent reading, students independently choose books that are at their reading levels; with guided reading, teachers work with small groups of students to help them with their particular reading problems. With whole group reading, the entire class reads the same text, and the teacher incorporates activities to help students learn phonics, comprehension, fluency, and vocabulary. In addition to these components of balanced literacy, teachers incorporate writing so that students can learn the structures of communicating through text.

Methods used to teach reading skills are often featured in a "balanced literacy" curriculum that focuses on the use of skills in various instructional contexts.

Sample Test Question and Rationale

(Rigorous)

1. **Which of the following is not a strategy of teaching reading comprehension?**

   A. Asking questions

   B. Utilizing graphic organizers

   C. Focusing on mental images

   D. Manipulating sounds

Answer: D. Manipulating sounds

Comprehension simply means that the reader can ascribe meaning to text. Teachers can use many strategies to teach comprehension, including questioning, asking students to paraphrase or summarize, utilizing graphic organizers, and focusing on mental images.

Demonstrating knowledge of characteristics and purposes of printed information and developmentally appropriate strategies for promoting students' familiarity with concepts of print

Development of the Understanding that Print Carries Meaning

This understanding is demonstrated every day in the elementary classroom when a teacher holds up a book to read it aloud to the class. The teacher is explicitly and deliberately thinking about how to hold the book, how to focus the class on looking at its cover, where to start reading, and in what direction to begin.

Even in writing the morning message on the board, the teacher is targeting the children by placing the message at its proper place at the top of the board and following it by additional activities and a schedule for the rest of the day.

When the teacher challenges children to make posters of items that begin with a single letter by using the items in the classroom, their home, or their general knowledge base, the children are making concrete the understanding that print carries meaning.

Strategies for Promoting Awareness of the Relationship Between Spoken and Written Language

- Put up a chart on which to write what the children are saying.

- Highlight and celebrate the meanings and uses of print products found in the classroom. These products include posters, labels, yellow sticky pad notes, labels on shelves and lockers, calendars, classroom rules, and directions.

- Make it a point to read big-print and oversized books to teach print conventions such as directionality.

- Practice the steps for reading to others (for K-2): how to hold the book, how to turn the pages, how to find the tops and bottoms of pages, and how to tell the difference between the front and back covers of a book.

- Search and discuss adventures in word awareness and close observation through which children are challenged to identify and talk about the length, appearance, boundaries of specific words, and the letters that comprise them.

- Have children match oral words to printed words by forming an echo chorus (where children echo the reading) as the teacher reads the story aloud. This often works best with poetry or rhymes.

- Have the children combine, manipulate, switch, and move letters to change words and spelling patterns.
- Work with letter cards to create messages and respond to the messages that they create.

The Role of Environmental Print in Developing Print Awareness

An environmental print book can be created for the children. The teacher can do this first—for example, creating a collage of the labels from the children's favorite lunch or breakfast foods. The teacher can then ask the students to bring in their own labels and alphabetically arrange them in the book. During the year, the students can cut out symbols and logos from additional sources of environmental print and place them in the book.

What is particularly effective in using environmental print is that it immediately transports the child from an ELL background into print awareness through the familiarity of commercial logos and packaging symbols used on a daily basis.

Newspapers are excellent sources of environmental print that are available every day. With food ads, clothing ads, and other child-centered products and personalities, newspapers are great for developing print awareness. Supermarket circulars and coupons distributed in chain drug stores are also excellent for engaging children in using environmental print as a reading device.

Development of Book Handling Skills

Have the children identify the front cover, the back cover, and the title page of a specific book. Model storytelling by holding the book so that the members of the audience can see the illustrations shown to them. Then have them demonstrate the skills for their peers.

Have children search through the class libraries for special features on the fronts or backs of books as they help return the books to their bins. Have the children display and talk about the special symbols they found.

Review with the children, in an age- and grade-appropriate format, additional parts of the book as they emerge through the minilessons and read-alouds. These additional parts of the book can include the title page, dedication page, foreword, appendix, credits, copyright date, table of contents, and so on.

Techniques for Promoting the Ability to Track Print in Connected Texts

Model directionality and one-to-one word matching by pointing to words while using a big book, a pocket chart, or a poem written out on a chart. As you repeatedly lead the children in this reading, they can follow along and eventually track the print and independently make one-to-one matches on the connected text. They can also practice by using their fingers to follow the words or a pointer, which children love doing because the fun of using the pointer becomes associated with reading. In general, children will happily vie to be the "point" person.

Copy a brief, familiar rhyme (perhaps from a favorite book or song) on a poster and hang it in the room at a child's eye level so the children can independently walk around and read it. Write a brief or familiar rhyme or a poem on individual word cards. You can challenge the children in small groups or independently to reassemble and display them on a pocket chart. As children "play" with constructing and reconstructing this pocket chart, they will develop an awareness of directionality, one-on-one matching of print to spoken word s, spacing, and punctuation.

Model interactive emergent writing with the class. While discussing and writing about the weather, deliberately ask and have the children suggest where the first word in that report should go.

- Should it go at the top or the bottom of the felt board?

- Will the first letter be uppercase or lowercase?

- What goes at the end of the sentence?

Create with the children rhythmic repetitions and rules for using capital letters, punctuation, and so on. Encourage the children to recite these phrases as soon as they see specific concepts of print in connected texts.

Model for children how when they are pointing at words, they can start at the top and move from left to right. Tell the children that when a sentence has more words after the first line of print, they should go back to the left and under the previous line. Young children enjoy practicing this kinesthetic "return sweep." You might want to teach them to identify the need to do this by saying, "Don't fall asleep at the page" or "It's time to get to the 'return sweep' stage!" Post this saying and encourage them to chant the phrase as they joyously take ownership of their reading.

Let beginning readers "read" through the text to find letters they recognize. Share some of the text that includes these specific letters to whet their appetite for more reading.

Strategies for Promoting Letter Knowledge and Letter Formation

Engage the children in a "Tale Trail" game. Use a story they have already heard or read. Ask the children to circle certain letters and then reread the story, sharing the letters they have circled. Give the children plenty of opportunities to do letter sorts. Pass out word cards that have the targeted letter on them. Ask the children to come up and display their answers to questions about the letter. As an example, consider the letter "R."

- *R* as the first letter—*rose, rise, ran*
- *R* as the last letter—*car, star, far*
- *R* with a "*t*" after it—*start, heart, part, smart*
- Two *R*s in the middle of a word—*carry, sorry, starry*

Play "What's in a Name?" Select a student's name—for example, William. Write the name on a sentence strip. Have the children count the number of letters in the name and how many of the letters appear twice. Allow them to talk about which letter is upper case and which letters are lower case. Have the students chant the name. Then rewrite the name on another sentence strip. Have the strip cut into separate letters and see if someone from the class can put the name back together correctly.

As you read a book along with or to the children, ask them to show you specific letters or lowercase or uppercase letters. Read the text first, and encourage as many children as possible to come up and identify the letters. Use a big book and have felt letters available for display as well. If this exercise is grade-, age-, and developmentally appropriate, have the children write the letter they identified themselves. (For even more fun, make the letter out of pipe cleaners, craft sticks, or colored markers, using different colors for upper- and lowercase letters.)

Play "Letter Leap" with the children, and have them look carefully at the room to identify labeled items that begin with a specific letter by "leaping" over to them and placing a large lettered placard next to them. Children who have advanced in letter formation can then be challenged to "leap" through the classroom when called upon to literally "letter" unlabeled objects.

Use of Reading and Writing Strategies for Teaching Letter-Sound Correspondence

Provide children with a sample of a single letter book (or create one from environmental sources, newspapers, coupons, circulars, magazines, or your own text ideas). Make sure that your selected or created sample includes a printed version of the letter in both upper- and lowercase forms. Make certain that each page contains a picture of something that starts with that specific letter and also has the word for the picture. The book that you select or create should be a predictable one in that when the picture is identified, the word can be read.

Once you have given the children your sample and have read it aloud to them, have them make their own single-letter book. It is often best to focus on familiar consonants or the first letter of the child's first name. Using the first letter of the child's name encourages them to create a book that tells something about themselves and the words they find. This is an excellent way for the reading workshop aspect of teaching alphabetic principles to complement and enhance the writing workshop.

Encourage children to be active writers and readers by finding words for their book on the classroom word wall, in alphabet books in the special alphabet book bin, and in grade- and age-appropriate pictionaries (dictionaries for younger children that are filled with pictures).

Of course, the richest resource in the reading and writing workshop classroom for teaching and fostering the alphabetic principle is using alphabet books as anchor books for inspiring students' writing. While young children in grades K–1 will do better with the single-letter book authoring activity, children in grades two and beyond can truly be inspired and motivated by alphabet books that enhance their own reading, writing, and alphabetic skills. Furthermore, using these books—which have and are being produced in a variety of formats to enhance social studies, science, and mathematical themes—gives even young children the opportunity to create a meaningful product that authenticates their content study while enhancing alphabetic skills and, of course, print awareness.

An annotated bibliography of some of the newest alphabet books has been provided in the bibliography section of this guide. It was limited by space considerations, but educators can catch up on the latest titles and identify those that are most appropriate for their grades by visiting a bookstore. Consider selecting an alphabet book that has a particularly inviting concept, art style, or adaptable format within the children's capacity to use as a model.

For example, author Tana Hoban uses actual color photographs of letters in her *26 Letters and 99 Cents*. Children may want to make clay letters or create letter sculptures that develop their own "in style of" alphabet book similar to Hoban's. If nutrition is the science topic, children might want to examine Lois Ehlert's very accessible *Eating the Alphabet: Fruits and Vegetables from A to Z*. This, combined with an examination of the fruits and vegetables in a local store (perhaps a pleasant walk from the school and a quick break from the routine local outing), can yield a wonderful alphabet book on fruits and vegetables that can also include fruits and vegetables eaten in various cultures (e.g., mangos, plantains, jicama, etc.).

The alphabet book can also offer the class a chance to work collaboratively within a template created by the teacher. Completion of this collaborative work can be

> *Encourage children to be active writers and readers by finding words for their single-letter books on the classroom word wall, in alphabet books in the special alphabet book bin, and in grade- and age-appropriate pictionaries.*

shared with peers in another class and with parents. It can also be kept as a model for the following year's class (of course, with the recognition and acceptance of the authors!).

> ### SKILL 1.3 Demonstrating knowledge of phonological awareness (i.e., awareness that oral language includes units such as spoken words and syllables)

PHONICS: method for teaching students to read, which relies on studying the rules and patterns found in language

PHONICS is a widely used method for teaching students to read. This method includes studying the rules and patterns found in language. By age five or six, children can typically begin to use phonics to begin to understand the connections between letters, their patterns, vowel sounds (e.g., short vowels or long vowels), and the collective sounds they all make.

The study of phonics is one that involves sound as well as sight. It is defined by the connection between hearing the sounds and seeing the letters on a page. In the beginning stages of phonics, students may use sight to see the word cat, but they use sound to break the word down to its letter components. It may require slowly speaking each letter before the students recognize that they actually said the word.

PHONOLOGICAL AWARENESS: the ability of the reader to recognize the sound of spoken language

PHONOLOGICAL AWARENESS means the ability of the reader to recognize the sound of spoken language. This recognition includes how these sounds can be blended together, segmented (divided up), and manipulated (switched around). This awareness then leads to phonics, a method for teaching children to read. It helps them to "sound out" the words.

Development of phonological skills may begin during the pre-Kindergarten years. Indeed, by the age of five, a child who has been exposed to rhyme can recognize a rhyme. Such a child can demonstrate phonological awareness by filling in the missing rhyming word in a familiar rhyme or rhymed picture book.

Children are taught phonological awareness when they are taught the sounds letters and combinations of letters make and how to recognize individual sounds in words.

Phonological awareness skills include:

- Rhyming and syllabification
- Blending sounds into words (such as *pic-tur-bo-k*)
- Identifying the beginning or starting sounds of words and the ending or closing sounds of words

- Breaking words down into sounds (also called "segmenting" words)
- Recognizing other, smaller words in the bigger word by removing starting sounds (recognizing the word *ear* in *hear*)

Explicit and Implicit Strategies for Teaching Phonics

Professor Uta Frith has done work on the sequence of children's phonic learning. Frith has identified the following three phases that describe the progression of children's phonic learning from ages four through eight.

The Logographic Phase	Children recognize whole words that have significance for them, such as their own names, the names of stores they frequent, or products their parents buy. Strategies that nurture development in this phase can include explicit labeling in the classroom using the children's names and the names of classroom objects, components, furniture, and materials. In addition, during snack time and lunchtime, explicit attention and talk can be focused on new brands of foods and drink. Toward the end of this phase, children start to notice initial letters in words and the sounds that they represent.
The Analytic Phase	During this phase, the children make associations between the spelling patterns in the words they know and the new words they encounter.
The Orthographic Phase	In this phase, children recognize words almost automatically. They can rapidly identify an increasing number of words because they know a good deal about the structure of words and how they're spelled.

To best support these phases and the development of emergent and early readers, teachers should focus on elements of phonics learning, which help children analyze words for their letters, spelling patterns, and structural components. The children need to be involved in activities where they can use what they know about words in order to learn new ones. For example, the teacher can build on what the children know to introduce new spelling patterns, vowel combinations, and short and long vowel investigations. The teacher must do this and be aware that these will be reintroduced again and again as needed.

Keep in mind that children's learning of phonics and other key components of reading is not linear but rather falls back to review and then flows forward to build new understandings.

Sorting words

This activity allows children to focus closely on the specific features of words and to begin to understand the basic elements of letter-sound relationships. Start with monosyllabic words. Have the children group them by length, common letters, common sounds, and/or spelling patterns.

Prepare for the activity by writing ten to fifteen words on oak-tag strips and placing them randomly on the sentence strip holder. These words should come from a book previously shared in the classroom or a language experience chart. Next, begin to sort out the word with the children, perhaps by focusing on where a particular letter appears in a word. While the children sort the position of a particular letter in a given word, they should also be coached (or facilitated) by the teacher to recognize that sometimes a letter in the middle of the word can still be the last sound that we hear and that some letters at the ends of words are silent (such as "e").

Children should be encouraged to make their own categories for word sorts and to share their own discoveries as they do the word sorts. The children's discoveries should be recorded and posted in the rooms with their names so they have ownership of their phonics learning.

Assessment of phonological awareness

These skills can be assessed by having the child listen to the teacher say two words. The child should then be asked to decide if these two words are the same word repeated twice or two different words. If you use two different words, make certain that they differ only by one phoneme, such as /d/ and /g/. Children can be assessed on words that are not real words or that they do not know. The words used can be make-believe.

Sample Test Question and Rationale

(Average)

1. **All of the following are true about phonological awareness EXCEPT:**

   A. It may involve print

   B. It is a prerequisite for spelling and phonics

   C. Children can do the activities with their eyes closed

   D. It starts before letter recognition is taught

Answer: A. It may involve print

The key word here is *EXCEPT*, which will be highlighted in uppercase on the test as well. All of the options are correct aspects of phonological awareness except answer A because phonological awareness *does not* involve print.

SKILL **Demonstrating knowledge of phonemic awareness** (*i.e., ability to*
1.4 *perceive and discriminate among the component sounds in a spoken word*)

PHONEMIC AWARENESS is the ability to break down and hear separate and/or different sounds and to distinguish among the sounds one hears. The terms phonics and phonemic awareness are different but are interdependent on each other. Phonemic awareness is required to begin the study of phonics, when students must be able to break down words into the smallest units of sound, known as phonemes, and to later identify syllables, blends, and patterns.

Phonemic awareness is based in a child's ability to acknowledge sounds and words. Unlike phonics, which uses both sight and sound, phonemic awareness can be done with the student's eyes closed. Phonemic awareness deals with sounds in words that are spoken.

Since the ability to distinguish among individual sounds or phonemes in words is a prerequisite for the association of sounds with letters and also for manipulating sounds to blend words—a fancy way of saying "reading"—the teaching of phonemic awareness is crucial to emergent literacy (early childhood K–2 reading instruction). Children need a strong background in phonemic awareness in order for phonics instruction (sound-spelling relationship printed materials) to be effective.

Theorist Marilyn Jager Adams, who researches early reading, has outlined five basic types of phonemic awareness tasks:

> **PHONEMIC AWARENESS:** the ability to break down and hear separate and/or different sounds and to distinguish among the sounds one hears

> To be phonemically aware means that the reader and listener can recognize and manipulate specific sounds in spoken words. The majority of phonemic awareness tasks, activities, and exercises are oral.

PHONEMIC AWARENESS TASKS	
Task 1	**The ability to hear rhymes and alliteration** For example, the children may listen to a poem, rhyming picture book, or song and identify rhyming words. The teacher then records or lists these words on an experiential chart.
Task 2	**The ability to do oddity tasks (recognize the member of a set that is different [odd] from the others in the group)** For example, the children may look at pictures of a blade of grass, a garden, and a rose and then determine which picture starts with a different sound.
Task 3	**The ability to orally blend words and split syllables** For example, the children can say the first sound of a word and then separately vocalize the rest of the word. They can then put it together as a single word.

Table continued on next page

Task 4	**The ability to orally segment words** For example, the children may focus on their abilities to count sounds. The children could be asked as a group to count the sounds in the word *hamburger*.
Task 5	**The ability to do phonics manipulation tasks** For example, the children may make sound replacements in common words. The teacher can ask them to replace the "r" sound in rose with a "p" sound.

Assessment of Phonemic Awareness

Teachers can maintain ongoing logs and rubrics for assessment throughout the year of phonemic awareness for individual children. Such assessments would identify particular stated reading behaviors or performance standards, the date the child's behavior (in this context, phonemic activity or exercise) was observed, and any comments.

The rubric or legend for assessing these behaviors might include descriptors such as demonstrates or exhibits reading behavior consistently, making progress/strides toward this reading behavior, and/or has not yet demonstrated or exhibited this behavior.

Depending on the particular phonemic task you are modeling, the performance task might include the following:

- Saying rhyming words in response to an oral prompt

- Segmenting a word spoken by the teacher into its beginning, middle, and ending sounds

- Correctly counting the number of syllables in a spoken word

Phonological awareness involves recognizing that spoken words are composed of a set of smaller units—including syllables and sounds. Phonemic awareness is a specific type of phonological awareness that focuses on the ability to distinguish, manipulate, and blend specific sounds or phonemes in a given word.

The Difference Between Phonological and Phonemic Awareness

Think of phonological awareness as an umbrella and phonemic awareness as a specific spoke under this umbrella. Phonics deals with printed words and the learning of sound-spelling correlations, whereas phonemic awareness activities are for the most part oral.

If you were, or are, a science or mathematics major, you need to remember in reviewing reading theory that the distinctions are not hard, fast, and absolute as are those in the mathematical and scientific fields. Many times they are semantic, and sometimes they are accepted and respected theories that change over time. The information and definitions in this guide are those accepted in the year of its publication and at the time of its authoring and updating. As changes occur in accepted theories, they will be made in the study guides and in the certification exams.

The Role of Phonemic Awareness in Reading Development

Children who have problems with phonics generally have not acquired or been exposed to phonemic awareness activities, which are usually fostered at home and in preschool. Examples of these activities include extensive songs, rhymes, and read-alouds.

Instructional methods

The following instructional methods may be effective for teaching phonemic awareness:

- Clapping syllables in words

- Distinguishing between a word and a sound

- Using visual cues and movements to help children understand when the speaker moves from one sound to another

- Incorporating oral segmentation activities that focus on easily distinguished syllables rather than sounds

- Singing familiar songs (e.g., "Happy Birthday" or "Knick Knack Paddy Whack") and replacing key words in them with words that have a different ending or middle sound (oral segmentation)

- Distributing picture cards and having the children sound out the words of the pictures on their cards or calling for a picture by asking for its first and second sounds

Consideration for ELL Learners

Given that the United States is becoming increasingly pluralistic and now has many citizens with English language learner) backgrounds, the likelihood that you will have one or more students whose first language is not English is about 75 percent. Therefore, as a conscientious educator, it is important that you understand the special factors involved in supporting their literacy development, including fostering progress in native language literacy as a perquisite for second language (English) reading progress.

Not all English phonemes are present in various ELL native languages. Some native language phonemes may, and do, conflict with English phonemes. It is recommended that all teachers of reading—particularly those who are working with ELL students—use meaningful, student-centered, and culture-customized activities. These activities may include language games, word walls, and poems. Some of these activities can also, if possible, be initiated in the child's first language and then reiterated in English.

Reading and the ELL learner

Research has shown that there is a positive and strong correlation between a child's literacy in his or her native language and his or her learning of English. The degree of native language proficiency and literacy is a strong predictor of English language development. Children who are literate and engaged readers in their native language can better transfer their skills to a second language (e.g., English).

What this means is that educators should not approach the needs of ELL learners in reading in the same manner that they would approach native English-speaking students. Those whose families are not from a focused oral literacy and reading culture in the native language will need additional oral language rhymes, read-alouds, and singing as support for reading skills development in both their native and the English language.

The Role of Phonological Processing in the Reading Development of Individual Students

English language learners (ELL)

Children who are raised in homes where English is not the first language and/or standard English is not spoken may have difficulty hearing the difference between similar-sounding words like *send* and *sent*. Any child who is not in a home, daycare, or preschool environment where English phonology operates may have difficulty perceiving and demonstrating the differences among English language phonemes. If children cannot hear the difference between words that sound the same, like *grow* and *glow*, they will get confused when they see these words in print. This confusion is very likely to impact their comprehension.

Research recommends that ELL children initially learn to read in their first language. It has also been found that a priority for ELL should be learning to speak English before being taught to read English. Research supports oral language development, since it lays the foundation for phonological awareness.

As a conscientious educator, it is important that you understand the special factors involved in supporting literacy development, including fostering progress in native language literacy as a perquisite for second language (English) reading progress.

When teaching phonological processing to ELL children, the teacher must understand that what works for the child who speaks English does not necessarily work for students who speak another language at home.

All phonological instruction programs must be tailored to the children's learning backgrounds. Rhymes and alliteration introduced to ELL children should be read or shared with them in their first language, if possible. If you do not speak the student's first language, find a paraprofessional or recruit an ELL educator to support your instruction in the first language.

Struggling readers

Among the causes that make reading a struggle for some children (and adults) is auditory trauma or ear infections that affect the ability to hear speech. Such children need one-on-one support with articulation and perception of different sounds. When a child says a word such as *parrot* incorrectly, repeat it back as a question with the correct pronunciation of the sounds. If the child says the word correctly after your question, you know that this type of extra support was all that was needed.

If the child still has difficulty with pronunciation, it may be necessary to consult with a speech therapist or audiologist. Early identification of medical conditions that affect hearing is crucial to reading development. Therefore, as an educator, you need to make the time to sit with struggling readers and play games such as "Same or Different" in order to identify those children who may be struggling due to a hearing difficulty.

POINTS TO PONDER ABOUT PHONOLOGICAL AWARENESS
It is auditory
It does not involve print
It must start before children have learned letter-sound correlations
It is the basis for the successful teaching of phonics and spelling
It can and must be taught and nurtured

SKILL 1.6 **Recognizing developmentally appropriate strategies for promoting students' phonological and phonemic awareness** (e.g., identifying rhyming words, segmenting words, and blending phonemes)

Using Phonics to Decode Words in Connected Text

Identifying new words

Some strategies to share with children during conferences or as part of shared reading include the following prompts:

Look at the beginning letter(s). What sound do you hear?

Stop to think about the text or story. What word with this beginning letter would make sense here?

Look at the book's illustrations. Do they provide you with help in figuring out the new word?

Think of which word would make sense, sound right, and match the letters that you see. Start the sentence over, making your mouth ready to say that word.

Skip the word, read to the end of the sentence, and then come back to the word. How does what you've read help you with the word?

Listen to whether what you are reading makes sense and matches the letters (this is asking the child to self-monitor). If it doesn't make sense, see if you can correct it on your own.

Look for spelling patterns you know from the spelling pattern wall.

Look for smaller words you might already know in the larger word.

Think of where you might have seen this word before in a story someone read to you or that you read or anyplace where you may have seen this word before.

Read on a little, and then return to the part that confused you.

Use of Semantic and Syntactic Cues

Semantic cues

Prompts that the teacher can use to alert the children to semantic cues include the following:

You said (the child's statement and incorrect attempt). Does that make sense to you?

If someone said (repeat the child's attempt), would you know what he or she meant?

You said (child's incorrect attempt). Would you write that?

Children need to use meaning to predict what the text says so the relevant information can prompt the correct words to surface as they identify the words.

If children come to a word they can't immediately recognize, they should try to figure it out by using their past reading (or being read to) experiences, background knowledge, and what they can deduce so far from the text itself.

Syntactic cues

The teacher can use the following prompts to alert the children to syntactic cues:

> You said (child's incorrect attempt). Does that sound right?
>
> You said (child's incorrect attempt). Can we say it like that?

Development of Phonics Skills in Individual Students

English language learners

In *On Solid Ground* (2000), researcher and educator Sharon Taberski said that it is much harder for children from ELL backgrounds and children from homes where other English dialects are spoken to use syntactic cues to attempt to self-correct. These children, through no fault of their own, do not have sufficient experience hearing standard English spoken to use this cueing system as they read. These children need a teacher who is sensitive to their linguistic or cultural background to guide them through these issues.

Highly proficient readers

Highly proficient readers can be paired as buddy tutors for ELL or special needs classroom members, or they can be used to assist the resource room teacher during their reading time. They can use the CVC Game developed by Jacki Montierth (explained in detail at the end of this skill) to support their peers, and they can even modify the game to meet the specific needs of classroom peers. This gives the highly proficient reader the opportunity to do a service learning project while still in elementary school. It also introduces the learner to another dimension of reading: the role of the reader as trainer and recruiter of other peers into the circle of readers and writers! These peer tutors can also maintain an ongoing reading progress journal for their tutees. This will be a wonderful way to realize the goals of the reading and writing workshop.

Blending letter sounds

A good strategy to use in working with individual children is to have them explain how they finally correctly identified a word that was giving them trouble. If prompted and habituated through one-on-one teacher/tutoring conversations, they can be quite clear about what they did to "get" the word. Here are some prompts you can use:

> *You said (the child's incorrect attempt). Does that match the letters you see?*
>
> *If it was (the word the child said), what would it have to start with?*
>
> *If it was (the word the child said), what would it have to end with?*
>
> *Look at the first letter(s) . . . middle letter(s) . . . last letter. What could the word be?*
>
> *If you were writing (the child's incorrect attempt), what letter would you write first? What letters would go in the middle? What letter would go last?*

If the children are already writing their own stories, the teacher might say to them: "When you write your own stories, you know you would never write any story that did not make sense. If you read something that doesn't make sense and doesn't match the letters, then it's probably not what the author wrote. This is the author's story, not yours, so go back and see if you can find out the author's story. Later on, you might write your own story."

Letter-Sound Correspondence and Beginning Decoding

Use this procedure for letter-sound investigations that support beginning decoding:

1. Focus on the particular letter(s) that you want the child to investigate. It is a good idea to choose one from a shared text that the children are familiar with. Make certain that the teachers' directions to the children are clear and focus on either looking for a specific letter or listening for sounds.

2. Begin a list of words that meet the task given to the children. Use chart paper to list the words that the children identify. This list can be continued into the next week as long as the children's focus is maintained on the list. This can be done by challenging the children with identifying a specific number of letters or sounds and then "daring" them as a class team to go beyond those words or sounds.

3. Continue to add to the list. Focus the children at the beginning of the day on their goal of individually adding to the list. Give them a sticky note on which they can individually write the words they find. Then they can attach their newly found words with their names on them to the chart. This provides the children with a sense of ownership and pride in their letter-sounding abilities. During shared reading, discuss the children's proposed additions and have the group decide if these meet the directed category. If all the children agree that they do meet the category, include the words on the chart.

4. Do a word sort from all of the words generated, and have the children put the words into categories that demonstrate similarities and differences. They can be prompted to see if the letter appeared at the beginning of the word

or in the middle of the word. They might also be prompted to see that one sound can have two different letter representations. The children can then "box" the word differences and similarities by drawing colors established in a chart key.

5. Before the children go off to read, ask them to look for new words in the texts that they can now recognize because of the letter-sound relationships on their chart. During shared reading, make certain that they have time to share the words they were able to decode because of their explorations.

Strategies for Helping Students Decode One-Syllable Words that Follow Common Patterns and Multisyllabic Words

This activity is presented in detail so it can actually be implemented with children in a classroom and also to provide detail for a potential constructed response question on a certification examination. The CVC Phonic Card game was developed by Jackie Montierth, a computer teacher in San Diego, for use with fifth- and sixth-grade students. It is a good activity to adapt to the needs of any group with appropriate modifications for age, grade level, and language needs.

To play the game, the children use the vehicle of the card game to practice and enhance their use of consonants and vowels. Their fluency in this will increase their ability to decode words. Potential uses beyond whole-classroom instruction include use as part of the small group word work component of the reading workshop and as part of cooperative team learning.

This strategy is also particularly helpful for grade four and beyond English language learners who are in a regular English language classroom setting. The card game works well because the practice of the content is implicit for transfer as the children continue to improve their reading skills. In addition, the card game format allows "instructional punctuation" using a student-centered high-interest exploration.

MATERIALS FOR THE CVC PHONIC CARD GAME

5" × 8" index cards or playing card–sized oak-tag cards to create a deck. For repeated use and durability, it is recommended that the deck be laminated.

The deck should consist of the following:

44 consonant cards (including the blends)

15 vowel cards (including three of each vowel)

5 wild cards (which can be used as any vowel)

6 final "e" cards

The design of this project can also focus on particular CVC words that are part of a particular book, topic, theme, or genre format (e.g., study of American history, grade four–appropriate or U.S. geography, Canada and Latin America, grades five through six). Before playing the game, children should be directed to review the words on the word wall or other words on a word map.

How to play the game

The game is best introduced first as part of a minilesson in which the teacher reads the rules and two children demonstrate the game step-by-step before the class plays the game for the first time. Have the children divide into pairs or small groups of no more than four. Each pair or group gets one deck of CVC cards,

Have each group choose a "dealer." The dealer shuffles the deck of cards and deals five cards to each player. The remaining cards are placed facedown for drawing during the game. One card is turned over to make the discard pile.

Players cannot show their cards to the other players. The first player to the left of the dealer looks at his/her cards and, if possible, puts down three cards that make a consonant-vowel-consonant word. To get more points, four cards that make a consonant-vowel-consonant word can be placed down. The player must then say the word and draw the number of cards he or she has put down. If that player is unable to form a word, he or she draws a card from either the draw pile or the discard pile and discards one card. All players must have five cards at all times.

The next player to the left now takes a turn, putting down any cards that form a C-V-C word. The player then says the word and draws the number of cards that he or she has put down. If the player cannot say the word that he or she has drawn from the pile, he or she then draws a card from the discard or the draw pile.

The game continues until one or more of the following happens:

1. There are no more cards in the draw pile

2. All players run out of cards

3. All players cannot form a word

The winner is the player who has put down the most cards during the game. Players may only put down words at the beginning of their turn. Proper names may not be used as words.

The game can also be played with teams of individuals in a small group of four or fewer competing against one another (excellent for special needs or resource room students). It can also be done as a whole-class activity where all of the students are divided into cooperative teams or small groups that compete against one another.

This second approach will work well with a heterogeneous classroom that includes special needs and/or ELL children.

Teachers of ELL learners can play this game in the students' native language first and then transition it into English, which will facilitate native language reading skills and second language acquisition. They can develop their own appropriate decks to meet the vocabulary needs of their children and to complement the curricula.

COMPETENCY 2
UNDERSTAND WORD IDENTIFICATION STRATEGIES, INCLUDING PHONICS

> **SKILL 2.1** Recognizing how beginning writers and readers learn to apply knowledge of the relationship between letters and letter combinations of written words and the sounds of spoken words

The Alphabetic Principle

The ALPHABETIC PRINCIPLE is sometimes called graphophonemic awareness. This multisyllabic technical reading foundation term details the understanding that written words are composed of patterns of letters that represent the sounds of spoken words. The alphabetic principle consists of two parts:

- An understanding that words are made up of letters and that each of these letters has a specific sound

- An understanding that the correspondence between sounds and letters leads to phonological reading; this consists of reading regular and irregular words as well as doing advanced analysis of words

Since the English language is based on the alphabet, being able to recognize and sound out letters is the first step for beginning readers. Simply relying on memorization for word recognition is not an effective way for children to learn to recognize words. Therefore, decoding is essential. The most important goal of beginning reading teachers is to teach students to decode text so they can read fluently and with understanding.

> **ALPHABETIC PRINCIPLE:** understanding that written words are composed of patterns of letters that represent the sounds of spoken words

THE FOUR BASIC FEATURES OF THE ALPHABETIC PRINCIPLE
Students need to be able to take apart spoken words and blend different sounds together to make new words
Students need to apply letter sounds to all of their reading
Teachers need to use a systematic, effective program in order to teach children to read
The teaching of the alphabetic principle usually begins in kindergarten

It is important to keep in mind that some children already know the letters and sounds before they come to school. Others may catch on to this quite quickly, while some may need one-on-one instruction in order to learn to read.

The following are the critical skills that students need to learn:

- Letter-sound correspondence

- How to sound out words

- How to decode text to make meaning

Assessment Throughout the Year of Graphophonemic Awareness

The teacher should maintain individual records of children's reading behaviors that demonstrate alphabetic principle/graphophonemic awareness. The following performance standards should be part of a record template form for each child in grades K–1 and beyond, as needed (depending on ELL or special needs):

- Match all consonant and short vowel sounds

- Read one's own name

- Read one-syllable words and high-frequency words

- Demonstrate the ability to read and understand that as letters in words change, so do the sounds

- Generate the sounds from all letters, including consonant blends and long-vowel patterns, and blend those different sounds into recognizable words

- Read common sight words

- Read common word families

- Recognize and use knowledge of spelling patterns when reading (*run/running, hop/hopping*)

- Decode (sound out) regular words with more than one syllable (*vacation, graduation*)

- Recognize regular abbreviations (Feb., Mr., P.S.)

Any record kept of an individual child's progress should include each date of observation and some legend or rubric detailing the level of performance, standard acquisition, or mastery. Some teachers use *Y* for "exhibits the reading behavior consistently," *M* for "making progress toward the standard," and *N* for "has not yet exhibited the behavior." Beyond this objective legend for the assessment, the teacher may want and should include any other comments that detail the child's progress in this awareness.

Development of Alphabetic Knowledge in Individual Students

Researchers Laura M. Justice and Helen K. Ezell of the University of Virginia conducted a study in 2002 that evaluated alphabetic knowledge and print awareness in preschool children from low-income households. Their research findings offer potential insights for educators who seek to foster the skills and capabilities of all of their students.

In their posttesting of children in the experimental group who had participated in shared reading sessions that emphasized a print focus, they found that the at-risk children outperformed their control group peers (other Head Start children) on three measures of print awareness: words in print, print recognition, and alphabetic knowledge.

Other researchers, including Chaney (1994), have demonstrated a statistically significant and inverse relationship between household income and children's performance on measures of print awareness and alphabetic principle. A study by Lonigan (1999) found that substantial group differences existed on a variety of preliteracy tasks administered to eighty-five preschool children from lower- and middle-income households. Measures of print awareness used included environmental print, print and book reading conventions, and alphabet knowledge.

Results showed that preschool children from middle-income households showed significantly higher levels of skill across all print awareness tasks in comparison with preschoolers from low-income households. Obviously, these data highlight the importance of extensive alphabetic knowledge activities and print awareness opportunities for children from low-income households in grades K–1 and, when necessary, beyond.

Two other studies undertaken by Ezell and Justice (2000) suggested that structuring adult-child shared book reading interactions to include an explicit print

Studies have shown that preschool children from middle-income households show significantly higher levels of skill across all print awareness tasks in comparison with preschoolers from low-income households.

awareness and alphabetic principle focus resulted in a substantial increase in children's verbal interactions with print. This work highlights the importance of not only classroom and preschool emphases on print awareness and alphabetic principle routines but also the need for teachers to reach out to parents to model for them these shared reading experiences so family life can parallel the classroom experiences.

Many schools currently have parent volunteers and reading buddy programs. Training of these volunteers, particularly in high-need, low-economic-income status communities, is certainly warranted.

Children with learning disabilities especially benefit from organized instruction that centers on letters, sounds, and the relations between sounds and letters.

David J. Chard and Jean Osborn (1999) reflected on the guidelines necessary for teachers to use in selecting supplemental phonics and word-recognition materials for addressing students with learning disabilities. They note that an important part of helping children with reading disabilities to figure out the system underlying the printed word is to lead them to understand the alphabetic principle. Children with learning disabilities (LD) especially benefit from organized instruction that centers on letters, sounds, and the relations between sounds and letters. They also benefit from word-recognition patterns instruction that offers practice with, for example, word families that share similar letter patterns.

Children who are LD also benefit from opportunities to apply what they are learning to the reading and rereading of stories and other texts. Such texts contain a high portion of words that reflect the letters, sounds, and spelling patterns that the children are learning.

For special needs children, a beginning reading program should include the following elements of alphabetic knowledge instruction:

- A variety of alphabetic knowledge activities in which the children learn to identify and name both upper- and lowercase letters

- Games, songs, and other activities that help children to learn to name the letters quickly

- Writing activities that encourage children to practice the letters they are writing

- A sensible sequence of letter introduction that can be adjusted to the needs of the children.

Sample Test Questions and Rationale

(Average)

1. Oral language development includes which of the following:

   A. Listening comprehension

   B. Storytelling

   C. Developing vocabulary

   D. All of the above

   Answer: D. All of the above

   Effective oral language development includes storytelling, listening comprehension, and an ever-increasing vocabulary.

(Average)

2. How do children make the transition from letter forms to invented spelling?

   A. Write strings of letters

   B. Organize group of letters

   C. Leave spaces

   D. All of the above

   Answer: D. All of the above

   Young children write strings of letters, organize them into groups, and then leave spaces between the groups. These are important steps in a child's early developmental stages of learning to read and write.

(Rigorous)

3. Which aspect of language is innate?

   A. Biological capability to articulate sounds that can be understood by other humans

   B. Cognitive ability to create syntactical structures

   C. Capacity for using semantics to convey meaning in a social environment

   D. Ability to vary inflections and accents

   Answer: A. Biological capability to articulate sounds understood by other humans

   Language ability is innate, and the biological capability to produce sounds lets children learn semantics and syntactical structures through trial and error. Linguists agree that language is a vocal system of word symbols that enable a human to communicate his or her feelings, thoughts, and desires to other human beings.

SKILL 2.2 Demonstrating knowledge of phonics skills and their application to decoding unfamiliar words

WORD ANALYSIS: the process readers use to figure out unfamiliar words based on written patterns

WORD ANALYSIS (a.k.a. phonics or decoding) is the process readers use to figure out unfamiliar words based on written patterns. Word recognition is the process of automatically determining the pronunciation and some degree of the meaning of an unknown word. In other words, fluent readers recognize most written words easily and correctly, without consciously decoding or breaking them down. These elements of literacy are skills that readers need for word recognition.

DECODE: to change communication signals into messages

To DECODE means to change communication signals into messages. Reading comprehension requires that the reader learn the code within which a message is written and be able to decode it to get the message. Encoding involves changing a message into symbols—for example, to encode oral language into writing (spelling), to encode an idea into words, or to encode a mathematical or physical idea into appropriate mathematical symbols.

Word meanings in context are definitions that a reader determines based on information from the surrounding text, such as other words, phrases, sentences, and/or paragraphs. Readers can also use words they already know to piece together possible meanings. They can use root words, antonyms, and word forms to help determine the meaning of an unfamiliar word.

For more information on phonics, see Skills 1.1, 1.3, and 1.6

Sample Test Questions and Rationale

(Easy)

1. To *decode* is to:

   A. Construct meaning

   B. Sound out a printed sequence of letters

   C. Use a special code to decipher a message

   D. None of the above

   Answer: A. Construct meaning

   Word analysis (phonics or decoding) is the process readers use to figure out unfamiliar words based on written patterns. Decoding is the process of constructing meaning of an unknown word.

(Easy)

2. To *encode* means that you:

   A. Decode a second time

   B. Construct meaning from a code

   C. Tell someone a message

   D. None of the above

   Answer: D. None of the above

   Encoding involves changing a message into symbols.

SKILL 2.3 **Applying knowledge of structural analysis as a word identification strategy** *(e.g., identifying prefixes, suffixes, and roots)*

Students will be better at comprehension if they have a stronger working vocabulary. Research has shown that students learn more vocabulary when it is presented in context rather than just in vocabulary lists. Furthermore, the more students are enabled to use particular words in context, the more they will remember each word and use the word in the comprehension of sentences that contain the words.

Auditory games and drills during which students recognize and manipulate the sounds of words, separate or segment the sounds of words, take out sounds, blend sounds, add new sounds, or take apart sounds to recombine them in new formations are good ways to foster phonological awareness.

Identification of Common Morphemes, Prefixes, and Suffixes

This aspect of vocabulary development is used to help students look for structural elements in words that they can use independently to help them determine meanings. The following terms are generally recognized as the key structural analysis components.

ROOT WORDS: a word from which another word is developed

BASE WORDS: a stand-alone linguistic unit that cannot be deconstructed or broken down into smaller words

CONTRACTIONS: shortened form of two words in which one or more letters have been deleted

PREFIXES: beginning units of meaning that can be added to a base word or root word

SUFFIXES: ending units of meaning that can be "affixed" or added onto the ends of root or base words

COMPOUND WORDS: occur when two or more base words are connected to form a new word

SECTIONAL ENDINGS: suffixes that impart a new meaning to the base or root word

- **ROOT WORDS:** A root word is a word from which another word is developed. The second word can be said to have its "root" in the first. This structural component nicely lends itself to an illustration of a tree with roots, which can concretize the meaning for students. Students may also want to literally construct root words using cardboard trees and/or actual roots from plants to create word family models. This is a wonderful way to help students own their root words.

- **BASE WORDS:** A base word is a stand-alone linguistic unit that cannot be deconstructed or broken down into smaller words. For example, in the word retell, the base word is tell.

- **CONTRACTIONS:** Contractions are shortened forms of two words in which one or more letters have been deleted. These deleted letters are then replaced by an apostrophe.

- **PREFIXES:** These are beginning units of meaning that can be added (the vocabulary word for this type of structural adding is "affixed") to a base word or root word. They cannot stand alone. They are also sometimes known as "bound morphemes," meaning that they cannot stand alone as a base word.

- **SUFFIXES:** These are ending units of meaning that can be "affixed" or added onto the ends of root or base words. Suffixes transform the original meanings of base and root words. Like prefixes, they are also known as "bound morphemes," because they cannot stand alone as words.

- **COMPOUND WORDS:** Compound words occur when two or more base words are connected to form a new word. The meaning of the new word is in some way connected with that of the base word.

- **SECTIONAL ENDINGS:** These are types are suffixes that impart a new meaning to the base or root word. In particular, these endings change the gender, number, tense, or form of the base or root words. Just like other suffixes, these are also termed "bound morphemes."

Sometimes a very familiar word can appear as a different part of speech as in the following examples:

You may have heard that fraud involves a criminal misrepresentation, so when it appears as the adjective form fraudulent —for example, "He was suspected of fraudulent activities"—you can make an educated guess as to the meaning.

You probably know that something out of date is obsolete; therefore, when you read about "built-in obsolescence," you can detect the meaning of the unfamiliar word.

SKILL 2.4 **Demonstrating knowledge of the use of spelling patterns and syllabication as techniques for decoding unfamiliar words**

Morphology, Syntax, and Semantics

MORPHOLOGY is the study of word structure. When readers develop morphemic skills, they are developing an understanding of patterns they see in words. For example, English speakers realize that *cat, cats,* and *caterpillar* share some similarities in structure. This understanding helps readers to recognize words at a faster and easier rate, since each word doesn't need individual decoding.

> **MORPHOLOGY:** the study of word structure

SYNTAX refers to the rules or patterned relationships that correctly create phrases and sentences from words. When readers develop an understanding of syntax, they begin to understand the structure of how sentences are built and eventually the beginning of grammar.

> **SYNTAX:** phrases and sentences from words

Example: I am going to the movies.

This statement is syntactically and grammatically correct.

Example: They am going to the movies.

This statement is syntactically correct because all of the words are in their correct place, but it is grammatically incorrect with the use of the word They rather than I.

SEMANTICS refers to the meaning expressed when words are arranged in a specific way. This is where connotation and denotation of words will eventually have a role with readers. All of these skill sets are important to eventually develop effective word recognition skills that help emerging readers to develop fluency.

> **SEMANTICS:** refers to the meaning expressed when words are arranged in a specific way

Using of Syllabification as a Word Identification Strategy

Strategy: Clap Hands, Count those Syllables as They Come!! (Taberski, 2000)

The objective of this activity is for children to understand that every syllable in a polysyllabic word can be studied for its spelling patterns in the same way that monosyllabic words are studied for their spelling patterns. The easiest way for the K–3 teacher to introduce this activity to the children is to share a familiar poem from the poetry chart (or to write out a familiar poem on a large experiential chart).

First, the teacher reads the poem with the children. As they are reading it aloud, the children clap the beats of the poem, and the teacher uses a colored marker to place a tic (/) above each syllable. Next, the teacher takes letter cards and selects one of the polysyllabic words from the poem that the children have already "clapped" out.

The children use letter cards to spell the word on the sentence strip holder, or the letter can be placed on a felt board or up against a window on display. Together, the children and teacher divide the letters into syllables and place blank letter cards between the syllables. The children identify spelling patterns they know.

Finally, and as part of continued small-group syllabification study, the children identify other polysyllabic words they clapped out from the poem. They make up the letter combinations of these words. Then they separate them into syllables with blank letter cards between the syllables.

Children who require special support in syllabification can be encouraged to use plenty of letter cards to create a large butcher paper syllabic (in letter cards with spaces) representation of the poem or at least a few lines of the poem. They can be told that this is for use as a teaching tool for others. In this way, they authenticate their study of syllabification with a real product that can actually be referenced by peers.

Techniques for Identifying Compound Words

Semantic feature analysis

This technique for enhancing vocabulary skills by using semantic cues is based on the research of Johnson and Pearson (1984) and Anders and Bos (1986). It involves young children who are instructed to set up a feature analysis grid of various subject content words. This grid is an outgrowth of their discussion about these words.

For instance, in Cooper's *Literacy—Helping Children Construct Meaning* (2004), the author includes a sample of a Semantic Features Analysis grid for vegetables.

Vegetables	Green	Have Peels	Eat Raw	Seeds
Carrots	−	+	+	−
Cabbage	+	−	+	−

Note the use of + for yes, − for no, and possible use of +/− if a vegetable like squash could be both green and yellow. This grid should be very accessible for young readers and something they can easily do on their own as part of their independent word analysis.

Teachers of children in grade one and beyond can design their own semantic analysis grids to meet their students' needs and to align with the topics the students are studying at the time. Select a category or class of words (e.g., planets, rodents, winter, weather). Use the left side of the grid to list at least three or more items that fit this category. The number of actual items listed will depend on the age and grade level of the children (typically three or four items for K–1 and up to ten or fifteen for grades five and six).

Brainstorm with the children, or if it is better suited to the class, the teacher may list the features that the items have in common. As in Cooper's table, common features such as vegetables' green color, peels, and seeds are usually pretty easy to identify. Show the children how to insert +, −, or even ? (if they are not certain) notations on the grid. The teacher might also explore with the children the possibility that an item could get both a + and a −. For example, a vegetable like broccoli might be eaten cooked or raw, depending on preference, and squash can be green or yellow.

Whatever the length of the grid when first presented to the children (perhaps a semantic cue lesson in and of itself tied to a text being read in class), make certain that the grid as presented and filled out is not the end of the activity. Children can use it as a model for developing their own semantic features grids and sharing them during the share time with the whole class. Child-developed grids can become part of a Word Work center in the classroom or even be published in a *Word Study Games* book by the class as a whole. Such a publication can be shared with parents during open school week and evening visits or with peer classes.

For information on context clues, see Skill 3.3

Sample Test Question and Rationale

(Average)

1. The arrangement and relationship of words in sentences or sentence structure best describes:

   A. Style

   B. Discourse

   C. Thesis

   D. Syntax

Answer: D. Syntax

Syntax is the grammatical structure of sentences.

SKILL 2.5 Applying knowledge of developmentally appropriate instruction and curriculum materials for promoting students' decoding skills and word identification strategies

In the 1960s and 1970s, many reading specialists, especially Fries (1962), believed that successful decoding resulted in reading comprehension. This meant that if children could sound out the words, they would then automatically be able to comprehend the words. Many teachers of reading and many reading texts still subscribe to this theory after over thirty years.

This out-of-date teaching style leaves no room for the concepts of decoding and encoding to achieve reading comprehension. As mentioned in Skill 2.2, readers do much more than simply create sounds from words. A word is composed of several constituents, each of which requires its own level of comprehension before the word can be understood at more than just the memorization level.

Although effective reading comprehension requires identifying words automatically (Adams, 1990; Perfetti, 1985), children do not have to be able to identify every single word or know the exact meaning of the every word in a text to understand it. Indeed, Nagy (1988) says that children can read a work with a high level of comprehension even if they do not fully know as many as 15 percent of the words in a given text. For these reasons, it is important to address issues of decoding, encoding, and word recognition at a very early level. These early teachings create a platform for future reading skills and word identification strategies; children then can extend their ability to decode to multisyllabic words, using the same learned abilities without returning to rote memorization or sounding out words.

Although effective reading comprehension requires identifying words automatically, children do not have to be able to identify every single word or know the exact meaning of the every word in a text to understand it.

Sample Test Question and Rationale

(Rigorous)

1. **Effective reading comprehension requires:**

   A. Encoding

   B. Decoding

   C. Both A and B

   D. Neither A nor B

Answer: C. Both A and B

Reading comprehension requires that the reader learn the code within which a message is written and be able to decode it to get the message.

COMPETENCY 3

UNDERSTAND THE DEVELOPMENT OF VOCABULARY KNOWLEDGE AND SKILLS ACROSS THE CURRICULUM

SKILL 3.1 Recognizing criteria for selecting appropriate words to increase students' vocabulary knowledge *(e.g., synonyms, antonyms, words with multiple meanings, idioms, and classifications)*

The simplest method that teachers can use to increase student vocabulary is by exposing students to many new words in the course of frequent reading and writing exercises. Students can also learn many words indirectly through independent reading. Teachers should emphasize that words are not separate, disconnected units that need to be learned in isolation but are related and interrelated.

Synonyms, antonyms, and root words are only three obvious examples of the connections that exist among words. When words are connected together in sentences, their individual meanings change and are enhanced by one another. However, teaching particular words—especially words with multiple meanings—before reading a text helps students with both vocabulary acquisition and reading comprehension. When providing instruction in the definitions of new vocabulary words, teachers should focus on the words' classification to other words.

Useful Criteria for Selecting Appropriate New Words in Vocabulary Instruction

- Provide opportunities for extensive reading

- Teach words in related clusters

- Teach key vocabulary words before assigning reading from a text

- Have dictionary and glossary resources available for the precise spelling of words

Student readers comprehend and learn when they are able to connect the new information in their reading material to what they already know. Vocabulary instruction, therefore, should help students make the connections between unknown words and the knowledge they already possess.

> **SKILL 3.2** Demonstrating knowledge of developmentally appropriate strategies for promoting and reinforcing students' oral and written vocabulary knowledge

The typical variation in literacy backgrounds that children bring to reading can make teaching difficult. Often a teacher must choose between focusing on the learning needs of a few students at the expense of the group or focusing on the group at the risk of leaving some students behind academically. This situation is particularly critical for children with gaps in their literacy knowledge, as they may be at risk in subsequent grades for becoming "diverse learners."

AREAS OF EMERGING EVIDENCE	
Experiences with Print (Through reading and writing) help preschool children to develop an understanding of the conventions, purposes, and functions of print	Children learn about print from a variety of sources; through the process, they come to realize that print carries a story. They also learn how text is structured visually (i.e., text begins at the top of the page, moves from left to right, and carries over to the next page when it is turned). While knowledge about the conventions of print enables children to understand the physical structure of language, the conceptual knowledge that printed words convey a message also helps children to bridge the gap between oral and written language.

Table continued on next page

Phonological Awareness and Letter Recognition	These contribute to initial reading acquisition by helping children to develop efficient word recognition strategies (e.g., detecting pronunciations and storing associations in memory). Phonological awareness and knowledge of print-speech relations play an important role in facilitating reading acquisition. Therefore, phonological awareness instruction should be an integral component of early reading programs. Within the emergent literacy research, viewpoints diverge on whether acquisition of phonological awareness and letter recognition are preconditions of literacy acquisition or whether they develop interdependently with literacy activities such as story reading and writing.
Storybook Reading Affects children's knowledge about, strategies for, and attitudes toward reading	Of all the strategies intended to promote growth in literacy acquisition, none is as commonly practiced or as strongly supported across the emergent literacy literature as storybook reading. Children in different social and cultural groups have differing degrees of access to storybook reading. For example, it is not unusual for a teacher to have students who have experienced thousands of hours of story reading time alongside other students who have had little or no such exposure.

Instructional Strategies

- Teacher-guided activities that require students to organize and to summarize information based on the author's explicit intent are pertinent strategies in middle grades. Evaluation techniques include oral and written responses to standardized or teacher-made worksheets.

- The reading of fiction introduces and reinforces skills in inferring meaning from narration and description. Teaching-guided activities focused on the process of reading for meaning should be followed by cooperative planning of the skills to be studied and of the selection of reading resources. Many printed reading for comprehension instruments, as well as individualized computer software programs, are available to monitor the progress of acquiring comprehension skills.

- Older middle school students should be given opportunities for more student-centered activities, such as individual and collaborative reading selection based on student interest, small-group discussions of selected works, and greater written expression. Evaluation techniques include teacher monitoring and the observation of discussions and written work samples.

- Certain students may begin some fundamental critical interpretation activities: recognizing fallacious reasoning in news media, examining the accuracy of news reports and advertising, or explaining their reasons for preferring one author's writing to another's. Development of these skills may require a more learning-centered approach in which the teacher identifies a number of objectives and suggested resources from which the student may choose his or her course of study. Self-evaluation through a reading diary should be stressed. Teacher and peer evaluation for creative projects resulting from such study is encouraged.

- Reading aloud before the entire class as a formal means of teacher evaluation should be phased out in favor of one-to-one tutoring or peer-assisted reading. The occasional sharing of favored selections by both teacher and willing students is a good oral interpretation basic.

SKILL 3.3 Applying knowledge of how context is used to determine the meaning of unfamiliar words

Contextual Redefinition

This strategy helps children to use context more effectively by presenting them with sufficient background *before* they begin reading. It models for the children the use of contextual clues to make informed guesses about word meanings.

To apply this strategy as a teacher, first select unfamiliar words for teaching. No more than two or three words should be selected for direct teaching. Write a sentence in which there are sufficient clues supplied for the child to successfully figure out the meaning. Among the types of context clues the teacher can use are compare/contrast, synonyms, and direct definition.

The next step is to present the words only on the experiential chart or as letter cards. Have the children pronounce the words. As they pronounce them, challenge them to come up with a definition for each word. After more than one definition is offered, encourage the children to decide as a whole group what the definition is. Write down their agreed-upon definition with no comment as to its true meaning.

Share with the children the contexts (sentences written with the words and explicit context clues). Ask the children to read the sentences aloud. Then have them offer suggestions for definitions of each word. Do not comment on their definitions, but ask the children to support their definitions with specific references to the context clues in the sentences. As the discussion continues, direct the children's attention to their previously agreed-upon definition of the word. Facilitate them in discussing the differences between their guesses about the word when they saw only the word itself and their guesses about the word when they read it in context. Finally, have the children check their use of context skills to correctly define the word by using a dictionary.

This type of direct teaching of word definitions is useful when the children have dictionary skills and the teacher is aware that there are not sufficient clues about the words in the context to help the students define it. In addition, struggling readers and students from ELL backgrounds may benefit tremendously from being walked through this same process, even though highly proficient and successful readers may apply it automatically. By using this strategy, the teacher can also "kid watch" and note their students' prior knowledge as they guess the word in isolation. The teacher can also actually witness and hear how various students use context skills.

Through their involvement in this strategy, struggling readers gain a feeling of community as they experience the ways in which their struggles and guesses resonate in other peers' responses to the text. They are also getting a chance to be "walked through" this maze of meaning and are learning how to use context clues in order to navigate it themselves.

Sample Test Question and Rationale

(Rigorous)

1. **Contextual redefinition is a strategy that encourages children to use the context more effectively by presenting them with sufficient vocabulary _____ reading the text.**

   A. after

   B. before

   C. while

   D. None of the above

Answer: B. before

Contextual redefinition is a strategy that encourages children to use the context more effectively by presenting them with sufficient context *before* they begin reading. To apply this strategy, the teacher should first select unfamiliar words for teaching. No more than two or three words should be selected for direct teaching.

SKILL 3.4 **Recognizing ways to help students identify and use references such as dictionaries and thesauri for various purposes** *(e.g., determining word meanings and pronunciations, finding alternative word choices)*

CONTENT AREA VOCABULARY is the specific vocabulary related to the particular concepts of various academic disciplines (e.g., social science, science, math, and art). While teachers tend to think of content area vocabulary as something that

> **CONTENT AREA VOCABULARY:** the specific vocabulary related to the particular concepts of various academic disciplines

should be focused on only at the secondary level (middle and high school), students go to different teachers for different subjects, so content-area vocabulary is very important. However, even elementary school–aged students studying various subjects will understand concepts better when the vocabulary used to describe them is explained in detail.

Some educators also believe that vocabulary should only be taught in language arts classes, not realizing that (1) students do not have enough time to learn all the necessary vocabulary in order to be successful with a standards-based education, and (2) teaching vocabulary that is related to a specific subject is a very good way to help students understand that subject better.

So how do content-area teachers teach vocabulary? First, content-area teachers help students to learn strategies to figure out the meanings of difficult vocabulary words when the students encounter them on their own. All teachers can do this by teaching students how to identify the meanings of words in context (usually through activities where the word is taken out and the students have to figure out a way to make sense of the sentence). In addition, dictionary skills must be taught in all subject areas.

> Teachers should consider that teaching vocabulary is not just the teaching of words, but rather, it is the teaching of complex concepts, each with histories and connotations.

When teachers explicitly teach vocabulary, it is best when they connect new words to ideas, other words, and experiences that students are already familiar with. This helps to reduce the strangeness of the new words. Furthermore, the more concrete the examples are, the more likely students will know how to use the words in context.

Finally, students need plenty of exposure to the new words. They need to be able to hear and use them in naturally produced sentences. The more one hears and uses a sentence in context, the more the word is solidified in the person's long-term vocabulary.

Like a dictionary, a thesaurus is an excellent resource to use when writing. Students can use a thesaurus to find appropriate synonyms, antonyms, and other related words to enhance their writing. However, it is important for teachers to model and instruct students in using a thesaurus so students do not simply replace words. Students need to learn about word connotations and the "between the lines" meanings of words to effectively use a thesaurus.

Sample Test Question and Rationale

(Average)

1. What is the best place for students to find appropriate synonyms, antonyms, and other related words to enhance their writing?

    A. Dictionary

    B. Spell check

    C. Encyclopedia

    D. Thesaurus

Answer: D. Thesaurus

Students need plenty of exposure to the new words. A thesaurus is an excellent resource to use when writing. Students can use a thesaurus to find appropriate synonyms, antonyms, and other related words to enhance their writing

---

COMPETENCY 4
UNDERSTAND READING FLUENCY AND COMPREHENSION ACROSS THE CURRICULUM

> **SKILL 4.1** Demonstrating knowledge of the concepts of rate, accuracy, expression, and phrasing in reading fluency and recognizing factors that affect fluency

When students practice fluency, they practice reading connected pieces of text. In other words, instead of looking at a word as just a word, they might read a sentence straight through. The point of this is that in order for the student to comprehend what he or she is reading, it is necessary to "fluently" and quickly piece together the words in a sentence.

If a student is *not* fluent in reading, he or she slowly sounds out each letter or word and pays more attention to the phonics of each word. A fluent reader, on the other hand, might read a sentence aloud, using appropriate intonations. The best way to test for fluency is to have a student read something out loud, preferably a few or more sentences in a row. Most students who are just learning to read will probably not be very fluent right away, but their fluency will improve with practice.

Even though fluency is not the same as comprehension, fluency is a good predictor of comprehension. If a student is focusing too much on sounding out each word, he or she is not going to be paying attention to the meaning behind them.

Accuracy

One of the best ways to evaluate reading fluency is to look at student accuracy. One method of accomplishing this involves keeping running records of students during oral reading. Calculating the reading level lets teachers know if the book is at a level where the child can read it independently or comfortably with guidance or if the book is at a level where reading it frustrates the child.

As part of the informal assessment of primary-grade reading, it is important to record the child's word insertions, omissions, requests for help, and attempts to determine the word. In informal assessment, the rate of accuracy can be estimated from the ratio of errors to total words read.

The results of keeping a running record informal assessment can be used for teaching based on text accuracy. For example, if a child reads from 95 to 100 percent correctly, the child is ready for independent reading. If the child reads from 92 to 97 percent correctly, the child is ready for guided reading. A score below 92 percent indicates that the child needs a read-aloud or shared reading activity.

Automaticity

Fluency in reading depends on automatic word identification, which assists the student in achieving comprehension of the material. Even slight difficulties in word identification can significantly increase the time it takes a student to read material, because the difficulties may require rereading parts or passages of the material and reduce the level of comprehension expected.

If the student experiences reading as a constant struggle or an arduous chore, he or she may avoid reading whenever possible and consider it a negative experience. Obviously, the ability to read for comprehension, and learning in general, will suffer if all aspects of reading fluency are not presented to the student as acquirable skills that will be readily accomplished with the appropriate effort.

Automatic reading involves the development of strong orthographic representations, which allows fast and accurate identification of whole words made up of specific letter patterns.

Automatic reading involves the development of strong orthographic representations, which allows fast and accurate identification of whole words made up of specific letter patterns. Most young students move easily from the use of alphabetic strategies to the use of orthographic representations that can be accessed automatically.

Initially, word identification is based on the application of phonic word accessibility strategies (letter-sound associations). These strategies are in turn based on the development of phonemic awareness, which is necessary to learn how to relate speech to print. One of the most useful devices for developing automaticity in young students is through the visual pattern provided in the six syllable types:

Syllable Type	Example	Explanation
CLOSED	NOT	Closed in by a consonant—vowel makes its **short** sound
OPEN	NO	Ends in a vowel—vowel makes its **long** sound
NOTE	SILENT "E"	Ends in vowel consonant "e"—vowel makes its **long** sound
NAIL	VOWEL COMBINATION	Two vowels together make the sound
BIRD	"R" CONTROLLED	Contains a vowel plus "r"—vowel sound is changed
TABLE	CONSONANT "L"-"E"	Applied at the end of a word

These orthographic (letter) patterns signal vowel pronunciation to the reader. Students must be able to apply their knowledge of these patterns to recognize the syllable types as well as to see these patterns automatically. This will ultimately allow students to read words as wholes.

The move from decoding letter symbols and identifying recognizable terms to automatic word recognition is a substantial move toward fluency. A significant aid for helping students move through this phase was developed by Anna Gillingham when she incorporated the Phonetic Word Cards activity into the Orton-Gillingham lesson plan (Gillingham and Stillman, 1997). This activity involves asking the students to practice reading words (and some nonwords) on cards as wholes, beginning with simple syllables and moving systematically through the syllable types to complex syllables and two-syllable words. The words should be divided into groups that correspond to the specific sequence of skills being taught.

The students' developments of the elements required by automaticity continually move through stages. One of the next important stages involves the automatic recognition of single graphemes as a step toward the development of the letter patterns that make up words or word parts. English orthography is made up of four basic word types:

1. Regular, for reading and spelling (e.g., *cat, print*)

2. Regular, for reading but not for spelling (e.g., *float, brain*—could be spelled *flote* or *brane*, respectively)

3. Rule based (e.g., *canning*—doubling rule, *faking*—drop the "e" rule)

4. Irregular (e.g., *beauty*)

Students must be taught to recognize all four types of words automatically in order to be effective readers. Repeated practice in pattern recognition is often necessary. Practice techniques for student development can include speed drills in which students read lists of isolated words with contrasting vowel sounds that are signaled by the syllable type. For example, several closed syllable and vowel-consonant-"e" words containing the vowel "a" can be arranged randomly on pages containing about twelve lines and read for one minute. Individual goals are established, and charts should be kept of the number of words read correctly in successive sessions. The same word lists are then repeated in sessions until the goal has been achieved for several succeeding sessions. When selecting words for these lists, the use of high-frequency words in a syllable category increases the likelihood of generalization to text reading.

True automaticity should be linked with prosody and anticipation to acquire full fluency. Concepts such as which syllable is accented or how word structure can be predictive are necessary to true automaticity and essential to complete fluency.

A student whose reading rate is slow, halting, or inconsistent is exhibiting a lack of reading fluency. According to an article by Mastropieri, Leinart, and Scruggs (1999), some students have developed accurate word pronunciation skills but read at a slow rate. They have not moved to the phase where decoding is automatic, and their limited fluency may affect performance in the following ways:

- They read less text peers and have less time to remember, review, or comprehend the text than their peers do.

- They expend more cognitive energy trying to identify individual words than their peers do.

- They may be less able to retain text in their memories and less likely to integrate those segments with other parts of the text

The simplest means of determining a student's reading rate is to have the student read aloud from a prescribed passage (which should be at the appropriate reading level for age and grade and contain a specified number of words). The passage should not be too familiar to the student (some will try to memorize or "work out" difficult parts ahead of time) and should not contain more words than can be read comfortably and accurately by a normal reader in one or two minutes.

Count only the words pronounced *correctly* on the first reading, and divide this word count into elapsed time to determine the student's reading rate. To determine the student's standing and progress, compare this rate with the norm for the

> *True automaticity should be linked with prosody and anticipation to acquire full fluency. Concepts such as which syllable is accented or how word structure can be predictive are necessary to true automaticity and essential to complete fluency.*

class and the average for all students who read fluently at that specific age/grade level.

The following general guidelines can be applied for reading lists of words with a speed drill and a one-minute timing:

- Thirty correct words per minute for first- and second-grade children

- Forty correct wpm for third-grade children

- Sixty correct wpm for mid-third-grade children

- Eighty wpm for students in fourth grade and higher

Various techniques are useful with students who have acquired some proficiency in decoding skill but whose levels of skill are lower than their oral language abilities. Such techniques have certain, common features:

- Students listen to text as they follow along with the book

- Students follow the print using their fingers as guides

- Reading materials are used that students would be unable to read independently

Experts recommend that a beginning reading program should incorporate partner reading, practice in reading difficult words prior to reading the text, timings for accuracy and rate, opportunities to hear books read, and opportunities to read to others.

Prosody concerns the versification of text and involves such matters as which syllable of a word is accented. As regards fluency, it is that aspect that translates reading into the same experience as listening in the reader's mind. Prosody involves intonation and rhythm through such devices as syllable accent and punctuation.

In their article for *Perspectives* (Winter, 2002), Pamela Hook and Sandra Jones proposed that teachers can begin to develop awareness of the prosodic features of language by introducing a short three-word sentence with each of the three different words underlined for stress:

_He_ is sick. He _is_ sick. He is _sick_.

The teacher can then model the three sentences while discussing the possible meaning for each variation. The students can practice reading them with different stresses until they are fluent. These simple three-word sentences can be modified and expanded to include various verbs, pronouns, and tenses:

You are sick. _I_ am sick. _They_ are sick.

This strategy can also be used while increasing the length of phrases and emphasizing the different meanings:

> *Get out of bed. Get out of bed. Get out of bed now.*

Teachers can also practice fluency with common phrases that frequently occur in text.

Prepositional phrases are also good syntactic structures for this type of work:

> *on the _____, in the _____, over the _____*

Teachers can pair these printed phrases with oral intonation patterns that include variations of rate, intensity, and pitch. Students can infer the intended meaning as the teacher presents different prosodic variations of a sentence. For example, when speakers want to stress a concept, they often slow their rate of speech and may speak in a louder voice:

> *Joshua, get-out-of-bed-**NOW**!*

Often, the only text marker for this sentence will be the exclamation point (!), but the speaker's intent will affect the manner in which it is delivered.

Practicing oral variations and then mapping the prosodic features onto the text will assist students in making the connection when reading. This strategy can also be used to alert students to the prosodic features present in punctuation marks.

In the early stages, using the alphabet helps to focus a student on the punctuation marks without having to deal with meaning. The teacher models for the students and then has them practice the combinations, using the correct intonation patterns to fit the punctuation mark:

> *ABC. DE? FGH! IJKL? or ABCD! EFGHI? KL.*

Teachers can then move to simple two-word or three-word sentences. The sentences are punctuated with a period, a question mark, and an exclamation point, and the differences in meaning that occur with each different punctuation mark are discussed:

> *Chris hops. Chris hops? Chris hops!*

It may help students to point out that the printed words convey the fact that someone named Chris is engaged in the physical activity of hopping, but the intonation patterns get their cue from the punctuation mark. The meaning extracted from an encounter with a punctuation mark depends on the students' ability to project an appropriate intonation pattern onto the printed text.

Keeping the text static while changing the punctuation marks helps students to see prosodic patterns. Students who read text word for word may benefit initially from practicing phrasing with the alphabet rather than words, since letters do not tax the meaning system. This is similar to using the alphabet to teach intonation patterns. To accomplish this task, letters are grouped, an arc is drawn underneath, and students recite the alphabet in chunks:

ABC DE FGH IJK LM NOP QRS TU VW XYZ.

Once students understand the concept of phrasing, it is recommended that teachers help students chunk text into syntactic (noun phrases, verb phrases, and prepositional phrases) or meaning units until they are proficient themselves. There are no hard and fast rules for chunking, but syntactic units are most commonly used.

For better readers, teachers can mark the phrasal boundaries with slashes for short passages. Eventually, the slashes will be used only at the beginning of long passages, and students will be asked to continue "phrase reading" even after the marks end. Marking phrases can be done together with students, or those on an independent level may divide passages into phrases themselves.

Comparisons can be made to clarify reasons for differences in phrasing. Another way to encourage students to focus on phrase meaning and prosody (in addition to word identification) is to provide tasks that require them to identify or supply a paraphrase of an original statement.

Sample Test Questions and Rationale

(Average)

1. If a student has a poor vocabulary, what should the teacher recommend?

    A. The student should read newspapers, magazines, and books on a regular basis

    B. The student should enroll in a Latin class

    C. The student should write the words frequently after looking them up in the dictionary

    D. The student should use a thesaurus to locate synonyms and incorporate them into his or her vocabulary

    Answer: A. The student should read newspapers, magazines, and books on a regular basis

    It is up to the teacher to help the student to choose reading material, but the student must be able to choose where he or she will search for the reading pleasure that is indispensable for enriching vocabulary.

(Easy)

2. Which of the following indicates that a student is a fluent reader?

    A. Reads texts with expression or prosody

    B. Reads word-to-word and haltingly

    C. Must intentionally decode a majority of the words

    D. In a writing assignment, sentences are poorly organized

    Answer: A. Reads texts with expression or prosody

    The teacher should listen to the children read aloud, but there are also clues to reading levels in their writing.

(Rigorous)

3. All of the following are examples of ongoing informal assessment techniques used to observe student progress *except*:

    A. Analysis of student work product

    B. Collection of data from assessment tests

    C. Effective questioning

    D. Observation of students

    Answer: B. Collection of data from assessment tests

    Assessment tests are formal progress-monitoring measures.

(Easy)

4. Which of the following is a formal reading level assessment?

    A. A standardized reading test

    B. A teacher-made reading test

    C. An interview

    D. A reading diary

    Answer: A. A standardized reading test

    If the assessment is standardized, it has to be objective, whereas B, C, and D are all subjective assessments.

SKILL 4.2 Analyzing the relationship between reading fluency and comprehension

Reading fluency refers to a student's speed, smoothness, and ease of oral reading. Fluent readers read rapidly and smoothly, allowing their minds to focus on comprehension of the text, thereby gaining meaning from the text they read. Because reading fluency leads to reading comprehension, fluent readers typically enjoy reading more than students who apply all their energy to just sounding out the words. Struggling readers often labor to identify each word on the page, becoming so occupied in the process of identifying words that they are unable to devote any attention to comprehending the text they are reading.

Strategies to Improve Reading Fluency	• Repeated oral reading with guidance • Graphing the student's reading rate over repeated readings • Buddy reading • Instructor modeling of fluent reading followed by student rereading
Reading Comprehension Skills	• Using prior knowledge and making connections • Determining the main idea, summarizing, and drawing conclusions • Analyzing, evaluating, and predicting • Distinguishing facts and opinions • Determining the author's purpose

In order to develop fluent readers, knowledgeable teachers should devote substantial instructional time to enhancing the reading fluency of students.

SKILL 4.3 Recognizing the effects of various factors (e.g., prior knowledge, context, vocabulary knowledge, graphic cues) on reading comprehension

Conspicuous Strategies

As an instructional priority, CONSPICUOUS STRATEGIES are a sequence of teaching events and teacher actions used to help students to learn new literacy information and relate it to their existing knowledge. Conspicuous strategies can be

CONSPICUOUS STRATEGIES: a sequence of teaching events and teacher actions used to help students to learn new literacy information and relate it to their existing knowledge

MEDIATED SCAFFOLDING: temporary support or guidance provided to students in the form of steps, tasks, materials, and personal support during initial learning

STRATEGIC INTEGRATION: when information is carefully combined with what the learner already knows and understands to produce a more generalizable, higher-order skill

BACKGROUND KNOWLEDGE: the basic knowledge most children bring to their learning experiences

incorporated in beginning reading instruction to ensure that all learners have basic literacy concepts. During storybook reading, teachers should show students how to recognize the fronts and backs of books, locate titles, or look at pictures and predict the story, rather than just assume that children will learn this through incidental exposure. Teachers can also teach students a strategy for holding a pencil appropriately or checking the form of their letters against an alphabet sheet on their desks or the classroom wall.

Mediated scaffolding

MEDIATED SCAFFOLDING can be accomplished in a number of ways to meet the needs of students with diverse literacy experiences. To link oral and written language, for example, teachers may use texts that simulate speech by incorporating oral language patterns or children's writing. Teachers can use daily storybook reading to discuss book-handling skills and directionality concepts that are particularly important for children who are unfamiliar with printed texts. Teachers can also use repeated readings to give students multiple exposures to unfamiliar words, extend opportunities to look at books with predictable patterns, and provide support by modeling the behaviors associated with reading. Teachers can act as *scaffolds* during these storybook reading activities by adjusting their demands, such as asking increasingly complex questions or encouraging children to take on portions of the reading, or by reading more complex text as students gain knowledge of beginning literacy components.

Strategic integration

Many children with diverse literacy experiences have difficulty making connections between old and new information. STRATEGIC INTEGRATION can be applied to help link old and new learning. For example, in the classroom, strategic integration can be accomplished by providing access to literacy materials in classroom writing centers and libraries. Students should also have opportunities to integrate and extend their literacy knowledge by reading aloud, listening to other students read aloud, and listening to tape recordings and videotapes in reading corners.

Primed background knowledge

All children bring some level of BACKGROUND KNOWLEDGE, such as how to hold a book, awareness of directionality of print, to beginning reading. Teachers can utilize the children's background knowledge to help them link their personal literacy experiences with beginning reading instruction while also closing the gap between students who have strong literacy experiences and those who have few such experiences.

Activities that draw upon background knowledge include incorporating oral language activities (which discriminate between printed letters and words) into daily read-alouds, as well as providing frequent opportunities to retell stories, look at books with predictable patterns, write messages with invented spellings, and respond to literature through drawing.

Emergent literacy

EMERGENT LITERACY research examines early literacy knowledge and the contexts and conditions that foster that knowledge. Despite differing viewpoints on the relation between emerging literacy skills and reading acquisition, there is strong evidence that early-childhood exposure to oral and written language is linked to the facility with which children learn to read.

> **EMERGENT LITERACY:** the early reading and writing behaviors that precede and develop into conventional literacy

Reading for comprehension of factual material, such as content area textbooks, reference books, and newspapers, is closely related to study strategies in the middle/junior high setting. Organized study models, such as the SQ3R method—a technique that makes it possible to learn the content of even large amounts of text (Survey, Question, Read, Recite, and Review Studying)—teach students to locate main ideas and supporting details, to recognize sequential order, to distinguish fact from opinion, and to determine cause-and-effect relationships.

SKILL 4.4 Distinguishing among literal, inferential, and evaluative comprehension

> **LITERAL COMPREHENSION:** the understanding of the basic facts of a given passage

LITERAL COMPREHENSION is the understanding of the basic facts of a given passage. This level of comprehension is the priority for the reader so that he or she can maintain coherence and a general understanding of what is being read.

INFERENTIAL COMPREHENSION is the ability to create or infer a hypothesis for a given statement based on collected facts and information. Research suggests that students must mentally "highlight" relevant information they might need later in order to relate and connect ideas from the passage. Understandings of concepts such as syntax, morphology, discourse, and pragmatics are all needed for students to effectively make inferences while reading.

> **INFERENTIAL COMPREHENSION:** the ability to create or infer a hypothesis for a given statement based on collected facts and information

EVALUATIVE COMPREHENSION is the ability to understand and sort facts, opinions, assumptions, persuasive elements, and the validity of a passage. Students with excellent evaluative comprehension skills cannot only infer meaning from the text but can also compare, contrast, and apply what is read.

> **EVALUATIVE COMPREHENSION:** the ability to understand and sort facts, opinions, assumptions, persuasive elements, and the validity of a passage

Sample Test Questions and Rationale

(Easy)

1. **Which of the following is an opinion?**

   A. A subjective evaluation based on personal bias

   B. A statement that is readily provable by objective empirical data

   C. The sky is blue

   D. Airplanes flew into the World Trade Center on September 11, 2001

   Answer: A. Subjective evaluation based on personal bias

   An opinion is a subjective evaluation based on personal bias.

(Easy)

2. **Which of the following is a fact?**

   A. It's going to rain

   B. John is a liar

   C. Joe said he believes John is a liar

   D. The world is going to the dogs

   Answer: C. Joe said he believes John is a liar

   The only answer that is a fact is C. Joe said he believes that John is a liar. It's a fact that he *said* it, even though what he said may not be a fact.

SKILL 4.5 Identifying strategies for promoting students' literal, inferential, and evaluative comprehension

The five key strategies to increase children's abilities to read informational/expository texts are as follows:

> **INFERENCING:** an evaluative process that involves the reader in making a reasonable judgment based on the information given and engages children in literally constructing meaning

1. **INFERENCING** is an evaluative process that involves the reader in making a reasonable judgment based on the information given and engages children in literally constructing meaning. In order to develop and enhance inferencing in children, a teacher may consider having a minilesson in which this key skill is demonstrated by reading an expository book aloud (e.g., one on skyscrapers for young children) and then demonstrating for them the following reading habits: looking for clues, reflecting on what the reader already knows about the topic ("activating" prior knowledge), and using the clues in the expository text to figure out what the author means.

2. Identifying main ideas in an expository text can be improved when children have an explicit strategy for identifying important information. They can be included in making this strategy part of their everyday reading style by being focused and "walked" through exercises as a part of a series of guided reading sessions. The child should read a passage so he or she can readily identify the topic.

3. The child should be asked to be on the lookout for a sentence in the expository passage that summarizes the key information in the paragraph or in the lengthier excerpt. The child should then read the rest of the passage or excerpt in light of this information and also note which information in the paragraph is not important. The child can then use the important information to formulate the author's main idea and may even want to use some of the author's own words to formulate that idea.

4. MONITORING means self-clarifying: As students read, they often realize that what they are reading doesn't make sense. The reader must then make a "plan" to figure out the meaning of the excerpt. Cooper and other balanced literacy advocates have a "stop and think" strategy that they use with children. The child is asked to consider, "Does this make sense to me?" If the child concludes that it does not, he or she then rereads the text, reads ahead in the text, looks up unknown words, or asks for help from the teacher.

MONITORING: means self-clarifying

5. What is important about monitoring is that some readers ask these questions and try these approaches without ever being explicitly taught them in school. However, the key philosophy of the reading theorists mentioned here is that these strategies need to be explicitly modeled and practiced under the guidance of the teacher by most, if not all, child readers.

6. SUMMARIZING engages the reader in pulling out the essential bits of information in a longer passage or excerpt of text and making them into a cohesive whole. Children can be taught to summarize informational or expository text by following these guidelines. First, they should look at the topic sentence of the paragraph or the text and delete the trivia. They should then search for information that has been mentioned more than once and make sure it is included only once in their summary. Students should find related ideas or items and group them under a unifying heading; they can then search for and identify a main idea sentence. Finally, they can put the summary together using all of these guidelines.

SUMMARIZING: engages the reader in pulling out the essential bits of information in a longer passage or excerpt of text and making them into a cohesive whole

Generating questions can motivate and enhance children's comprehension of reading in that they become actively involved in generating their own questions and then answering these questions based on their reading.

In order to generate meaningful questions that trigger constructive reading in expository texts, children should preview the text by reading the titles and subheads (they should also look at the illustrations and the pictures). Students may then begin to read the first paragraph. These first previews should yield an impressive batch of specific questions.

Next, children should get into their "Dr. Seuss mode" by asking themselves a "think" question. For younger children, having a "think" hat in the classroom that the children can put on can be very effective.

Teachers should make certain that the children write down the "think" question and encourage them to read to find important information to answer it. The children should be asked to write down the answer they found and to copy the sentence or sentences where they found the answer. Also, children should be encouraged to consider whether, in light of their further reading through the text, their original question was a good one or not.

The teacher should ask the students to be prepared to explain why or why not their original question was a good one. Once the children have answered their original "think" question, they can generate additional ones.

SKILL 4.6 **Applying knowledge of strategies** *(e.g., predicting, rereading, retelling)* **that facilitate comprehension before, during, and after reading**

Making Predictions

One approach to teaching reading that gained currency in the late 1960s and the early 1970s involved asking the readers inferential and critical thinking questions that would challenge and engage them in the text. This approach to reading went beyond the literal level of what was stated in the text to an inferential level of using text clues to make predictions, and it extended further to a critical level of involving the child in evaluating the text. While asking engaging and thought-provoking questions is still considered an important part of teaching reading, it is currently viewed only as one component.

Prior Knowledge

PRIOR KNOWLEDGE can be defined as all of an individual's prior experiences, education, and development that precede his or her entrance into a specific learning situation or his or her attempts to comprehend a specific text. At times, prior knowledge can be erroneous or incomplete. If there are misconceptions in a child's prior knowledge, these must be corrected so that the child's overall comprehension skills can continue to progress. Prior knowledge even at the kindergarten level includes accumulated positive and negative experiences both in and out of school.

Prior knowledge might range from family travels, watching television, and visiting museums and libraries to visiting hospitals, prisons, and struggling with poverty. Whatever the prior knowledge the child brings to the school setting, the independent reading and writing the child does in school immeasurably expands his or her prior knowledge, hence broadening his or her reading comprehension capabilities.

Literary response skills are also dependent on SCHEMATA, which are those structures that represent generic concepts stored in the memory. Effective textual comprehension, whether done by adults or children, uses schemata and prior knowledge in addition to the ideas from the printed text for reading comprehension; graphic organizers help to organize this information.

> **PRIOR KNOWLEDGE:** all of an individual's prior experiences, education, and development that precede his or her entrance into a specific learning situation or his or her attempts to comprehend a specific text

> **SCHEMATA:** structures that represent generic concepts stored in the memory

Graphic Organizers

Graphic organizers solidify in a chart format a visual relationship among various reading and writing ideas. These ideas include sequence, timelines, character traits, fact and opinion, main ideas and details, differences, and likenesses (generally done using a Venn diagram of interlocking circles, a KWL chart, etc.). These charts and formats are essential for providing scaffolding for instruction by activating pertinent prior knowledge.

KWL (Know, Want, Learn) charts are very useful for reading comprehension because they outline what children *know*, what they *want* to know, and what they've *learned* after reading. Students are asked to activate prior knowledge about a topic and further develop their knowledge about a topic using this organizer. Teachers often opt to display and maintain KWL charts throughout a classroom to continually record pertinent information about students' reading.

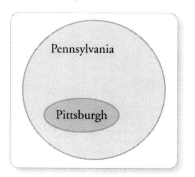

KWL		
What I know	**What I want to know**	**What I have learned**
•	•	•
•	•	•
•	•	•

The most interesting fact I learned was:

_____

_____

When the teacher first introduces the KWL strategy, the children should be allowed sufficient time to brainstorm in response to the first question: What do they already know about the topic? The children should have a three-columned KWL worksheet template for their journals, and a chart should be available to record the responses from class or group discussions. The children can write under each column in their own journal, and they should also help their teacher with notations on the chart. This strategy involves the children in actually gaining experience in note taking and in creating a concrete record of new data and information gleaned from the passage about the topic.

Depending on the grade level of the participating children, the teacher may also want to channel them into considering categories of information they hope to find out from the expository passage. For instance, they may be reading a book on animals to find out more about the animal's habitats during the winter or about the animal's mating habits. When the children are working on the middle column—what they want to know about the reading—the teacher may want to help them to express it in question format.

KWL is a useful tool and can even be introduced as early as second grade with extensive teacher discussion and support. It not only serves to support the child's comprehension of a particular expository text, but it also models for children a format for note taking. In addition, when the teacher wants to introduce report writing, the KWL format provides excellent outlines and question introductions for at least three paragraphs of a report.

Cooper (2004) recommends this strategy for use with thematic units and reading chapters in required science, social studies, or health text books. In addition to its usefulness with thematic unit study, KWL is wonderful for providing the teacher with a concrete format to assess how well children have absorbed pertinent new knowledge in the passage (by looking at the third L section). Ultimately, it is hoped that students will learn to use this strategy not only under explicit teacher direction with templates of KWL sheets but also on their own by informally writing questions they want to find out about in their journals and then going back and answering them after the reading.

Note Taking

Older children should take notes in their reading journals, while younger children and those more in need of explicit teacher support may contribute their ideas and responses as part of the discussion in class. Their responses should be recorded on the experiential chart.

Connecting Texts

The concept of readiness is generally regarded as a developmentally based phenomenon. Various abilities, whether cognitive, affective, or psychomotor, are perceived to be dependent on the mastery or development of certain prerequisite skills or abilities. Readiness, then, implies that prior to accomplishing the knowledge, experience, and readiness prerequisites, children should not yet engage in the new task.

Readiness for subject area learning is dependent not only on prior knowledge but also on affective factors such as interest, motivation, and attitude. These factors are often more influential on student learning than the preexisting cognitive base. When texts relate to a student's life or other reading materials or areas of study, they become more meaningful and relevant to students' learning. Students typically enjoy seeing reading material that connects to their lives, other subject areas, and other reading material.

> Readiness for subject area learning is dependent not only on prior knowledge but also on affective factors such as interest, motivation, and attitude.

Discussing the Text

Discussion is an activity in which the children (this activity works well from grades three through six and beyond) conclude a particular text. Among the prompts, the teacher-coach might suggest that the children focus on words of interest they encountered in the text. These can also be words that they heard if the text was read aloud.

Children can be asked to share something funny, upsetting, or unusual about the words they have read. Through this focus on children's responses to words as the center of the discussion circle, peers become more interested in word study. Furthermore, in the current teaching of literacy, reading, writing, thinking, listening, viewing, and discussing are not viewed as separate activities or components of instruction but rather as simultaneous and interactive elements of reading comprehension.

COMPETENCY 5

UNDERSTAND COMPREHENSION STRATEGIES FOR LITERARY AND INFORMATIONAL TEXTS ACROSS THE CURRICULUM

SKILL 5.1 Recognizing types and characteristics of literary and informational texts

Fiction versus Nonfiction

Students often misrepresent the differences between fiction and nonfiction. They mistakenly believe that stories are always examples of fiction. The simple truth is that stories are both fiction and nonfiction. The primary difference is that fiction is made up by the author and nonfiction is generally fact (or an opinion).

It is harder for students to understand that nonfiction entails an enormous range of material, from textbooks and true stories to newspaper articles and speeches. Fiction, on the other hand, is fairly simple, consisting of made-up stories, novels, and so on. However, it is also important for students to understand that most of fiction throughout history has been based on true events. In other words, authors use their own life experiences to help them create works of fiction.

In understanding fiction, it is important to recognize the artistry in telling a story to convey a point. When students see that an author's choice in a work of fiction is for the sole purpose of conveying a viewpoint, they can make better sense of the specific details in the work of fiction. To understand nonfiction, it is important to realize what is truth and what is perspective. Often, a nonfiction writer will present an opinion, and that opinion may be very different from the truth. Knowing the difference between the two is very crucial.

In comparing fiction to nonfiction, students need to learn about the conventions of each. In fiction, students can generally expect to see plot, characters, settings, and themes. In nonfiction, students may also see these features, but they will also see interpretations, opinions, theories, research, and other elements.

Over time, students may begin to see patterns that identify fiction from nonfiction. Often, the more fanciful or unrealistic a story is, the more likely it is fiction. On the other hand, the saying "truth is stranger than fiction" is reinforced by the outrageous true events that sometimes comprise the basis of nonfiction.

> *To understand nonfiction, it is important to realize what is truth and what is perspective.*

Therefore, it is vital for students to have a strong framework of understanding for the literary conventions that separate the two genres.

> ### SKILL 5.2 Identifying characteristics and functions of literary elements and devices *(e.g., plot, point of view, setting)*

Most works of fiction contain a common set of elements that make them come alive to readers. In a way, even though writers do not consciously think about each of these elements when they sit down to write, all stories essentially contain these "markers" that make them the stories that they are. However, even though all stories share these elements, they are a lot like fingerprints: Each story's elements are different.

Let's look at a few of the most commonly discussed elements. The most commonly discussed story element in fiction is plot, which is the series of events in a story. Typically, but not always, plot moves in a predictable fashion:

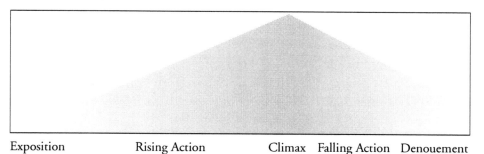

Exposition   Rising Action   Climax   Falling Action   Denouement

> **Exposition** *is when characters and their situations are introduced.*
> **Rising action** *is the point at which conflict starts to occur.*
> **Climax** *is the highest point of conflict, often a turning point.*
> **Falling action** *is the result of the climax.*
> **Denouement** *is the final resolution of the plot.*

CHARACTER is another commonly studied story element. In stories, we often find heroes, villains, comedic characters, dark characters, and so on. When we examine the characters of a story, we look to see who they are and how their traits contribute to the story. Often, because of their characteristics, plot elements become more interesting. For example, authors may pair unlikely characters together in a way that creates specific conflict.

> **CHARACTER:** the person, such as a hero or villain, represented in a story

SETTING: the place or location where a story occurs

The **SETTING** of a story is the place or location where it occurs. Often, the specific place is not as important as some of the specifics about the setting. For example, the setting of *The Great Gatsby*—New York—is not as significant as the fact that it takes place among incredible wealth. Conversely, *The Grapes of Wrath*, although it takes place in Oklahoma and California, has the more significant setting of poverty. In fact, as the story takes place *around* other migrant workers, the setting is even more significant. In a way, the setting serves as a reason for various conflicts to occur.

THEMES: the underlying messages, above and beyond all plot elements, that writers want to convey

THEMES of stories are the underlying messages, above and beyond all plot elements, that writers want to convey. Very rarely will one find that good literature is without a theme, a lesson, a message, or an ideal. The best writers in the English language all seem to want to convey something about human nature or the world, and they turn to literature in order to do that. Common themes in literature are jealousy, money, love, and citizen against corporation or government. These themes are never explicitly stated; rather, they are the result of the portrayal of characters, settings, and plots. Readers get the message even if the theme is not directly stated.

MOOD: the atmosphere or attitude the writer conveys through descriptive language

Finally, the **MOOD** of a story is the atmosphere or attitude the writer conveys through descriptive language. Often, mood fits nicely with theme and setting. For example, in Edgar Allan Poe's stories, we often find a mood of horror and darkness. We get that from the descriptions of characters and the settings, as well as from specific plot elements. Mood simply helps us to better understand the writer's theme and intentions through descriptive, stylistic language.

Sample Test Questions and Rationale

(Rigorous)

1. **Which is an untrue statement about a theme in literature?**

   A. The theme is always stated directly somewhere in the text

   B. The theme is the central idea in a literary work

   C. All parts of the work (plot, setting, mood) should contribute to the theme in some way

   D. By analyzing the various elements of the work, the reader should be able to arrive at an indirectly stated theme

   Answer: A. The theme is always stated directly somewhere in the text

   The theme may be stated directly, but it can also be implicit in various aspects of the work, such as the interaction among characters, symbolism, or description.

(Rigorous)

2. **Exposition occurs in a story:**

   A. After the rising action

   B. After the denouement

   C. Before the rising action

   D. Before the setting

   Answer: C. Before the rising action

   Exposition is where characters and their situations are introduced. Rising action is the point at which conflict starts to occur and is often a turning point. Denouement is the final resolution of the plot.

SKILL 5.3 Applying strategies for developing students' literary response skills *(e.g., making connections between texts and personal experiences)*

While literature is a vehicle for teaching reading comprehension and writing, it is often overlooked that a very important reason for teaching literature is to help students understand how to appreciate written text, complex ideas, poetic language and ideas, and unique perspectives. However, just presenting good literature

A very important reason for teaching literature is to help students understand how to appreciate written text, complex ideas, poetic language and ideas, and unique perspectives.

to students is not enough. They need the opportunity to be actively involved with the literature and the chance to respond to the literature in a variety of ways. Response helps students to personalize the literature (in other words, to understand that the literature comes from human instincts and issues), to make sense of the meaning, and to appreciate it more.

Appropriate responses to literature come in many forms. Many students learn a lot by responding with additional works of art—other literature (poetry, fiction, science fiction), art, or music. For example, students can write a poem expressing the mood of a character or draw a picture that portrays a scene in a novel. They can even be asked to rewrite the ending of a story. Giving students the opportunity to be creative in these ways helps them to "enter" into the literature more fully. It gives them a real opportunity to interact with the book's ideas, characters, settings, and author.

Analytic writing is another good way to respond to literature. Of course, this may not seem as much fun from the student perspective, but analytic writing allows students to see that there is not just one way to view literature. They often learn best when they understand that their possibly unconventional ways of understanding literature must be defended with clear examples from the text.

Drama is another very effective tool for responding to literature. When students act out scenes from a novel, for example, they begin to understand the characters' motives more clearly.

The list of appropriate responses to literature could go on and on, but it is important for teachers to match up appropriate responses with the literature and their students. Not every type of response will work well for all students and for all pieces of literature, so careful selection is important.

Sample Test Questions and Rationale

(Easy)

1. **Which of the following are important reasons for teaching literature?**

   A. Active involvement with the literature

   B. Appreciate written text

   C. Make sense of meaning

   D. All of the above

   Answer: D. All of the above

   Children need active involvement with the literature. Students also can understand how to appreciate written text.

(Easy)

2. **Which of the following is not a characteristic of a fable?**

   A. Animals that feel and talk like humans

   B. Happy solutions to human dilemmas

   C. Teaches a moral or standard for behavior

   D. Illustrates specific people or groups without directly naming them

   Answer: D. Illustrates specific people or groups without directly naming them

   A fable is a short tale with animals, humans, gods, or even inanimate objects as characters. Fables often conclude with a moral, delivered in the form of an epigram (a short, witty, and ingenious statement in verse). Fables are among the oldest forms of writing in human history: it appears in Egyptian papyri of c. 1500 BCE. The most famous fables are those of Aesop, a Greek slave who lived about 600 BCE. In India, the *Pantchatantra* appeared in the third century. The most famous modern fables are those of seventeenth-century French poet Jean de La Fontaine.

Major Literary Genres

- **Allegory:** A story in verse or prose with characters representing virtues and vices. An allegory can have a symbolic or literal meaning. John Bunyan's *Pilgrim's Progress* is the most renowned of this genre.

- **Ballad:** An *in medias res* (Latin for "in the middle of things") story told or sung, usually in verse and accompanied by music. Literary devices found in ballads include the refrain, or repeated section, and incremental repetition, or anaphora, for effect. The earliest forms were anonymous folk ballads. Later forms include Coleridge's Romantic masterpiece "Rime of the Ancient Mariner."

- **Drama:** Plays—comedy, modern, or tragedy—typically conducted in five acts. Traditionalists and neoclassicists adhere to Aristotle's unities of time, place, and action. Plot development is advanced through dialogue. Literary devices include asides, soliloquies, and the chorus representation of public opinion. William Shakespeare is considered by many to be the greatest of all dramatists/playwrights. Other notable dramaturges include Ibsen, Williams, Miller, Shaw, Stoppard, Racine, Molière, Sophocles, Aeschylus, Euripides, and Aristophanes.

- **Epic:** A long poem usually of book length that reflects values inherent in the generative society. Epic devices include an invocation to a muse for inspiration, an overall purpose for writing, a universal setting, a protagonist and antagonist who possess supernatural strength and acumen, and the interventions of a supreme being or the gods. Overall, there are very few epics. Some of the most notable include Homer's *Iliad* and *Odyssey*, Virgil's *Aeneid*, Milton's *Paradise Lost*, Spenser's *The Faerie Queene*, Barrett Browning's *Aurora Leigh*, and Pope's mock-epic *The Rape of the Lock*.

- **Epistle:** A letter that is not always originally intended for public distribution but, due to the fame of the sender and/or recipient, becomes public domain. For example, the apostle Paul wrote epistles that were later placed in the Bible.

- **Essay:** Typically, a limited-length prose work that focuses on a topic and propounds a definite point of view through an authoritative tone. Great essayists include Carlyle, Lamb, DeQuincy, Emerson, and Montaigne, who is credited with defining this genre.

- **Fable:** A terse tale offering up a moral or exemplum. Chaucer's *The Nun's Priest's Tale* is a fine example of a bête fabliau (beast fable), in which animals speak and act characteristically human, illustrating human foibles.

- **Legend:** A traditional narrative or collection of related narratives, popularly regarded as historically factual but actually a mixture of fact and fiction.

- **Myth:** Stories that are more or less universally shared in a culture to explain its history and traditions.

- **Novel:** The longest form of fictional prose containing a variety of characterizations, settings, local color, and regionalism. Most have complex plots, expanded descriptions, and attention to detail. Some of the great novelists include Austen, the Brontës, Twain, Tolstoy, Hugo, Hardy, Dickens, Hawthorne, Forster, and Flaubert.

- **Poem:** A work in which the only requirement is rhythm. Subgenres include fixed types of literature such as sonnets, elegies, odes, pastorals, and villanelle. Unfixed types of literature include blank verse and dramatic monologue.

- **Romance:** A highly imaginative tale set in a fantastical realm dealing with the conflicts between heroes and villains and/or monsters. "Knight's Tale" from *Chaucer's The Canterbury Tales, Sir Gawain and the Green Knight*, and Keats's "The Eve of St. Agnes" are prime examples.

- **Short Story:** Typically a terse narrative with less developmental background about characters but that still includes description, point of view, and tone. Poe emphasized that a successful short story should create one focused impact. Considered among the greatest short story writers are Hemingway, Faulkner, Twain, Joyce, Jackson, O'Connor, de Maupassant, Saki, Poe, and Pushkin.

Children's literature

Children's literature is a genre of its own that emerged as a distinct and independent form in the second half of the eighteenth century. *The Visible World in Pictures* by John Amos Comenius, a Czech educator, was one of the first printed works and the first picture book. For the first time, educators acknowledged that children are different from adults in many respects. Modern educators agree that introducing elementary students to a wide range of reading experiences plays an important role in their mental, social, and psychological developments. Some common forms of literature that are specifically for children include the following.

Traditional literature

Traditional literature opens up a world where right wins out over wrong, where hard work and perseverance are rewarded, and where helpless victims find vindication—all worthwhile values that children identify with even as early as kindergarten. In traditional literature, children are introduced to fanciful beings, humans with exaggerated powers, talking animals, and heroes who will inspire them. For younger elementary children, these stories in Big Book format are ideal for providing predictable and repetitive elements that can be easily grasped.

- Folktales/Fairy Tales: Some examples include "The Three Bears," "Little Red Riding Hood," "Snow White," "Sleeping Beauty," "Puss-in-Boots," "Rapunzel," and "Rumpelstiltskin." Adventures of animals or humans and the supernatural characterize these stories. The hero is usually on a quest and is aided by other-worldly helpers. More often than not, the story focuses on good and evil and reward and punishment.

- Fables: Animals that act like humans are featured in these stories; they usually reveal human foibles or sometimes teach a lesson. One example is *Aesop's Fables*.

- Myths: These stories about events from the earliest times, such as the origin of the world, are considered true in their own societies.

- Legends: These are similar to myths except that they tend to deal with events that happened more recently. One example is Arthurian legends.

- Tall Tales: Paul Bunyan, John Henry, and Pecos Bill are all characters in tall tales. These are purposely exaggerated accounts of individuals with superhuman strength.

- Modern Fantasy: Many of the themes found in these stories are similar to those in traditional literature. The stories start out based in reality, which makes it easier for the reader to suspend disbelief and enter worlds of unreality. Little people live in the walls in *The Borrowers*, and time travel is possible in *The Trolley to Yesterday*. Including some fantasy tales in the curriculum helps elementary-grade children to develop their senses of imagination. Fantasy literature often appeals to ideals of justice and issues having to do with good and evil. Because children tend to identify with the characters, the message is more likely to be retained.

- Science Fiction: Robots, spacecraft, mystery, and civilizations from other ages and planets often appear in these stories. Most presume advances in science on other planets or in a future time. Most children like these stories because of their interest in space and the "what if" aspect of the stories. Some examples of science fiction books are *Outer Space and All That Junk* and *A Wrinkle in Time*.

- Modern Realistic Fiction: These stories are about real problems that real children face. When children see that their hopes and fears are shared by others, they can find insight into their own problems. Young readers also tend to experience a broadening of interests as the result of this kind of reading. It's good for them to know that a child can be brave and intelligent and can solve difficult problems.

- Historical Fiction: *Rifles for Watie* by Harold Keith is an example of this kind of story. Presented in a historically accurate setting, this book is about a young boy (sixteen years old) who serves in the Union army during the Civil War. He experiences great hardship but discovers that his enemy is an admirable human being. It provides a good opportunity to introduce younger children to history in a beneficial way.

- Biography: Reading about inventors, explorers, scientists, political and religious leaders, social reformers, artists, sports figures, doctors, teachers, writers, and war heroes helps children to see that one person can make a difference. They also open new vistas for children to think about when they choose an occupation to consider for their own futures.

- Informational Books: These are ways to learn more about something you are interested in or something that you know nothing about. Encyclopedias are good resources, of course, but a book like *Polar Wildlife* by Kamini Khanduri shows pictures and facts that capture the imaginations of young children.

Sample Test Questions and Rationale

(Average)

1. **Which of the following is an example of alliteration?**

   A. "The City's voice itself is soft like Solitude."

   B. "Both in one faith unanimous; though sad."

   C. "By all their country's wishes blest!"

   D. "In earliest Greece to thee with partial choice."

Answer: A. "The City's voice itself is soft like Solitude."

Alliteration is the repetition of consonant sounds in two or more neighboring words or syllables, usually the beginning sound but not always. This line from Shelley's *Stanzas Written in Dejection Near Naples* is an especially effective use of alliteration using the sibilant s not only at the beginning of words but also within words. Alliteration usually appears in prosody, but effective use of alliteration can be found in other genres.

(Average)

2. **Which of the following is a ballad?**

   A. "The Knight's Tale"

   B. *Julius Caesar*

   C. *Paradise Lost*

   D. "Rime of the Ancient Mariner"

Answer: D. "Rime of the Ancient Mariner"

"The Knight's Tale" is a Romantic poem from the longer *Canterbury Tales* by Chaucer. *Julius Caesar* is a Shakespearian play. *Paradise Lost* is an epic poem in blank verse. A ballad is an *in media res* story told or sung, usually in verse and accompanied by music, and usually with a refrain. Typically, ballads are based on folk stories.

(Average)

3. **Which of the following is an epic?**

   A. *On the Choice of Books*

   B. *The Faerie Queene*

   C. *Northanger Abbey*

   D. *A Doll's House*

Answer: B. *The Faerie Queene*

An epic is a long poem, usually of book length, reflecting the values of the society in which it was produced. *On the Choice of Books* is an essay by Thomas Carlyle. *Northanger Abbey* is a novel written by Jane Austen, and *A Doll's House* is a play written by Henrik Ibsen.

(Average)

4. **The children's literature genre came into its own in the:**

   A. Seventeenth century

   B. Eighteenth century

   C. Nineteenth century

   D. Twentieth century

Answer: B. Eighteenth century

Children's literature is a genre of its own that emerged as a distinct and independent form in the second half of the eighteenth century. *The Visible World in Pictures* by John Amos Comenius, a Czech educator, was one of the first printed works and the first picture book.

| SKILL 5.5 | Recognizing common patterns of organization in informational texts *(e.g., chronological, cause and effect)* |

Main Idea

A TOPIC of a paragraph or story is what the paragraph or story is about. The MAIN IDEA of a paragraph or story states the important idea(s) that the author wants the reader to know about a topic. The topic and main idea of a paragraph or story are sometimes directly stated. There are times, however, when the topic and main idea are not directly stated but are only implied. For example, look at the following paragraph:

> *Henry Ford was an inventor who developed the first affordable automobile. The cars that were being built before Ford created the Model-T were very expensive. Only rich people could afford to have cars.*

The topic of this paragraph is Henry Ford. The main idea is that Henry Ford built the first affordable automobile.

The TOPIC SENTENCE indicates what the passage is about. It is the subject of that portion of the narrative. The ability to identify the topic sentence in a passage enables the student to focus on the concept being discussed and to better comprehend the information provided.

You can find the main ideas by looking at the way in which paragraphs are written. A paragraph is a group of sentences about one main idea. Paragraphs usually have two types of sentences: a topic sentence, which contains the main idea, and two or more detail sentences that support, prove, provide more information, explain, or give examples. You can tell if you have a detail or topic sentence by comparing the sentences with each other. Look at this sample paragraph:

> *Fall is the best of the four seasons. The leaves change colors to create a beautiful display of golds, reds, and oranges. The air turns crisp and windy. The scents of pumpkin muffins and apple pies fill the air. Finally, Halloween marks the start of the holiday season. Fall is my favorite time of year!*

Here is a breakdown of these sentences:

TOPIC: a paragraph or story is what the paragraph or story is about

MAIN IDEA: a paragraph or story states the important idea(s) that the author wants the reader to know about a topic

TOPIC SENTENCE: indicates what the passage is about

Fall is the best of the four seasons. (TOPIC SENTENCE)

The leaves change colors to create a beautiful display of golds, reds, and oranges. (DETAIL)

The air turns crisp and windy. (DETAIL)

The scents of pumpkin muffins and apple pies fill the air. (DETAIL)

Finally, Halloween marks the start of the holiday season. (DETAIL)

Fall is my favorite time of year! *(CLOSING SENTENCE—This is often a restatement of the topic sentence.)*

Tips for finding the topic sentence

- The topic sentence is usually first, although it could be in any position in the paragraph.

- A topic is usually more "general" than the other sentences; that is, it addresses many things and looks at the big picture. Sometimes it refers to more than one thing. Plurals and the words *many, numerous,* or *several* often signal a topic sentence.

- Detail sentences are usually more "specific" than the topic; that is, they usually address one single idea or one side of an idea. Also, the words *for example, that is, first, second, third,* and *finally* often signal a detail.

- Most of the detail sentences support, give examples, prove, talk about, or point toward the topic in some way.

How can you be sure that you have a topic sentence? Try this trick: Switch the sentence you think is the topic sentence into a question. If the other sentences seem to "answer" the question, then you've got it. Here is an example:

Reword the topic sentence "Fall is the best of the four seasons" in one of the following ways:

Why is fall the best of the four seasons?

Which season is the best season?

Is fall the best season of the year?

Then, as you read the remaining sentences (the ones you didn't pick), you will find that they answer (support) your question.

If you attempt this with a sentence other than the topic sentence, it won't work. Suppose you select "Halloween marks the start of the holiday season," and you reword it in the following way:

Which holiday is the start of the holiday season?

You will find that the other sentences fail to help you answer (support) your question.

Summary Statements

The INTRODUCTORY STATEMENT should be at the beginning of the passage. An introductory statement provides a bridge between any previous, relevant text and the content to follow. It provides information about the text and also sets the tone and parameters. The old axiom regarding presenting a body of information suggests that you should always "tell them what you are going to tell them; tell it to them; tell them what you just told them." In accordance with this, the introductory statement is where the writer "tell[s] them what [he or she is] going to tell them," the content portion (the main body of the narrative) is where the writer "tell[s] it to them," and the SUMMARY STATEMENT is where the writer "tell[s] them what [he or she] just told them." In short, the summary statement should be at or near the end of the passage; it is a concise presentation of the essential data from that passage.

> **INTRODUCTORY STATEMENT:** provides a bridge between any previous, relevant text and the content to follow; it provides information about the text and also sets the tone and parameters

> **SUMMARY STATEMENT:** a concise presentation of the essential data from that passage

Restating the main idea

An accurate restatement of the main idea from a passage will usually summarize the concept in a concise manner; it will often present the same idea from a different perspective. A restatement should always demonstrate complete comprehension of the main idea.

To select an accurate restatement, identifying the main idea of the passage is essential (see Skill 5.2). Once a reader comprehends the main idea of a passage, it is important to evaluate the choices to see which statement restates the main idea while eliminating statements that only restate a supporting detail. Go through the steps after the sample paragraph from Skill 5.2 to see how to select the accurate restatement.

> *An accurate restatement of the main idea from a passage will usually summarize the concept in a concise manner; it will often present the same idea from a different perspective.*

Sample paragraph

> *Fall is the best of the four seasons. The leaves change colors to create a beautiful display of golds, reds, and oranges. The air turns crisp and windy. The scents of pumpkin muffins and apple pies fill the air. Finally, Halloween marks the start of the holiday season. Fall is my favorite time of year!*

Steps

> 1. *Identify the main idea. (Answer: "Fall is the best of the four seasons.")*
> 2. *Decide which of the following statements restates the topic sentence:*
>   A. *The changing leaves turn gold, red, and orange.*
>   B. *The holidays start with Halloween.*
>   C. *Of the four seasons, fall is the greatest of them all.*
>   D. *Crisp wind is a fun aspect of fall.*

The answer is *C* because it rewords the main idea of the first sentence (the topic sentence).

Supporting details

SUPPORTING DETAILS:
are sentences that give more information about the topic and the main idea

The **SUPPORTING DETAILS** are sentences that give more information about the topic and the main idea. The supporting details in the preceding paragraph about Henry Ford include (1) he was an inventor, and (2) before he created the Model-T, only rich people could afford cars because they were so expensive.

Organization

The organization of a written work includes two factors: the order in which the writer has chosen to present the different parts of the discussion or argument and the relationships he or she constructs between these parts. Written ideas need to be presented in a **LOGICAL ORDER** so a reader can follow the information easily and quickly. A series of ideas can be ordered in several different ways, but they all have one thing in common: to lead the reader along a desired path while avoiding backtracking or skipping around. The goal is to give a clear, strong presentation of the writer's main idea. The following are some of the ways a paragraph can be organized.

LOGICAL ORDER: so a reader can follow the information easily and quickly

SEQUENCE OF EVENTS: details are presented in the order in which they have occurred

STATEMENT SUPPORT: the main idea is stated and the rest of the paragraph explains or proves it

- **SEQUENCE OF EVENTS:** In this type of organization, the details are presented in the order in which they have occurred. One idea is connected or depends on the next based on how they fit together in a chronological sequence. Paragraphs that describe a process or procedure, give directions, or outline a given period of time (such as a day or a month) are often arranged chronologically.

- **STATEMENT SUPPORT:** In this type of organization, the main idea is stated and the rest of the paragraph explains or proves it. This is also referred to as relative importance. This type of order may be organized most to least, least to most, most-least-most, and least-most-least.

- **COMPARISON-CONTRAST:** In this type of organization, the compare-contrast pattern is used when a paragraph describes the differences or similarities of two or more ideas, actions, events, or things. The topic sentence usually describes the basic relationship between the ideas or items, and the rest of the paragraph explains this relationship.

- **CLASSIFICATION:** In this type of organization, the paragraph presents grouped information about a topic. The topic sentence usually states the general category, and the rest of the sentences show how various elements of the category have a common base as well as how they differ from the common base.

- **CAUSE AND EFFECT:** This pattern describes how two or more events are connected. The main sentence usually states the primary cause(s) and the primary effect(s) and how they are basically connected. The rest of the sentences explain the connection, or how one event caused the next event. Many times, all of these organizations follow the basic P.I.E sequence:

> *P—The point, or main idea, of the paragraph*
>
> *I—The information (e.g., data, details, facts) that supports the main idea*
>
> *E—The explanation or analysis of the information and how it proves, is related to, or is connected to the main idea*

- Even if the sentences that make up a given paragraph or passage are arranged in logical order, the document as a whole can still seem choppy or the various ideas disconnected.

- **TRANSITIONS**, words that signal relationships between ideas, can help to improve the flow of a document. Transitions can help to achieve clear and effective presentation by establishing connections among sentences, paragraphs, and sections of a document. With transitions, each sentence builds on the ideas in the last, and each paragraph has clear links to the preceding one. As a result, the reader receives clear directions on how to piece together the writer's ideas in a logically coherent argument. By signaling how to organize, interpret, and react to information, transitions allow writers to effectively and elegantly explain their ideas.

COMPARISON-CONTRAST: when a paragraph describes the differences or similarities of two or more ideas, actions, events, or things

CLASSIFICATION: the paragraph presents grouped information about a topic

CAUSE AND EFFECT: this pattern describes how two or more events are connected

TRANSITIONS: words that signal relationships between ideas can help to improve the flow of a document

Logical Relationship	Transitional Expression
Comparison	*also, in the same way, just as, so too, likewise, similarly*
Exception/Contrast	*but, however, in spite of, on the one hand, on the other hand, nevertheless, nonetheless, notwithstanding, in contrast, on the contrary, still, yet*
Sequence/Order	*first, second, third, next, then, finally*
Time	*after, afterward, at last, before, currently, during, earlier, immediately, later, meanwhile, now, recently, simultaneously, subsequently, then*
Example	*for example, for instance, namely, specifically, to illustrate*
Emphasis	*even, indeed, in fact, of course, truly*
Place/Position	*above, adjacent, below, beyond, here, in front, in back, nearby, there*
Cause and Effect	*accordingly, consequently, hence, so, therefore, thus*
Additional Support or Evidence	*additionally, again, also, and, as well, besides, equally important, further, furthermore, in addition, moreover, then*
Conclusion/ Summary	*finally, in a word, in brief, in conclusion, in the end, in the final analysis, on the whole, thus, to conclude, to summarize, in sum, in summary*

Sample Test Question and Rationale

(Average)

1. A sixth-grade science teacher has given her class a paper to read on the relationship between food and weight gain. The writing contains signal words such as "because," "consequently," "this is how," and "due to." This paper has which text structure?

    A. Cause and effect

    B. Compare and contrast

    C. Description

    D. Sequencing

Answer: A. Cause and effect

Cause and effect is the relationship between two things when one thing makes something else happen. Writers use this text structure to show order, to inform, to speculate, and to change behavior. This text structure uses the process of identifying potential causes of a problem or issue in an orderly way.

SKILL 5.6 **Applying knowledge of strategies for promoting comprehension of informational texts** (e.g., identifying the main idea and explicit and implicit supporting details, using a glossary, using a graphic organizer)

The point of comprehension instruction is not necessarily to focus only on the text(s) that the students are using at that moment of instruction but rather to help them to learn the strategies they can use independently with any other text. Some of the most common methods of teaching instruction are as follows:

- SUMMARIZATION: This is where, either in writing or verbally, students go over the main point of the text, along with strategically chosen details that highlight the main point. This is not the same as *paraphrasing*, which is saying the same thing in different words. Teaching students how to summarize is very important, because it will help them to look for the most critical areas in a text. For example, it will help them to distinguish between main arguments and examples. In fiction, it helps students to learn how to focus on the main characters and events and to distinguish those from the lesser characters and events.

- QUESTION ANSWERING: While this tends to be overused in many classrooms, it is still a valid method of teaching students to comprehend. As the name implies, students answer questions regarding a text, either out loud in small groups, or individually on paper. The best questions are those that make the students think about the text (rather than just find the answer in the text).

- QUESTION GENERATING: This is the opposite of question answering, although students can then be asked to answer their own questions or the questions of peer students. In general, students should constantly question texts as they read. This is important because it causes students to become more critical readers. When you teach students to generate questions, it helps them to learn the types of questions they can ask, and it gets them thinking about how best to be critical of texts.

- GRAPHIC ORGANIZERS: Graphic organizers are graphical representations of the content in a text. For example, Venn diagrams can be used to highlight the difference between two characters in a novel or two similar political concepts in a social studies textbook. A teacher can also use flowcharts with students to talk about the steps in a process (for example, the steps of setting up a science experiment or the chronological events of a story). Semantic organizers are similar in that they graphically display information. The difference, however, is that semantic organizers focus on words or concepts. For example, a word web can help students to make sense of a word by mapping from the central word all of the similar and related concepts to that word.

SUMMARIZATION: students go over the main point of the text, along with strategically chosen details that highlight the main point

QUESTION ANSWERING: students answer questions regarding a text, either out loud in small groups, or individually on paper

QUESTION GENERATING: the opposite of question answering, where students learn to ask questions and think critically about texts

GRAPHIC ORGANIZERS: graphical representations of the content in a text

TEXT STRUCTURE: the use of headings, sidebars, etc., that give important clues to the reader about what to look for in a story

MONITORING COMPREHENSION: making certain that the text is making sense to the reader

TEXTUAL MARKING: where students interact with the text as they read (for example, with sticky notes) to help them focus on the importance of small things and provide a reference point for review

DISCUSSION: the process by which students are encouraged to see the range of possibilities in a text by sharing their thoughts about it in a group

- **TEXT STRUCTURE:** In nonfiction—particularly textbooks (and sometimes fiction)—text structures can give important clues to readers about what to look for. Often, students do not know how to make sense of all the types of headings in a textbook and do not realize that, for example, the sidebar story about a character in history is not the main text on a particular page in the history textbook. Teaching students how to interpret text structures gives them the tools to tackle similar texts.

- **MONITORING COMPREHENSION:** Students need to be aware of their comprehension, or lack of it, in particular texts. As such, it is important to teach students what to do when text suddenly stops making sense. For example, students can go back and reread the description of a character, or they can go back to the table of contents or the first paragraph of a chapter to see where they are headed.

- **TEXTUAL MARKING:** This is where students interact with the text as they read. For example, armed with sticky notes, students can insert questions or comments regarding specific sentences or paragraphs in the text. This helps students to focus on the importance of the small things, particularly when they are reading larger works (such as novels in high school). It also gives students a reference point on which to go back to the text when they need to review something.

- **DISCUSSION:** Small-group or whole-class discussion stimulates thoughts about texts and gives students a larger picture of the impact of those texts. For example, teachers can strategically encourage students to discuss related concepts to the text. This helps students to learn to consider texts within larger societal and social concepts. Teachers can also encourage students to provide personal opinions during discussions. By listening to various students' opinions, all of the students in the class are encouraged to see the wide range of possible interpretations and thoughts regarding one text.

Many people mistakenly believe that the terms research-based, research-validated, or evidence-based relate mainly to specific programs, such as early reading textbook programs. While research does validate that some of these programs are effective, much research has been conducted regarding the effectiveness of particular instructional strategies.

In reading, many of these strategies have been documented in the report from the National Reading Panel (2000). However, just because a strategy has not been validated as effective by research does not necessarily mean that it is not effective with certain students in certain situations. It is not possible for researchers to test the effectiveness of the enormous number of strategies that are presented today. Some of the preceding strategies have been validated by rigorous research, while others have been shown consistently to help improve students' reading abilities in localized situations. Space does not allow mention of all of the strategies that have been proven effective, but those cited here are most often cited as effective in a variety of situations.

Sample Test Question and Rationale

(Average)

1. A teacher has taught his students several strategies to monitor their reading comprehension. These strategies include identifying where in the passage they are having difficulty, identifying what the difficulty is, and restating the difficult sentence or passage in their own words. These strategies are examples of:

    A. Graphic and semantic organizers

    B. Metacognition

    C. Recognizing story structure

    D. Summarizing

Answer: B. Metacognition

Metacognition may be defined as "thinking about thinking." Good readers use metacognitive strategies to think about and maintain control over their reading. Before reading, they might clarify their purpose for reading and preview the text. During reading, they might monitor their understanding, adjusting their reading speed to fit the difficulty of the text, and try to fix any comprehension problems they have. After reading, they check their understanding of what they read.

COMPETENCY 6

UNDERSTAND SKILLS AND STRATEGIES INVOLVED IN WRITING FOR VARIOUS PURPOSES ACROSS THE CURRICULUM

SKILL 6.1 Recognizing developmental stages of writing, including the use of pictures and developmental spelling

See Skill 6.3 for the writing process

Developmental Spelling

Spelling instruction should include learning to correctly spell commonly mis-spelled words, generalizing spelling knowledge, and mastering objectives in progressive phases of development.

THE DEVELOPMENTAL STAGES OF SPELLING	
Prephonemic Spelling	Children know that letters stand for a message, but they do not know the relationship between spelling and pronunciation.
Early Phonemic Spelling	Children are beginning to understand spelling. They usually write the beginning letter correctly, while the rest of the word is composed of consonants or long vowels.
Letter-Name Spelling	Some words are consistently spelled correctly. The student is developing a sight vocabulary and a stable understanding of letters as representing sounds. Long vowels are usually used accurately, but silent vowels are omitted. Unknown words are spelled by the child attempting to match the name of the letter to the sound.
Transitional Spelling	This phase is typically entered in late elementary school. Short vowel sounds are mastered, and some spelling rules are known. Students are developing a sense of which spellings are correct and which are not.
Derivational Spelling	Usually reached from high school to adulthood, this is the stage where spelling rules are mastered.

SKILL 6.2 **Analyzing factors to consider in writing for various audiences and purposes, and in writing materials in various genres, formats** (e.g., essay, poem), **and modes** (e.g., descriptive, persuasive, evaluative)

Discourse, whether in speaking or writing, falls naturally into four different forms: narrative, descriptive, expository, and persuasive. The first question to ask yourself when you are reading a piece of literature, listening to a presentation, or writing is "What's the point?" This is usually called the thesis. For example, when you finish reading an essay, you should be able to say something like "The point of this piece is that the foster care system in America is a disaster." If you have read a play, you should also be able to say, "The point of that play is that good overcomes evil." The same is true of any written document or performance. If it doesn't make a point, the reader/listener/viewer may become confused and feel that it's not worth the effort. It is helpful to keep this in mind when you sit down to write a document—be it an essay, a poem, or a speech—as these forms have been the structure of Western thinking since the Greek rhetoricians.

PERSUASION is a piece of writing whose purpose is to change the minds of the audience members or to get them to do something. This can be achieved in many ways:

1. The credibility of the writer/speaker might lead the listeners/readers to a change of mind or a recommended action.

2. Reasoning is important in persuasive discourse. No one wants to believe that she should accept a new viewpoint or go out and take action just because she likes and trusts the person who recommended it. Logic comes into play in reasoning that is persuasive.

3. The third, and most powerful, force that leads to acceptance or action is emotional appeal. Even if a person has been persuaded logically and reasonably that he should believe in a different way, he is unlikely to act on it unless he is moved emotionally. For example, an individual might be convinced that people suffered in New Orleans after Hurricane Katrina, but she is not likely to do anything about it until she is moved emotionally by their plight. Sermons are good examples of persuasive discourse.

EXPOSITION is discourse whose only purpose is to inform. Expository writing is not interested in changing anyone's mind or getting anyone to take a certain action. It exists to give information. Some examples include directions to get to a particular place or for putting together a toy. The writer doesn't care whether the readers do or do not follow the directions but only wants to be sure the information is available in case they do need it.

NARRATION is discourse that is arranged chronologically—something happened, and then something else happened, and then something else happened. It is also called a story. News reports are often narrative in nature, as are records of trips.

DESCRIPTION is discourse whose purpose is to make an experience available through one of the five senses: seeing, smelling, hearing, feeling (as with the fingers), and tasting. Descriptive words are used to make it possible for the reader to "see" with his own mind's eye, "hear" through his own mind's ear, "smell" through his own mind's nose, "taste" with his own mind's tongue, and "feel" with his own mind's fingers. This is how language moves people. Only by experiencing an event can the emotions become involved. Poets are experts in descriptive language.

PERSUASION: a piece of writing whose purpose is to change the minds of the audience members or to get them to do something

EXPOSITION: discourse whose only purpose is to inform

NARRATION: discourse that is arranged chronologically

DESCRIPTION: discourse whose purpose is to make an experience available through one of the five senses

Persuasive writing often uses all forms of discourse. The introduction may be a history or a background of the idea being presented—exposition. Details supporting some of the points may be stories—narrations. Descriptive writing is used to make sure that the point is established emotionally.

Paraphrasing is the rewording of a piece of writing. The result is not necessarily shorter than the original, because it uses different vocabulary and possibly a different arrangement of details. Sometimes paraphrases are used to clarify a complex piece of writing or to compose material that cannot be copied due to copyright restraints.

Summarizing is distilling the elements of a piece of writing or speech. It is much shorter than the original. To write a good summary, the writer must determine what the "bones" of the original piece are. What is its structure? What are its thesis and subpoints? A summary does not make judgments about the original but simply reports the original in condensed form.

Letters are often expository in nature, since their purpose is to give information. However, letters are also often persuasive—the writer wants to persuade or get the recipient to do something. They are also sometimes descriptive or narrative—the writer may share an experience or tell about an event.

Research reports are a special kind of expository writing. A topic is researched—explored by some appropriate means such as searching literature, interviewing experts, or even conducting experiments—and the findings are written up in such a way that the audience learns what was discovered. They can be very simple, such as delving into the history of an event, or very complex, such as a report on a scientific phenomenon that requires complicated testing and reasoning to explain. A research reports often reports possible conclusions but puts forth one as the best answer to the question that inspired the research in the first place, which is what becomes the thesis of the report.

Sample Test Questions and Rationale

(Easy)

1. A student has written a paper with the following characteristics: written in first person; characters, setting, and plot; some dialogue; and events organized in chronological sequence with some flashbacks. In what genre has the student written?

   A. Expository writing

   B. Narrative writing

   C. Persuasive writing

   D. Technical writing

   Answer: B. Narrative writing

   All of these are characteristics of narrative writing. Expository writing is intended to give information, such as an explanation or directions, and the information is logically organized. Persuasive writing gives an opinion in an attempt to convince the reader that this point of view is valid or tries to persuade the reader to take a specific action. The goal of technical writing is to clearly communicate a select piece of information to a targeted reader or group of readers.

(Rigorous)

2. Which of the following should not be included in the opening paragraph of an informative essay?

   A. Thesis sentence

   B. Details and examples supporting the main idea

   C. A broad general introduction to the topic

   D. A style and tone that grabs the reader's attention

   Answer: B. Details and examples supporting the main idea

   The introductory paragraph should introduce the topic, capture the reader's interest, state the thesis, and prepare the reader for the main points in the essay. Details and examples, however, should be given in the second part of the essay to help develop the thesis.

(Rigorous)

3. *Our borders must be protected from illegal immigrants.* Which of the following does *not* support this thesis?

   A. Terrorists can get across the border undetected

   B. Illegal drugs flow across the unprotected borders

   C. Illegal immigrants are a drain on the American economy

   D. Illegal immigrants make good citizens

   Answer: D. Illegal immigrants make good citizens

   D does not support the thesis statement. Good questions to ask to determine whether a point supports the statement are "How?" and "Why?" For example: Our borders must be protected from illegal immigrants. Why? Because terrorists can get across the border undetected.

Sample Test Questions and Rationale

(Rigorous)

4. **Which of the following are good ways to support a thesis?**

    A. Reasons

    B. Examples

    C. Answers to the question *"Why?"*

    D. All of the above

    Answer: D. All of the above

    When you answer "Why?", you are giving reasons, but those reasons need to be supported with examples.

(Easy)

5. **Which of the following is a good definition for the *purpose* of an essay?**

    A. To get a good grade

    B. To fulfill an assignment

    C. To change the minds of the readers

    D. The point of the writing

    Answer: D. The point of the writing

    The purpose is what you want your writing to achieve. It is based on the four forms of discourse: expository, descriptive, narrative, and persuasive.

(Average)

6. **Which of the following is *not* an approach to keep students ever conscious of the need to write for audience appeal?**

    A. Pairing students during the writing process

    B. Reading all rough drafts before the students write the final copies

    C. Having students compose stories or articles

    D. Writing letters to friends or relatives

    Answer: B. Reading all rough drafts before the students write the final copies

    Reading all of the rough drafts will not encourage the students to take control of their text and might even inhibit their creativity. On the contrary, pairing students will foster their sense of responsibility, and having them compose stories for literary magazines will boost their self-esteem as well as their organization skills. As for writing letters, the works of authors such as Madame de Sevigne in the seventeenth century are good examples of epistolary literary work.

SKILL **Demonstrating knowledge of the writing process** *(e.g., prewriting,*
6.3 *drafting, revising, editing)* **and strategies for promoting students' writing skills**

Writing is a recursive process. As students engage in the various stages of writing, they develop and improve not only their writing skills but their thinking skills as well.

THE STAGES OF THE WRITING PROCESS	
Prewriting	Students gather ideas before writing. Prewriting may include clustering, listing, brainstorming, mapping, freewriting, and charting. Providing many ways for a student to develop ideas on a topic will increase his or her chances for success.
Writing	Students compose the first draft.
Revising	Students examine their work and make changes in sentences, wording, details, and ideas. *Revise* comes from the Latin word *revidere*, meaning "to see again."
Editing	Students proofread the draft for punctuation and mechanical errors.
Publishing	Students may have their work displayed on a bulletin board, read aloud in class, or printed in a literary magazine or school anthology. It is important to realize that these steps are recursive; as a student engages in each aspect of the writing process, he or she may begin with prewriting, writing, revising, writing, revising, editing, and publishing. They do not engage in this process in a lockstep manner; it is more circular.

Teaching the Composing Process

Prewriting activities

1. Have a class discussion about the topic

2. Map out ideas, questions, and graphic organizers on the chalkboard

3. Break into small groups to discuss different ways of approaching the topic, develop an organizational plan, and create a thesis statement

4. Research the topic, if necessary

Drafting/revising

1. Students write a first draft in class or at home

2. Students engage in peer response and class discussion

3. Using checklists or a rubric, students critique one another's writing and make suggestions for revising the writing

4. Students revise the writing

Editing and proofreading

1. Students, working in pairs, analyze sentences for variety

2. Students work in groups to read papers for punctuation and mechanics

3. Students perform final edit

Sample Test Questions and Rationale

(Average)

1. **Which of the following is *not* a technique of prewriting?**

   A. Clustering

   B. Listing

   C. Brainstorming

   D. Proofreading

   Answer: D. Proofreading

   Proofreading cannot be a method of prewriting because it is done on texts that have already been written.

(Rigorous)

2. **Which is *not* a true statement concerning an author's literary tone?**

   A. Tone is partly revealed through the selection of details

   B. Tone is the expression of the author's attitude toward his or her subject

   C. Tone in literature is usually satiric or angry

   D. Tone in literature corresponds to the tone of voice a speaker uses

   Answer: C. Tone in literature is usually satiric or angry

   Tone in literature conveys a mood and can be as varied as the tone of voice of a speaker (e.g., sad, nostalgic, whimsical, angry, formal, intimate, satirical, sentimental).

> **SKILL 6.4** **Demonstrating knowledge of the use of writing strategies and language to achieve various effects** (*e.g., creating a point of view, showing author's voice, persuading, establishing setting, describing sensory details*)

See also Skill 5.5

Fact and Opinion

A FACT is something that is true and can be proved. An OPINION is something that a person believes, thinks, or feels. Look at the following examples:

> *Joe DiMaggio, a Yankees' center-fielder, was replaced by Mickey Mantle in 1952.*

This is a fact. If necessary, evidence can be produced to support this.

> *First-year players are more ambitious than seasoned players.*

This is an opinion. There is no proof to support that everyone feels this way.

FACT: something that is true and can be proved

OPINION: something that a person believes, thinks, or feels

Author's purpose

An author may have more than one purpose in writing, which may be to entertain, to persuade, to inform, to describe, or to narrate. There are no tricks or rules to follow when attempting to determine an author's purpose. It is up to the reader to use his or her own judgment. Consider the following paragraph:

> *Charles Lindbergh had no intention of becoming a pilot. He was a student at the University of Wisconsin, but then a flying lesson changed the course of his life. He began his career as a pilot by performing daredevil stunts at fairs.*

The author wrote this paragraph primarily to:

> A. Describe
> B. Inform
> C. Entertain
> D. Narrate

Because the author is simply telling us or informing us about the life of Charles Lindbergh, the correct answer here is *B*.

Author's tone and point of view

The author's tone is his or her attitude as reflected in the statement or passage. The author's choice of words helps the reader to determine the overall tone of a statement or passage. Read the following paragraph:

> *I was shocked by your article in which you said that sitting down to breakfast was a thing of the past. Many families consider breakfast time as family time. Children need to realize the importance of having a good breakfast. It is imperative that they be taught this at a young age. I cannot believe that a writer with your reputation has difficulty comprehending this.*

The author's tone in this passage is one of:

> A. Concern
> B. Panic
> C. Excitement
> D. Disbelief

Because the author directly states that he "cannot believe" that the writer feels this way, the answer is *D*.

Inferences and conclusions

In order to draw inferences and make conclusions, a reader must use prior knowledge and apply it to the current situation. A conclusion or inference is never stated. The reader must rely on his or her common sense. Read the following passage:

> *The Smith family waited patiently around carousel number seven for their luggage to arrive. They were exhausted after their five-hour trip and were anxious to get to their hotel. After about an hour, they realized that they no longer recognized any of the other passengers' faces. Mrs. Smith asked the person who appeared to be in charge if they were at the right carousel. The man replied, "Yes, this is it, but we finished unloading that baggage almost half an hour ago."*

From the man's response we can infer that:

> A. The Smiths were ready to go to their hotel
> B. The Smith's luggage was lost
> C. The man had their luggage
> D. They were at the wrong carousel

Because the Smiths were still waiting for their luggage, we know that they were not yet ready to go to their hotel. From the man's response, we know that they were not at the wrong carousel and that he did not have their luggage. Therefore, though not directly stated, it appears that their luggage was lost, so *B* is the correct answer.

Figurative Language

- FIGURATIVE LANGUAGE, which appears in both fiction and nonfiction, is language that uses creative or poetic methods to convey points and is used for effect and to make a point stand out. The most common examples of figurative language include hyperbole, metaphor, personification, simile, and idiom.

- HYPERBOLE: Hyperbole is the literary version of exaggeration. When authors exaggerate in their text, they are using hyperbole. Hyperbole is often used as irony, often to overemphasize a point.

- METAPHOR: A metaphor is any time one thing is used in place of something else in text, signifying some sort of resemblance. For example, we might say, "It is raining cats and dogs." Hopefully, this is not literally true—ever! Instead, we use this to signify heavy rain. Authors use metaphors for emphasis, creativity, and often clarity. Sometimes, metaphors provide a better picture than accurate language does.

- PERSONIFICATION: Whenever an author gives human life to an inanimate item, that's personification. For example, we might say, "The wind is whistling." Authors use personification to provide a more poetic look at common events.

- SIMILE: Similes are comparisons between two objects (or between a person and an object) that use the words *like* or *as* to identify the similarities. An example of a simile is "Love is like a rose."

- IDIOM: Idioms are phrases or words used only in specific locations or cultures. For example, a common American idiom is "Break a leg," which is a wish for good luck. However, each region of the country has its own distinctive idioms as well. Idioms are generally used in writing to spice up the language with local flavor. Often, idioms are used to make characters seem more real or even to indicate where in the country the action is taking place.

FIGURATIVE LANGUAGE: language that uses creative or poetic methods to convey points

HYPERBOLE: the literary version of exaggeration

METAPHOR: any time one thing is used in place of something else in text, signifying some sort of resemblance

PERSONIFICATION: whenever an author gives human life to an inanimate item

SIMILE: comparisons between two objects (or between a person and an object) that use the words *like* or *as* to identify the similarities

IDIOM: phrases or words used only in specific locations or culture

SKILL 6.5 Applying revision strategies to improve the unity, organization, clarity, precision, and effectiveness of written materials

Revision is probably the most important step in the writing process. Here, students examine their work and make changes in wording, details, and ideas. Often, students will write a draft and believe they are finished writing. Students, however, must be encouraged to develop, change, and enhance their writing once they've completed the draft, as well as during the initial composition.

Effective teachers realize that revision and editing go hand in hand. They also know that students often move back and forth between these two stages during the course of one written work. These stages are often best practiced in small groups or pairs, as well as on an individual basis. Students must learn to analyze and improve their own work as well as the works of their peers. Here are some methods to use:

- Students work in pairs to analyze sentences for variety

- Students work in pairs or groups to ask questions about unclear areas or to help in adding details, information, and so on

- Students perform their final edit

Many teachers hold a writer's workshop to help students to maximize learning about the writing process. Writer's workshops vary across classrooms, but the main idea is for students to become comfortable with the writing process. A basic writer's workshop includes a block of classroom time committed to writing various projects (e.g., narratives, memoirs, book summaries, fiction, book reports, etc.). Students use this time to write, meet with others to review/edit writing, make comments on writing, revise their own work, proofread, meet with the teacher, and publish their work.

Teachers who facilitate effective writer's workshops are able to meet with students one at a time and can guide each student in his or her individual writing needs. This approach allows the teacher to differentiate instruction for each student's writing level.

Clarifying Writing

Writing introductions

It is important to remember that in the writing process, the introduction should be written last. Until the body of the paper has been determined, including the thesis and its development, it is difficult to make strategic decisions regarding the introduction. The Greek rhetoricians called this part of a discourse *exordium*, or "leading into."

> Effective teachers realize that revision and editing go hand in hand. They also know that students often move back and forth between these two stages during the course of one written work.

> It is important to remember that in the writing process, the introduction should be written last. Until the body of the paper has been determined, including the thesis and its development, it is difficult to make strategic decisions regarding the introduction.

The basic purpose of the introduction, then, is to lead the audience into the discourse. It can let the reader know what the purpose of the discourse is, and it can condition the audience to be receptive to what the writer wants to say. It can be very brief, or it can take up a large percentage of the total word count. Aristotle said that the introduction can be compared to the flourishes that flute players make before their performance—an overture in which the musicians display what they can play best in an attempt to gain the favor and attention of the audience for the main performance.

In order to do this, the writer must first know what to say; who the readership is likely to be; what the social, political, and economic climate is; what preconceived notions the audience is likely to have regarding the subject; and how long the discourse is going to be. This can be done in many ways:

- Show that the subject is important

- Show that although the points being presented may seem improbable, they are true

- Show that the subject has been neglected, misunderstood, or misrepresented in the past

- Explain an unusual mode of development

- Forestall any misconception of the purpose

- Apologize for a deficiency

- Arouse interest in the subject with an anecdotal lead-in

- Ingratiate oneself with the readership

- Establish one's own credibility

The introduction often ends with the thesis—the point or purpose of the paper. The thesis may open the body of the discussion, or it may conclude the discourse. The most important thing to remember is that the purpose and structure of the introduction should be deliberate if it is to serve the purpose of "leading the reader into the discussion."

Writing conclusions

It is easier to write a conclusion after the decisions regarding the introduction have been made. Aristotle taught that the conclusion should strive to do five things:

1. Inspire the reader with a favorable opinion of the writer

2. Amplify the force of the points made in the body of the paper

3. Reinforce the points made in the body

4. Rouse appropriate emotions in the reader

5. Restate in a summary way what has been said

The conclusion may be short or long, depending on its purpose in the paper. Recapitulation, a brief restatement of the main points (or of the thesis), is the most common form of effective conclusion writing. A good example is the closing argument in a court trial.

> *Recapitulation, a brief restatement of the main points (or of the thesis), is the most common form of effective conclusion writing.*

Text organization

In studies of professional writers and how they produce their successful works, it has been shown that writing is a process that can be clearly defined (although, in practice, it must have enough flexibility to allow for creativity). The teacher must be able to define the various stages that a successful writer goes through in order to make a statement that has value.

There must be a discovery stage when ideas, materials, and supporting details are deliberately collected. These may come from many possible sources: the writer's own experience and observations, deliberate research of written sources, interviews, television presentations, or the Internet.

The next stage is organizing where the purpose, thesis, and supporting points will be. Most writers will present more than one possible thesis; in the next stage, the writing of the paper, they will then settle on one as the result of trial and error.

Once the paper is written, the editing stage is probably the most important stage. This is not just the polishing stage. At this point, decisions must be made regarding whether the reasoning is cohesive—does it hold together? Is the arrangement the best possible one, or should the points be rearranged? Are there holes that need to be filled in? What form will the introduction take? Does the conclusion lead the reader out of the discourse, or is it inadequate or too abrupt?

It is important to remember that the best writers engage in all of these stages recursively. They may go back to discovery at any point in the process. They may go back and rethink the organization even if they are almost finished. To help students become effective writers, teachers need to give them adequate practice in the various stages. Students must be encouraged to engage deliberately in the creative thinking that makes writers successful.

Assessing writing

Students need to be trained to become effective at proofreading, revising, and editing strategies. Begin by training them using both deskside and scheduled conferences. The following are some strategies to use to guide students through the final stages of the writing process (and these can easily be incorporated into the writer's workshop).

- Provide some guide sheets or forms for students to use during peer responses

- Allow students to work in pairs, and limit the agenda

- Model the use of the guide sheet or form for the entire class

- Give students a time limit or number of written pieces to be completed in a specific amount of time

- Have the students read their classmates' papers, and ask at least three who, what, when, why, and how questions (the students should answer the questions and use them as a place to begin discussing the piece)

- At this point in the writing process, a mini-lesson that focuses on some of the problems students are having is appropriate

To help students revise, provide them with a series of questions that will assist them in revising their writing:

- Do the details give a clear picture? Add details that appeal to more than just the sense of sight.

- How effectively are the details organized? Reorder the details if necessary.

- Are the thoughts and feelings of the writer included? Add personal thoughts and feelings about the subject.

As teachers discuss revision, they should begin by discussing what it means to revise. Also, it is important to state that *all* writing must be revised to improve it. After students have revised their writing, it is time for the final editing and proofreading to be performed.

SKILL 6.6 Demonstrating knowledge of the use of research skills and computer technology to support writing

Students must be able to research effectively in order to write about a specific assignment. Students need the skills to collect information, sort data, and make a decision as to what facts they will incorporate into their assignment or project.

STUDENT RESEARCH SKILLS
Learn to generate questions about a topic
Form a research plan using a variety of strategies
Restate factual information in the student's own words
Collect and organize information on various topics
Write grade-level-appropriate research drafts

Computer technology, in the form of word processing programs, with the capability to add, delete, and rearrange text are supportive of writing programs. The use of computer technology can lead to better writing outcomes.

THE BENEFITS OF USING COMPUTERS TO WRITE
Longer written samples
Greater variety of word usage
More variety of sentence structure
More accurate mechanics and spelling
Better understanding of the writing process
Better attitudes toward writing

Batey (1986) and Bialo and Sivin (1990)

Computer technology

Teachers should evaluate and select educational software based on problem solving, critical thinking, and curriculum standards. In so doing, they can create an environment where students are encouraged to research and write effectively while applying a variety of technology processes.

Locating information for research projects and compiling research sources using both print and electronic resources are vital steps in the construct of written documents. The resources that are available in today's school communities include a large database of Internet resources and World Wide Web access, both of which provide individual navigation for print and electronic information. Research sources include looking at traditional commercial databases and using the Electronic Library to print and cite a diversity of informational resources.

One vital aspect of the research process includes learning to analyze the applicability and validity of the massive amounts of accessible information in cyberspace. Verifying and evaluating electronic resources should be a part of the writing process, as should sorting through the downloaded hard copies or scrolling through the electronic databases. In using a diversity of research sources, the user must be able to discern authentic sources of information from the mass collections of Web sites and information databases with less than reputable sources.

One vital aspect of the research process includes learning to analyze the applicability and validity of the massive amounts of accessible information in cyberspace.

In primary research, selecting a topic and setting up an outline for research information precedes using the secondary research of both print and electronic resources. Using conceptual Venn diagrams to center the topic and brainstorm the peripheral information pertaining to the topic clarifies the purpose of the research. Secondary research involves two actions: using print sources and using electronic research tools.

Print sources provide guides on locations for specific or general information resources. Libraries have floors or designated areas dedicated to the collection of encyclopedias, specific resource manuals, card catalogs, and periodical indexes that provide information on the projected topic. Electronic research tools include a list of the latest and most effective search engines like Google, Yahoo!, and Ask to find the topic of research, along with peripheral support information. Electronic databases that contain extensive resources help the user with selecting resources, choosing effective keywords, and constructing search strategies. The world of electronic research opens up a global library of resources for both print and electronic information.

Major online services, such as Microsoft, provide users with specialized information that is either free or has a minimal charge assessed for that specific service or Web site. Online resources teach effective ways to bookmark sites of interest and provide information on how to cut and paste relevant information onto Word documents for citation and reference.

Bookmarking favorite Internet searches that contain correct sources for reference can save a lot of research time. Web sites that are visited frequently can be stored under the "Favorites" feature.

Online search engines and Web portals create avenues of navigating the World Wide Web. Web portals provide linkages to other Web sites and are typically subdivided into other categories for searching. Portals are also specific to certain audience interests that index parts of the Web. Search engines can provide additional strategic site searches.

COMPETENCY 7

UNDERSTAND THE CONVENTIONS OF STANDARD ENGLISH GRAMMAR, USAGE, AND MECHANICS

SKILL 7.1 Demonstrating knowledge of the parts of speech

In conventional use, English grammar classifies words based on the following eight parts of speech:

- **Verb:** Essential to a sentence, a verb asserts something about the subject of the sentence and expresses an action, event, or state of being. The verb is the critical element of the predicate of a sentence.

- **Noun:** A noun is a word used to name or identify a person, animal, place, thing, or abstract idea. Within the structure of a sentence, a noun can function as a subject, a direct or indirect object, a subject or object complement, an appositive, an adjective, or an adverb.

- **Pronoun:** This can be substituted for a noun or another pronoun. Pronoun classifications include the personal pronoun, the demonstrative pronoun, the interrogative pronoun, the indefinite pronoun, the relative pronoun, the reflexive pronoun, and the intensive pronoun. The appropriate use of pronouns (e.g., *he, which, none, you*) can make sentences less cumbersome and less repetitive (and, therefore, more readable).

- **Adjective:** An adjective modifies a noun or a pronoun by describing, identifying, or quantifying other words. An adjective usually precedes the noun or the pronoun that it modifies.

- **Adverb:** An adverb can modify a verb, an adjective, another adverb, a phrase, or a clause. An adverb indicates manner, time, place, cause, or degree; it answers questions such as "how," "when," "where," or "how much." While some adverbs can be identified by the characteristic *-ly* suffix, most adverbs must be identified by analyzing the grammatical relationships in the sentence or the clause as a whole. Unlike the adjective, the adverb can be found in various places in the sentence.

- **Preposition:** This word links nouns, pronouns, and phrases to other words in a sentence. The word or phrase that the preposition introduces is the object of the preposition. A preposition usually indicates the temporal, spatial, or logical relationship of its object to the rest of the sentence (e.g., *on, beneath, against, beside, over, during*).

- Conjunction: A conjunction is used to link words, phrases, or clauses. For independent clauses, phrases, and individual words, coordinating conjunctions (e.g., *and, but, or, nor, for, so, yet*) are used. To introduce a dependent clause and indicate the nature of a relationship between the independent clause and dependent clause, a subordinating conjunction (e.g., *after, although, as, because, before, how, if, once, since, than, that, though, until, when, where, whether, while*) is used. Equivalent sentence elements are linked with correlative conjunctions, which always appear in pairs (e.g., *both . . . and, either . . . or, neither . . . nor, not ... only, but ... also, so . . . as, whether . . . or*). Strictly speaking, correlative conjunctions consist simply of a coordinating conjunction linked to an adjective or adverb.

- Interjection: This is a word that is added to a sentence to convey emotion, often ending the sentence with an exclamation mark. It is not grammatically related to any other part of the sentence. Some examples include "Ouch," "Hey," "Wow," and "Oh no!"

- It is important to remember that each part of speech explains not what the word is but how the word is used. For example, in some instances, the same word can be used as a noun in one sentence and as a verb or adjective in another.

SKILL 7.2 Demonstrating knowledge of elements of appropriate grammar and usage *(e.g., subject verb agreement, noun-pronoun agreement, verb tense, correct pronoun usage in prepositional phrases)*

Subject-Verb Agreement

A verb agrees in number with its subject. Making the two agree relies on the ability to properly identify the subject.

One of the boys *was playing* too rough.

No one in the class—neither the teacher nor the students—*was listening* to the message from the intercom.

The *candidates*, including a grandmother and a teenager, *are debating* some controversial issues.

If two singular subjects are connected by *and*, the verb must be plural.

> *A man and his dog <u>were jogging</u> on the beach.*

If two singular subjects are connected by *or* or *nor*, a singular verb is required.

> *Neither Dot nor Joyce <u>has missed</u> a day of school this year.*
> *Either Fran or Paul <u>is</u> missing.*

If one singular subject and one plural subject are connected by *or* or *nor*, the verb agrees with the subject nearer to the verb.

> *Neither the coach nor the <u>players were</u> able to sleep on the bus.*

If the subject is a collective noun, its sense of number in the sentence determines the verb—singular if the noun represents a group or unit and plural if the noun represents individuals.

> *The House of Representatives has adjourned for the holidays.*
> *The House of Representatives have failed to reach an agreement on the subject of adjournment.*

Pronoun-Antecedent Agreement

A noun is any word that names a person, place, thing, idea, animal, quality, or activity. A pronoun is a word that is used in place of a noun or more pronouns. The word or word group that a pronoun stands for (or refers to) is called its ANTECEDENT.

We use pronouns in many of the sentences that we write. Pronouns add variety to writing by enabling the writer to avoid a monotonous repetition of nouns. Pronouns also help to maintain coherence within and among sentences. Pronouns must agree with their antecedents in number and person. Therefore, if the antecedent is plural, a plural pronoun must be used; if the antecedent is feminine, a feminine pronoun must be used. The pronouns must show a clear reference to their antecedents as well.

In order to aid students in revising their texts to correct errors, teachers should have them complete the following steps:

- Read with a focus only on pronouns
- Circle each pronoun and draw an arrow to its antecedent

ANTECEDENT: the word or word group that a pronoun stands for (or refers to)

The nine types of pronouns are personal, possessive, indefinite, reflexive, reciprocal, intensive, interrogative, relative, and demonstrative.

- Replace the pronoun with a noun to eliminate a vague pronoun reference

- Supply missing antecedents where needed

- Place the pronoun so the nearest noun is its antecedent

Once the students focus on pronoun antecedent agreement a few times, they will progress from correcting errors to avoiding errors. The only way to develop a student's skill with pronoun reference is to focus clear attention on pronouns until it becomes a habit of his or her writing.

Other agreement

Possessive nouns are used in context to show that something is owned and belongs within a contextual framework of the sentence or the passage. Nouns have common usages in describing people, places, or things; they also provide the collective thought and meaning of the sentence. Nouns provide singular or plural contextual identity to the subject matter being addressed in sentences. The specificity of nouns can describe a diversity of familiar names, places, and things: New York, Statue of Liberty, Coca-Cola, Pacific Ocean, Mom, Dad, student, teacher, life, and America. Nouns provide a common language for the reader in understanding the context of information.

In contrast, pronouns are supportive descriptors that take the place of nouns in a sentence. Pronouns, like nouns, can either be singular or plural in usage. The first person pronoun in a sentence that can take the place of a name in the singular sense include I, me, or my; in the plural sense, the pronoun descriptor becomes we, us, or our. In second person, pronoun terms include *you* or *yours* (singular and plural, respectively), whereas in the third person usage, the singular words *he/she*, *him/her*, or *his/hers* become *they*, *them*, or *their*. Pronouns can become subjects in sentences and direct or indirect objects in sentences—for example, "I work with a great professor, and I like her!"

Adjectives modify (or help to describe) people, places, or things. They are typically located in front of the noun or pronoun they describe in a sentence.

> The *sick* child stayed in the bed.

Like an adjective works in connection with nouns and pronouns, adverbs work as descriptors of verbs, adjectives, or other adverbs.

> Mary *barely* gets to work on time each day.

Adjectives and adverbs can be either comparative forms or superlative forms when comparisons occur in sentences:

> *This book is lighter than the* <u>*last*</u> *book.*
> *She is the* <u>*funniest*</u> *sister in the family."*

Verbs that show action and the state of being can take many forms. They can be present, present participle, past, or past participle. For example, in the sentence

> *She eats*

the verbs become (respectively)

> *She is eating*
> *She ate*
> *She has eaten*

Irregular verbs used in sentences commonly contain *is*, *were*, and *been*.

The importance of using possessive nouns, pronouns, verbs, adjectives, and adverbs correctly is crucial if the meaning of the text is to be clear. In connecting the reader with the written information, understanding how the information is presented creates an access to understanding the contextual aspect of the words. Using correct forms of support words is crucial in creating informative and accessible text.

Use of Verbs (Tense)

PRESENT TENSE is used to express an action that is currently happening or is always true.

> *Randy is playing the piano.*
> *Randy plays the piano like a pro.*

PAST TENSE is used to express an action that occurred in a past time.

> *Randy learned to play the piano when he was six years old.*

FUTURE TENSE is used to express an action or a condition of future time.

> *Randy will probably earn a music scholarship.*

PRESENT TENSE: expresses an action that is currently happening or is always true

PAST TENSE: expresses an action that occurred in a past time

FUTURE TENSE: expresses an action or a condition of future time

PRESENT PERFECT TENSE is used to express an action or a condition that started in the past and is continued to or completed in the present.

> Randy has practiced piano every day for the last ten years.
>
> Randy has never been bored with practice.

PAST PERFECT TENSE expresses an action or a condition that occurred as a precedent to some other action or condition.

> Randy had considered playing clarinet before he discovered the piano.

FUTURE PERFECT TENSE expresses action that started in the past or the present and will conclude at some time in the future.

> By the time he goes to college, Randy will have been an accomplished pianist for more than half of his life.

Use of Verbs (Mood)

INDICATIVE MOOD is used to make unconditional statements; SUBJUNCTIVE MOOD is used for conditional clauses or wish statements that pose untrue conditions. Verbs in subjunctive mood are plural for both singular and plural subjects.

> If I were a bird, I would fly.
>
> I wish I were as rich as Donald Trump.

Verb conjugation

The conjugation of verbs follows the patterns used in the preceding discussion of tense. However, the most frequent problems in verb use stem from the improper formation of past and past participial forms.

Regular verbs: believe, believed, (have) believed

Irregular verbs: run, ran, run; sit, sat, sat; teach, taught, taught

Other problems arise from the use of verbs that are the same in some tenses but have different forms and different meanings in other tenses.

PRESENT PERFECT TENSE: expresses an action or a condition that started in the past and is continued to or completed in the present

PAST PERFECT TENSE: expresses an action or a condition that occurred as a precedent to some other action or condition

FUTURE PERFECT TENSE: expresses an action that started in the past or the present and will conclude at some time in the future

INDICATIVE MOOD: used to make unconditional statements

SUBJUNCTIVE MOOD: used for conditional clauses or wish statements that pose untrue conditions

> *I lie on the ground. I lay on the ground yesterday. I have lain down.*
>
> *I lay the blanket on the bed. I laid the blanket there yesterday. I have laid the blanket there every night.*
>
> *The sun rises. The sun rose. The sun has risen.*
>
> *He raises the flag. He raised the flag. He had raised the flag.*
>
> *I sit on the porch. I sat on the porch. I have sat on the porch.*
>
> *I set the plate on the table. I set the plate there yesterday. I had set the table before dinner.*

Two other verb problems often stem from misusing the preposition of for the verb auxiliary have and misusing the verb ought (now rare).

Incorrect: *I should of gone to bed.*

Correct: *I should have gone to bed.*

Incorrect: *He hadn't ought to get so angry.*

Correct: *He ought not to get so angry.*

Use of Pronouns

A pronoun used as a subject of a predicate nominative occurs in the nominative case.

> *She was the drum majorette. The lead trombonists were Joe and he. The band director accepted whoever could march in step.*

A pronoun used as a direct object, an indirect object, or as the object of a preposition occurs in the objective case.

> *The teacher praised him. She gave him an "A" on the test. Her praise of him was appreciated. The students whom she did not praise will work harder next time.*

Common pronoun errors typically occur from the misuse of reflexive pronouns:

Singular: myself, yourself, herself, himself, itself

Plural: ourselves, yourselves, themselves

Incorrect: *Jack cut hisself shaving.*

Correct: *Jack cut himself shaving.*

Incorrect: *They backed theirselves into a corner.*

Correct: *They backed themselves into a corner.*

Use of Adjectives

An adjective should agree with its antecedent in number.

> Those apples are rotten. This one is ripe. These peaches are hard.

Comparative adjectives end in *-er* and superlatives in *-est*, with some exceptions like worse and worst. Some adjectives that cannot easily make comparative inflections are preceded by *more* and *most.*

> Mrs. Carmichael is the <u>better</u> of the two basketball coaches.
>
> That is the <u>hastiest</u> excuse you have ever contrived.

Avoid Double Comparisons

Incorrect: *This is the worstest headache I ever had.*

Correct: *This is the worst headache I ever had.*

When comparing one thing to others in a group, exclude the thing under comparison from the rest of the group.

Incorrect: *Joey is larger than any baby I have ever seen. (Since you have seen him, he cannot be larger than himself.)*

Correct: *Joey is larger than <u>any other</u> baby I have ever seen.*

Include all necessary words to make a comparison clear in meaning.

> I am as tall as my mother. I am as tall as she (is).
>
> My cats are better behaved than those of my neighbor.

Plurals

The multiplicity and complexity of spelling rules based on phonics, letter doubling, and exceptions to rules—not mastered by adulthood—should be replaced by a good dictionary. Because spelling mastery is also difficult for adolescents, the recommendation is the same. Learning the use of a dictionary and thesaurus is, overall, a rewarding use of time.

Most plurals of nouns that end in hard consonants or hard consonant sounds followed by a silent e are made by adding *s*. Some words ending in vowels only add *s*. For example:

> *fingers, numerals, banks, bugs, riots, homes, gates, radios, bananas*

For nouns that end in soft consonant sounds *s, j, x, z, ch,* and *sh*, add *es*. Some nouns ending in *o* also add *es*.

> *dresses, waxes, churches, brushes, tomatoes*

For nouns ending in *y* and preceded by a vowel, just add *s*.

> *boys, alleys*

For nouns ending in *y* and preceded by a consonant, change the *y* to *i* and add *es*.

> *babies, corollaries, frugalities, poppies*

Some nouns' plurals are formed irregularly or remain the same.

> *sheep, deer, children, leaves, oxen*

Some nouns derived from foreign words, especially Latin, may make their plurals in two different ways—one of them Anglicized. Sometimes, the meanings are the same; other times, the two plurals are used in slightly different contexts. It is always wise to consult the dictionary.

> *appendices, appendixes*
> *criterion, criteria*
> *indexes, indices*
> *crisis, crises*

Make the plurals of closed (solid) compound words in the usual way except for words ending in ful, which make their plurals on the root word.

> *timelines, hairpins, cupsful*

Make the plurals of open or hyphenated compounds by adding the change in inflection to the word that changed in number.

> *fathers-in-law, courts-martial, masters of art, doctors of medicine*

Make the plurals of letters, numbers, and abbreviations by adding *s*.

> *fives and tens, IBMs, 1990s, As and Bs (Note that letters are italicized.)*

Possessives

Make the possessives of singular nouns by adding an apostrophe followed by the letter *s* (*'s*).

> *baby's bottle, father's job, elephant's eye, teacher's desk, sympathizer's protests, week's postponement*

Make the possessive of singular nouns ending in *s* by adding either an apostrophe or an *'s*, depending on the common usage or sound. When making the possessive is difficult, use a prepositional phrase instead. Even with the sibilant ending, it is advisable to use the *'s* construction (with a few exceptions).

> *dress's color, species' characteristics or characteristics of the species, James' hat or James's hat, Delores's shirt*

Make the possessive of plural nouns ending in *s* by adding the apostrophe after the *s*.

> *horses' coats, jockeys' times, four days' time*

Make possessives of plural nouns that do not end in *s* the same as singular nouns by adding *'s*.

> *children's shoes, deer's antlers, cattle's horns*

Make possessives of compound nouns by adding the inflection at the end of the word or phrase.

> *the mayor of Los Angeles's campaign, the mailman's new truck, the mailmen's new trucks, my father-in-law's first wife, the keepsakes' values, daughters-in-law's husbands*

Note: Because a gerund functions as a noun, any noun preceding it and operating as a possessive adjective must reflect the necessary inflection. However, if the gerundive following the noun is a participle, no inflection is added.

The general was perturbed by the private's sleeping on duty. (The word sleeping is a gerund, the object of the preposition by.)

but

The general was perturbed to see the private sleeping on duty. (The word sleeping is a participle modifying private.)

Sample Test Question and Rationale

(Rigorous)

1. **Which of the following contains an error in possessive inflection?**

   A. Doris's shawl

   B. Mother's-in-law frown

   C. Children's lunches

   D. Ambassador's briefcase

Answer: B. Mother's-in-law frown

Mother-in-law is a compound common noun, and the inflection should be at the end of the word: *mother-in-law's*.

SKILL 7.3 Demonstrating knowledge of appropriate mechanics in writing *(e.g., capitalization, punctuation)*

The candidate should be cognizant of proper rules and conventions of punctuation, capitalization, and spelling. Competency exams will generally test the ability to apply more advanced skills, so a limited number of more frustrating rules are presented here. Rules should be applied according to the American style of English—for example, *theater* instead of *theatre* and placing terminal marks of punctuation almost exclusively within other marks of punctuation.

Capitalization

Capitalize all proper names of persons (including specific organizations or agencies of government); places (countries, states, cities, parks, and specific geographical areas); things (political parties, structures, historical and cultural terms, and calendar and time designations); and religious terms (any deity, revered person or group, and sacred writings).

> *Percy Bysshe Shelley, Argentina, Mount Rainier National Park,*
> *Grand Canyon, League of Nations, Birmingham,*
> *Lyric Theater, Americans, Midwest, Democrats, Renaissance,*
> *Boy Scouts of America, Thanksgiving, Koran*

Capitalize proper adjectives and titles used with proper names.

> *California gold rush, President Barack Obama, Homeric epic, Romanesque architecture,*
> *King Richard*

Note: Some words that represent titles and offices are not capitalized unless used with a proper name.

Capitalized: Representative McKay, Commander Alger, Queen Elizabeth

Not capitalized: the representative from Florida, the commander of the Pacific Fleet, the queen of England

Capitalize all main words in titles of works of literature, art, and music.

Punctuation

Using terminal punctuation in relation to quotation marks

In a quoted statement that is either declarative or imperative, place the period inside the closing quotation marks.

> *"The airplane skidded on the runway during takeoff."*

If the quotation is followed by other words in the sentence, place a comma inside the closing quotation marks and a period at the end of the sentence.

> *"The airplane skidded on the runway during takeoff," said the announcer.*

In most instances in which a quoted title or expression occurs at the end of a sentence, the period is placed before either the single or double quotation marks.

> *"The students had difficulty understanding Bryant's poem 'Thanatopsis.'"*
> *Early book-length adventure stories like Don Quixote and The Three Musketeers were known as "picaresque novels."*

In sentences that are interrogatory or exclamatory, the question mark or exclamation point should be positioned outside the closing quotation marks if the quote itself is a statement, command, or cited title.

> Who decided to lead us in the recitation of the "Pledge of Allegiance"?
>
> Why was Tillie shaking as she began her recitation, "Once upon a midnight dreary . . ."?
>
> I was so embarrassed when Mrs. White said, "You have spinach stuck in your teeth"!

In sentences that are declarative but the quotation is a question or an exclamation, place the question mark or exclamation point inside the quotation marks.

> The hall monitor yelled, "Fire! Fire!"
>
> "Fire! Fire!" yelled the hall monitor.
>
> Cory shrieked, "Is there a mouse in the room?" (In this instance, the question supersedes the exclamation.)

Using periods with parentheses or brackets

Place the period inside the parentheses or brackets if they enclose a complete sentence, independent of the other sentences around it.

> Stephen Crane was a confirmed alcohol and drug addict. (He admitted as much to other journalists in Cuba.)

If the parenthetical expression is a statement inserted within another statement, the period in the enclosure is omitted.

> Mark Twain used the character Indian Joe (Joe also appeared in The Adventures of Tom Sawyer) as a foil for Jim in The Adventures of Huckleberry Finn.

When enclosed matter comes at the end of a sentence requiring quotation marks, place the period outside the parentheses or brackets.

> "The secretary of state consulted with the ambassador [Albright]."

Using Commas

Separate two or more coordinate adjectives modifying the same word and three or more nouns, phrases, or clauses in a list.

Maggie's hair was dull, dirty, and shapeless.

Dickens portrayed the Artful Dodger as skillful pickpocket, loyal follower of Fagin, and defender of Oliver Twist.

Ellen couldn't wait to get out of the rain, take a shower, and eat a hot dinner.

In Elizabethan England, Ben Johnson wrote comedies, Christopher Marlowe wrote tragedies, and William Shakespeare wrote both.

Use commas to separate antithetical or complimentary expressions from the rest of the sentence.

The veterinarian, not his assistant, would perform the delicate surgery.

The more he knew about her, the less he wished he knew.

Randy hopes to, and probably will, get an appointment to the Naval Academy.

His thorough, though esoteric, scientific research could not easily

be understood by high school students.

Using Double Quotation Marks with Other Punctuation

Quotations—whether words, phrases, or clauses—should be punctuated according to the rules of the grammatical function they serve in the sentence.

The works of Shakespeare, "the bard of Avon," have been contested as originating with other authors.

"You'll get my money," the old man warned, "when Hell freezes over!"

Sheila cited the passage that began "Four score and seven years ago. . . ." (Note the ellipsis followed by an enclosed period.)

"Old Ironsides" inspired the preservation of the U.S.S. Constitution.

Use quotation marks to enclose the titles of shorter works: songs, short poems, short stories, essays, and chapters of books.

"The Tell-Tale Heart"

"Casey at the Bat"

"America the Beautiful"

Using Semicolons

Use semicolons to separate independent clauses when the second clause is introduced by a transitional adverb. (These clauses may also be written as separate sentences, preferably by placing the adverb within the second sentence.)

> *The Elizabethans modified the rhyme scheme of the sonnet; thus, it was called the English sonnet.*
>
> **or**
>
> *The Elizabethans modified the rhyme scheme of the sonnet. It was thus called the English sonnet.*

Use semicolons to separate items in a series that are long and complex or have internal punctuation.

> *The Italian Renaissance produced masters in the fine arts: Dante Alighieri, author of the Divine Comedy; Leonardo da Vinci, painter of The Last Supper; and Donatello, sculptor of the Quattro Coronati, the four saints.*
>
> *The leading scorers in the WNBA were Zheng Haixia, who averaged 23.9 points per game; Lisa Leslie, 22; and Cynthia Cooper, 19.5.*

When using a semicolon in conjunction with quotation marks, the semicolon falls outside the final quotation mark (even when a period applied in the same situation falls inside the final quotation mark).

> *Paul McCartney wrote the hit song "Hey Jude."*
>
> **but**
>
> *Paul McCartney wrote the hit song "Hey Jude"; some consider it his best song.*

Using Colons

Place a colon at the beginning of a list of items.

> *The teacher directed us to compare Faulkner's three symbolic novels: Absalom, Absalom; As I Lay Dying; and Light in August.*

Do not use a colon if the list is preceded by a verb.

> *Three of Faulkner's symbolic novels are Absalom, Absalom!; As I Lay Dying, and Light in August.*

Using Dashes

Use dashes to denote sudden breaks in thought.

> *Some periods in literature—the Romantic Age, for example—spanned different time periods in different countries.*

Use dashes instead of commas if commas are already used elsewhere in the sentence for amplification or explanation.

> *The Fireside Poets included three Brahmans—James Russell Lowell, Henry David Wadsworth, Oliver Wendell Holmes— and John Greenleaf Whittier.*

Use italics to punctuate the titles of long works of literature, names of periodical publications, musical scores, works of art, motion pictures, and television and radio programs. (When unable to type in italics, students should be instructed to underline titles where italics are required.)

> *The Idylls of the King*
>
> *Hiawatha*
>
> *The Sound and the Fury*
>
> *Dancing with the Stars*
>
> *Newsweek*
>
> *The Nutcracker Suite*

SKILL 7.4 Identifying appropriate corrections of errors in sentence structure *(e.g., run-on sentences, misplaced modifiers, sentence fragments)*

Fragments

Fragments occur (1) if word groups standing alone are missing either a subject or a verb, and (2) if word groups that have a subject, have a verb, and are standing alone are actually made dependent because of the use of subordinating conjunctions or relative pronouns.

Incorrect:	*The teacher waiting for the class to complete the assignment.*
Problem:	This sentence is incomplete because an *-ing* word alone does not function as a verb. When a helping verb is added (for example, was waiting), it forms a sentence.
Correct:	*The teacher was waiting for the class to complete the assignment.*

Sentence completeness

Avoid fragments and run-on sentences. Recognizing sentence elements necessary to make a complete thought, properly using independent and dependent clauses (see "Use Correct Coordination and Subordination"), and using correct punctuation will amend such errors.

Sentence structure

Recognize simple, compound, complex, and compound-complex sentences. Use dependent (subordinate) and independent clauses correctly to create these sentence structures.

> **Simple:** *Nadia wrote a letter.*
>
> **Compound:** *Nadia wrote a letter, and Pablo drew a picture.*
>
> **Complex:** *While Nadia wrote a letter, Pablo drew a picture.*
>
> **Compound/Complex:** *When Lindsey asked them to demonstrate their newfound skills, Nadia wrote a letter, and Pablo drew a picture.*

Note: Do not confuse compound sentence elements with compound sentences.

Simple sentence with compound subject:

> <u>Veronica</u> and <u>Uri</u> wrote letters.
>
> The <u>girl</u> in row three and the <u>boy</u> next to her were passing notes across the aisle.

Simple sentence with compound predicate:

> Ian wrote letters and drew pictures.
>
> The captain of the high school debate team graduated with honors and studied broadcast journalism in college.

Simple sentence with compound object of preposition:

> Dawn graded the students' essays for <u>style</u> and <u>mechanical accuracy</u>.

Parallelism

Recognize parallel structures using phrases (prepositional, gerund, participial, and infinitive) and omissions from sentences that create the lack of parallelism.

Prepositional phrase/single modifier

Incorrect: *Tracy ate the ice cream with enthusiasm and hurriedly.*

Correct: *Tracy ate the ice cream with enthusiasm and in a hurry.*

Correct: *Tracy ate the ice cream enthusiastically and hurriedly.*

Participial phrase/infinitive phrase

Incorrect: *After hiking for hours and to sweat profusely, Ahmet sat down to rest and drinking water.*

Correct: *After hiking for hours and sweating profusely, Ahmet sat down to rest and drink water.*

Recognition of dangling modifiers

Dangling phrases are attached to sentence parts in a way that creates ambiguity and incorrect meaning.

Participial phrase

Incorrect: *Hanging from her skirt, Tasha tugged at a loose thread.*

Correct: *Tasha tugged at a loose thread hanging from her skirt.*

Incorrect: *Relaxing in the bathtub, the telephone rang.*

Correct: *While I was relaxing in the bathtub, the telephone rang.*

Infinitive Phrase

Incorrect: *To improve his behavior, the dean warned Fred.*

Correct: *The dean warned Fred to improve his behavior.*

Prepositional phrase

Incorrect: *On the floor, Shazia saw the dog eating table scraps.*

Correct: *Shazia saw the dog eating table scraps on the floor.*

Recognition of syntactical redundancy or omission

These errors occur when superfluous words have been added to a sentence or key words have been omitted from a sentence.

Redundancy

Incorrect: *Deanna made sure that when her plane arrived that she retrieved all of her luggage.*

Correct: *Deanna made sure that when her plane arrived she retrieved all of her luggage.*

Incorrect: *Norris was a mere skeleton of his former self.*
Correct: *Norris was a skeleton of his former self.*

Omission

Incorrect: *Debbie opened her book, recited her textbook, and answered the teacher's subsequent question.*

Correct: *Debbie opened her book, recited from the textbook, and answered the teacher's subsequent question.*

Avoidance of double negatives

This error occurs from positioning two negatives that, in fact, cancel each other out in meaning.

Incorrect: *Janelle didn't have no double negatives in her paper.*
Correct: *Janelle didn't have any double negatives in her paper.*

Sample Test Question and Rationale

(Rigorous)

1. Which of the following sentences contains an error in agreement?

    A. Jennifer is one of the women who writes for the magazine.

    B. Each of their sons plays a different sport.

    C. This band has performed at the Odeum many times.

    D. The data are available online at the listed Web site.

Answer: A. Jennifer is one of the women who writes for the magazine.

"Women" is the plural subject of the verb, so the correct verb is "write."

SKILL 7.5 Demonstrating knowledge of various types of sentence structures (e.g., declarative, interrogative)

Teachers can instruct students to classify a sentence structure according to its purpose. Have the students ask themselves, "Why did the writer write this sentence this way?" The answer is then likely to lead them to the function of the sentence classification. Students can then classify sentences based on their purpose.

Four types of sentences:

1. A declarative sentence makes a statement and ends with a period. Declarative sentences consist of a subject and a predicate.

2. An interrogative sentence asks a question and ends with a question mark, in addition to having a different tonal pattern (often a raised tone near the end of the sentence).

3. An imperative sentence gives a command or makes a request. Sometimes the subject of an imperative sentence (you) is understood without being written.

4. An exclamatory sentence emphasizes a statement (either declarative or imperative), shows strong feeling, and ends with an exclamation mark.

Declarative, imperative, or interrogative sentences can be made into exclamatory sentences by punctuating them with an exclamation point. Students should be taught to use different sentence types in their writing in order to create and combine diverse sentences for writing effective paragraphs.

COMPETENCY 8

UNDERSTAND SKILLS AND STRATEGIES INVOLVED IN SPEAKING, LISTENING, AND VIEWING ACROSS THE CURRICULUM

> **SKILL** **Applying knowledge of conventions of one-on-one and group**
> **8.1** **verbal interactions** *(e.g., turn taking, responding to questions with appropriate information)*

Listening is not a skill that is talked about much, except when someone clearly does not listen. The truth is, however, that listening is a very specific skill for very specific circumstances. Two aspects of listening warrant attention: *comprehension*—which is simply understanding what someone says, the purposes behind the message, and the context in which it is said—and *purpose*.

While someone may completely understand a message, what is the listener supposed to do with it? Just nod and smile? Go out and take action? While listening comprehension is indeed a significant skill in itself that deserves a lot of focus in the classroom (much in the same way that reading comprehension does), we will focus on purpose here. Often, when we understand the purpose of listening in various contexts, comprehension will be much easier. Furthermore, when we know the purpose of listening, we can better adjust our comprehension strategies.

First, when complex or new information is provided to us orally, we must analyze and interpret that information:

- What is the author's most important point?

- How do the figures of speech impact meaning?

- How are conclusions made?

Often, making sense of this information can be tough when presented orally— first, because we have no place to go back and review material already stated, and second, because oral language is so much less predictable than written language. However, when we focus on extracting the meaning, message, and speaker's purpose (rather than just "listening" and waiting for things to make sense for us—in other words, when we are more "active" in our listening), we have greater success in interpreting speech.

Second, listening is often done for the purpose of enjoyment. We like to listen to stories, poetry, and radio dramas and theater. Listening to literature can also be a great pleasure. The problem today is that students have not learned to extract great pleasure on a widespread scale from listening to literature, poetry, or language that is read aloud. Perhaps that is because we have not done a good job of showing students how listening to literature (or other oral communications) can indeed be more interesting than television or video games. In the classrooms of exceptional teachers, we will often find that students are captivated by the reading aloud of good literature. It is refreshing and enjoyable to just sit and soak in the language, story, and poetry of literature when it is read to us.

Finally, we will discuss listening in both large- and small-group conversations. The difference here is that conversation requires more than just listening: it also involves feedback and active involvement. This can be particularly challenging because in our culture we are trained to move conversations along, to discourage silence in a conversation, and to always get in the last word.

In a discussion, for example, when we are preparing our next response—rather than listening to what others are saying—we do a large disservice to the entire discussion. Students need to learn how listening carefully to others in discussions actually promotes better responses on the part of subsequent speakers. One way teachers can encourage this in both large- and small-group discussions is to expect students to respond *directly* to the previous student's comments before moving ahead with their new comments. This will encourage them to pose their new comments in light of the comments that came just before them.

> We must teach students **how** to listen and enjoy such work. We do this by making it fun and giving many possibilities and alternatives to capture the wide array of interests in each classroom.

> In group discussions, teachers should encourage students to respond directly to the previous student's comments before moving ahead with their new comments. This will encourage them to pose their new comments in light of the comments that came just before them and promote better listening skills.

Sample Test Question and Rationale

(Rigorous)

1. **Which of the following is a valid conclusion?**

   A. Based on the evidence, I believe John Jones stole the car.

   B. I suspect that John Jones stole the car.

   C. John Jones looks guilty, so he must have stolen the car.

   D. Of the two suspects, John Jones's cynical expression makes me think that he's guilty.

Answer: A. Based on the evidence, I believe John Jones stole the car.

Valid conclusions are based on evidence.

SKILL 8.2 Analyzing ways in which verbal cues (*e.g., word choice, tone, volume*) and nonverbal cues (*e.g., body language, eye contact*) affect communication in various situations

Analyzing the speech of others is a very good technique for helping students to improve their own public speaking abilities. In most circumstances, because students cannot view themselves as they give speeches and presentations, they begin to learn what works and what doesn't work in effective public speaking when they get the opportunity to critique, question, and analyze others' speeches. However, a very important word of warning: *Do not* have students critique one another's public speaking skills. It could be very damaging to a student to have his or her peers point out what did not work in a speech. Instead, video is a great tool teachers can use. Any appropriate source of public speaking can be used in the classroom for students to analyze and critique.

Here are some of the things students should pay attention to when speaking:

- Volume: A speaker should use an appropriate volume—not too loud to be annoying but not too soft to be inaudible.

- Pace: The rate at which words are spoken should be appropriate—not too fast to make the speech incomprehensible but not too slow so as to put listeners to sleep.

- Pronunciation: A speaker should make sure words are spoken clearly. Listeners do not have a text to refer to, and they cannot reread things they didn't catch.

- Body language: While animated body language can help a speech, too much of it can be distracting. Body language should help to convey the message, not detract from it.

- Word choice: The words speakers choose should be consistent with their intended purpose as well as the audience.

- Visual aids: Visual aids, like body language, should enhance a message. Many visual aids can be distracting, which can detract from the message.

Overall, instead of telling students to keep these factors in mind when presenting information orally, it may be beneficial to have them observe speakers who do these things both well and poorly. Watching other speakers will help students to remember the "rules" the next time they give a speech.

SKILL 8.3 Demonstrating knowledge of strategies for promoting effective listening skills

Oral speech can be very difficult to follow, as listeners typically have no written record in which to "reread" things they didn't hear or understand. In addition, oral speech can be much less structured than written language. At the same time, many of the skills and strategies that help students in reading comprehension can help them in listening comprehension. For example, as soon as we start listening to something new, we should tap into our prior knowledge in order to attach new information to what we already know. This will not only help in understanding, but it will also assist in remembering the material.

We can also look for transitions between ideas. Sometimes, in oral speech, this is fairly simple to find (such as when voice tone or body language change). Although we don't have the luxury of looking at paragraphs in oral language, we do have the animation that comes along with live speech. Human beings have to try very hard to be completely nonexpressive in their speech. Listeners should take advantage of this and notice how the speaker changes character and voice to signal a transition of ideas.

Listeners can also better comprehend the underlying intent of a speaker when they notice nonverbal cues. For example, looking to see an expression on the face of a speaker that signals irony is often simpler than trying to extract irony from written words. Another good way to follow oral speech is to take notes, outlining the major points. Because oral speech can be more circular (as opposed to linear) than written text, it can be of great assistance to keep track of an author's message. Students can practice this strategy in many ways in the classroom, including taking notes during the teacher's oral messages as well as other students' presentations and speeches.

Listeners can better comprehend the underlying intent of a speaker by paying attention to nonverbal cues.

Additional classroom methods can help students to learn good listening skills. For example, teachers can have students practice following complex directions. They can also have students orally retell stories or retell (in writing or in oral speech) oral presentations of stories or other materials. These activities give students direct practice in the very important skills of listening. They provide students with outlets in which they can slowly improve their abilities to comprehend oral language; they also allow students to take decisive action based on oral speech.

SKILL 8.4 Recognizing types, characteristics, and roles of visual and oral media (e.g., television, radio, film, electronic media)

The use of the media, television, radio, film, Internet resources, and other electronic sources has become an asset in teaching because they encourage students to practice critical thinking. The use of media offers new ways of engaging students in learning and in making connections among themselves, between school and life, and between educators and the outside world. Teachers should utilize a variety of media because it is through the media that our culture largely expresses itself.

Media literacy is an informed, critical understanding gleaned from verbal and visual symbols that are experienced every day through television, radio, computers, and other electronic sources. Teachers should be aware of the need for students to develop critical viewing abilities along with critical *thinking* abilities when *viewing* various types of media. Critical viewing involves examining the techniques and characteristics that are involved in media production, critically analyzing media messages, and recognizing the roles that audiences play in deriving meaning from those messages.

When listening to a radio program, viewing a film, or watching a television program, students should ask themselves some key questions:

- What is this program's point of view?

- What persuasive techniques are used?

- What evidence is used to support the program's argument?

- Is there a media stereotyping, or are there correct representations of gender, race, and ethnicity?

Teachers should have an understanding of how to select, evaluate, and use information from television, radio, film, and electronic media sources. The key component of media literacy is understanding the symbols, information, ideas, values, and messages that emanate from the media. Teachers should choose appropriate media selection by analyzing the various instructional media programs available. This will help them to achieve learning goals, which, after all, is the motivation for the use of technology.

SKILL 8.5 Demonstrating knowledge of the structures and elements of oral, visual, and multimedia presentations for diverse audiences and for various purposes

The media's impact on today's society is immense, and it is growing all the time. As children, we watch programs on television that are amazingly fast-paced and visually rich. Parents' roles as verbal and moral teachers are diminishing in response to the much more stimulating guidance of the television set. Adolescence, which used to be the time for going out and exploring the world firsthand, is now consumed by the allure of MTV, popular music, and video games. At the same time, the media's effect on society is also beneficial and progressive. In particular, its effect on education provides special challenges and opportunities for both teachers and students.

Thanks to satellite technology, instructional radio and television programs can be received by urban classrooms and rural villages. CD-ROMs allow students to learn information through a virtual reality experience. The Internet allows instant access to unlimited data and connects people across cultures. Educational media, when used in a productive way, enriches instruction and makes it more individualized, accessible, and economical.

MULTIMEDIA TEACHING MODEL	
Step 1. Diagnose	• Figure out what students need to know. • Assess what students already know.
Step 2. Design	• Design tests of learning achievement. • Identify effective instructional strategies. • Select suitable media. • Sequence learning activities within the program. • Plan introductory activities. • Plan follow-up activities.
Step 3. Procure	• Secure materials at hand. • Obtain new materials.

Table continued on next page

Step 4. Produce	• Modify existing materials.
	• Craft new materials.
Step 5. Refine	• Conduct a small-scale test of the program.
	• Evaluate procedures and achievements.
	• Revise the program accordingly.
	• Conduct a classroom test of the program.
	• Evaluate procedures and achievements.
	• Revise the program in anticipation of the next school term.

TIPS FOR USING PRINT MEDIA AND VISUAL AIDS
Use pictures instead of words whenever possible.
Present one key point per visual.
Use no more than three or four colors per visual to avoid clutter and confusion.
Use contrasting colors, such as dark blue and bright yellow.
Use a maximum of twenty-five to thirty-five numbers per visual aid.
Use bullets instead of paragraphs whenever possible.
Make sure it is student-centered, not media-centered. The delivery is just as important as the media presented.

TIPS FOR USING MOVIES AND TELEVISION
Study the programs in advance.
Obtain supplementary materials such as printed transcripts of the narrative or study guides.
Provide students with background information, explain unfamiliar concepts, and anticipate outcomes.

Table continued on next page

Assign outside readings based on the students' viewing.
Ask cuing questions.
Watch along with the students.
Observe the students' reactions.
Follow up the viewing with discussions and related activities.

The Media and Culture

Research is beginning to document the ways in which cultural minority parents interact with their children to support learning. The research mostly focuses on how these interactions differ from more mainstream or middle-class approaches.

One recent study explored the nontraditional ways in which Hispanic parents are involved in their children's education—ways that are not necessarily recognized by educators as parent involvement. However, further research is needed to delve more deeply into the connections that diverse families create, as traditional indicators do not always recognize effective interactions. More studies are also needed to consider the reasons why some diverse families might not be involved in the more traditional ways.

Building a body of knowledge about the specific practices of various cultural groups may support the validation of those practices by school personnel, and this research may even support sharing effective practices across cultural groups.

Interactive Homework Assignments

The development of interactive homework assignments (homework that requires parent-child interaction as part of the activity) has shown promise as a way of supporting parent involvement and student achievement. Homework activities that are explicitly designed to be interactive have shown positive results for increasing achievement in several subject areas, including science and the language arts.

Well-designed interactive assignments can have a number of positive outcomes: They can help students to practice study skills, prepare for class, participate in learning activities, and develop personal responsibility for homework. These assignments may also promote parent-child relations, develop parent-teacher communication, and fulfill policy directives from administrators.

School Support of Parental Homework Help

Although parents express positive feelings about homework, many have concerns about their children's homework, including their personal limitations in subject matter knowledge and effective helping strategies. More research is needed on how school personnel can effectively support parental homework help.

Teachers have a critical role to play in encouraging multicultural experiences. They have an opportunity to incorporate activities that reflect our nation's increasing diversity by allowing students to share their similarities, develop a positive cultural identity, and appreciate the unique contributions of all cultures. For example, one of the best ways to incorporate multicultural literature (depicting African-American, Asian, Arabic, Native American, and Hispanic heritage) is to integrate it into the established reading program rather than to teach it as a separate or distinct area of study.

DOMAIN II
SOCIAL STUDIES

PERSONALIZED STUDY PLAN

PAGE	COMPETENCY AND SKILL	KNOWN MATERIAL/ SKIP IT
129	**9: Understand important events, concepts, and methods of inquiry related to Georgia, U.S., and world history**	☐
	9.1: Recognizing chronological relationships among historical events	☐
	9.2: Demonstrating knowledge of people, events, issues, and developments in Georgia, U.S., and world history	☐
	9.3: Demonstrating knowledge of early Native American cultures in North America	☐
	9.4: Analyzing various events, issues, and developments in Georgia, U.S., and world historys	☐
	9.5: Demonstrating knowledge of historical inquiry	☐
175	**10: Understand major concepts, principles, and methods of inquiry related to geography**	☐
	10.1: Applying knowledge of basic concepts of geography	☐
	10.2: Demonstrating knowledge of major physical and human-constructed features of the earth	☐
	10.3: Analyzing interactions between physical systems and human systems	☐
	10.4: Applying knowledge of maps, globes, and other geographic toolss	☐
	10.5: Demonstrating knowledge of strategies and resources for geographic inquiry	☐
190	**11: Understand major concepts, principles, and methods of inquiry related to U.S. Government and civics**	☐
	11.1: Demonstrating knowledge of the functions and the basic principles of the U.S. government	☐
	11.2: Identifying the roles and interrelationships of national, state, and local governments in the United States	☐
	11.3: Recognizing the roles and powers of the executive, legislative, and judicial branches	☐
	11.4: Demonstrating knowledge of the Declaration of Independence, the U.S. Constitution, and the Bill of Rights	☐
	11.5: Identifying the rights and responsibilities of U.S. citizenship	☐
	11.6: Demonstrating knowledge of strategies and resources for inquiry related to government and civics	☐

PERSONALIZED STUDY PLAN

KNOWN MATERIAL/ SKIP IT

PAGE	COMPETENCY AND SKILL	
201	**12: Understand major concepts, principles, and methods of inquiry related to economics**	☐
	12.1: Recognizing basic economic concepts and the purposes and functions of currency	☐
	12.2: Demonstrating knowledge of the basic structure of the U.S. economy	☐
	12.3: Recognizing the roles and interactions of consumers and producers	☐
	12.4: Identifying the functions of private business, banks, and the government	☐
	12.5: Identifying the skills necessary to make responsible financial decisions	☐
	12.6: Demonstrating knowledge of strategies and resources for inquiry related to economics	☐

COMPETENCY 9

UNDERSTAND IMPORTANT EVENTS, CONCEPTS, AND METHODS OF INQUIRY RELATED TO GEORGIA, U.S., AND WORLD HISTORY

SKILL 9.1 Recognizing chronological relationships among historical events

CHRONOLOGY is the ordering of events through time. Chronologies are often listed along a timeline or in a list by date. Chronologies allow for an easy visualization of a wide expanse of history. Information condensed this way allows a student to quickly get an overview of the major events and changes over time. By focusing on important related events, the causes and effects of major developments can be emphasized. In addition, in placing chronologies for different societies parallel to one another, comparisons in relative development can be quickly interpreted, providing material for further historical exploration.

HISTORIC CAUSATION is the concept that events in history are linked to one another by an endless chain of cause and effect. The root causes of major historical events cannot always be seen immediately; they are often only apparent when looking back from many years later.

When Columbus landed in the New World in 1492, the full effect of his discovery could not have been measured at that time. By opening the Western Hemisphere to economic and political developments from Europeans, Columbus changed the face of the world. The American Indian populations that resided in those areas were quickly decimated by disease and warfare after Columbus's arrival. Over the following century, the Spanish conquered most of South and Central America, and English and French settlers arrived in North America, eventually displacing the native people. This gradual displacement took place over many years and could not have been foreseen by those early explorers. Nevertheless, looking back, it can be said that Columbus caused a series of events that greatly impacted world history.

In some cases, individual events do have an immediate, clear effect. In 1941, Europe was embroiled in war. On the Pacific Rim, Japan was engaged in a military occupation of Korea and other Asian countries. The United States took a position of isolation, choosing not to become directly involved with the conflicts. This position changed rapidly, however, when on the morning of December 7, 1941, Japanese forces launched a surprise attack on a U.S. naval base at Pearl

CHRONOLOGY: the ordering of events through time; often listed along a timeline or in a list by date

HISTORIC CAUSATION: the concept that events in history are linked to one another by an endless chain of cause and effect

Harbor in Hawaii. The United States immediately declared war on Japan and became involved in Europe shortly afterward. The entry of the United States into the Second World War undoubtedly contributed to the eventual victory of the Allied forces in Europe and the defeat of Japan after the United States dropped two atomic bombs there. The surprise attack on Pearl Harbor affected the outcome of the war and the shape of the modern world.

Interactions among cultures—either by exploration, migration, or war—often contribute directly to major historical events; however, other forces can influence the course of history as well.

- Religious movements, such as the rise of Catholicism in the Middle Ages, created social changes throughout Europe and culminated in the Crusades and the expulsion of Muslims from Spain.

- Technological developments lead to major historical events, as in the case of the Industrial Revolution, which was driven by the replacement of water power with steam power.

- Social movements caused major historical shifts. For example, between the Civil War and the early 1960s in the United States, racial segregation was practiced legally in many parts of the country through "Jim Crow" laws. Demonstrations and activism opposing segregation began to escalate during the late 1950s and early 1960s, eventually leading to the passage in the U.S. Congress of the Civil Rights Act of 1964, effectively ending legal segregation in the United States.

Even now, all of these examples of historical occurrences can be changed by the passage of time. Viewed in light of the entire scope of U.S. history, the events of fifty years ago are still incredibly pertinent to today's society. Viewed in light of the entire scope of world history, the events of five hundred years ago may have less of an overall impact than those changes wrought five thousand years ago. Chronology, like time, is relative.

Students must have a grasp of how events relate to one another and to history as a whole in order to understand what the events mean in a greater context.

Sample Test Questions and Rationale

(Easy)

1. Which of the following were results of the Age of Exploration?

   A. More complete and accurate maps and charts

   B. New and more accurate navigational instruments

   C. Proof that the earth is round

   D. All of the above

Answer: D. All of the above

The importance of the Age of Exploration was not only the discovery and colonization of the New World but also better maps and charts; new, more accurate navigational instruments; increased knowledge; great wealth; new and different foods and items; a new hemisphere as a refuge from poverty, persecution, and a place to start a new and better life; and proof that Asia could be reached by sea and that the earth was round.

(Rigorous)

2. What was the long-term importance of the Mayflower Compact?

   A. It established the foundation of all later agreements with the Native peoples

   B. It established freedom of religion in the original English colonies

   C. It ended the war in Europe involving Spain, France, and England

   D. It established a model of small, town-based government that was adopted throughout the New England colonies

Answer: D. Established a model of small, town-based government

Before setting foot on land in 1620, the Pilgrims aboard the *Mayflower* agreed to a form of self-government by signing the Mayflower Compact. The Compact served as the basis for governing the Plymouth colony for many years and set an example of small, town-based government that would proliferate throughout New England. The present-day New England town meeting is an extension of this tradition. This republican ideal was later to clash with the policies of British colonial government.

HISTORY: the study of
the past, especially aspects
of human past: political
incidents, economic
events, and cultural and
social conditions

HISTORY is the study of the past, especially aspects of human past: political incidents, economic events, and cultural and social conditions. Students study history through textbooks, research, field trips to museums and historical attractions, and other hands-on methods. Most nations set requirements in history around the study of their own country's heritage, usually to develop an awareness and feeling of loyalty and patriotism.

For better comprehension, history can be divided into three main classifications:

- Time periods

- Nations (in terms of a group of peoples sharing political and social boundaries, not necessarily nations as we know them today),

- Specialized topics.

In the following pages, all of the provided historical information for study falls into one of these three divisions. Note that the three categories can and do overlap in some of their content; this is a natural outcome of the complex details that make up our world's history. For example, Imperial and Feudal Japan can fall under the categories of both time period and nation. It is a time period in that there were definite years when Imperialism and Feudalism were common forms of government. At the same time, the provided information deals only with those forms of government in Japan. In order to understand history in a greater context, the reader must grasp that when it comes to history, all things are relative; comparisons and chronologies can be manipulated to provide evidence for any line of reasoning the reader wishes to take.

Examples of Time Periods

Prehistory

PREHISTORY: the period
of mankind's achievements
before the development of
writing

PREHISTORY is defined as the period of mankind's achievements before the development of writing. In the Stone Age cultures, there were three different periods: the Lower Paleolithic Period, which is characterized by the use of crude tools; the Upper Paleolithic Period, which exhibited a greater variety of more intricate tools and implements, the adoption of wearing clothing, a highly organized group life, and skills in art; and the Neolithic Period, during which the people domesticated animals; formalized food production; practiced the arts of knitting, spinning, and weaving cloth; learned how to start fires with friction; built domestic shelters; and developed the institutions of family, religion, and government.

The Tang Dynasty

The Tang Dynasty extended from 618 to 907 CE. Its capital was the most heavily populated of any city in the world at the time. Buddhism was adopted by the imperial family (Li) and became an integral part of Chinese culture. The emperor, however, feared the monasteries and began to take action against them in the tenth century. Confucianism experienced a rebirth during the time of this dynasty as an instrument of state administration.

Following a civil war, the central government lost control of local areas. Warlords arose in 907, and China was divided into North and South. These areas came to be ruled by short-lived minor dynasties. A major political accomplishment of this period was the creation of a class of career government officials who functioned between the populace and the government. This class of "scholar-officials" continued to fulfill this function in government and society until 1911.

The period of the Tang Dynasty is generally considered a pinnacle of Chinese civilization. Through contact with the Middle East and India, the period was marked by great creativity in many areas.

- Block printing was invented, which made information and literature available to a much wider audience.

- In science, astronomers calculated the paths of the sun and the moon as well as the movements of the constellations. This facilitated the development of the calendar.

- In agriculture, such technologies as land cultivation by setting it on fire, the curved-shaft plow, separate cultivation of seedlings, and sophisticated irrigation systems increased productivity.

- Hybrid breeds of horses and mules were created to strengthen the labor supply.

- In medicine, there were achievements like the understanding of the circulatory and digestive systems, as well as great advances in pharmacology.

- In ceramics, a new type of glazing was invented that gave the dynasty's porcelain and earthenware its unique appearance through three-colored glazing.

- In literature, the poetry of the period is generally considered the best in the entire history of Chinese literature. The rebirth of Confucianism led to the publication of many commentaries on his classical writings. Encyclopedias on several subjects were produced, as well as histories and philosophical works.

The Middle Ages

In Europe, the system of FEUDALISM was one of loyalty and protection. The strong and wealthy protected the weak, who in turn provided services in farm labor, military service, and lifelong allegiances. Life was typically lived on a vast estate, owned by a nobleman and his family, called a manor. It was a complete village that supported a few hundred people, mostly peasants. Improved tools and farming methods made life more bearable, although most people never left the manor or traveled from their village during their entire lifetimes.

In feudal societies, a very small number of people owned land. Instead, they held it as a hereditary trust from some social or political superior in return for services. The superiors were a small percentage of the people; they were a fighting and ruling aristocracy. The vast majority of the people were simply workers. One of the largest landowners of the time was the Roman Catholic Church. It was estimated that during the twelfth and thirteenth centuries, the Church controlled one-third of the useable land in Western Europe.

In addition to the tremendous influence of the Church, the era of knighthood and its code of chivalry also came into importance at this time. Until the period of the Renaissance, the Church was the only place where people could be educated. The Bible and other books were hand-copied by monks in the monasteries. Cathedrals were built and decorated with art depicting religious subjects.

With the increase in trade and travel, cities sprang up and began to grow. Craft workers in the cities developed their skills to a high degree, eventually organizing guilds to protect the quality of the work and to regulate the buying and selling of their products. City government, centered on strong town councils, developed and flourished. The wealthy businessmen who made up the rising middle class were the most active in city government and town councils.

The end of the feudal manorial system was sealed by the outbreak and spread of the infamous BLACK DEATH, which killed over one-third of the total population of Europe. Those who survived and were skilled in any job or occupation were in demand; for the first time, many serfs and peasants found freedom and (for that time period) a decidedly improved standard of living. Strong nation-states became powerful, and people developed a renewed interest in life and learning.

Imperial and Feudal Japan

From its beginnings, Japan operated under an Imperial form of government. The divine emperor was believed to do no wrong and, therefore, served for his entire life. Kyoto, the capital, became one of the largest and most powerful cities in the world. As in Europe, however, the rich and powerful landowners—the nobles—grew powerful over time. Eventually, the nobles had more power than the emperor, which required a change in attitude in the minds of the Japanese people.

The nobles of Japan, called DAIMYOS, were lords of great lands. They were of the highest social class, and people of lower social classes worked for them. The workers included the lowly peasants, who had few privileges other than being allowed to work for the great men that the Daimyos told everyone they were. Serving them, the Daimyos had warriors known as SHOGUN, who were answerable only to the Daimyos. The Shogun code of honor was an exemplification of the overall Japanese belief that every man was a soldier and a gentleman. The contradiction that the emerging social classes identified didn't seem to get noticed much, nor did the needs of women.

The main economic difference between Imperial and Feudal Japan was that the money that continued to flow into the country from trade with China, Korea, and other Asian countries (and from good old-fashioned plundering on the high seas) made its way into the pockets of the Daimyos rather than the emperor's coffers.

Feudalism developed in Japan later than it did in Europe, and it lasted longer as well. Japan dodged one huge historical bullet when a huge Mongol invasion was driven away by the famed KAMIKAZE, or "divine wind," in the twelfth century. Japan was thus free to continue to develop itself as it saw fit and to refrain from interacting with the West. This isolation lasted until the nineteenth century.

The Scientific Revolution

The SCIENTIFIC REVOLUTION was characterized by a shift in scientific approaches and ideas. Near the end of the sixteenth century, Galileo Galilei introduced a radical approach to the study of motion. He moved from attempts to explain the general reasons why objects move the way they do and began to use experiments to describe precisely how they move. He also used experimentation to describe how forces affect nonmoving objects. Other scientists continued in the same approach.

Outstanding scientists of the period also included Johannes Kepler, Evangelista Torricelli, Blaise Pascal, Isaac Newton, and Gottfried Wilhelm Leibniz. This was the period when experiments dominated scientific study. This method was particularly applied to the study of physics.

The Agricultural Revolution

The AGRICULTURAL REVOLUTION occurred first in England. It was marked by experimentation that resulted in the increased production of crops as well as a new and more technical approach to the management of agriculture. This revolution was hugely enhanced by the Industrial Revolution and the invention of the steam engine. The introduction of steam-powered tractors greatly increased crop

DAIMYOS: Japanese lords of great lands, who were of the highest social classes

SHOGUN: Japanese warriors who served the Daimyos and who followed a strict code of honor

KAMIKAZE: a typhoon that dispersed a Mongol invasion fleet threatening Japan from the west in 1281; in World War II this term was used to describe Japanese pilots who deliberately crashed their planes into enemy targets

SCIENTIFIC REVOLUTION: the period beginning in the sixteenth century that was dominated by scientific study, particular applied to the study of physics

AGRICULTURAL REVOLUTION: experimentation that resulted in the increased production of crops as well as a new and more technical approach to the management of agriculture production and significantly decreased labor costs. Developments in agriculture were also enhanced by the Scientific Revolution and the process of learning from experimentation (which ultimately led to philosophies of crop rotation and soil enrichment). Improved systems of irrigation and harvesting also contributed to the growth of agricultural production.

Industrial Revolution

The **INDUSTRIAL REVOLUTION**, which began in Great Britain and spread elsewhere, was the development of power-driven machinery (fueled by coal and steam). This revolution led to the accelerated growth of industry, with large factories replacing homes and small workshops as work centers. The lives of people changed drastically, and a largely agricultural society changed to an industrial one. In Western Europe, the period of colonialism began. The industrialized nations seized and claimed parts of Africa and Asia in an effort to control and provide the raw materials needed to feed the industries and machines in the "mother country." Later developments included power based on electricity and internal combustion, which replaced coal and steam.

> **INDUSTRIAL REVOLUTION:** the development of power-driven machinery (fueled by coal and steam)

1920s America

Many refer to the decade of the 1920s as the Jazz Age. The decade was a time of optimism and of exploring new boundaries. In many ways, it was a clear movement away from conventionalism. Jazz music, uniquely American, was the country's popular music at the time. Jazz is essentially free-flowing improvisation on a simple theme with a four-beat rhythm; this musical style perfectly typified the mood of society. Jazz originated in the poor districts of New Orleans as an outgrowth of the blues. The leading jazz musicians of the time included Buddy Bolden, Joseph "King" Oliver, Duke Ellington, Louis Armstrong, and Jelly Roll Morton.

As jazz grew in popularity and in intricacy of the music, it gave birth to swing and the era of big band jazz. Some of the most notable musicians of the Big Band era were: Bing Crosby, Frank Sinatra, Don Redman, Fletcher Henderson, Count Basie, Benny Goodman, Billie Holiday, Ella Fitzgerald, and the Dorsey Brothers.

Information Revolution

The **INFORMATION REVOLUTION** refers to the sweeping changes during the latter half of the twentieth century as a result of technological advances and a new respect for the knowledge provided by trained, skilled, and experienced professionals in a variety of fields. This approach to understanding a number of social and economic changes in global society arose from the ability to make computer

> **INFORMATION REVOLUTION:** the sweeping changes during the latter half of the twentieth century as a result of technological advances and a new respect for the knowledge provided by trained, skilled, and experienced professionals in a variety of fields

technology both accessible and affordable. In particular, the development of the computer chip led to such technological advances as the Internet, the cell phone, cybernetics, wireless communication, and the related ability to disseminate and access a massive amount of information quite readily.

In terms of economic theory and segmentation, it is now very much the norm to think of three basic economic sectors: agriculture and mining, manufacturing, and "services." Indeed, labor is now often divided between manual labor and informational labor. When businesses became involved in the production, distribution, processing, and transmission of information, it created a new business sector.

The Information Revolution has clearly changed modern life in many ways, including by introducing devices and processes that actually control much of the world as it is experienced by the average person.

It has most certainly revolutionized the entertainment industry, as well as influenced the way people spend their time. In education, new technology has made information on virtually any subject instantly accessible. It has also thoroughly altered the way people can get minute-to-minute information about world events. Sixty years ago, news from the war front became available by radio for the first time. Visual images, however, were primarily available through the weekly newsreels shown in motion picture theaters. Today, live pictures from the battlefield are instantly available to people anywhere in the world. This technology has also made it possible for "smart wars" to be fought, reducing the number of civilian casualties.

Examples of nations

Ancient civilizations were those cultures which developed to a greater degree and were considered advanced. These included the following eleven with their major accomplishments.

Egypt

Egypt made numerous significant contributions including construction of the great pyramids; development of hieroglyphic writing; preservation of bodies after death; making paper from papyrus; contributing to developments in arithmetic and geometry; the invention of the method of counting in groups of 1–10 (the decimal system); completion of a solar calendar; and laying the foundation for science and astronomy.

The ancient civilization of the Sumerians invented the wheel; developed irrigation through use of canals, dikes, and devices for raising water; devised the system of cuneiform writing; learned to divide time; and built large boats for trade. The Babylonians devised the famous CODE OF HAMMURABI, a code of laws.

CODE OF HAMMURABI:
a Babylonian code of laws

The ancient Assyrians were warlike and aggressive due to a highly organized military and used horse drawn chariots.

The Hebrews, also known as the ancient Israelites, instituted MONOTHEISM, which is the worship of one God, Yahweh, and combined the sixty-six books of the Hebrew and Christian Greek scriptures into the Bible we have today.

MONOTHEISM: the worship of one God

The Minoans had a system of writing using symbols to represent syllables in words. They built palaces with multiple levels containing many rooms, water, and sewage systems with flush toilets, bathtubs, hot and cold running water, and bright paintings on the walls.

The Mycenaeans changed the Minoan writing system to aid their own language and used symbols to represent syllables.

The Phoenicians were sea traders well known for their manufacturing skills in glass and metals and the development of their famous purple dye. They became so very proficient in the skill of navigation that they were able to sail by the stars at night. Further, they devised an alphabet using symbols to represent single sounds, which was an improved extension of the Egyptian writing system.

India

In India, the caste system was developed, the principle of zero in mathematics was discovered, and the major religion of Hinduism was begun. In India, Hinduism was a continuing influence along with the rise of Buddhism. Industry and commerce developed along with extensive trading with the Near East. Outstanding advances in the fields of science and medicine were made along with being one of the first to be active in navigation and maritime enterprises during this time.

China

China began building the Great Wall, practiced crop rotation and terrace farming, increased the importance of the silk industry, and developed caravan routes across Central Asia for extensive trade. Also, the Chinese increased proficiency in rice cultivation and developed a written language based on drawings or pictographs (no alphabet symbolizing sounds as each word or character had a form different from all others). China is considered by some historians to be the oldest uninterrupted civilization in the world and was in existence around the same time as the ancient civilizations founded in Egypt, Mesopotamia, and the Indus Valley. The Chinese studied nature and weather; stressed the importance of education, family, and a strong central government; followed the religions of Buddhism, Confucianism, and Taoism; and invented such things as gunpowder, paper, printing, and the magnetic compass.

The Tang Dynasty extended from 618 to 907. Its capital was the most heavily populated of any city in the world at the time. Buddhism was adopted by the imperial family (Li) and became an integral part of Chinese culture. The emperor, however, feared the monasteries and began to take action against them in the tenth century. Confucianism experienced a rebirth during the time of this dynasty as an instrument of state administration.

Following a civil war, the central government lost control of local areas. Warlords arose in 907, and China was divided into north and south. These areas came to be ruled by short-lived minor dynasties. A major political accomplishment of this period was the creation of a class of career government officials, who functioned between the populace and the government. This class of "SCHOLAR-OFFICIALS" continued to fulfill this function in government and society until 1911.

> **SCHOLAR-OFFICIALS:** a class of career government officials, who functioned between the populace and the government

The period of the Tang Dynasty is generally considered a pinnacle of Chinese civilization. Through contact with the Middle East and India, the period of the Tang Dynasty was marked by great creativity in many areas. Block printing was invented, and made much information and literature available to wide audiences.

In science, astronomers calculated the paths of the sun and the moon and the movements of the constellations. This facilitated the development of the calendar. In agriculture, such technologies as cultivating the land by setting it on fire, the curved-shaft plow, separate cultivation of seedlings, and sophisticated irrigation system increased productivity. Hybrid breeds of horses and mules were created to strengthen the labor supply. In medicine, there were achievements like the understanding of the circulatory system and the digestive system and great advances in pharmacology. Ceramics was another area in which great advances were made. A new type of glazing was invented that gave Tang Dynasty porcelain and earthenware its unique appearance through three-colored glazing.

In literature, the poetry of the period is generally considered the best in the entire history of Chinese literature. The rebirth of Confucianism led to the publication of many commentaries on the classical writings. Encyclopedias on several subjects were produced, as well as histories and philosophical works.

Persia
The ancient Persians developed an alphabet; contributed the religions/philosophies of Zoroastrianism, Mithraism, and Gnosticism; and allowed conquered peoples to retain their own customs, laws, and religions.

Greece
The classical civilization of Greece reached the highest levels in man's achievements based on the foundations already laid by such ancient groups as the Egyptians, Phoenicians, Minoans, and Mycenaeans.

Among the more important contributions of Greece were the Greek alphabet derived from the Phoenician letters that formed the basis for the Roman alphabet and our present-day alphabet. Extensive trading and colonization resulted in the spread of the Greek civilization. The love of sports, with emphasis on a sound body, led to the tradition of the Olympic Games. Greece was responsible for the rise of independent, strong city-states. Note the complete contrast between independent, freedom-loving Athens with its practice of pure democracy (i.e., direct, personal, active participation in government by qualified citizens) and the rigid, totalitarian, militaristic Sparta. Other important areas that the Greeks are credited with influencing include drama, epic and lyric poetry, fables, myths centered on the many gods and goddesses, science, astronomy, medicine, mathematics, philosophy, art, architecture, and recording historical events. The conquests of Alexander the Great spread Greek ideas to the areas he conquered and brought to the Greek world many ideas from Asia including the value of ideas, wisdom, curiosity, and the desire to learn as much about the world as possible.

A most interesting and significant characteristic of the Greek, Hellenic, and Roman civilizations was SECULARISM, where emphasis shifted away from religion to the state. Men were not absorbed in or dominated by religion as had been the case in Egypt and the nations located in Mesopotamia. Religion and its leaders did not dominate the state and its authority was greatly diminished.

> **SECULARISM:** when emphasis shifts away from religion to the state

Japan
Civilization in Japan appeared during this time, having borrowed much of their culture from China. It was the last of these classical civilizations to develop. Although they used, accepted, and copied Chinese art, law, architecture, dress, and writing, the Japanese refined these into their own unique way of life, including incorporating the religion of Buddhism into their culture.

Africa
The civilizations in Africa south of the Sahara were developing the refining and use of iron, especially for farm implements and later for weapons. Trading was overland using camels and at important seaports. The Arab influence was extremely important, as was their later contact with Indians, Christian Nubians, and Persians. In fact, their trading activities were probably the most important factor in the spread of and assimilation of different ideas and stimulation of cultural growth.

Vikings
The Vikings had a lot of influence at this time, spreading their ideas and knowledge of trade routes and sailing, accomplished first through their conquests and later through trade.

Byzantium and the Saracens

In other parts of the world were the Byzantine and Saracenic (or Islamic) civilizations, both dominated by religion. The major contributions of the Saracens were in the areas of science and philosophy. Included were accomplishments in astronomy, mathematics, physics, chemistry, medicine, literature, art, trade, manufacturing, agriculture, and a marked influence on the Renaissance period of history. The Byzantines (Christians) made important contributions in art and the preservation of Greek and Roman achievements including architecture (especially in Eastern Europe and Russia), the Code of Justinian, and Roman law.

Ghana

The ancient empire of Ghana occupied an area that is now known as Northern Senegal and Southern Mauritania. There is no absolute certainty regarding the origin of this empire. Oral history dates the rise of the empire to the seventh century BCE. Most believe, however, that the date should be placed much later. Many believe the nomads who were herding animals on the fringes of the desert posed a threat to the early Soninke people, who were an agricultural community. In times of drought, it is believed the nomads raided the agricultural villages for water and places to pasture their herds. To protect themselves, it is believed that these farming communities formed a loose confederation that eventually became the empire of ancient Ghana.

The empire's economic vitality was determined by geographical location. It was situated midway between the desert, which was the major source of salt, and the gold fields. This location along the trade routes of the camel caravans provided exceptional opportunity for economic development. The caravans brought copper, salt, dried fruit, clothing, manufactured goods, and other items. For these goods, the people of Ghana traded kola nuts, leather goods, gold, hides, ivory, and slaves. In addition, the empire collected taxes on every trade item that entered the boundaries of the empire. With the revenue from the trade goods tax, the empire supported a government, an army that protected the trade routes and the borders, the maintenance of the capital, and primary market centers. But it was control of the gold fields that gave the empire political power and economic prosperity. The location of the gold fields was a carefully guarded secret. By the tenth century, Ghana was very rich and controlled an area about the size of the state of Texas. Demand for this gold sharply increased in the ninth and tenth centuries as the Islamic states of Northern Africa began to mint coins. As the gold trade expanded, so did the empire. The availability of local iron ore enabled the early people of the Ghana kingdom to make more efficient farm implements and effective weapons.

The United States

The Industrial Revolution had spread from Great Britain to the United States. Before 1800, most manufacturing activities were done in small shops or in homes. However, starting in the early 1800s, factories with modern machines were built making it easier to produce goods faster. The eastern part of the country became a major industrial area although some developed in the West. At about the same time, improvements began to be made in building roads, railroads, canals, and steamboats. The increased ease of travel facilitated the westward movement and boosted the economy with faster and cheaper shipment of goods and products, covering larger areas. Some of the innovations include the Erie Canal connecting the interior and Great Lakes with the Hudson River and the coastal port of New York.

Westward expansion occurred for a number of reasons, most importantly economic ones. Cotton had become most important to most of the people who lived in the southern states. The effects of the Industrial Revolution, which began in England, were now being felt in the United States. With the invention of power-driven machines, the demand for cotton fiber greatly increased for the yarn needed in spinning and weaving. Eli Whitney's cotton gin made the separation of the seeds from the cotton much more efficient and faster. This, in turn, increased the demand and more and more farmers became involved in the raising and selling of cotton.

The innovations and developments of better methods of long-distance transportation moved the cotton in greater quantities to textile mills in England as well as the areas of New England and Middle Atlantic states in the United States. As prices increased along with increased demand, southern farmers began expanding by clearing increasingly more land to grow more cotton. Movement, settlement, and farming headed west to utilize the fertile soils. This, in turn, demanded increased need for a large supply of cheap labor. The system of slavery expanded, both in numbers and in the movement to lands west of the South.

Cotton farmers and slave owners were not the only ones heading west. Many, in other fields of economic endeavor, began the migration: trappers, miners, merchants, ranchers, and others were all seeking their fortunes. The Lewis and Clark expedition stimulated the westward push. Fur companies hired men, known as Mountain Men, to go westward, searching for the animal pelts to supply the market and meet the demands of the East and Europe. These men in their own way explored and discovered the many passes and trails that would eventually be used by settlers in their trek to the west. The California gold rush also had a very large influence on the movement west.

In the American Southwest, the results were exactly the opposite. Spain had claimed this area since the 1540s, had spread northward from Mexico City and, in the 1700s, had established missions, forts, villages, towns, and very large ranches. After the purchase of the Louisiana Territory in 1803, Americans began moving into Spanish territory. A few hundred American families in what is now Texas were allowed to live there but had to agree to become loyal subjects to Spain. In 1821, Mexico successfully revolted against Spanish rule, won independence, and chose to be more tolerant toward the American settlers and traders. The Mexican government encouraged and allowed extensive trade and settlement, especially in Texas. Many of the new settlers were Southerners and brought with them their slaves. Slavery was outlawed in Mexico and technically illegal in Texas, although the Mexican government looked the other way.

The Red River Cession was the next acquisition of land and came about as part of a treaty with Great Britain in 1818:

- It included parts of North and South Dakota and Minnesota.

- In 1819, Florida, both east and west, was ceded to the United States by Spain along with parts of Alabama, Mississippi, and Louisiana.

- Texas was annexed in 1845.

- After the war with Mexico in 1848 the government paid $15 million for what would become the states of California, Utah, Nevada, and parts of four other states.

- In 1846, the Oregon Country was ceded to the United States, which extended the western border to the Pacific Ocean. The northern U.S. boundary was established at the 49th parallel. The states of Idaho, Oregon, and Washington were formed from this territory.

- In 1853, the Gadsden Purchase rounded out the present boundary of the forty-eight conterminous states with payment to Mexico of $10 million for land that makes up the present states of New Mexico and Arizona.

The election of Andrew Jackson as president signaled a swing of the political pendulum from government influence of the wealthy, aristocratic Easterners to the interests of the Western farmers and pioneers and the era of the "common man." Jacksonian democracy was a policy of equal political power for all. After the War of 1812, Henry Clay and supporters favored economic measures that came to be known as the American System. This involved tariffs protecting American farmers and manufacturers from having to compete with foreign products, stimulating industrial growth and employment. With more people working, more farm products would be consumed, prosperous farmers would be able to buy more manufactured goods, and the additional monies from tariffs would make it possible for the government to make needed internal improvements. To get this going, in 1816, Congress not only passed a high tariff, but also chartered a second Bank of the United States. Upon becoming President, Jackson fought to get rid of the bank.

Many social reform movements began during this period, including:

- Education
- Women's rights
- Labor and working conditions
- Temperance
- Prisons and insane asylums

But the most intense and controversial was the abolitionists' efforts to end slavery, an effort alienating and splitting the country, hardening Southern defense of slavery, and leading to four years of bloody war. The abolitionist movement had political fallout, affecting admittance of states into the Union and the government's continued efforts to keep a balance between total numbers of free and slave states. Congressional legislation after 1820 reflected this.

Robert Fulton's *Clermont*, the first commercially successful steamboat, led the way in the fastest way to ship goods, making it the most important way to do so. Later, steam-powered railroads soon became the biggest rival of the steamboat as a means of shipping, eventually being the most important transportation method opening the West. With expansion into the interior of the country, the United States became the leading agricultural nation in the world. The hardy pioneer farmers produced a vast surplus and emphasis went to producing products with a high-sale value. These implements, such as the cotton gin and reaper, improved production. Travel and shipping were greatly assisted in areas not yet touched by railroad or, by improved or new roads, such as the National Road in the East and in the West the Oregon and Santa Fe Trails.

People were exposed to works of literature, art, newspapers, drama, live entertainment, and political rallies. With better communication and travel, more information was desired about previously unknown areas of the country, especially the West. The discovery of gold and other mineral wealth resulted in a literal surge of settlers and even more interest.

Public schools were established in many of the states with more and more children being educated. With more literacy and more participation in literature and the arts, the young nation was developing its own unique culture becoming less and less influenced by and dependent on that of Europe.

More industries and factories required more and more labor. Women, children, and, at times, entire families worked the long hours and days, until the 1830s. By that time, the factories were getting even larger and employers began hiring immigrants who were coming to America in huge numbers. Before then, efforts were made to organize a labor movement to improve working conditions and increase wages. It never really caught on until after the Civil War, but the seed had been sown.

In between the growing economy, expansion westward of the population, and improvements in travel and mass communication, the federal government did face periodic financial depressions. Contributing to these downward spirals were land speculations, availability and soundness of money and currency, failed banks, failing businesses, and unemployment. Sometimes conditions outside the nation would help trigger it; at other times, domestic politics and presidential elections affected it. The growing strength and influence of two major political parties with opposing philosophies and methods of conducting government did not ease matters at times.

As 1860 began, the nation had extended its borders north, south, and west. Industry and agriculture were flourishing. Although the United States did not involve itself actively in European affairs, the relationship with Great Britain was much improved and it and other nations that dealt with the young nation accorded it more respect and admiration. Nevertheless, war was on the horizon. The country was deeply divided along political lines concerning slavery and the election of Abraham Lincoln.

As African-Americans left the rural South and migrated to the North in search of opportunities, many settled in Harlem in New York City. By the 1920s, Harlem had become a center of life and activity for people of color. The music, art, and literature of this community gave birth to a cultural movement known as the Harlem Renaissance. The artistic expressions that emerged from this community in the 1920s and 1930s celebrated the black experience, black traditions, and the voices of black America. Major writers and works of this movement included Langston Hughes (*The Weary Blues*), Nella Larsen (*Passing*), Zora Neale Hurston (*Their Eyes Were Watching God*), Claude McKay, Countee Cullen, and Jean Toomer.

Hispanic-Americans have contributed to American life and culture since before the Civil War. Mexicans taught Californians to pan for gold and introduced the technique of using mercury to separate silver from worthless ores. Six state names are of Hispanic origin.

Native Americans have made major contributions to the development of the nation and have been contributors, either directly or indirectly, in almost every area of political and cultural life. In the early years of European settlement, the Native Americans were both teachers and neighbors. Even during periods of extermination and relocation, their influence was profound.

Numerous conflicts, often called the Indian Wars, broke out between the U.S. army and many different Native American tribes during the nineteenth century. Many treaties were signed with the various tribes, but most were broken by the government for a variety of reasons. Two of the most notable battles were the Battle of Little Bighorn in 1876, in which the Natives defeated General Custer and his forces, and the massacre of Native Americans in 1890 at Wounded Knee. In 1876, the U.S. government ordered all surviving tribes to move to reservations.

Asian-Americans, particularly in the West and in large cities, have made significant contributions despite immigration bans, mistreatment, and confinement. Asians were particularly important in constructing the transcontinental railroad, mining metals, and providing other kinds of labor and services.

Examples of Specialized Topics

Nationalism

During the eighteenth and especially the nineteenth centuries, NATIONALISM emerged as a powerful force in Europe and elsewhere in the world. Strictly speaking, nationalism was a belief in one's own nation, or country, people. The people of the European nations began to think in terms of a nation of people who had similar beliefs, concerns, and needs. This was partly a reaction to a growing discontent with the autocratic governments of the day and also just a general realization that there was more to life than the individual. People could feel a part of something like their nation, making themselves more than just an insignificant soul struggling to survive.

> **NATIONALISM:** a belief in one's own nation, or country, people

Nationalism precipitated several changes in government, most notably in France; it also brought large groups of people together, as with the unifications of Germany and Italy. What it didn't do, however, is provide sufficient outlets for this sudden rise in national fervor. Especially in the 1700s and 1800s, European powers and people began looking to Africa and Asia in order to find colonies—rich sources of goods, trade, and cheap labor. Africa, especially, suffered at the hands of European imperialists, bent on expanding their reach outside the borders of Europe. Asia suffered colonial expansion, most notably in India and Southeast Asia.

This colonial expansion would come back to haunt the European imperialists in a very big way, as colonial skirmishes spilled over into alliance that dragged the European powers into World War I. Some of these colonial battles were still being fought as late as the start of World War II as well.

The following are just a few of the Americans who contributed their leadership and talents in various fields and reforms throughout history:

NINETEENTH CENTURY CULTURAL CONTRIBUTORS	
American	**Contribution**
Lucretia Mott and Elizabeth Cady Stanton	women's rights
Emma Hart Willard, Catharine Esther Beecher, and Mary Lyon	education for women
Dr. Elizabeth Blackwell	the first woman doctor
Antoinette Louisa Blackwell	the first female minister
Dorothea Lynde Dix	reforms in prisons and insane asylums
Elihu Burritt and William Ladd	peace movements
Robert Owen	a Utopian society
Horace Mann, Henry Barmard, Calvin E. Stowe, Caleb Mills, and John Swett	public education
Benjamin Lundy, David Walker, William Lloyd Garrison, Isaac Hooper, Arthur and Lewis Tappan, Theodore Weld, Frederick Douglass, Harriet Tubman, James G. Birney, Henry Highland Garnet, James Forten, Robert Purvis, Harriet Beecher Stowe, Wendell Phillips, and John Brown	the Underground Railroad and abolition of slavery
Louisa May Alcott, James Fenimore Cooper, Washington Irving, Walt Whitman, Henry David Thoreau, Ralph Waldo Emerson, Herman Melville, Richard Henry Dana, Nathaniel Hawthorne, Henry Wadsworth Longfellow, John Greenleaf Whittier, Edgar Allan Poe, Oliver Wendell Holmes	famous writers
John C. Fremont, Zebulon Pike, Kit Carson	explorers
Henry Clay, Daniel Webster, Stephen Douglas, John C. Calhoun	statesmen

Table continued on next page

American	Contribution
Robert Fulton, Cyrus McCormick, Eli Whitney	inventors
Noah Webster	American dictionary and spellers

U.S. Civil Rights

In 1957, the formation of the Southern Christian Leadership Conference by Martin Luther King Jr., John Duffy, Rev. C. K. Steele, Rev. T. J. Jemison, Rev. Fred Shuttlesworth, Ella Baker, A. Philip Randolph, Bayard Rustin, and Stanley Levison provided training and assistance to local efforts fighting segregation. Nonviolence was its central doctrine as well as its major method of fighting segregation and racism—a belief or doctrine that biological differences determine success or cultural achievement and that one's own race is superior, thereby possessing the right to rule over others.

The American Political Parties

During the colonial period, political parties, as the term is now understood, did not exist. The many issues that divided the people were centered on the relations of the colonies to the mother country. There was initially little difference of opinion on these issues. About the middle of the eighteenth century, after England began to develop a harsher colonial policy, two factions arose in America. One favored the attitude of home government, and the other declined to obey and demanded a constantly increasing level of self-government. The former came to be known as the Tory party, and the latter the Whigs. During the course of the American Revolution, a large number of Tories left the country either to return to England or move to Canada.

From the beginning of the Confederation, opinions varied about the new government. One faction favored a loose confederacy in which the individual state would retain all powers of sovereignty except the absolute minimum required for the limited cooperation of all the states. The other faction, which steadily gained influence, demanded that the central government be granted all the essential powers of sovereignty and that states could only possess limited powers of local self-government. The inadequacy of the Confederation demonstrated that the latter were promoting a more effective point of view.

The first real party organization developed soon after the inauguration of George Washington as president of the United States. His cabinet included people of both factions. Alexander Hamilton was the leader of the Nationalists (also known as the Federalist Party), and Thomas Jefferson was the spokesman for the Anti-Federalists, later known as Republicans, Democratic-Republicans, and, finally, the Democrats. Several other parties formed over the years, including the Anti-Masonic Party and the Free Soil Party (who existed for the 1848 and 1852 elections only). The Liberty Party of this period was abolitionist.

The American Party was called the Know-Nothings. They lasted from 1854 to 1858 and were opposed to Irish-Catholic immigration. The Constitution Union Party was formed in 1860. It was made up of entities from other extinguished political powers. They claimed to support the Constitution above all and thought this would do away with the slavery issue. The National Union Party of 1864 was formed only for the purpose of the Lincoln election. Although these parties provide a good sampling of those that have been in existence throughout American history, many more were to follow.

Religion

Religion has always been a factor in American life. Many early settlers came to America in search of religious freedom. Religion, particularly Christianity, was an essential element of the value and belief structure shared by the Founding Fathers. Yet the Constitution prescribes a separation of Church and State.

- The First Great Awakening was a religious movement within American Protestantism in the 1730s and 1740s. This was primarily a movement among Puritans seeking a return to strict interpretation of morality and values as well as emphasizing the importance and power of personal religious or spiritual experience. Many historians believe the First Great Awakening unified the people of the original colonies and supported the independence of the colonists.

- The Second Great Awakening (the Great Revival) was a broad movement within American Protestantism that led to several kinds of activities that were distinguished by region and denominational tradition. In general terms, the Second Great Awakening, which began in the 1820s, was a time of recognition that "awakened religion" must weed out sin on both a personal and a social level. It inspired a wave of social activism. In New England, the Congregationalists established missionary societies to evangelize the West. Publication and education societies arose, most notably the American Bible Society. This social activism gave rise to the temperance movement, prison reform efforts, and help for the handicapped and mentally ill. This period was particularly notable for the abolition movement. In the Appalachian region, the camp meeting was used to revive religion. The camp meeting became a primary method of evangelizing new territory.

- The Third Great Awakening (the Missionary Awakening) gave rise to the Social Gospel Movement. This period (1858 to 1908) resulted in a massive growth in membership of all major Protestant denominations through their missionary activities. This movement was partly a response to claims that the Bible was fallible. Many churches attempted to reconcile or change biblical teaching to fit scientific theories and discoveries. Colleges associated with Protestant churches began to appear rapidly throughout the nation. In terms of social and political movements, the Third Great Awakening was the most expansive and profound. Coinciding with many changes in production and labor, it won battles against child labor and stopped the exploitation of women in factories. Compulsory elementary education for children came from this movement, as did the establishment of a set work day. Much was also done to protect and rescue children from abandonment and abuse, to improve the care of the sick, and to prohibit the use of alcohol and tobacco, as well as numerous other "social ills."

The History of Georgia

During the seventeenth century, the east coast of North America was rapidly being settled by European colonists in the north and by the Spanish in the south. In 1670, the British colony of South Carolina was founded directly north of Spanish-controlled Florida, creating a tense frontier in what is now Georgia. Military conflict followed until the Spanish missions were withdrawn in 1704 and the area occupied by Yamasee Native Americans became more welcoming to the British.

However, relations grew sour between the Yamasee and the British in 1715 over the fur trade, and the Yamasee began attacking British colonists. The colonists responded with force, and the Yamasee were driven out of the area toward Florida. This largely depopulated the coastal region between Charleston, the capital of British Carolina, and St. Augustine, the capital of Spanish Florida.

In the early 1730s, James Oglethorpe, a British member of Parliament, was engaged in a campaign of prison reform in England. English citizens who fell into debt could be thrown into debtor's prisons under deplorable conditions, where they were usually mistreated and often died. Oglethorpe presented a plan to colonize the newly available land in North America with some of these debtors to give them an opportunity to escape the horrors of prison and start over in the New World.

King George II approved Oglethorpe's scheme, and on June 9, 1732, he granted a royal charter to Oglethorpe and a group of twenty other philanthropists to found a colony in North America. These twenty-one trustees called the new colony "Georgia" in honor of the king.

In the end, the first people chosen to go to the new colony were not debtors but individuals chosen by the trustees based on their skills, professions, and potential usefulness in the new colony. The first group of 114 people, including Oglethorpe, sailed from England on the *Anne* in November 1732 and arrived in Charleston two months later. Oglethorpe scouted ahead into the Georgia region and selected a bluff on the Savannah River to build the first settlement, which became Savannah.

Oglethorpe and the trustees wished to avoid duplicating England's strict class system in the new colony, as they felt it had led to the practice of imprisoning debtors. They implemented a series of rules in the colony that prohibited slavery and required each man to work his own land. Identical houses were built on equal-sized lots to emphasize the equality of all.

The peaceful agrarian community that was envisioned by Oglethorpe grew happily for a time, but positioned as it was on the British frontier with the Spanish, the realities of potential warfare occupied the colony's attentions. Oglethorpe successfully petitioned the British government to grant him military authority in the area and to provide him with a regiment of British troops to defend the frontier. Oglethorpe unsuccessfully attempted to capture St. Augustine, spurring a series of battles between the Spanish and the British allied troops under Oglethorpe. The British emerged victorious after holding the line at the Battle of Bloody Marsh in 1742, after which the Spanish did not try to invade Georgia again.

As dissatisfaction with taxation increased in the northern colonies, similar rumblings began in Georgia, which joined the other colonies in 1765 in renouncing the STAMP ACT. Georgia had prospered under its royal charter, however, and many Georgians believed that they needed British protection from neighboring Native Americans.

When news of the Battle of Lexington and Concord reached Georgia, patriotic resolve was strengthened; in May of 1775, a group of patriots raided the arsenal at Savannah and took a supply of British gunpowder. Georgian colonists set up their own government shortly thereafter and joined the association of colonies in enforcing a ban on trade with the British. While British governor James Wright was still the official authority in Georgia, the provincial government founded in July 1775 gave executive authority to Council of Safety, which held the real power.

Wright was eventually expelled in 1776, after being held hostage by the colonists once British warships approached Savannah. Without a governor, provincial congress was convened at Augusta in April 1776, and a set of rules and regulations was adopted, outlining a simple structure of government. Three delegates were sent to the Second Continental Congress in Philadelphia in time to sign the Declaration of Independence in July.

STAMP ACT: the first direct tax on British colonists in America

Battle of Lexington

Battle of Lexington. Engraving by Nicolas Ponce after Francois Godefroy, 1784.

Three months later, a convention was called in Savannah to provide for a more permanent form of government in Georgia. The result of this convention was Georgia's first constitution, the Constitution of 1777. The new constitution created a single elected assembly that, in turn, chose a governor.

The constitution was remarkable for its time in granting voting rights to a wide group of citizens, although only white men were allowed to vote. The Georgia Constitution also provided for future amendments by state convention. This provision, which was not included in all state constitutions at the time, eventually became common practice throughout the United States. However, the Constitution of 1777 lacked many of the internal balances of political power that would be included in the U.S. Constitution, and serious movements began in 1788 to redraft it.

BILL OF RIGHTS: the first ten amendments to the U.S. Constitution that spell out limits on governmental authority

Following the American victory in the Revolutionary War, Georgia engaged with the rest of the new states in the debate over a federal constitution. Along with its southern neighbors, Georgia opposed a strong central government advocated by the Federalists, fearing the concentration of political power in the northern states. The BILL OF RIGHTS, the first ten amendments to the U.S. Constitution that spell out limits on governmental authority, were included in the proposed constitution to ensure the rights of the states. In this way, Georgia and the other southern states greatly influenced the shape of the U.S. Constitution, which Georgia ratified in January 1788.

NEW SOUTH: a term sometimes used to describe the South after the Civil War; it refers to a South no longer dependent on slave labor and based on industry instead

NEW SOUTH is a term sometimes used to describe the South after the Civil War; it refers to a South no longer dependent on slave labor and based on industry instead. In Georgia, Henry Grady is closely associated with the New South movement of the 1880s. This movement sought to bring northern investments and industry to the state, particularly in the Atlanta region.

The New South was more of an ideal than a reality for Georgia farmers, who found themselves stressed by falling cotton prices after the Civil War. The growing Populist movement in the 1890s blamed the entrenched Democratic Party for many of the farmers' woes and mounted a challenge to the party. Georgia populists sought to include blacks in the movement and called for prison reform. By the turn of the century, Populism as a movement had largely faded from Georgia politics, although it did have lasting effects.

JIM CROW LAWS: laws enacted after the Civil War that resulted in the segregation of whites and blacks, with blacks being forced to use inferior facilities

JIM CROW LAWS were laws enacted after the Civil War that resulted in the segregation of whites and blacks, with blacks being forced to use inferior facilities. During Reconstruction, southern states were forced to adopt protections for free black citizens. Once the Reconstruction governments were replaced with "Redeemer" governments, laws were enacted that required separate schools and public facilities for blacks and whites, thereby replacing the Black Codes that had been in effect prior to the Civil War. Jim Crow laws had the effect of denying voting rights to many black citizens by requiring the payment of a poll tax. The Democratic Party also discouraged black participation in politics and elections.

Despite these prejudices, many blacks prospered after the war, especially in the growing industrial center of Atlanta. As the white elite witnessed the emergence of a black economic elite in Atlanta, some argued that allowing blacks to vote had caused them to consider themselves equal to whites, so the vote should be taken away from them.

Tension grew between the races, eventually erupting in violence in Atlanta in 1906. Unsubstantiated reports circulated that black men had attacked four white women. A mob of white men and boys gathered and raided black neighborhoods, destroying businesses and killing several people. The state militia was called in to control the mob, which eventually subsided. As a result of the riot, even further restrictions were placed on black voting rights.

World War I greatly impacted Georgia, which became the location of several military training camps. Thousands of troops from all over the country passed through Georgia on their way to war. In 1918, the troop ship Otranto sunk tragically, killing almost four hundred men. One hundred and thirty of them were from Georgia.

When President Wilson instituted the draft, many white Georgians (especially landowners who employed black sharecroppers) tried to prevent black men from being called into service. Not wanting to lose their labor force, they would sometimes not deliver draft notices and prevent blacks from registering. Many blacks were arrested and jailed for evading the draft as a result.

Agriculture during this time was threatened by more than just the potential loss of farm labor. The boll weevil, an insect that destroys cotton plants, began its spread northward from Mexico in the late nineteenth century and reached Georgia around 1915. Within ten years, the number of acres planted in cotton in Georgia halved because of the pest. The boll weevil forced farmers to diversify their crops, leading to the rise of peanut farming, which became an important agricultural product.

Eugene Talmadge began his career in state politics as the Commissioner of Agriculture in 1926. Outspoken and opinionated, Talmadge won popular support from the rural community and rapidly became a polarizing influence in the Democratic Party. He was elected governor in 1932 and reelected in 1934. After unsuccessful bids for the U.S. Senate, Talmadge was again elected governor in 1940.

Boll Weevil

Boll weevil, *Anthonomus grandis*, on a young cotton boll. Photo by Rob Flynn. Courtesy of the USDA-ARS.

Talmadge was a forceful leader who bypassed legislative action and removed appointees who disagreed with his views. He attempted to remove from the state university system any faculty members who he suspected wanted to integrate the schools or believed in racial equality. As a result of his raid on the system, the university lost its accreditation. The more moderate Ellis Arnall challenged Talmadge in the gubernatorial race of 1942, promising to restore accreditation, and won. Talmadge was reelected as governor in 1946, but he died before taking office.

> **NEW DEAL:** a series of public programs beginning in 1933 that were designed to assist Depression-wracked Americans and to promote economic recovery

Talmadge was a major opponent of President Franklin Roosevelt's NEW DEAL, a series of public programs beginning in 1933 that were designed to assist Depression-wracked Americans and to promote economic recovery. Talmadge and others saw the New Deal as federal interference with local affairs, but the program, which provided farm subsidies, built new infrastructure, and provided direct assistance to poor Georgians, was popular among the people. President Roosevelt himself was popular in Georgia, having adopted Warm Springs as a second home during his time in office.

Although the New Deal did help many poor southerners, it failed to bring the dramatic turnaround that had been hoped for in the South. It was World War II and the related boom in the war industry that transformed Georgia's economy. Defense contractors found a large and willing labor force in Georgia, and shipbuilding and aircraft manufacturing became important industries that employed hundreds of thousands of people. With many men away in the military, women entered the workforce in large numbers for the first time. African-American workers also benefited from the labor shortage, entering positions that had formerly been reserved for white men. Segregation, however, was still enforced.

New methods of agriculture made farming a viable endeavor once again, but Georgia was no longer entirely dependent on agriculture. The city of Atlanta made an early commitment to develop air travel when it establishment an airfield in 1925. The airfield grew throughout the twentieth century; under the administration of Mayor Maynard Jackson, it was transformed into the Hartsfield International Airport, a huge building project that opened in 1980. Later named the Hartsfield-Jackson International Airport, the facility is currently the busiest airport in the world.

Ellis Arnall was elected as the governor of Georgia in 1942 at the age of thirty-five. Arnall made several significant reforms, including eliminating poll taxes and lowering the voting age. He also proposed checks to the power of the governor, feeling that Eugene Talmadge had previously abused his power. Arnall left office in 1947, although he ran again in 1966 against the segregationist Lester Maddox. Maddox emerged the victor in that race and served as governor until 1971.

Herman Talmadge was the only son of former governor Eugene Talmadge.

He ran his father's successful campaign for governor in 1946 and was briefly appointed to the position by the legislature when his father died before taking office. Herman Talmadge was himself elected governor in 1948. Talmadge supported segregation and worked to bring industry to Georgia. He served as governor until 1954, when he ran for the U.S. Senate and was elected. Talmadge served in the Senate until 1981.

Between Reconstruction and the 1960s, the Democratic Party dominated Georgia politics. Republicans had been installed by the federal government during Reconstruction, but they were quickly replaced by Democrats after the federal troops that supported the Republican state governments were withdrawn. The civil rights era began drawing sharp lines between old-line Democrats and more moderate Democrats, sometimes splitting the vote and allowing Republicans to gain footholds.

Another change in Georgia politics in the 1960s was the end of the county unit system of conducting state primaries. Under this system, all of a county's unit votes were awarded to the candidate that received the most individual votes in that county. This system favored rural counties and allowed for the election of candidates who had actually lost the popular vote, as was the case in 1946 when Eugene Talmadge won the primary for governor. Primary politics were important in Georgia. Because of the dominance of the Democratic Party, winning the primary virtually ensured winning the general election. The U.S. Supreme Court declared the county unit system illegal in 1963.

In 1962, Jimmy Carter was elected to the Georgia legislature after challenging fraudulent returns in his election. He went on to serve as the governor of Georgia and was elected president of the United States in 1976, defeating President Gerald Ford.

Sample Test Questions and Rationale

(Easy)

1. **The end of the feudal manorial system was caused by:**

   A. The Civil War

   B. The Black Plague

   C. The Christian Riots

   D. Westward Expansion

Answer: B. The Black Plague

The end of the feudal manorial system was sealed by the outbreak and spread of the infamous Black Death, which killed over one-third of the total population of Europe.

(Average)

2. **What intellectual movement during the period of North American colonization contributed to the development of public education and the founding of the first colleges and universities?**

   A. Enlightenment

   B. Great Awakening

   C. Libertarianism

   D. The Scientific Revolution

Answer: A. Enlightenment

Enlightenment thinking quickly traveled across the Atlantic Ocean. It valued human reason and the importance of education, knowledge, and scholarly research. Education in the middle colonies was influenced largely by the Enlightenment movement, which emphasized scholarly research and public service. Benjamin Franklin embodied these principles in Philadelphia, which became a center of learning and culture, owing largely to its economic success and ease of access to European books and tracts.

(Rigorous)

3. **In 1957, the formation of the Southern Christian Leadership Conference was started by:**

   A. Martin Luther King Jr.

   B. Rev. T. J. Jemison

   C. Ella Baker

   D. All of the above

Answer: D. All of the above

In 1957, the formation of the Southern Christian Leadership Conference by Martin Luther King Jr., John Duffy, Reverend C. D. Steele, Reverend T. J. Jemison, Reverend Fred Shuttlesworth, Ella Baker, A. Philip Randolph, Bayard Rustin, and Stanley Levison provided training and assistance to local efforts to fight segregation.

(Average)

4. **In the early 1730s, James Oglethorpe, a British Member of Parliament, engaged in a campaign to bring _____ to America.**

   A. Soldiers

   B. Farmers

   C. Prisoners

   D. Parliament

Answer: C. Prisoners

Oglethorpe presented a plan to colonize the newly available land in North America with prisoners in order to give them an opportunity to escape the horrors of prison and start over in the New World.

Sample Test Questions and Rationale (cont.)

(Average)

5. Which of the following contributed to the severity of the Great Depression?

   A. An influx of Chinese immigrants

   B. The dust bowl, which drove people out of the cities

   C. An influx of Mexican immigrants

   D. An influx of Oakies

Answer: D. An influx of Oakies

The Dust Bowl of the Great Plains destroyed agriculture in the area. People living in the plains areas lost their livelihood, and many lost their homes and possessions in the great dust storms that resulted from a period of extended drought. People from these states made their way to California in search of a better life. Because the majority of the people were from Oklahoma, they were all referred to as "Oakies." These migrants brought with them their distinctive plains culture. The great influx of people seeking jobs exacerbated the effects of the Great Depression in California.

SKILL 9.3 **Demonstrating knowledge of early Native American cultures in North America and their interactions with early explorers**

Native American tribes lived throughout what we now call the United States in varying degrees of togetherness. They had established cultures long before Columbus or any other European explorer arrived on the scene. The tribes adopted different customs, pursued different avenues of agriculture and food gathering, and made slightly different weapons. They also fought among themselves and with other groups.

Perhaps the most famous of the Native American tribes is the Algonquians. Historians know much about this tribe because it was one of the first to interact with the newly arrived English settlers in Plymouth (and elsewhere). The Algonquians lived in wigwams and wore clothing made from animal skins. They

Powhatan

Detail from *A Map of Virginia* by Captain John Smith, 1612.

were proficient hunters, gatherers, and trappers who also knew quite a bit about farming.

Beginning with a brave man named Squanto, the Algonquians shared their agricultural knowledge with the English settlers, including how to plant and cultivate corn, pumpkins, and squash. Other famous Algonquians include Pocahontas and her father, Powhatan—both of whom are immortalized in English literature—and Tecumseh and Black Hawk, known foremost for their fierce fighting abilities. To the overall Native American culture, they were responsible for contributing wampum and dream catchers.

Another group of tribes who lived in the Northeast were the Iroquois, who were fierce fighters but also forward thinkers. They lived in long houses and wore clothes made of buckskin. They, too, were expert farmers, growing the Three Sisters (corn, squash, and beans). Five of the Iroquois tribes formed a Confederacy, which functioned as a shared form of government. The Iroquois also formed the False Face Society, a group of medicine men who shared their medical knowledge with others but kept their identities secret while doing so. The masks they wore are one of the enduring symbols of the Native American era.

Among those living in the Southeast were the Seminoles and Creeks, a huge collection of people who lived in chickees (open, bark-covered houses) and wore clothes made from plant fibers. They were expert planters and hunters and proficient at making and paddling dugout canoes. The beaded necklaces they created were some of the most beautiful in the continent. They are best known, however, for their struggles against Spanish and English settlers, especially those struggles led by the great Osceola.

The Cherokee also lived in the Southeast and were one of the most advanced tribes, living in domed houses and wearing deerskin and rabbit furs. Accomplished hunters, farmers, and fishermen, the Cherokee were known the continent over for their intricate and beautiful basketry and clay pottery. They also played a game called lacrosse, which survives to this day in countries around the world.

In the middle of the continent lived the Plains tribes, which included the Sioux, Cheyenne, Blackfeet, Comanche, and Pawnee. These peoples lived in teepees and wore buffalo skins and feather headdresses. (It is this image of the Native American that has made its way into most movies depicting the period.) They hunted wild animals on the plains, especially buffalo. They were well known for their many ceremonies, including the Sun Dance, and for the peace pipes that they smoked. Famous Plains people include Crazy Horse and Sitting Bull, authors of the Custer Disaster; Sacagawea, who guided the Lewis and Clark expedition; and Chief Joseph, the famous Nez Perce leader.

Dotting the deserts of the Southwest were a handful of tribes, including the famous Pueblo, who lived in houses that bear their tribe's name, wore clothes made of wool and woven cotton, farmed crops in the middle of desert land, created exquisite pottery and Kachina dolls, and had one of the most complex religions of all the tribes. They are perhaps best known for the challenging vista-based villages that they constructed out of the sheer faces of cliffs and rocks as well as for their adobes, which were mud-brick buildings that housed their living and meeting quarters. Theirs was perhaps one of the oldest representative governments in the world; the Pueblos chose their own chiefs.

Another well-known southwestern tribe included the Apache, with their famous leader Geronimo. The Apache lived in homes called wickiups, which were made of bark, grass, and branches. They wore cotton clothing and were excellent hunters and gatherers. Adept at basketry, the Apache believed that everything in nature had special powers and that they were honored just to be part of it all.

The Navajo, also residents of the Southwest, lived in hogans (round homes built with forked sticks) and wore clothes of rabbit skin. Their major contribution to the overall culture of the continent was in sand painting, weapon making, silversmithing, and weaving. Some of the most beautiful woven rugs were crafted by Navajo hands.

Living in the Northwest were the Inuit, who lived in tents made from animal skins or, in some cases, igloos. They wore clothes also made from animal skins, usually seals or caribou. They were excellent fisherfolk and hunters and built efficient kayaks and umiaks to take them through waterways and harpoons they used to hunt animals. The Inuit are perhaps best known for their great carvings, including ivory figures and totem poles.

Colonists from England, France, Holland, Sweden, and Spain all settled in North America on lands once frequented by Native Americans. Spanish colonies were mainly in the south, French colonies were mainly in the extreme north and in the middle of the continent, and the rest of the European colonies were in the northeast and along the Atlantic coast. These colonists got along with their new neighbors with varying degrees of success.

Of all of them, the French colonists seemed the most willing to work with the Native Americans. Even though their pursuit of animals to fill the growing demand for the fur trade was overpowering, they managed to find a way to keep their new neighbors happy. The French and Native Americans even fought on the same side of the war against England.

The Dutch and Swedish colonists were mainly interested in surviving in their new homes. However, they didn't last long in their struggles against England. The

Geronimo

Geronimo. Photoprint by A.B. Canady, 1907.

English and Spanish colonists had the worst relations with the Native Americans, mainly because the Europeans made a habit of taking land, signing and then breaking treaties, massacring, and otherwise abusing their new neighbors. The Native Americans were only too happy to share their agriculture and jewel-making secrets with the Europeans, but they got only grief and deceit in return. The term MANIFEST DESTINY meant nothing to the Native Americans, who believed they lived on land that their gods had given to them.

MANIFEST DESTINY: the nineteenth-century doctrine that the United States had the right and duty to expand throughout the North American continent

The conflicts between Europeans and the various Native American groups carved an incredibly large portion of early U.S. history; the repercussions of many of these conflicts are still evident in society today.

SKILL 9.4 Analyzing various perspectives, interpretations, and implications of events, issues, and developments in Georgia, U.S., and world history

The practice of dividing time into a number of discrete periods or blocks of time is called PERIODIZATION. Because history is continuous, all systems of periodization are arbitrary to a greater or lesser extent. However, dividing time into segments facilitates understanding of changes that occur over time and identifying similarities of events, knowledge, and experience within the defined period. Further, some divisions of time into these periods apply only under specific circumstances.

PERIODIZATION: the practice of dividing time into a number of discrete periods or blocks of time

Divisions of time may be determined by date, by cultural advances or changes, by historical events, by the influence of particular individuals or groups, or by geography. The "World War II" era defines a particular period of time in which key historical, political, social, and economic events occurred. The "Jacksonian Era," however, has meaning only in terms of American history. Defining the "Romantic period" makes sense only in England, Europe, and countries under their direct influence.

Many of the divisions of time that are commonly used are open to some controversy and discussion. The use of BC and AD dating, for example, has clear reference only in societies that account time according to the Christian calendar. Similarly, "the year of the pig" has greatest meaning in China.

An example of the kind of questions that can be raised about designations of time periods can be seen in the use of "Victorian." Is it possible to speak of a Victorian era beyond England? Is literature that is written in the style of the English poets and writers "Victorian" if it is written beyond the borders of England? Some designations also carry both positive and negative connotations. "Victorian" is an example of potential negative connotations, as well. The term is often used to refer to class conflict, sexual repression, and heavy industry. These might be negative connotations. The term "Renaissance" is generally read with positive connotations.

Sometimes several designations can be applied to the same period. The period known as the "Elizabethan Period" in English history is also called the "English Renaissance." In some cases the differences in designation refer primarily to the specific aspect of history that is being considered. For example, one designation may be applied to a specific period of time when one is analyzing cultural history, while a different designation is applied to the same period of time when considering military history.

Civil War

In 1833, Congress lowered tariffs, this time at a level acceptable to South Carolina. Although President Jackson believed in states' rights, he also firmly believed in and determined to keep the preservation of the Union. A constitutional crisis had been averted but sectional divisions were getting deeper and more pronounced. The abolition movement was growing rapidly, becoming an important issue in the North. The slavery issue was at the root of every problem, crisis, event, decision, and struggle from then on. The next crisis involved the issue concerning Texas. By 1836, Texas was an independent republic with its own constitution. During its fight for independence, Americans were sympathetic to and supportive of the Texans and some recruited volunteers who crossed into Texas to help the struggle. Problems arose when the state petitioned Congress for statehood. Texas wanted to allow slavery but Northerners in Congress opposed admission to the Union because it would disrupt the balance between free and slave states and give Southerners in Congress increased influence.

A few years later, Congress took up consideration of new territories between Missouri and present-day Idaho. Again, heated debate over permitting slavery in these areas flared up. Those opposed to slavery used the MISSOURI COMPROMISE to prove their point showing that the land being considered for territories was part of the area the Compromise had been designated as banned to slavery. On May 25, 1854, Congress passed the infamous KANSAS-NEBRASKA ACT which nullified the provision creating the territories of Kansas and Nebraska. This provided for the people of these two territories to decide for themselves whether or not to permit slavery to exist there. Feelings were so deep and divided that any further attempts to compromise would meet with little, if any, success. Political and social turmoil swirled everywhere. Kansas was called "Bleeding Kansas" because of the extreme violence and bloodshed throughout the territory because two governments existed there—one pro-slavery and the other anti-slavery.

Coming up:
- *The Second World War*
- *The Korean War*
- *The Vietnam War*
- *The Cold War*

MISSOURI COMPROMISE: Congressional solution to the addition of slave states to the union; it forbade slavery to areas north of latitude 36° 30'N

KANSAS-NEBRASKA ACT: Congressional act that allowed the territories of Kansas and Nebraska to decide for themselves whether to allow slavery; it repealed the Missouri Compromise

The Supreme Court, in 1857, handed down a decision guaranteed to cause explosions throughout the country. Dred Scott was a slave whose owner had taken him from slave state Missouri, to free state Illinois, then into Minnesota Territory—free under the provisions of the Missouri Compromise—and then finally back to slave state Missouri. Abolitionists pursued the dilemma by presenting a court case, stating that since Scott had lived in a free state and free territory, he was in actuality a free man. Two lower courts had ruled before the Supreme Court became involved, one ruling in favor and one against. The Supreme Court decided that residing in a free state and free territory did not make Scott a free man because Scott (and all other slaves) was not a U.S. citizen or a state citizen of Missouri. Therefore, he did not have the right to sue in state or federal courts.

The Court went a step further and ruled that the old Missouri Compromise was now unconstitutional because Congress did not have the power to prohibit slavery in the Territories.

In 1858, Abraham Lincoln and Stephen A. Douglas were running for the office of U.S. Senator from Illinois and participated in a series of debates, which directly affected the outcome of the 1860 Presidential election. Douglas, a Democrat, was up for reelection and knew that if he won this race, he had a good chance of becoming President in 1860. Lincoln, a Republican, was not an abolitionist, but he believed that slavery was morally wrong, and he supported the Republican Party principle that slavery must not be allowed to extend any further.

The final straw came with the election of Lincoln to the presidency the next year. Due to a split in the Democratic Party, there were four candidates from four political parties. With Lincoln receiving a minority of the popular vote and a majority of electoral votes, the Southern states, one by one, voted to secede from the Union, as they had promised they would do if Lincoln and the Republicans were victorious. The die was cast.

It is ironic that South Carolina was the first state to secede from the Union and the first shots of the war were fired on Fort Sumter in Charleston Harbor. Both sides quickly prepared for war. The North had more in its favor: a larger population; superiority in finances and transportation facilities; and manufacturing, agricultural, and natural resources. The North possessed most of the nation's gold, had about ninety-two percent of all industries, and almost all known supplies of copper, coal, iron, and various other minerals. Most of the nation's railroads were in the North and Midwest, men and supplies could be moved wherever needed; food could be transported from the farms of the Midwest to workers in the East and to soldiers on the battlefields. Trade with nations overseas could go on as usual due to control of the navy and the merchant fleet. The Northern states numbered twenty-four and included western states (California and Oregon) and border states (Maryland, Delaware, Kentucky, Missouri, and West Virginia).

The eleven states of the Southern Confederacy were:

- South Carolina
- Mississippi
- North Carolina
- Georgia
- Louisiana
- Tennessee
- Florida
- Texas
- Arkansas
- Alabama
- Virginia

Although outnumbered in population, the South was completely confident of victory. They knew that all they had to do was fight a defensive war and protect their own territory.

The North had to invade and defeat an area almost the size of Western Europe. Another advantage of the South was that a number of its best officers had graduated from the U.S. Military Academy at West Point and had had long years of army experience. Many had exercised varying degrees of command in the Indian Wars and the war with Mexico. Men from the South were conditioned to living outdoors and were more familiar with horses and firearms than men from northeastern cities. Since cotton was such an important crop, Southerners felt that British and French textile mills were so dependent on raw cotton that they would be forced to help the Confederacy in the war.

The South won decisively until the Battle of Gettysburg, July 1 through 3, 1863. Until Gettysburg, Lincoln's commanders, McDowell and McClellan, were less than desirable; Burnside and Hooker, not what was needed. Lee, on the other hand, had many able officers: Jackson and Stuart were depended on heavily by him. Jackson died at Chancellorsville and was replaced by Longstreet. Lee decided to invade the North and depended on J.E.B. Stuart and his cavalry to keep him informed of the location of Union troops and their strengths.

The day after Gettysburg, on July 4, Vicksburg, Mississippi, surrendered to Union General Ulysses Grant, thus severing the western Confederacy from the eastern part. In September 1863, the Confederacy won its last important victory at Chickamauga. In November, the Union victory at Chattanooga made it possible for Union troops to go into Alabama and Georgia, splitting the eastern Confederacy in two. Lincoln gave Grant command of all Northern armies in March of 1864. Grant led his armies into battles in Virginia while Phil Sheridan and his cavalry did as much damage as possible. In a skirmish at a place called Yellow Tavern, Virginia, Sheridan's and Stuart's forces met. Stuart was fatally wounded.

The Civil War took more American lives than any other war in history, the South losing one-third of its soldiers in battle compared to about one-sixth for the North. More than half of the total deaths were caused by disease and the horrendous conditions of field hospitals. Both sides paid a tremendous economic price, but the South suffered more severely from direct damages. Destruction was pervasive, with towns, farms, trade, industry, lives, and homes of men, women, children all destroyed, and an entire Southern way of life was lost. The South had no voice in the political, social, and cultural affairs of the nation, lessening to a great degree the influence of the more traditional Southern ideals. The Northern Yankee Protestant ideals of hard work, education, and economic freedom became the standard of the United States and helped influence the development of the nation into a modern, industrial power.

The effects of the Civil War were tremendous. It changed the methods of waging war and has been called the first modern war. It introduced weapons and tactics that, when later improved, were used extensively in wars of the late 1800s and 1900s.

- Civil War soldiers were the first to fight in trenches, first to fight under a unified command, and first to wage a defense called "major cordon defense," a strategy of advance on all fronts

- They were also the first to use repeating and breech loading weapons

- Observation balloons were first used during the war along with submarines, ironclad ships, and mines

- Telegraphy and railroads were put to use first in the Civil War

It was considered a modern war because of the vast destruction and because it was "total war," involving the use of all resources of the opposing sides. There was no way it could have ended other than total defeat and unconditional surrender of one side or the other.

By executive proclamation and constitutional amendment, slavery officially ended, although there remained deep prejudice and racism, still raising its ugly head today. Also, the Union was preserved and the states were finally truly united. Sectionalism, especially in the area of politics, remained strong for another hundred years, but not to the degree and with the violence as existed before 1861. It has been noted that the Civil War may have been American democracy's greatest failure because from 1861 to 1865, calm reason—basic to democracy—fell to human passion. Yet, democracy did survive.

The victory of the North established that no state has the right to end or leave the Union. Because of unity, the United States became a major global power. Lincoln never proposed to punish the South. He was most concerned with restoring the South to the Union in a program that was flexible and practical rather than rigid and unbending. In fact he never really felt that the states had succeeded in leaving the Union but that they had left the "family circle" for a short time.

World Wars

The American isolationist mood was given a shocking and lasting blow in 1941 with the Japanese attack on Pearl Harbor. The nation arose and forcefully entered the international arena as never before. Declaring itself "the arsenal of democracy," it entered the Second World War and emerged not only victorious, but also as the strongest power on the Earth. It would now have a permanent and leading place in world affairs.

In the aftermath of the Second World War, with the Soviet Union emerging as the second strongest power on Earth, the United States embarked on a policy known as "containment" of the Communist menace. This involved what came to be known as the Marshall Plan and the Truman Doctrine. The MARSHALL PLAN involved the economic aid that was sent to Europe in the aftermath of the Second World War aimed at preventing the spread of communism. To that end, the United States has devoted a larger and larger share of its foreign policy, diplomacy, and economic and military might to combating it.

The TRUMAN DOCTRINE offered military aid to those countries that were in danger of communist upheaval. This led to the era known as the COLD WAR in which the United States took the lead along with the Western European nations against the Soviet Union and the Eastern Bloc countries. It was also at this time that the United States finally gave up on George Washington's advice against "European entanglements" and joined the North Atlantic Treaty Organization (NATO). This was formed in 1949 and was composed of the United States and several Western European nations for the purposes of opposing communist aggression.

The UNITED NATIONS was formed in 1945 to replace the defunct League of Nations for the purposes of ensuring world peace. Even with American involvement, it would prove largely ineffective in its goals. In the 1950s, the United States embarked on what was called the "Eisenhower Doctrine," after the then-President Eisenhower. This aimed at trying to maintain peace in a troubled area of the world, the Middle East. However, unlike the Truman Doctrine in Europe, it would have little success.

The United States also became involved in a number of world conflicts in the ensuing years. Each had at the core the struggle against communist expansion. Among these were the Korean War (1950–1953), the Vietnam War (1965–1975), and various continuing entanglements in Central and South America and the Middle East. By the early 1970s under the leadership of then-Secretary of State Henry Kissinger, the United States and its allies embarked on the policy that came to be known as DÉTENTE. This was aimed at the easing of tensions between the United States and its allies and the Soviet Union and its allies.

MARSHALL PLAN: U.S. program for rebuilding the economic foundation of Western Europe following WWII

TRUMAN DOCTRINE: President Harry S. Truman's foreign policy declaring the United States "leader of the free world"

COLD WAR: the state of political tension and military rivalry between the Soviet Union and the West from the end of WWII to the 1980s

UNITED NATIONS: an international organization composed of most countries of the world and dedicated to promoting peace, security, and economic development

DÉTENTE: the easing of tensions or strained relations between rivals

By the 1980s, the United States embarked on what some saw as a renewal of the Cold War. This owed to the fact that the United States was becoming more involved in trying to prevent communist insurgency in Central America. A massive expansion of its armed forces and the development of space-based weapons systems were undertaken at this time. As this occurred, the Soviet Union, with a failing economic system and a foolhardy adventure in Afghanistan, found itself unable to compete. By 1989, events had come to a head. This ended with the breakdown of the Communist Bloc, the virtual end of the monolithic Soviet Union, and the collapse of the communist system by the early 1990s.

Now the United States remains active in world affairs in trying to promote peace and reconciliation, with a new specter rising to challenge it and the world—the specter of nationalism.

Sample Test Questions and Rationale

(Rigorous)

1. **The first real party organization developed soon after the inauguration of Washington as president. It included which of the following:**

    A. Democrats

    B. Republicans

    C. Nationalists

    D. All of the above

    Answer: D. All of the above

    Washington's cabinet included people of both factions. Hamilton was the leader of the Nationalists (the Federalist Party), and Jefferson was the spokesman for the Anti-Federalists, later known as Republicans, Democratic-Republicans, and finally Democrats.

(Rigorous)

2. **What was the name of the cultural revival after the Civil War?**

    A. The Revolutionary War

    B. The Second Great Awakening

    C. The Harlem Renaissance

    D. The Gilded Age

    Answer: C. The Harlem Renaissance

    As African-Americans left the rural South and migrated to the North in search of opportunity, many settled in Harlem in New York City. By the 1920s, Harlem had become a center of life and activity for persons of color. The music, art, and literature of this community gave birth to a cultural movement known as the Harlem Renaissance. (A) The Revolution War (1776) occurred prior to the Civil War. (B) The Second Great Awakening occurred in the 1920s, but like the (D) Gilded Age (1878–1889), it affected the entire United States.

Sample Test Questions and Rationale (cont.)

(Average)

3. **Which one of the following is *not* a reason why Europeans came to the New World?**

   A. To find resources in order to increase wealth

   B. To establish trade

   C. To increase a ruler's power and importance

   D. To spread Christianity

   Answer: B. To establish trade

   The Europeans came to the New World for a number of reasons; they often came to find new natural resources to extract for manufacturing. The Portuguese, Spanish, and English were sent over to increase the monarch's power and to spread influences such as religion (Christianity) and culture. Therefore, the only reason given that Europeans didn't come to the New World was to establish trade.

(Average)

4. **The Westward Expansion occurred for a number of reasons, but the most important reason was:**

   A. Colonization

   B. Slavery

   C. Independence

   D. Economics

   Answer: D. Economics

   The Westward Expansion occurred for a number of reasons, the most important being economic.

(Rigorous)

5. **The year 1619 was memorable for the colony of Virginia. Three important events occurred, resulting in lasting effects on U.S. history. Which one of the following is *not* one of the events?**

   A. Twenty African slaves arrived

   B. The London Company granted the colony a charter, making it independent

   C. The colonists were given the right by the London Company to govern themselves through representative government in the Virginia House of Burgesses

   D. The London Company sent to the colony sixty women, who quickly married, establishing families and stability in the colony

   Answer: B. The London Company granted the colony a charter making it independent

   In the year 1619, the southern colony of Virginia had an eventful year, including the first arrival of twenty African slaves, the right to self-governance through representative government in the Virginia House of Burgesses (their own legislative body), and the arrival of sixty women sent to marry and establish families in the colony. The London Company did not, however, grant the colony a charter in 1619.

Sample Test Questions and Rationale (cont.)

(Rigorous)

6. The "divine right" of kings was the key political characteristic of:

   A. The Age of Absolutism

   B. The Age of Reason

   C. The Age of Feudalism

   D. The Age of Despotism

Answer: A. The Age of Absolutism

The "divine right" of kings was the key political characteristic of the Age of Absolutism and was most visible in the reign of King Louis XIV of France, as well as during the times of King James I and his son, Charles I. The divine right doctrine claims that kings and absolute leaders derive their right to rule by virtue of their birth alone. They see this as both a law of God and a law of nature.

(Rigorous)

7. During the 1920s, the United States almost completely stopped all immigration. One of the reasons was:

   A. Plentiful cheap, unskilled labor was no longer needed by industrialists

   B. War debts from World War I made it difficult to render financial assistance

   C. European nations were reluctant to allow people to leave, since there was a need to rebuild populations and economic stability

   D. The United States did not become a member of the League of Nations

Answer: A. Plentiful cheap, unskilled labor was no longer needed by industrialists

The primary reason that the United States almost completely stopped all immigration during the 1920s was because their once much needed cheap, unskilled labor jobs, made available by the once booming industrial economy, were no longer needed. This had much to do with the increased use of machines to do the work once done by those laborers.

(Average)

8. Which one of the following would *not* be considered a result of World War II?

   A. Economic depressions and slow resumption of trade and financial aid

   B. Western Europe was no longer the center of world power

   C. The beginnings of new power struggles not only in Europe but in Asia as well

   D. Territorial and boundary changes for many nations, especially in Europe

Answer: A. Economic depressions and slow resumption of trade and financial aid

Following World War II, the economy was vibrant and flourished from the stimulant of war and an increased dependence of the world on U.S. industries. Therefore, World War II didn't result in economic depressions and slow resumption of trade and financial aid. Western Europe was no longer the center of world power. New power struggles arose in Europe and Asia, and many European nations underwent changing territories and boundaries.

Sample Test Questions and Rationale (cont.)

(Easy)

9. The belief that the United States should control all of North America was called:

   A. Westward Expansion

   B. Pan Americanism

   C. Manifest Destiny

   D. Nationalism

Answer: C. Manifest Destiny

This idea fueled much of the violence and aggression toward those already occupying the lands, such as the Native Americans. Manifest Destiny was certainly driven by sentiments of (D) nationalism and gave rise to (A) Westward Expansion.

SKILL 9.5 **Demonstrating knowledge of strategies** *(e.g., formulating research questions)* **and resources for historical inquiry**

Historical Data

Historical data can come from a wide range of sources, beginning with LIBRARIES—small local ones or very large university libraries. Records and guides are almost universally digitally organized and available for instant searching by era, topic, event, personality, or area. Libraries offer resources such as survey information from various departments and bureaus of the federal and state government, magazines and periodicals in a wide range of topics, artifacts, encyclopedias, and other reference materials, and usually access to the Internet.

The Internet offers unheard of possibilities for finding even the most obscure information. However, even with all these resources available, nothing is more valuable than a visit to the site being researched, including a visit to historical societies, local libraries, or sometimes even local schools.

The same things could be said about geographical data. It's possible to find a map of almost any area online; however, the best maps will be available locally, as will knowledge and information about the development of the area.

Scientific Method

The SCIENTIFIC METHOD is the process by which researchers over time endeavor to construct an accurate (that is, reliable, consistent, and nonarbitrary)

> **LIBRARIES:** offer resources such as survey information from various departments and bureaus of the federal and state government, magazines and periodicals in a wide range of topics, artifacts, encyclopedias and other reference materials, and usually access to the Internet

> **SCIENTIFIC METHOD:** the process by which researchers over time endeavor to construct an accurate representation of the world

representation of the world. Recognizing that personal and cultural beliefs influence both our perceptions and our interpretations of natural phenomena, standard procedures and criteria minimize those influences when developing a theory.

The scientific method has four steps:

1. Observation and description of a phenomenon or group of phenomena

2. Formulation of a hypothesis to explain the phenomena

3. Use of the hypothesis to predict the existence of other phenomena or to predict quantitatively the results of new observations

4. Performance of experimental tests of the predictions by several independent experimenters and properly performed experiments

While the researcher may bring certain biases to the study, it's important that bias not be permitted to enter into the interpretation. It's also important that data that don't fit the hypothesis not be ruled out. This is unlikely to happen if the researcher is open to the possibility that the hypothesis might turn out to be null. Another important caution is to be certain that the methods for analyzing and interpreting are flawless. Abiding by these mandates is important if the discovery is to make a contribution to human understanding.

The phenomena that interest social scientists are usually complex. Capturing that complexity more fully requires the assessment of simultaneous covariations along the following dimensions: the units of observation, their characteristics, and time. This is how behavior occurs. For example, to obtain a richer and more accurate picture of the progress of school children requires measuring changes in their attainment over time together with changes in the school over time. This acknowledges that changes in one arena of behavior are usually contingent on changes in other areas. Models used for research in the past were inadequate to handle the complexities suggested by multiple covariations. However, the evolution of computerized data processing has taken away that constraint.

While descriptions of the research project and presentation of outcomes along with analysis must be a part of every report, graphs, charts, and sometimes maps are necessary to make the results clearly understandable.

Demography

DEMOGRAPHY is the branch of science of statistics most concerned with the social well-being of people. Demographic tables may include:

- Analysis of the population on the basis of age, parentage, physical condition, race, occupation, and civil position, giving the actual size and the density of each separate area

DEMOGRAPHY: the branch of science of statistics most concerned with the social well-being of people

- Changes in the population as a result of birth, marriage, and death

- Statistics on population movements and their effects and their relations to given economic, social, and political conditions

- Statistics of crime, illegitimacy, and suicide

- Levels of education and economic and social statistics

Such information is also similar to that area of science known as vital statistics and as such is indispensable in studying social trends and making important legislative, economic, and social decisions. Such demographic information is gathered from census, registrar, reports and the like, and by state laws such information, especially the vital kind, is kept by physicians, attorneys, funeral directors, members of the clergy, and similar professional people. In the United States such demographic information is compiled, kept and published by the Public Health Service of the United States Department of Health, Education, and Welfare.

The most important element of this information is the so-called rate, which customarily represents the average of births and deaths for a unit of one thousand people in a population over a given calendar year. These general rates are called crude rates, which are then subdivided into sex, color, age, occupation, locality, and so on. They are then known as refined rates.

Statistics

In examining STATISTICS and the sources of statistical data, one must also be aware of the methods of statistical information gathering. For instance, there are many good sources of raw statistical data. Books such as *The Statistical Abstract of the United States*, published by the United States Chamber of Commerce; *The World Fact Book*, published by the Central Intelligence Agency; or *The Monthly Labor Review*, published by the United States Department of Labor are excellent examples that contain much raw data.

Simply put, statistics is the mathematical science that deals with the collection, organization, presentation, and analysis of various forms of numerical data and with the problems such as interpreting and understanding such data. The raw materials of statistics are sets of numbers obtained from enumerations or measurements collected by various methods of extrapolation, such as census taking, interviews, and observations.

One important idea to understand is that statistics usually deal with a specific model, hypothesis, or theory that is being attempted to be proven. One should be aware, however, that a theory could never actually be proved correct; it can only be CORROBORATED. One should also be aware that what is known as

> **STATISTICS:** the mathematical science that deals with the collection, organization, presentation, and analysis of various forms of numerical data

> **CORROBORATED:** the data presented is more consistent with this theory than with any other theory

CORRELATION: the joint movement of various data points

CAUSATION: the change in one of those data points caused the other data points to change

CORRELATION does not infer CAUSATION. It is important that one take these aspects into account so that one can be in a better position to appreciate what the collected data are really saying.

Tests of reliability are used, bearing in mind the manner in which the data have been collected and the inherent biases of any artificially created model to be used to explain real world events. Indeed the methods used and the inherent biases and reasons actually for doing the study by the individual(s) involved must never be discounted.

Conducting a research project once involved the use of punch cards, microfiche, and other manual means of storing data in a retrievable fashion. Today, high-powered computers are available to anyone who chooses to conduct research, so organizing data has become revolutionized. Creating multilevel folders, copying and pasting into the folders, making ongoing additions to the bibliography at the exact moment a source is consulted, and using search-and-find functions make this stage of the research process much faster. The results of these new sorting methods equal less frustration and a decrease in the likelihood that important data might be overlooked.

Serious research requires high-level analytical skills. A degree in statistics (or at least a graduate-level concentration) is very useful. A team approach to a research project typically includes a statistician in addition to those members who are knowledgeable in the social sciences.

Sample Test Questions and Rationale

(Easy)

1. *Capitalism* and *communism* are alike in that they are both:

   A. Organic systems

   B. Political systems

   C. Centrally planned systems

   D. Economic systems

Answer: D. Economic systems

While economic and (B) political systems are often closely connected, capitalism and communism are primarily (D) economic systems. Capitalism is a system of economics that allows the open market to determine the relative value of goods and services. Communism is an economic system where the market is planned by a central state. While communism is a (C) centrally planned system, this is not true of capitalism. (A) Organic systems are studied in biology, a natural science.

(Easy)

2. An *economist* might engage in which of the following activities?

   A. An observation of the historical effects of a nation's banking practices

   B. The application of a statistical test to a series of data

   C. Introduction of an experimental factor into a specified population to measure the effect of the factor

   D. An economist might engage in all of these

Answer: D. An economist might engage in all of these

Economists use statistical analysis of economic data, controlled experimentation, and historical research in their field of social science.

(Average)

3. The advancement of understanding in dealing with human beings has led to a number of interdisciplinary areas. Which of the following interdisciplinary studies would *not* be considered under the social sciences?

   A. Molecular biophysics

   B. Peace studies

   C. African-American studies

   D. Cartographic information systems

Answer: A. Molecular biophysics

Molecular biophysics is an interdisciplinary field combining the fields of biology, chemistry, and physics. These are all natural sciences, not social sciences.

Sample Test Questions and Rationale (cont.)

(Average)

4. **For the historian studying Ancient Egypt, which of the following would be least useful?**

   A. The record of an ancient Greek historian on Greek–Egyptian interaction

   B. Letters from an Egyptian ruler to his or her regional governors

   C. Inscriptions on stele of the Fourteenth Egyptian Dynasty

   D. Letters from a nineteenth-century Egyptologist to his wife

Answer: D. Letters from a nineteenth-century Egyptologist to his wife

Historians use primary sources from the actual time they are studying whenever possible. (A) Ancient Greek records of interaction with Egypt, (B) letters from an Egyptian ruler to regional governors, and (C) inscriptions from the Fourteenth Egyptian Dynasty are all primary sources created at or near the actual time being studied. (D) Letters from a nineteenth-century Egyptologist would not be considered primary sources, as they were created thousands of years after the fact and may not actually be about the subject being studied.

COMPETENCY 10
UNDERSTAND MAJOR CONCEPTS, PRINCIPLES, AND METHODS OF INQUIRY RELATED TO GEOGRAPHY

SKILL **Applying knowledge of basic concepts of geography** (e.g., location,
10.1 movement of people, interaction among peoples)

Geography

GEOGRAPHY involves studying location and how living things and Earth's features are distributed throughout the Earth. It includes where animals, people, and plants live and the effects of their relationship with Earth's physical features. Geographers also explore the locations of Earth's features, how they got there, and why it is so important.

GEOGRAPHY: the study of location and how living things and Earth's features are distributed throughout the Earth

AREAS OF GEOGRAPHICAL STUDY	
Regional	Elements and characteristics of a place or region
Topical	One Earth feature or one human activity occurring throughout the entire world
Physical	Earth's physical features, what creates and changes them, their relationships to each other, as well as human activities
Human	Human activity patterns and how they relate to the environment including political, cultural, historical, urban, and social geographical fields of study

Two of the most important terms in the study of geography are absolute and relative location. First, what is location? We want to know this in order to determine where something is and where we can find it. We want to point to a spot on a map and say, "That is where we are" or "That is where we want to be." In another way, we want to know where something is as compared to other things. It is very difficult for many people to describe something without referring to something else. Associative reasoning is a powerful way to think.

- Absolute location is the exact whereabouts of a person, place, or thing, according to any kind of geographical indicators you want to name. You could be talking about latitude and longitude or GPS or any kind of indicators at all. For example, Paris is at 48 degrees north longitude and 2 degrees east latitude. You can't get much more exact than that. If you had a map that showed every degree of latitude and longitude, you could pinpoint exactly where Paris was and have absolutely no doubt that your geographical depiction was accurate.

- Relative location, on the other hand, is always a description that involves more than one thing. When you describe a relative location, you tell where something is by describing what is around it. The same description of where the nearest post office is in terms of absolute location might be this: "It's down the street from the supermarket, on the right side of the street, next to the dentist's office."

Ecology

ECOLOGY: the study of how living organisms interact with the physical aspects of their surroundings (their environment), including soil, water, air, and other living things

BIOGEOGRAPHY: the study of how the surface features of the Earth—form, movement, and climate—affect living things

ECOLOGY is the study of how living organisms interact with the physical aspects of their surroundings (their environment), including soil, water, air, and other living things. BIOGEOGRAPHY is the study of how the surface features of the Earth—form, movement, and climate—affect living things.

THREE LEVELS OF ENVIRONMENTAL UNDERSTANDING	
Ecosystem	A community (of any size) consisting of a physical environment and the organisms that live within it.
Biome	A large area of land with characteristic climate, soil, and mixture of plants and animals. Biomes are made up of groups of ecosystems. Major biomes are: desert, chaparral, savanna, tropical rain forest, temperate grassland, temperate deciduous forest, taiga, and tundra.
Habitat	The set of surroundings within which members of a species normally live. Elements of the habitat include soil, water, predators, and competitors.

Within habitats interactions between members of the species occur. These interactions occur among members of the same species and among members of different species. Interaction tends to be of three types:

1. Competition: Competition occurs between members of the same species or between members of different species for resources required to continue life, to grow, or to reproduce. For example, competition for acorns can occur between squirrels or it can occur between squirrels and woodpeckers. One species can either push out or cause the demise of another species if it is better adapted to obtain the resource. When a new species is introduced into a habitat, the result can be a loss of the native species and/or significant change

to the habitat. For example, the introduction of the Asian plant Kudzu into the American South has resulted in the destruction of several species because Kudzu grows and spreads very quickly and smothers everything in its path.

2. Predation: Predators are organisms that live by hunting and eating other organisms. The species best suited for hunting other species in the habitat will be the species that survives. Larger species that have better hunting skills reduce the amount of prey available for smaller and/or weaker species. This affects both the amount of available prey and the diversity of species that are able to survive in the habitat.

3. Symbiosis: Symbiosis is a condition in which two organisms of different species are able to live in the same environment over an extended period of time without harming one another. In some cases one species may benefit without harming the other. In other cases both species benefit.

BIODIVERSITY refers to the variety of species, organisms, and habitats available on the Earth. Biodiversity provides the life-support system for the various habitats and species. The greater the degree of biodiversity, the more species and habitats will continue to survive.

> **BIODIVERSITY:** the variety of species, organisms and habitats available on the Earth

When human and other population and migration changes, climate changes, or natural disasters disrupt the delicate balance of a habitat or an ecosystem, species either adapt or become extinct.

Natural changes can occur that alter habitats—floods, volcanoes, storms, earthquakes. These changes can affect the species that exist within the habitat, either by causing extinction or by changing the environment in a way that will no longer support the life systems. Climate changes can have similar effects. Inhabiting species, however, can also alter habitats, particularly through migration. Human civilization, population growth, and efforts to control the environment can have many negative effects on various habitats. Humans change their environments to suit their particular needs and interests. This can result in changes that result in the extinction of species or changes to the habitat itself. For example, deforestation damages the stability of mountain surfaces. One particularly devastating example is in the removal of the grasses of the Great Plains for agriculture. Tilling the ground and planting crops left the soil unprotected. Sustained drought dried out the soil into dust. When windstorms occurred, the topsoil was stripped away and blown all the way to the Atlantic Ocean.

SKILL 10.2 Demonstrating knowledge of major physical and human-constructed features of the earth

SIX THEMES OF GEOGRAPHY	
Location	Including relative and absolute location. A relative location refers to the surrounding geography, e.g., "on the banks of the Mississippi River." Absolute location refers to a specific point, such as 41 degrees North latitude, 90 degrees West longitude, or 123 Main Street.
Spatial Organization	A description of how things are grouped in a given space. In geographical terms, this can describe people, places, and environments anywhere and everywhere on Earth. The most basic form of spatial organization for people is where they live. The vast majority of people live near other people, in villages, towns, cities, and settlements. These people live near others in order to take advantage of the goods and services that naturally arise from cooperation. These villages, towns, cities, and settlements are, to varying degrees, near bodies of water. Water is a staple of survival for every person on the planet and is also a good source of energy for factories and other industries, as well as a form of transportation for people and goods. For example, in a city, where are the factories and heavy industry buildings? Are they near airports or train stations? Are they on the edge of town, near major roads? What about housing developments? Are they near these industries, or are they far away? Where are the other industry buildings? Where are the schools and hospitals and parks? What about the police and fire stations? How close are homes to each of these things? Towns and especially cities are routinely organized into neighborhoods, so that each house or home is near to most things that its residents might need on a regular basis. This means that large cities have multiple schools, hospitals, grocery stores, fire stations, etc.
Place	A place has both human and physical characteristics. Physical characteristics include features such as mountains, rivers, and deserts. Human characteristics are the features created by human interaction with their environment such as canals and roads.
Human-Environmental Interaction	The theme of human-environmental interaction has three main concepts: humans adapt to the environment (wearing warm clothing in a cold climate); humans modify the environment (planting trees to block a prevailing wind); and humans depend on the environment (for food, water, and raw materials).

Table continued on next page

Movement	The theme of movement covers how humans interact with one another through trade, communications, immigration, and other forms of interaction.
Regions	A region is an area that has some kind of unifying characteristic, such as a common language or a common government. There are three main types of regions. Formal regions are areas defined by actual political boundaries, such as a city, county, or state. Functional regions are defined by a common function, such as the area covered by a telephone service. Vernacular regions are less formally defined areas that are formed by people's perception, e.g., the Middle East, and the South.

Human Geography

Geography involves studying location and how living things and Earth's features are distributed throughout the Earth. It includes where animals, people, and plants live and the effects of their relationship with Earth's physical features.

Geographers also explore the locations of Earth's features, how they got there, and why it is so important. Another way to describe where people live is by the geography and topography around them. The vast majority of people on the planet live in areas that are very hospitable. Yes, people live in the Himalayas and in the Sahara, but the populations in those areas are small indeed when compared to the plains of China, India, Europe, and the United States. People naturally want to live where they won't have to work really hard just to survive, and world population patterns reflect this.

Human communities subsisted initially as gatherers—gathering berries, leaves, etc. With the invention of tools it became possible to dig for roots, hunt small animals, and catch fish from rivers and oceans. Humans observed their environments and soon learned to plant seeds and harvest crops. As people migrated to areas in which game and fertile soil were abundant, communities began to develop. When people had the knowledge to grow crops and the skills to hunt game, they began to understand division of labor. Some of the people in the community tended to agricultural needs while others hunted game.

As habitats attracted larger numbers of people, environments became crowded and there was competition. The concept of division of labor and sharing of food soon followed. Groups of people focused on growing crops while others concentrated on hunting. Experience led to the development of skills and of knowledge that make the work easier. Farmers began to develop new plant species and hunters began to protect animal species from other predators for their own use.

This ability to manage the environment led people to settle down, to guard their resources, and to manage them.

Camps soon became villages. Villages became year-round settlements. Animals were domesticated and gathered into herds that met the needs of the village. With the settled life it was no longer necessary to "travel light." Pottery was developed for storing and cooking food.

By 8000 BCE, culture was beginning to evolve in these villages. Agriculture was developed for the production of grain crops, which led to a decreased reliance on wild plants. Domesticating animals for various purposes decreased the need to hunt wild game. Life became more settled. It was then possible to turn attention to such matters as managing water supplies, producing tools, and making cloth. There was both the social interaction and the opportunity to reflect upon existence. Mythologies arose and various kinds of belief systems. Rituals arose that reenacted the mythologies that gave meaning to life.

As farming and animal husbandry skills increased, the dependence upon wild game and food gathering declined. With this change came the realization that a larger number of people could be supported on the produce of farming and animal husbandry.

CIVILIZATION: a high level of cultural and technological development

CULTURE: the set of values, conventions, or social practices associated with a particular group

Two things seem to have come together to produce CIVILIZATIONS and CULTURES: a society and culture based on agriculture and the development of centers of the community with literate social and religious structures, respectively.

The members of these hierarchies then managed water supplies and irrigation and ritual and religious life and exerted their own right to use a portion of the goods produced by the community for their own subsistence in return for their management.

Sharpened skills; development of more sophisticated tools; commerce with other communities; increasing knowledge of their environment and the resources available to them; and responses to the needs to share goods, order community life, and protect their possessions from outsiders led to further division of labor and community development.

As trade routes developed and travel between cities became easier, trade led to specialization. Trade enables a people to obtain the goods they desire in exchange for the goods they are able to produce. This, in turn, leads to increased attention to refinements of technique and the sharing of ideas. The knowledge of a new discovery or invention provides knowledge and technology that increases the ability to produce goods for trade. As each community learns the value of the goods it produces and improves its ability to produce the goods in greater quantity, industry is born.

SKILL 10.3 **Analyzing interactions between physical systems and human systems** (e.g., economic, cultural, political)

Agricultural Revolution

The Agricultural Revolution, which was initiated by the invention of the plow, led to a thorough transformation of human society by making large-scale agricultural production possible and facilitating the development of agrarian societies. At the same time the plow was invented, the wheel, numbers, and writing were also invented. Coinciding with the shift from hunting wild game to the domestication of animals, this period was one of dramatic social and economic change.

Numerous changes in lifestyle and thinking accompanied the development of stable agricultural communities. Rather than gathering a wide variety of plants as hunter-gatherers, agricultural communities depended on a limited number of plants and crops. Subsistence is vulnerable to the weather and dependent on planting and harvesting times. Agriculture also required a great deal of physical labor as well as a sense of discipline. Agricultural communities are also more sedentary and stable in terms of location. This made the construction of dwellings possible—especially dwellings relatively close together, creating villages and towns.

Stable communities also freed people from the need to carry everything with them when moving from hunting ground to hunting ground. In addition to pottery, this facilitated the invention of larger, more complex tools. As new tools were envisioned and developed, it began to make sense to have some specialization within the society.

In the beginning of the transition to agriculture, the tools that were used for hunting and gathering were sufficient for agricultural tasks. The initial challenge was in adapting to a new way of life. Once that challenge was met, attention turned to the development of more advanced tools and sources of energy. Six thousand years ago, the first plow, which was pulled by animals, was invented in Mesopotamia. With this invention, agriculture became possible on a much larger scale. Soon, tools were developed that made basic tasks like gathering seeds, planting, and cutting grain faster and easier.

It also becomes necessary to maintain social and political stability to ensure that planting and harvesting times were not interrupted by internal discord or a war with a neighboring community. It was also necessary to develop ways to store the crop and to prevent its destruction by the elements and animals (not to mention protection from thieves).

Settled communities that produced the necessities of life were largely self-supporting. Advances in agricultural technology and the ability to produce a surplus of crops created two opportunities: trading the surplus goods for other desired goods and vulnerability to theft. Protecting domesticated livestock and surplus crops become an issue for the early communities. This in turn led to the construction of walls and other fortifications around the community.

The ability to produce surplus crops also created the opportunity to trade or barter with other communities in exchange for desired goods. Traders and trade routes began to develop between villages and cities. With the expansion of trade and travel between communities came the exchange of ideas and knowledge.

Industrial Revolution

The Industrial Revolution of the eighteenth and nineteenth centuries resulted in even greater changes in human civilization by creating opportunities for trade, increased production, and the exchange of ideas and knowledge. The first phase of the Industrial Revolution (1750–1830) saw the mechanization of the textile industry; vast improvements in mining with the invention of the steam engine; and numerous improvements in transportation with the development and improvement of turnpikes, canals, and the invention of the railroad.

The second phase (1830–1910) resulted in improvements in a number of industries that had already been mechanized through such inventions as the Bessemer steel process and steamships. New industries arose as a result of the new technological advances, including photography, electricity, and chemical processes. New sources of power were harnessed and applied, including petroleum and hydroelectric power. Precision instruments were developed, and engineering was launched. It was during this second phase that the Industrial Revolution spread to other European countries, Japan, and the United States.

The direct results of the Industrial Revolution, particularly as they affected industry, commerce, and agriculture, included the following:

- Enormous increases in productivity

- Huge increases in world trade

- Specialization and division of labor

- Standardization of parts

- Mass production

- Growth of giant business conglomerates and monopolies

- A new revolution in agriculture facilitated by the steam engine, machinery, chemical fertilizers, processing, canning, and refrigeration

The political results included the following:

- Growth of complex government by technical experts

- Centralization of government, including regulatory administrative agencies

- Advantages to democratic development, including the extension of franchise to the middle class (and later to all elements of the population), mass education to meet the needs of an industrial society, and the development of media of public communication, including radio, television, and cheap newspapers

- Dangers to democracy, including the risk of media manipulation, the facilitation of dictatorial centralization and totalitarian control, the subordination of the legislative function to administrative directives, greater efforts to achieve uniformity and conformity, and social impersonalization

The economic results included the following:

- The conflict between free trade and low tariffs and protectionism

- The issue of free enterprise against government regulation

- Struggles between labor and capital, including the trade-union movement

- The rise of socialism

- The rise of the utopian socialists

- The rise of Marxian or scientific socialism

The social results of the Industrial Revolution included the following:

- Increase of population, especially in industrial centers

- Advances in science applied to agriculture, sanitation, and medicine

- Growth of great cities

- Disappearance of the difference between city dwellers and farmers

- Faster tempo of life and increased stress from the monotony of the work routine

- The emancipation of women

- The decline of religion

- The rise of scientific materialism

- Darwin's theory of evolution

Increased mobility produced a rapid diffusion of knowledge and ideas and also resulted in widescale immigration to industrialized countries. Cultures clashed and cultures melded.

Trade organizations

The General Agreement on Tariffs and Trade (GATT), the North Atlantic Free Trade Agreement (NAFTA), the World Trade Organization (WTO), and the European Union (EU) are all forms of trade liberalization. The GATT was founded in 1947; today, as the WTO (established in 1995), it has 147 member nations. It was based on three principles:

1. Most favored nation status for all members, which meant that trade should be based on comparative advantage without tariffs or trade barriers

2. Elimination of quotas

3. Reduction of trade barriers through multilateral trade negotiations

Today, the WTO's object is to promote free trade. As such, it administers trade agreements, settles disputes, and provides a forum for trade discussions and negotiations.

NAFTA and the EU are both forms of regional economic integration. Economic integration is a method of trade liberalization on a regional basis.

NAFTA represents the lowest form or first step in the regional trade integration process. Through it, a free trade area exists for two or more countries that abolishes tariffs and other trade barriers but allows the countries to maintain their own trade barriers against the rest of the world. It allows for specialization and trade on the basis of comparative advantage within the area.

The next stage in the integration process is a customs union, which is a free trade area that has common external tariffs against nonmembers.

The third stage is a common market, which is a customs union with free factor mobility within the area. Factors migrate where they find the best payment in the area.

The fourth state is an economic union in which the market members have common or coordinated economic and social policies.

The final stage is a monetary union in which the area has a common currency. This is what Europe is working toward. They have a common market with elements of the fourth and fifth stages of integration.

The WTO does not change or blur the significance of political borders and territorial sovereignty in the same way that economic integration does, although the WTO is a way of settling trade disputes that arise from the different integration agreements. In the advanced stages of economic integration, the political borders remain but economic and social policies are common or coordinated.

In a monetary union, there is one common currency. Each nation is its own independent entity, but each gives up some sovereignty in the interest of having a successful union.

Trade agreements proliferate in the world today. The Smoot Hawley Tariffs and the rounds of retaliation in the 1930s are what laid the basis for today's WTO and EU. The GATT and the beginnings of what is now the EU came into being as organizations trying to undo the effects of the Great Depression and the First World War.

Free trade without trade barriers typically results in the most efficient use of resources, with higher consumption, employment, and income levels for all participants. This is why there are so many free trade agreements being negotiated in today's world.

SKILL 10.4 Applying knowledge of maps (e.g., political, physical, topographic, resource), globes, and other geographic tools (e.g., compass rose, legend, map scale)

Physical locations of the Earth's surface features include the four major hemispheres and the parts of the Earth's continents in them. Political locations are the political divisions, if any, within each continent. Both physical and political locations are precisely determined in two ways:

1. Surveying is done to determine boundary lines and distance from other features.

2. Exact locations are precisely determined by imaginary lines of latitude (parallels) and longitude (meridians). The intersection of these lines at right angles forms a grid, making it impossible to pinpoint an exact location of any place using any two grip coordinates.

The process of putting the features of the Earth onto a flat surface is called projection. All maps are really map projections. There are many different types. Each one deals in a different way with the problem of distortion. Map projections are made in a number of ways. Some are done using complicated mathematics. However, the basic ideas behind map projections can be understood by looking at the three most common types:

COMMON MAP PROJECTIONS	
Cylindrical Projections	These are done by taking a cylinder of paper and wrapping it around a globe. A light is used to project the globe's features onto the paper. Distortion is least where the paper touches the globe. For example, suppose that the paper was wrapped so that it touched the globe at the equator, the map from this projection would have just a little distortion near the equator. However, in moving north or south of the equator, the distortion would increase as you moved further away from the equator. The best known and most widely used cylindrical projection is the Mercator Projection. It was first developed in 1569 by Gerardus Mercator, a Flemish mapmaker.
Conical Projections	The name for these maps come from the fact that the projection is made onto a cone of paper. The cone is made so that it touches a globe at the base of the cone only. It can also be made so that it cuts through part of the globe in two different places. Again, there is the least distortion where the paper touches the globe. If the cone touches at two different points, there is some distortion at both of them. Conical projections are most often used to map areas in the middle latitudes. Maps of the United States are most often conical projections. This is because most of the country lies within these latitudes.
Flat-Plane Projections	These are made with a flat piece of paper. It touches the globe at one point only. Areas near this point show little distortion. Flat-plane projections are often used to show the areas of the north and south poles. One such flat projection is called a Gnomonic Projection. On this kind of map all meridians appear as straight lines, Gnomonic projections are useful because any straight line drawn between points on it forms a Great-Circle Route.

Great-circle routes can best be described by thinking of a globe and, when using the globe, the shortest route between two points on it can be found by simply stretching a string from one point to the other. However, if the string was extended in reality, so that it took into effect the globe's curvature, it would then make a great-circle. A great-circle is any circle that cuts a sphere, such as the globe, into two equal parts. Because of distortion, most maps do not show great-circle routes as straight lines. Gnomonic projections, however, do show the shortest distance between the two places as a straight line, and because of this they are valuable for navigation. They are called great-circle sailing maps.

Reading Maps

To properly analyze a given map, one must be familiar with the various parts and symbols that most modern maps use. For the most part, this is standardized, with different maps using similar parts and symbols. These can include:

COMMON MAP SYMBOLS	
The Title	All maps should have a title, just like all books should. The title tells you what information is to be found on the map.
The Legend	Most maps have a legend. A legend tells the reader about the various symbols that are used on that particular map and what the symbols represent (also called a map key).
The Grid	A grid is a series of lines that are used to find exact places and locations on the map. There are several different kinds of grid systems in use however most maps do use the longitude and latitude system, known as the Geographic Grid System.
Directions	Most maps have some directional system to show which way the map is being presented. Often on a map, a small compass will be present, with arrows showing the four basic directions: north, south, east, and west.
The Scale	This is used to show the relationship between a unit of measurement on the map versus the real world measure on the Earth. Maps are drawn to many different scales. Some maps show a lot of detail for a small area. Others show a greater span of distance. Whichever is being used one should always be aware of just what scale is being used. For instance the scale might be something like 1 inch = 10 miles for a small area or for a map showing the whole world it might have a scale in which 1 inch = 1,000 miles. The point is that one must look at the map key in order to see what units of measurements the map is using.

Maps have four main properties. They are

1. The size of the areas shown on the map

2. The shapes of the areas

3. Consistent scales

4. Straight line directions

A map can be drawn so that it is correct in one or more of these properties. No map can be correct in all of them.

TYPES OF MAPS	
Equal Areas	One property that maps can have is that of equal areas. In an equal area map, the meridians and parallels are drawn so that the areas shown have the same proportions as they do on the Earth. For example, Greenland is about 118th the size of South America, thus it will be show as 118th the size on an equal area map. The Mercator projection is an example of a map that does not have equal areas. In it, Greenland appears to be about the same size of South America. This is because the distortion is very bad at the poles and Greenland lies near the North Pole.
Conformal Map	A second map property is conformal, or correct shapes. There are no maps that can show very large areas of the Earth in their exact shapes. Only globes can really do that; however, conformal maps are as close as possible to true shapes. The United States is often shown by a Lambert Conformal Conic Projection Map.
Consistent Scales	Many maps attempt to use the same scale on all parts of the map. Generally, this is easier when maps show a relatively small part of the Earth's surface. For example, a map of Florida might be a Consistent Scale Map. Generally maps showing large areas are not consistent-scale maps. This is so because of distortion. Often such maps will have two scales noted in the key. One scale, for example, might be accurate to measure distances between points along the Equator. Another might be then used to measure distances between the North Pole and the South Pole. Maps showing physical features often try to show information about the elevation or relief of the land. Elevation is the distance above or below the sea level. The elevation is usually shown with colors, for instance, all areas on a map which are at a certain level will be shown in the same color.
Relief Maps	These show the shape of the land surface, flat, rugged, or steep. Relief maps usually give more detail than simply showing the overall elevation of the land's surface. Relief is also sometimes shown with colors, but another way to show relief is by using contour lines. These lines connect all points of a land surface that are the same height surrounding the particular area of land.
Thematic Maps	These are used to show more specific information, often on a single theme, or topic. Thematic maps show the distribution or amount of something over a certain given area—things such as population density, climate, economic information, cultural, political information, etc.

SKILL 10.5 Demonstrating knowledge of strategies (e.g., interpreting maps) and resources for geographic inquiry

ATLAS: a collection of maps, usually bound into a book, that contains geographic features, political boundaries, and perhaps social, religious, and economic statistics

An ATLAS is a collection of maps, usually bound into a book, that contains geographic features, political boundaries, and perhaps social, religious, and economic statistics. Atlases can be found at most libraries, but they are also widely available on the Internet. The U.S. Library of Congress holds more than 53,000 atlases; it is most likely the largest and most comprehensive collection in the world.

Statistical surveys are used in the social sciences to collect information on a sample of the population. With any kind of information, care must be taken to accurately record information so the results are not skewed or distorted.

Opinion polls are used to represent the opinions of a population by asking a number of people a series of questions about a product, place, person, or event and then using the results to apply the answers to a larger group or population. Polls, like surveys, are subject to errors in the process. Errors can occur based on who is asked the question, where they are asked, the time of day, or the biases one may hold in relevance to the poll being taken.

Illustrations of various sorts are used because it is often easier to demonstrate a given idea visually instead of orally. This is especially true in the areas of education and research because humans tend to be visually stimulated; most ideas presented visually are easier to understand and to comprehend than those presented verbally. Among the more common illustrations used in political and social sciences are various types of maps, graphs, and charts.

Photographs and globes are useful as well, but because they are limited in what kind of information they can show, they are rarely used for statistical purposes, unless something like a photograph of a particular political figure is necessary for visualization purposes. Although maps have advantages over globes and photographs, they do have a major disadvantage: Issues of distortion limit the truthfulness of the information that maps relay.

Distance is the measurement between two points of location on a map. Measurement can be in terms of feet, yards, miles, meters, or kilometers (just to name a few). Distance is often correct on equidistant maps only in the direction of latitude.

Another method for measuring curvilinear map distances is to use a mechanical device called an opisometer. This device uses a small rotating wheel that records the distance traveled. The recorded distance is measured by this device either in centimeters or inches.

Direction is usually measured relative to the location of the North or South Pole. Directions determined from these locations are said to be relative to "true north" or "true south." The magnetic poles can also be used to measure direction. However, these points on the earth are located in spatially different spots from the geographic North and South Poles. The north magnetic pole is located at 78.3° north, 104.0° west. In the southern hemisphere, the south magnetic pole is located in Commonwealth Day, Antarctica, and has a geographical location of 65° south, 139° east. The magnetic poles are not fixed; over time, they shift their spatial position.

COMPETENCY 11

UNDERSTAND MAJOR CONCEPTS, PRINCIPLES, AND METHODS OF INQUIRY RELATED TO U.S. GOVERNMENT AND CIVICS

SKILL
11.1
Demonstrating knowledge of the functions of government and the basic principles of the U.S. government as a republic

Many of the core values in the U.S. democratic system can be found in the opening words of the Declaration of Independence. This includes the important beliefs in equality and the rights of citizens to "life, liberty and the pursuit of happiness."

The Declaration was a condemnation of the British king's tyrannical government, and these words emphasized the American colonists' belief that a government received its authority to rule from the people, and its function should not be to suppress the governed but to protect the rights of the governed, including protection from the government itself. These two ideals, **POPULAR SOVEREIGNTY** and the **RULE OF LAW**, are basic core values of democracy.

Popular sovereignty grants citizens the ability to directly participate in their own government by voting and running for public office. This ideal is based on a belief of equality that holds that all citizens have an equal right to engage in their own governance. The ideal of equality has changed over the years, since women and nonwhite citizens were not always allowed to vote or to bring suit in court. Now, all U.S citizens age eighteen and over are allowed to vote. This expansion of rights since the adoption of the Constitution demonstrates an American value of respect for minority rights.

The democratic system of election and representation is based on majority rule. In the case of most public elections, the candidate who receives the most votes is awarded the office. Majority rule is also used to pass legislation in Congress. Majority rule is meant to ensure that authority cannot be concentrated in one small group of people.

The rule of law is the ideal that the law applies not only to the governed but to the government as well. This core value gives authority to the justice system, which grants citizens protection from the government by requiring that any accusation of a crime be proved by the government before a person is punished.

POPULAR SOVEREIGNTY: grants citizens the ability to directly participate in their own government by voting and running for public office

RULE OF LAW: the ideal that the law applies not only to the governed but to the government as well

This is called due process, and it ensures that any accused person will have an opportunity to confront his accusers and provide a defense. Due process follows from the core value of a right to liberty. The government cannot take away a citizen's liberty without reason or without proof. The correlating ideal is also a core value—that someone who does harm to another or breaks a law will receive justice under the democratic system. The ideal of justice holds that a punishment will fit the crime and that any citizen can appeal to the judicial system if he feels he has been wronged.

Central to the ideal of justice is an expectation that citizens will act in a way that promotes the common good, meaning that they will treat one another with honesty and respect and will exercise self-discipline in their interactions with others. These are among the basic responsibilities of a citizen of a democracy.

SKILL 11.2 Identifying the roles and interrelationships of national, state, and local governments in the United States

POWERS DELEGATED TO THE FEDERAL GOVERNMENT
1. To tax
2. To borrow and coin money
3. To establish postal service
4. To grant patents and copyrights
5. To regulate interstate and foreign commerce
6. To establish courts
7. To declare war
8. To raise and support the armed forces
9. To govern territories
10. To define and punish felonies and piracy on the high seas
11. To fix standards of weights and measures
12. To conduct foreign affairs

POWERS RESERVED TO THE STATES
1. To regulate intrastate trade
2. To establish local governments
3. To protect general welfare
4. To protect life and property
5. To ratify amendments
6. To conduct elections
7. To make state and local laws

Concurrent powers of the federal government and states

1. Both Congress and the states may tax

2. Both may borrow money

3. Both may charter banks and corporations

4. Both may establish courts

5. Both may make and enforce laws

6. Both may take property for public purposes

7. Both may spend money to provide for the public welfare

Implied powers of the federal government

1. To establish banks or other corporations to tax, borrow, and regulate commerce

2. To spend money for roads, schools, health, insurance, and so on; to establish post roads; to tax to provide for general welfare and defense; and to regulate commerce

3. To create military academies to raise and support an armed force

4. To locate and generate sources of power and sell surplus to dispose of government property, commerce, and war powers

5. To assist and regulate agriculture to tax and spend for general welfare and to regulate commerce

SKILL 11.3 Recognizing the roles and powers of the executive, legislative, and judicial branches of government

At the U.S. federal level:

- **Legislative:** Article I of the Constitution established the legislative, or law-making, branch of the government called the Congress. It is made up of two houses: the House of Representatives and the Senate. Voters in all states elect the members who serve in each house. The legislative branch is responsible for making laws, raising and printing money, regulating trade, establishing the postal service and federal courts, approving the president's appointments, declaring war, and supporting the armed forces. The Congress also has the power to change the Constitution itself, and to impeach (bring charges against) the president. Charges for impeachment are brought by the House of Representatives and are then tried in the Senate.

- **Executive:** Article II of the Constitution created the executive branch of the government, headed by the president, who leads the country. This branch recommends new laws and can veto bills passed by the legislative branch. As the chief of state, the president is responsible for carrying out the laws of the country as well as the treaties and declarations of war passed by the legislative branch. The president also appoints federal judges and is commander in chief of the military when it is called into service. Other members of the executive branch include the vice president, who is also elected, and various cabinet members as the president might appoint: ambassadors, presidential advisors, members of the armed forces, and other appointed and civil servants of government agencies, departments, and bureaus. Though the president appoints them, they must be approved by the legislative branch.

- **Judicial:** Article III of the Constitution established the judicial branch of government headed by the Supreme Court. The Supreme Court has the power to rule that a law passed by the legislature, or an act of the executive branch, is illegal and unconstitutional. Citizens, businesses, and government officials can, in an appeal capacity, ask the Supreme Court to review a decision made in a lower court if they believe that the ruling by a judge is unconstitutional. The judicial branch also includes lower federal courts known as federal district courts that have been established by the Congress. These courts try lawbreakers and review cases referred from other courts.

The System of Checks and Balances

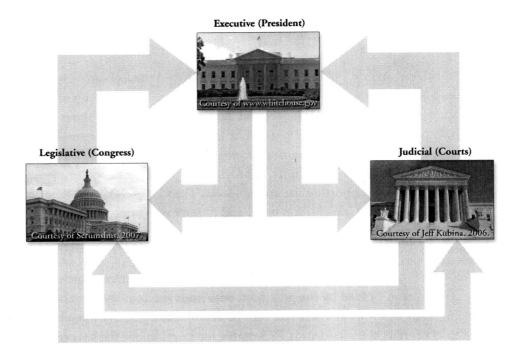

Executive (President)

Legislative (Congress)

Judicial (Courts)

SKILL 11.4 **Demonstrating knowledge of the Declaration of Independence, the U.S. Constitution, and the Bill of Rights**

The Declaration of Independence

The beginnings of civil liberties and the idea of civil rights in the United States go back to the ideas of the ancient Greeks. This was illustrated by the early struggle for civil rights against the British and by the very philosophies that led people to come to the New World in the first place. Religious freedom, political freedom, and the right to live one's life as one sees fit are basic to the American ideal. These were embodied in the ideas expressed in the Declaration of Independence and the Constitution.

The Declaration of Independence was adopted on July 4, 1776. It laid out the reasons and justifications for separating from Britain, but it was also used as a founding document to later form the United States of America. It was a joint work created by some of America's most important founding fathers, including John Adams, Benjamin Franklin, Roger Sherman, Robert Livingston, and Thomas Jefferson.

Influences for the Declaration of Independence included the Dutch Oath of Abjuration and philosophies of the Enlightenment period, in addition to those of early Greek democratic processes.

The U.S. Constitution

The U.S. Constitution is the supreme law of the United States of America. Its first draft was written in 1787 by the Constitutional Convention in Philadelphia, Pennsylvania. It is composed of a preamble (a statement of purpose), seven articles, and twenty-seven amendments. The seven articles include information on the following:

SEVEN ARTICLES OF THE CONSTITUTION			
Article One:	Legislative power	**Article Five:**	Process of Amendments
Article Two:	Executive power	**Article Six:**	Federal power
Article Three:	Judicial power	**Article Seven:**	Ratification
Article Four:	States' powers and limits		

The Bill Of Rights

The first ten of the twenty-seven amendments to the U.S. Constitution are known as the Bill of Rights. They outline information on civil liberties and civil rights. James Madison was credited with writing a majority of them.

SKILL 11.5 Identifying the rights and responsibilities of U.S. citizenship

---

The cause of human rights has been advanced significantly since the eighteenth century, both in theory and in fact. Several fundamental statements of human rights in the United States have extended and established human rights throughout the world.

The U.S. Declaration of Independence, ratified in 1776, declared that certain truths are self-evident: All men are created equal, and they are inherently endowed with certain unalienable rights that no government should ever violate.

These rights include the right to life, liberty, and the pursuit of happiness. When a government infringes upon those rights or fails to protect those rights, it is both the right and the duty of the people to overthrow that government and to establish in its place a new government that will protect those rights.

The Declaration of the Rights of Man and of the Citizen is a document created by the French National Assembly and issued in 1789. It sets forth the "natural, inalienable and sacred rights of man." It proclaims the following rights:

- Men are born and remain free and equal in rights. Social distinctions may only be founded upon the general good.

- The aim of all political association is the preservation of the natural and imprescriptible rights of man: liberty, property, security, and resistance to oppression.

- All sovereignty resides essentially in the nation. No body or individual may exercise any authority that does not proceed directly from the nation.

- Liberty is the freedom to do everything that injures no one else; hence, the exercise of these rights has no limits except those that ensure to the other members of the society the enjoyment of the same rights. These limits can only be determined by law.

- Law can only prohibit such actions as are hurtful to society.

- Law is the expression of the general will. Every citizen has a right to participate in the formation of law. It must be the same for all. All citizens, being equal in the eyes of the law, are equally eligible to all dignities and to all public positions and occupations, according to their abilities.

- No person shall be accused, arrested, or imprisoned except in the cases and according to the forms prescribed by law.

- The law shall provide for such punishments only as are strictly and obviously necessary.

- All persons are held innocent until they have been declared guilty. If it is necessary to arrest a person, all harshness not essential to the securing of the prisoner's person shall be severely repressed by law.

- No one shall be disquieted on account of his or her opinions, including religious views, provided their manifestation does not disturb the peace.

- The free communication of ideas and opinions is one of the most precious of the rights of man.

- The security of the rights of man and of the citizen requires public military force. These forces are, therefore, established for the good of all and not for the personal advantage of those to whom they shall be entrusted.

- A common contribution is essential for the maintenance of the public forces and for the cost of administration. This should be equitably distributed among all the citizens in proportion to their means.

- All citizens have a right to decide, either personally or by their representatives, as to the necessity of the public contribution.

- Society has the right to require of every public agent an account of his administration.

- A society in which the observance of the law is not ensured, nor the separation of powers defined, has no constitution at all.

- Since property is an inviolable and sacred right, no one shall be deprived thereof except where public necessity, legally determined, shall clearly demand it, and then only on condition that the owner shall have been previously and equitably indemnified.

The United Nations Declaration of Universal Human Rights

(1948) opens with the words "Whereas recognition of the inherent dignity and of the equal and inalienable rights of all members of the human family is the foundation of freedom, justice, and peace in the world. Whereas disregard and contempt for human rights have resulted in barbarous acts which have outraged the conscience of mankind, and the advent of a world in which human beings shall enjoy freedom of speech and belief and freedom from fear and want has been proclaimed as the highest aspiration of the common people." It sets out these articles:

1. All human beings are born free and equal in dignity and rights. They are endowed with reason and conscience and should act toward one another in a spirit of brotherhood.

2. Everyone is entitled to all the rights and freedoms set forth in this Declaration, without distinction of any kind.

3. Everyone has the right to life, liberty, and security of person.

4. No one shall be held in slavery or servitude.

5. No one shall be subjected to torture or to cruel, inhuman, or degrading treatment or punishment.

6. Everyone has the right to recognition everywhere as a person before the law.

7. All are equal before the law and are entitled without any discrimination to equal protection of the law.

8. Everyone has the right to an effective remedy by the competent national tribunals for acts violating the fundamental rights granted by the constitution of by law.

9. No one shall be subjected to arbitrary arrest, detention, or exile.

10. Everyone is entitled in full equality to a fair and public hearing by an independent and impartial tribunal, in the determination of rights and obligations and of any criminal charges.

11. All people charged with a penal offense have the right to be presumed innocent until proved guilty according to law in a public trial at which they have had all the guarantees necessary for their defense. No one shall be held guilty of any penal offense on account of any act or omission that did not constitute a penal offence, under national or international law, at the time when it was committed.

12. No one shall be subjected to arbitrary interference with privacy, family, home, or correspondence, or to attacks upon honor and reputation.

13. Everyone has the right to freedom of movement and residence within the borders of each state. All people have the right to leave any country, including their own, and to return to their country.

14. Everyone has the right to seek and to enjoy in other countries asylum from persecution. This right may not be invoked in the case of prosecutions genuinely arising from nonpolitical crimes or from acts contrary to the purposes and principles of the United Nations.

15. Everyone has the right to a nationality. No one shall be arbitrarily deprived of his nationality or denied the right to change nationality.

16. Men and women of full age have the right to marry and to found a family. They are entitled to equal rights as to marriage, during marriage, and at its dissolution. Marriage shall be entered into only with the free and full consent of the intending spouses. The family is the natural and fundamental group unit of society and is entitled to protection by society and the State.

17. Everyone has the right to own property alone or in association with others. No one shall be arbitrarily deprived of his property.

18. Everyone has the right to freedom of thought, conscience, and religion, including the right to change religion or belief, and freedom to manifest religion or belief in teaching, practice, worship, and observance.

19. Everyone has the right to freedom of opinion and expression.

20. Everyone has the right to freedom of peaceful assembly and association. No one may be compelled to belong to an association

21. Everyone has the right to take part in the government of his or her country, directly or through freely chosen representatives. Everyone has the right of equal access to public service in his or her country. The will of the people shall be the basis of the authority of government.

22. Everyone has the right to social security and is entitled to realization of the economic, social, and cultural rights indispensable for dignity and the free development of personality.

23. Everyone has the right to work. Everyone, without any discrimination, has the right to equal pay for equal work. Everyone who works has the right to just and favorable remuneration. Everyone has the right to form and to join trade unions for the protection of interests.

24. Everyone has the right to rest and leisure, including reasonable limitation of working hours and periodic holidays with pay.

25. All people have the right to a standard of living adequate for the health and well-being of themselves and their families, and the right to security in the event of unemployment, sickness, disability, widowhood, old age, or other lack of livelihood in circumstances beyond their control. Motherhood and childhood are entitled to special care and assistance. All children shall enjoy the same social protection.

26. Everyone has the right to education. Education shall be directed to the full development of the human personality and to the strengthening of respect for human rights and fundamental freedoms. Parents have a prior right to choose the kind of education that shall be given to their children.

27. Everyone has the right to freely participate in the cultural life of the community. All people have the right to the protection of the moral and materials interests resulting from any scientific, literary, or artistic production of which they are the author.

28. Everyone is entitled to a social and international order in which the rights and freedoms set forth in this Declaration can be fully realized.

The United Nations Convention on the Rights of the Child brings together the rights of children as they are enumerated in other international documents. In this document, those rights are clearly and completely stated, along with the explanation of the guiding principles that define the way society

views children. The goal of the document is to clarify the environment that is necessary to enable every human being to develop to his or her full potential. The Convention calls for resources and contributions to be made to ensure the full development and survival of all children. The document also requires the establishment of appropriate means to protect children from neglect, exploitation, and abuse. The document also recognizes that parents have the most important role in raising children.

SKILL 11.6 Demonstrating knowledge of strategies and resources (e.g., Internet, mass communication) for inquiry related to government and civics

Primary sources are works, records, and so on that were created during the period being studied or immediately after it. Secondary sources are works written significantly after the period being studied; they are based upon primary sources. Suppose an individual is preparing for a presentation on the Civil War and intends to focus on causes, an issue that has often been debated. If examining the matter of slavery as a cause, a graph of the increase in the number of slaves by area of the country for the previous 100 years would be very useful in the discussion. If focusing on the economic conditions that were driving the politics of the age, graphs of the gross domestic product (GDP), the distribution of wealth geographically and individually, and the relationship of wealth to ownership of slaves would be useful.

In that same manner, if discussing the war in Iraq, detailed maps with geopolitical elements would help to clarify not only the day-to-day happenings but also the historical features that led up to it. A map showing the number of oil fields and where they are situated with regard to the various political factions and charts showing output of those fields historically would be useful.

As another example, when teaching the history of space travel, photos of the most famous astronauts can add interest to the discussion. Graphs showing the growth of the industry, and charts showing discoveries and their relationship to the lives of everyday Americans might also be helpful.

Geography and history classes are notoriously labeled by students as dull. With all the visual resources available nowadays, however, those classes have the potential for being the most exciting courses in the curriculum.

COMPETENCY 12

UNDERSTAND MAJOR CONCEPTS, PRINCIPLES, AND METHODS OF INQUIRY RELATED TO ECONOMICS

SKILL 12.1 **Recognizing basic economic concepts** *(e.g., scarcity, supply and demand, needs and wants, opportunity cost, productivity, trade)* **and the purposes and functions of currency**

The fact that resources are scarce is the basis for the existence of economics. Economics is defined as a study of how scarce resources are allocated to satisfy unlimited wants. Resources refer to the four factors of production: labor, capital, land, and entrepreneurship. The individual has the right to supply whatever resources he wants to the market. The fact that the supply of these resources is finite means that society cannot have as much of everything that it wants. There is a constraint on production and consumption and on the kinds of goods and services that can be produced and consumed.

Scarcity means that choices have to be made. If society decides to produce more of one good, this means that there are fewer resources available for the production of other goods. Assume a society can produce two goods, good A and good B. The society uses resources in the production of each good. If producing one unit of good A results in an amount of resources used to produce three units of good B, then producing one more unit of good A results in a decrease in three units of good B. In effect, one unit of good A "costs" three units of good B.

This cost is referred to as opportunity cost. OPPORTUNITY COST is the value of the sacrificed alternative—in the above examples the value of what had to be given up in order to have the output of good A. Opportunity cost does not just refer to production. Your opportunity cost of studying with this guide is the value of what you are not doing because you are studying, whether it is watching TV, spending time with family, working, or whatever. Every choice has an opportunity cost.

The supply curve represents the selling and production decisions of the seller and is based on the costs of production. The costs of production of a product are based on the costs of the resources used in its production. The costs of resources are based on the scarcity of the resource. The scarcer a resource is, relatively speaking, the higher its price. A diamond costs more than paper because diamonds are scarcer than paper is. All of these concepts are embodied in the seller's supply curve. The same thing is true on the buying side of the market. The buyer's

Teaching economics:

http://fte.org/teachers/ lessons/lessons.htm

http://www. teachingeconomics.org/

http://ecedweb.unomaha. edu/teachsug.htm

http://lessonplanz.com/ Lesson_Plans/Social_ Studies/__Grades_K-2/ Economics/index.shtml

OPPORTUNITY COST: the value of the sacrificed alternative

Supply curve

preferences, tastes, income, etc.—all of his or her buying decisions—are embodied in the demand curve.

Where the demand and supply curves intersect is where the buying decisions of buyers are equal to the selling decisions of sellers. The quantity that buyers want to buy at a particular price is equal to the quantity that sellers want to sell at that particular price. The market is in equilibrium.

CASE STUDY

What happens when there is a change? Suppose a new big oil field is found. Also suppose there is a technology that allows its recovery and refining at a fraction of the present costs. The result is a big increase in the supply of oil at lower costs, as reflected by a rightward shifting oil supply curve. Oil is used as an input into almost all production. Firms now have lower costs. This means that the firm can produce the same amount of output at a lower cost or can produce a larger amount of output at the same cost. The result is a rightward shift of the firm's and, therefore, the industry supply curve. This means that sellers are willing and able to offer for sale larger quantities of output at each price. Assuming buyers' buying decisions stay the same, there is a new market equilibrium, or new point of intersection of the shifted supply curve with the buyers' demand curve. The result is a lower price with a larger quantity of output. The market has achieved a new equilibrium based on the increase in the quantity of a resource.

Firms in markets tend to grow over time. If there is a market for the firm's product, as it grows it experiences economies of scale, or lower per-unit costs. As firms grow they tend to become large relative to the market and the smaller more inefficient firms tend to go out of business. Larger firms have more market power and are able to influence their price and output. They can become monopolistic. Government counters this lessening of competition in a market by enacting antitrust legislation to protect the competitive nature of the market.

SKILL 12.2 Demonstrating knowledge of the basic structure of the U.S. economy and ways in which the U.S. economy relates to and interacts with the economies of other nations

TRADITIONAL ECONOMY: an economy based on traditional ways of doing things

The TRADITIONAL ECONOMY is one based on custom. This usually describes the situation that exists in many less-developed countries. The people do things the way their ancestors did so they are not too technologically advanced. Since their whole mindset is directed toward tradition, they are not very interested in technology, equipment, or new ways of doing things. Technology and equipment are viewed as a threat to the old way of doing things and to their tradition. There is very little upward mobility for the same reason.

The model of CAPITALISM is based on private ownership of the means of production and operates on the basis of free markets, on both the input and output side. The free markets function to coordinate market activity and to achieve an efficient allocation of resources. Laissez-faire capitalism is based on the premise of no government intervention in the economy. The market will eliminate any unemployment or inflation that occurs. Government needs only to provide the framework for the functioning of the economy and to protect private property. The role of financial incentives is crucial for it results in risk-taking and research and development. Capitalist economies tend to have democratic forms of government because the system is based on competition and individual freedoms.

A COMMAND ECONOMY is almost the exact opposite of a market economy. A command economy is based on government ownership of the means of production and the use of planning to take the place of the market. Instead of the market determining the output mix and the allocation of resources, the bureaucracy fulfills this role by determining the output mix and establishing production target for the enterprises, which are publicly owned. The result is inefficiency. There is little interest in innovation and research because there is no financial reward for the innovator. A command economy tends to have an authoritarian form of government because a planning mechanism that replaces the market requires a planning authority to make decisions supplementing the freedom of choice of consumers and workers.

A MIXED ECONOMY uses a combination of markets and planning, with the degree of each varying according to country. The real world can be described as mixed economies, each with varying degrees of planning. The use of markets results in the greatest efficiency since markets direct resources in and out of industries according to changing profit conditions. However, government is needed to perform various functions. The degree of government involvement in the economy can vary in mixed economies. Government is needed to keep the economy stable during periods of inflation and unemployment.

All of the major economies of the world are mixed economies. They use markets but have different degrees of government involvement in the functioning of the markets and in the provision of public goods. For example, in some countries health care and education are provided by government and are not a part of the private sector. In the United States, most health care and higher education is private and at the expense of the consumer.

CAPITALISM: an economic system based on private ownership of capital

COMMAND ECONOMY: an economy in which decisions about production and allocation are made by the governement

MIXED ECONOMY: an economy in which certain sectors are left to private ownership and the free market, while others are regulated by the government

SKILL 12.3 Recognizing the roles and interactions of consumers and producers in the U.S. economy

The U.S. economy consists of the household or consumer sector, the business sector, and the government sector. Households earn their incomes by selling their factors of production in the input market. Businesses hire their inputs in the factor market and use them to produce outputs. Households use their incomes earned in the factor market to purchase the output of businesses. Both households and businesses are active participants in both the input and output market. Households do not spend all of their income; they save some of it in banks. A well-organized, smoothly functioning banking system is required for the operation of the economy.

The function of organized labor is to help obtain a higher-factor income for workers. Organized labor negotiates the work agreement, or contract, for their union members. This collective bargaining agreement is a contract between the worker and the employer; it states the terms and conditions of employment for the length of the contract.

MACROECONOMICS:
refers to the functioning of the economy on the national level, as well as the functioning of the aggregate units that comprise the national economy

MACROECONOMICS refers to the functioning of the economy on the national level, as well as the functioning of the aggregate units that comprise the national economy. Macroeconomics is concerned with a study of the economy's overall economic performance, or what is called the GROSS DOMESTIC PRODUCT (GDP). The GDP is a measure of the economy's output during a specified time period. Tabulating the economy's output can be measured in two ways, both of which give the same result: the expenditures approach and the incomes approach. Basically, what is spent on the national output by each sector of the economy is equal to what is earned producing the national output by each of the factors of production.

GROSS DOMESTIC PRODUCT: a measure of the economy's output during a specified time period

The macroeconomy consists of four broad sectors: consumers, businesses, government, and the foreign sector. In the expenditures approach, the GDP is determined by the amount of spending in each sector. The GDP is equal to the consumption expenditures of consumers (C), plus the investment expenditures of businesses (I), plus the spending of all three levels of government (G), plus the net export spending in the foreign sector. It can be determined by the equation

$$GDP = C + I + G + (X - M)$$

When the economy is functioning smoothly, the amount of national output produced, or the aggregate supply, is just equal to the amount of national output purchased, or aggregate demand. It is at this point that we have an economy in a period of prosperity without economic instability. However, market economies experience the fluctuations of the business cycle (the ups and downs in the level of economic activity). There are four phases: boom (period of prosperity), recession (a period of declining GDP and rising unemployment), trough (the low point of the recession), and recovery (a period of lessening unemployment and rising prices). There are no rules pertaining to the duration or severity of any of the phases. The phases result in periods of unemployment and periods of inflation. Inflation results from too much spending in the economy; it occurs when buyers want to buy more than sellers can produce and bid up prices for the available output. Unemployment occurs when there is not enough spending in the economy; sellers have produced more output than buyers are buying, and the result is a surplus situation. Firms faced with surplus merchandise then lower their production levels and lay off workers. The result is unemployment. These are situations that require government policy actions.

The U.S. economy is based on the concepts of individual freedom of choice and competition. Economic agents are free to pursue their own interests. They can choose their occupation and undertake entrepreneurial ventures. If they are successful, they gain in the form of profits. The profit incentive is very important because people and businesses are willing to take risks for the possibility of gaining profit. The U.S. economy is one of the most successful economies in the world, with the highest total GDP. Like any market economy, it is subject to the business cycle and temporary bouts of inflation and/or unemployment. When they do occur, appropriate policies are typically implemented in time to counteract them.

SKILL 12.4 Identifying the functions of private business, banks, and the government in the U.S. economy

Households, businesses, and government are related through the circular flow diagram. They are all integral parts of the macroeconomy, and they contain two markets. The input market exists when factor owners sell their factors and employers hire their inputs. Sometimes, labor is organized into labor unions in the input market. The purpose of the labor union is to negotiate the work contract with the employer and to establish a procedure for grievances. Unions typically hope to acquire a larger share of income for their members. The output market exists when firms sell the output they produce with their inputs. It is wherein factors owners spend their incomes on goods and services.

There are two sectors of the macroeconomy: households and businesses. Households sell their factors in the input market and use their income to purchase goods and services in the output market. Therefore, wages, interest, rents, and profits flow from the business sector to the household sector. Because factor incomes are based on the scarcity of the factor as well as the contribution of the factor, there is often an unequal distribution of income; not all factors are equal.

Households that earn their factor incomes in the factor market spend their incomes on goods and services produced by businesses and sold in the output market. Receipts for goods and services flow from households to businesses. The government receives tax payments from households and businesses, and then provides services to businesses and households. Each of these three exchanges of factors is a component of the aggregate sectors of the economy; as such, they all make a contribution to the GDP.

Adding financial institutions to the picture demonstrates how the Federal Reserve implements monetary policy. There are three components of monetary policy: the reserve ratio, the discount rate, and open market operations. Changes in any of these three components affect the amount of money in the banking system and, thus, the level of spending in the economy. The reserve ratio refers to the portion of deposits that banks are required to hold as vault cash or on deposit with the Federal Reserve. The purpose of this reserve ratio is to give the Federal Reserve a way to control the money supply. These funds can't be used for any other purpose. When the Federal Reserve changes the reserve ratio, it changes the money creation and lending ability of the banking system. When the Federal Reserve wants to expand the money supply, it lowers the reserve ratio, leaving banks with more money to loan. This is one aspect of expansionary monetary policy. When the reserve ratio is increased, the result is that banks have less money to make loans with, which is considered a form of contractionary monetary policy. This type of policy leads to a lower level of spending in the economy.

Another way in which monetary policy is implemented is by changing the discount rate. When banks have temporary cash shortages, they can borrow from the Federal Reserve. The interest rate on the funds they borrow is called the discount rate. Raising and lowering the discount rate is a way of controlling the money supply. Lowering the discount rate encourages banks to borrow from the Federal Reserve, instead of restricting their lending to deal with the temporary cash shortage. By encouraging banks to borrow, their lending ability is increased; this results in a higher level of spending in the economy. Lowering the discount rate is another form of expansionary monetary policy. Discouraging bank lending by raising the discount rate is another form of contractionary monetary policy. In this way, a well-developed banking system is necessary for capital formation and investment purposes.

> **SKILL 12.5** Identifying the knowledge and skills necessary to make reasoned and responsible financial decisions as a consumer, producer, saver, and borrower in a market economy

ECONOMICS is the study of how a society allocates its scarce resources to satisfy what are basically unlimited and competing wants. Economics can also be defined as a study of the production, consumption, and distribution of goods and services. Both of these definitions are the same. A fundamental fact of economics is that resources are scarce and that wants are infinite. The fact that scarce resources have to satisfy unlimited wants means that choices have to be made, whether the entity is a consumer, producer, saver, or investor. As mentioned in an example in Skill 12.1, if society uses its resources to produce good A, then it doesn't have those resources to produce good B. More of good A means less of good B.

On the consumption side of the market, consumers buy the goods and services that give them satisfaction, or utility. They want to obtain the most utility they can for their dollar. The quantity of goods and services that consumers are willing and able to purchase at different prices during a given period of time is referred to as DEMAND. Since consumers buy the goods and services that give them satisfaction, this means that, for the most part, they don't buy the goods and services that they don't want or that don't give them satisfaction. Consumers are, in effect, voting for the goods and services that they want with their dollars—what is called DOLLAR VOTING. Consumers are basically signaling firms as to how they want society's scarce resources used with their dollar votes.

A good that society wants acquires enough dollar votes for the producer to experience profits—a situation in which the firm's revenues exceed the firm's costs. The existence of profits indicates to the firm that it is producing the goods and services that consumers want and that society's scarce resources are being used in accordance with consumer preferences.

This process through which consumers vote with their dollars is called CONSUMER SOVEREIGNTY. Consumers are directing the allocation of scarce resources in the economy with their dollar spending. Firms, who are in business to earn profit, then hire resources, or inputs, in accordance with consumer preferences. This is the way in which resources are allocated in a market economy, with consumers basing their decisions on the utility or satisfaction they receive from buying goods.

SUPPLY is based on production costs. The supply of a good or service is defined as the quantities of a good or service that a producer is willing and able to sell at different prices during a given period of time. Remember, market equilibrium occurs when the buying decisions of buyers are equal to the selling decision of seller, or where the demand and supply curves intersect. At this point, the

ECONOMICS: the study of how a society allocates its scarce resources to satisfy what are basically unlimited and competing wants; a study of the production, consumption, and distribution of goods and services

DEMAND: the quantity of goods and services that consumers are willing and able to purchase at different prices during a given period of time

DOLLAR VOTING: consumers, in effect, voting for the goods and services that they want with their dollars

CONSUMER SOVEREIGNTY: process through which consumers vote with their dollars

SUPPLY: the quantities of a good or service that a producer is willing and able to sell at different prices during a given period of time

quantity that sellers want to sell at a price is equal to the quantity the buyers want to buy at that same price. This is the market equilibrium price.

The price of an input or output allocates that input or output to those who are willing and able to transact at the market price. Those who can transact at the market price or better are included in the market; those who can't or won't transact at the market price are excluded from the market.

The fundamental characteristics of the U.S. economic system are the uses of competition and markets. Profit and competition all go together in the U.S. economic system. Competition is determined by market structure. Since the cost curves are the same for all the firms, the only difference comes from the revenue side. Each firm maximizes profit by producing at the point where marginal cost equal marginal revenue. The existence of economic profits, an above-normal rate of return, attracts capital to an industry and results in expansion.

MONOPOLY: when a single company owns all or nearly all of the market for a given type of product or service

Whether new firms can enter the market depends on the barriers to entry. Firms can enter easily in perfect competition, and the expansion will continue until economic profits are eliminated and firms earn a normal rate of return. The significant barriers to entry in monopoly serve to keep firms out, so the monopolist continues to earn an above-normal rate of return. Some firms will be able to enter in monopolistic competition but won't have a MONOPOLY over the existing firm's brand name. The competitiveness of the market structure determines whether new firms or capital can enter in response to profits.

PROFIT: positive gain from an investment or business operation after subtracting for all expenses

PROFIT functions as a financial incentive for individuals and firms. The possibility of earning profit is why individuals are willing to undertake entrepreneurial ventures and why firms are willing to spend money on research and development, and innovation. Without these kinds of financial incentives, new product development or technological advancement would not take place.

Savings represents delayed consumption. Savers must be paid a price for delaying consumption. This price is called the interest rates. Savers will save more money at higher interest rates than at lower interest rates. The interest rate is the price of borrowing to the investor. Investors will borrow more funds at lower interest rates than at higher interest rates. The equilibrium rate of interest is the rate at which the amount savers want to save is equal to the amount borrowers want to borrow for investment purposes.

SKILL 12.6 Demonstrating knowledge of strategies *(e.g., interpreting graphs and tables)* and resources for inquiry related to economics

In measuring the social significance of an event or issue, one of the first questions to ask is how many people are affected. Major events such as wars, natural disasters, and revolutions are significant partly because they can change the way of life for many people in a short time. However, some significant changes take place over long periods of time, so it is also important to look at the long-term effects of an event or phenomenon, following the chain of causes and effects. In this way, events that seem insignificant at the time they occur or those that affect only a small number of people can be linked directly to large societal changes.

Participation in self-government is one of the United States' core democratic values. By participating in democratic institutions, citizens become better informed of their rights and responsibilities in a democracy and thus better citizens. While elementary students are too young to participate directly by voting, classroom activities that simulate elections can help to develop a sense of the importance of participating. Encouraging structured discussions or debates on issues that directly affect the students can help to establish respect for minority viewpoints and the importance of free expression—both core democratic values.

There are many different ways to find ideas for research problems. One of the most common ways is through experiencing and assessing relevant problems in a specific field. Researchers are often involved in the fields in which they choose to study and thus encounter practical problems related to their areas of expertise on a daily basis. They can then use their knowledge, expertise, and research ability to examine their selected research problem. For students, all that this entails is being curious about the world around them. Research ideas can come from one's background, culture, education, or experiences. Another way to get research ideas is by exploring literature in a specific field and coming up with a question that extends or refines previous research.

Once a topic is decided upon, a research question must be formulated. A research question is a relevant, researchable, feasible statement that identifies the information to be studied. Once this initial question is formulated, it is a good idea to think of specific issues related to the topic. This will help to create a hypothesis. A research HYPOTHESIS is a statement of the researcher's expectations for the outcome of the research problem. It is a summary statement of the problem to be addressed in any research document. A good hypothesis states, clearly and concisely, the researchers' expected relationship between the variables that they are investigating. Once a hypothesis is decided, the rest of the research paper should focus on analyzing a set of information or arguing a specific point. Thus, there are two types of research papers: analytical and argumentative.

> **HYPOTHESIS:** a statement of the researcher's expectations for the outcome of the research problem; a summary statement of the problem to be addressed in any research document

Analytical papers focus on examining and understanding the various parts of a research topic and reformulating them in a new way to support your initial statement. In this type of research paper, the research question is used as both a basis for investigation as well as a topic for the paper. Once a variety of information is collected on the given topic, it is coalesced into a clear discussion

Argumentative papers focus on supporting the question or claim with evidence or reasoning. Instead of presenting research to provide information, an argumentative paper presents research in order to prove a debatable statement and interpretation.

DOMAIN III
MATHEMATICS

PERSONALIZED STUDY PLAN

✗

KNOWN MATERIAL/ SKIP IT

✗

PERSONALIZED STUDY PLAN

KNOWN MATERIAL/ SKIP IT

COMPETENCY 13
UNDERSTAND PROCESSES AND APPROACHES FOR EXPLORING MATHEMATICS AND SOLVING PROBLEMS

> **SKILL** Identifying effective strategies *(e.g., determining relevant information,*
> **13.1** *simplifying, estimating)* for solving single-step and multi-step problems
> in mathematical and other contexts

Successful math teachers introduce their students to multiple problem-solving strategies. They create classroom environments where free thought and experimentation are encouraged. Teachers can promote problem solving among their students by allowing them to make multiple attempts at problems, giving credit for reworking test or homework problems, and encouraging students to share their ideas through class discussion. To maximize efficacy, there are several specific problem-solving skills with which teachers should be familiar.

The GUESS-AND-CHECK STRATEGY calls for students to make an initial guess at the solution, check the answer, and use that outcome to guide the next guess. With each successive guess, the student should get closer to the correct answer. Constructing a table from the guesses can help to organize the data.

> **GUESS-AND-CHECK STRATEGY:** calls for students to make an initial guess at the solution, check the answer, and use that outcome to guide the next guess

Example: There are 100 coins in a jar. 10 are dimes. The rest are pennies and nickels. There are twice as many pennies as nickels. How many pennies and nickels are in the jar?

There are 90 total nickels and pennies in the jar (100 coins—10 dimes).

There are twice as many pennies as nickels. Students can take guesses that fulfill the criteria and adjust these guesses based on the answer found. They can continue until they find the correct answer: 60 pennies and 30 nickels.

NUMBER OF PENNIES	NUMBER OF NICKELS	TOTAL NUMBER OF PENNIES AND NICKELS
40	20	60
80	40	120

Table continued on next page

| 70 | 35 | 105 |
| 60 | 30 | 90 |

The WORKING BACKWARD STRATEGY requires students to determine a starting point when solving a problem where the final result and the steps to reach the result are given.

Example: John subtracted 7 from his age and then divided the result by 3. The final result was 4. What is John's age?
Work backwards by reversing the operations.

$4 \times 3 = 12;$
$12 + 7 = 19$
John is 19 years old.

The strategy of ESTIMATING AND TESTING FOR REASONABLENESS draws on related skills that students should employ prior to and after solving a problem. These skills are particularly important when students use calculators to find answers.

Example: Find the sum of 4387 + 7226 + 5893.
$4300 + 7200 + 5800 = 17300$ Estimation.
$4387 + 7226 + 5893 = 17506$ Actual sum.

By comparing their estimate to the sum that they actually computed, students can determine whether their answer is reasonable.

Many times, the description of a problem may contain more information than is needed to solve the problem. Some of the information may actually be irrelevant. It is important to focus on what information is relevant to the problem.

Example: Jonathan went to the mall and bought a baseball cap for $14, gloves for $10, a stocking cap for $8, a headband for $7, and an umbrella for $15. What was the average price of the headwear that Jonathan bought?
In this problem, we are interested only in the items Jonathan bought that could be worn on the head: a baseball cap, a stocking cap, and a headband. We are not interested in the gloves or the umbrella. Therefore, we average $14, $8, and $7 to get $9.67.

The strategy of SIMPLIFYING is used when the best way to solve a problem is to break it into a series of simpler problems. This may be most appropriate when:

• A direct solution to the problem is too complicated

• The problem involves numbers that are either too small or too large

- The student needs to understand the problem better

- The computations are too complex

- The problem involves a diagram or a large array

Example: There are 20 people at a party. If each person shakes hands with every other person, how many handshakes will there be?
We could take the long approach by determining that the first person shakes hands with 19 other people, the second person has 18 other people with whom to shake hands, the third person has 17 other people with whom to shake hands, etc., and then adding all of these numbers together.

A simpler approach would be to break the problem down into a smaller problem—such as 4 people at a party. We determine that the first person would shake hands with 3 other people, the second would shake hands with 2 other people, and the third person would shake hands with 1 other person. We can represent this as

$$(4 - 1) + (4 - 2) + (4 - 3) = 3 + 2 + 1 = 6$$

or

$$(n - 1) + (n - 2) + (n - 3) = 3n - 6 = 6$$

where n = the total number of people at the party. If we set the answer equal to x, we can solve for x as follows:

$$(n - 1)n - x = x$$
$$(20 - 1)(20) = 2x$$
$$(19)(20) = 2x$$
$$380 = 2x$$
$$190 = x$$

Sample Test Questions and Rationale

(Easy)

1. $\left(\frac{-4}{9}\right) + \left(\frac{-7}{10}\right) =$

   A. $\frac{23}{90}$

   B. $\frac{-23}{90}$

   C. $\frac{103}{90}$

   D. $\frac{-103}{90}$

Answer: D.

Find the LCD of $\frac{-4}{9}$ and $\frac{-7}{10}$. The LCD is 90, so you get $\frac{-40}{90} + \frac{63}{90} = \frac{-103}{90}$, which is answer D.

Sample Test Questions and Rationale (cont.)

(Average)

2. $(5.6) \times (-0.11) =$

   A. -0.616

   B. 0.616

   C. -6.110

   D. 6.110

Answer: A. -0.616

This is simple multiplication. The answer will be negative because a positive times a negative is a negative number. $5.6 \times -0.11 = -0.616$, which is answer A.

SKILL 13.2 Demonstrating knowledge of strategies for investigating, developing, and evaluating mathematical arguments

Write Simple Proofs in Two-Column Form

In a two-column proof, the left side should consist of the given information, or statements that could be proven by deductive reasoning. The right column should consist of the methods used to determine that each statement to the left is verifiably true. The right side can identify given information or state theorems, postulates, definitions, or algebraic properties used to prove that each particular line of the proof is true.

Write Indirect Proofs

Assume the opposite of the conclusion. Keep the hypothesis and the given information the same. Proceed to develop the steps of the proof, looking for a statement that contradicts the original assumption or some other known fact. This contradiction indicates that the assumption made at the beginning of the proof was incorrect; therefore, the original conclusion has to be true.

Classify Conclusions as Examples of Inductive or Deductive Thinking

INDUCTIVE THINKING: the process of finding a pattern from a group of examples

INDUCTIVE THINKING is the process of finding a pattern from a group of examples. That pattern is the conclusion that this set of examples seemed to indicate. It may be a correct conclusion, or it may be an incorrect conclusion because other examples may not follow the predicted pattern.

DEDUCTIVE THINKING is the process of arriving at a conclusion on the basis of other statements that are all known to be true, such as theorems, axioms, or postulates. Conclusions found by deductive thinking based on true statements will always be true.

Examples:

Suppose:

On Monday Mr. Peterson eats breakfast at McDonald's.
On Tuesday Mr. Peterson eats breakfast at McDonald's.
On Wednesday Mr. Peterson eats breakfast at McDonald's.
On Thursday Mr. Peterson eats breakfast at McDonald's.

Conclusion:

On Friday Mr. Peterson will eat breakfast at McDonald's again.

This is a conclusion based on inductive reasoning. On the basis of several days' observations, it can be concluded that Mr. Peterson will eat at McDonald's the next day as well. This may or may not be true, but it is a conclusion developed by inductive thinking.

Make Conditional Statements

CONDITIONAL STATEMENTS are frequently written in **"if-then"** form. The "if" clause of the conditional is known as the hypothesis, and the "then" clause is called the conclusion. In a proof, the hypothesis is the information that is assumed to be true, while the conclusion is what is to be proven true. A conditional is considered to be of the form:

If p, then q

p is the hypothesis. q is the conclusion.

Conditional statements can be diagrammed using a Venn diagram. A diagram can be drawn with one figure inside another figure. The inner portion represents the hypothesis. The outer portion represents the conclusion. If the hypothesis is taken to be true, then you are located inside the inner circle. If you are located in the inner circle then you are also inside the outer circle, so that proves the conclusion is true.

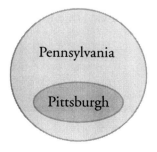

> **DEDUCTIVE THINKING:** the process of arriving at a conclusion on the basis of other statements that are all known to be true, such as theorems, axioms, or postulates

> **CONDITIONAL STATEMENTS:** frequently written in "if-then" form

Example: If an angle has a measure of 90°, then it is a right angle.
In this statement "an angle has a measure of 90°" is the hypothesis.
In this statement "it is a right angle" is the conclusion.

Example: If you are in Pittsburgh, then you are in Pennsylvania.
In this statement "you are in Pittsburgh" is the hypothesis.
In this statement "you are in Pennsylvania" is the conclusion.

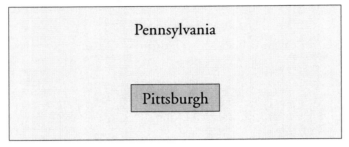

Conditional: If p, then q
    p is the hypothesis. q is the conclusion.

Inverse: If ~ p, then ~ q.
    Negate both the hypothesis (If not p, then not q) and the conclusion from the
    original conditional.

Converse: If q, then p.
    Reverse the two clauses.
    The original hypothesis becomes the conclusion.
    The original conclusion then becomes the new hypothesis.

Contrapositive: If ~ q, then ~ p.
    Reverse the two clauses. The "If not q, then not p" original hypothesis
    becomes the conclusion.
    The original conclusion then becomes the new hypothesis.
    THEN negate both the new hypothesis and the new conclusion.

Example: Given the conditional: If an angle has 60°, then it is an acute angle.
Its **inverse**, in the form "If ~ p, then ~ q," would be:
    If an angle doesn't have 60°, then it is not an acute angle.
    **Notice that the inverse is not true, even though the conditional statement
    was true.**

Its **converse**, in the form "If q, then p," would be:
    If an angle is an acute angle, then it has 60°.
    **Notice that the converse is not true, even though the conditional statement
    was true.**

Its **contrapositive**, in the form "If ~ q, then ~ p," would be:

If an angle isn't an acute angle, then it doesn't have 60°.

Notice that the contrapositive is true, assuming original conditional statement was true.

Find the inverse, converse, and contrapositive of the following conditional statement. Also determine if each of the four statements is true or false.

Conditional: If $x = 5$, then $x^2 - 25 = 0$. TRUE

Inverse: If $x \neq 5$, then $x^2 - 25 \neq 0$. FALSE, x could be -5

Converse: If $x^2 - 25 = 0$, then $x = 5$. FALSE, x could be -5

Contrapositive: If $x^2 - 25 \neq 0$, then $x \neq 5$. TRUE

Conditional: If $x = 5$, then $6x = 30$. TRUE

Inverse: If $x \neq 5$, then $6x \neq 30$. TRUE

Converse: If $6x = 30$, then $x = 5$. TRUE

Contrapositive: If $6x \neq 30$, then $x \neq 5$. TRUE

Sometimes, as in this example, all four statements can be logically equivalent; however, the only statement that will always be logically equivalent to the original conditional is the contrapositive.

The use of Venn diagrams (explained above) can help you visualize this process. Suppose that the following statements were given to you, and you were asked to try to reach a conclusion.

All swimmers are athletes.

All athletes are scholars.

In "if-then" form, these would be:

If you are a swimmer, then you are an athlete.

If you are an athlete, then you are a scholar.

Clearly, if you are a swimmer, then you are also an athlete. This includes you in the group of scholars.

Suppose that these statements were given to you, and you are asked to try to reach a conclusion. The statements are:

All swimmers are athletes.

All wrestlers are athletes.

In "if-then" form, these would be:

If you are a swimmer, then you are an athlete.

If you are a wrestler, then you are an athlete.

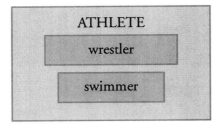

Clearly, if you are a swimmer or a wrestler, then you are also an athlete. This does NOT allow you to come to any other conclusions.

A swimmer may or may NOT also be a wrestler. Therefore, NO CONCLUSION IS POSSIBLE.

Suppose that these statements were given to you, and you are asked to try to reach a conclusion. The statements are:

All rectangles are parallelograms.

Quadrilateral ABCD is not a parallelogram.

In "if-then" form, the first statement would be:

If a figure is a rectangle, then it is also a parallelogram.

Note that the second statement is the negation of the conclusion of statement one. Remember also that the contrapositive is logically equivalent to a given conditional. That is, "**If ~ q, then ~ p.**" Since "ABCD is NOT a parallelogram" is like saying "**If ~ q,**" then you can come to the conclusion "**then ~ p.**" Therefore, the conclusion is ABCD is not a rectangle.

Looking at the Venn diagram below, if all rectangles are parallelograms, then rectangles are included as part of the parallelograms. Since quadrilateral ABCD is not a parallelogram, that it is excluded from anywhere inside the parallelogram box. This allows you to conclude that ABCD can not be a rectangle either.

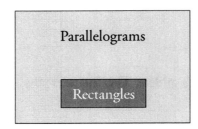

A **COUNTEREXAMPLE** is an exception to a proposed rule or conjecture that disproves the conjecture. For example, the existence of a single nonbrown dog disproves the conjecture "all dogs are brown." Thus, any nonbrown dog is a counterexample.

In searching for mathematic counterexamples, one should consider extreme cases near the ends of the domain of an experiment as well as special cases where an additional property is introduced. Examples of extreme cases are numbers near zero and obtuse triangles that are nearly flat. A square is an example of a special case for a problem involving rectangles, because a square is a rectangle with the additional property of symmetry.

Example: Identify a counterexample for the following conjectures.

If n is an even number, then $n + 1$ is divisible by 3.

$n = 4$

$n + 1 = 4 + 1 = 5$

5 is not divisible by 3.

If n is divisible by 3, then $n^2 - 1$ is divisible by 4.

$n = 6$

$n^2 - 1 = 6^2 - 1 = 35$

35 is not divisible by 4.

The **QUESTIONING TECHNIQUE** is a mathematic process in which students devise questions to clarify the problem, eliminate possible solutions, and simplify the problem-solving process. By developing and attempting to answer simple questions, students can tackle difficult and complex problems.

Sometimes, the discourse may be teacher-guided though a process in which the teacher asks questions to generate dialogue and lead discussions. Other times, the students might be encouraged to generate their own inquiry discussions by sharing their questions and thoughts among themselves. A third type of discourse can take place in small groups, where the students work both independently and collaboratively.

Teachers might ask the following types of questions to encourage higher-order thinking:

- Questions that require manipulation of prior knowledge

- Questions that ask students to state ideas or definitions in their own words

- Questions that require students to solve a problem

- Questions that require observations and/or descriptions of an object or event

- Questions that call for comparison and contrast

COUNTEREXAMPLE: an exception to a proposed rule or conjecture that disproves the conjecture

QUESTIONING TECHNIQUE: a mathematic process in which students devise questions to clarify the problem, eliminate possible solutions, and simplify the problem-solving process

It is also recommended that teachers give students enough time to attempt to answer the question before calling on another student. When a student is having trouble responding to a question, a teacher should ask probing questions such as:

- Asking for clarification
- Rephrasing the question
- Asking related questions
- Restating the student's ideas

(Ornstein, 1995)

Sample Test Questions and Rationale

(Average)

1. An item that sells for $375 is put on sale at $120. What is the percent of decrease?

   A. 25%

   B. 28%

   C. 68%

   D. 34%

   Answer: C. 68%

   Use $(1 - x)$ as the discount. $375i. = 120$.

   $375(1 - x) = 120 \rightarrow 375 - 375x = 120 \rightarrow$ $375x = 255 = \rightarrow x = 0.68 = 68\%$, which is answer C.

(Average)

2. Two mathematics classes have a total of 410 students. The 8:00 am class has 40 more than the 10:00 am class. How many students are in the 10:00 am class?

   A. 123.3

   B. 370

   C. 185

   D. 330

   Answer: C. 185

   Let x = # of students in the 8 am class and $x - 40$ = # of students in the 10 am class. So there are 225 students in the 8 am class, and $225 - 40 = 185$ in the 10 am class, which is answer C.

SKILL Demonstrating knowledge of how the language and vocabulary of 13.3 mathematics are used to communicate ideas precisely

Mathematical concepts and procedures can take many different forms. Students of mathematics must be able to recognize different forms of equivalent concepts.

For example, the slope of a line can be represented graphically, algebraically, verbally, and numerically. A line drawn on a coordinate plane will show the slope. In the equation of a line, $y = mx + b$, the term m represents the slope. The slope of a line can be defined in several different ways; it is the change in the value of y divided by the change in the value of x over a given interval. Alternatively, the slope of a line is the ratio of "rise" to "run" between two points. The numerical value of the slope can be calculated by using the verbal definitions and the algebraic representation of the line.

In order to understand mathematics and to solve problems, it is important to know the definitions of basic mathematic terms and concepts. Additionally, one must use the language of mathematics correctly and precisely to communicate concepts and ideas.

For example, the statement "minus 10 times minus 5 equals plus 50" is incorrect because "minus" and "plus" are arithmetic operations, not numerical modifiers. The statement should read "negative 10 times negative 5 equals positive 50."

For a list of definitions and explanations of basic math terms, visit the following Web site:

http://home.blarg. net/~math/deflist.htm

Sample Test Questions and Rationale

(Easy)

1. **What measure could be used to report the distance traveled in walking around a track?**

    A. Degrees

    B. Square meters

    C. Kilometers

    D. Cubic feet

    Answer: C. Kilometers

    Degrees measure angles, square meters measure area, cubic feet measure volume, and kilometers measure length. Kilometers is the only reasonable answer.

(Rigorous)

2. **What is the area of a square whose side is 13 feet?**

    A. 169 feet

    B. 169 square feet

    C. 52 feet

    D. 52 square feet

    Answer: B. 169 square feet

    Area = length times width (lw)
    Length = 13 feet

    Width = 13 feet (square, so length and width are the same)

    Area = 13 × 13 = 169 square feet

    Area is measured in square feet. The answer is B.

Demonstrating knowledge of the variety of materials, models, and methods used to explore mathematical concepts and solve problems

Manipulatives

MANIPULATIVES:
objects a student can use
to reinforce a lesson

MANIPULATIVES can foster learning for all students. The subject of mathematics needs to be derived from something that is real to the learner. If the learner can "touch" it, he or she will better understand and remember it. Students can use fingers, ice cream sticks, tiles, and paper folding (as well as commercially available manipulatives) to visualize operations and concepts. The teacher needs to solidify concrete examples into abstract mathematics.

Example: Using tiles to demonstrate both geometric ideas and number theory.
Give each group of students 12 tiles and instruct them to build rectangles. Students draw their rectangles on paper.

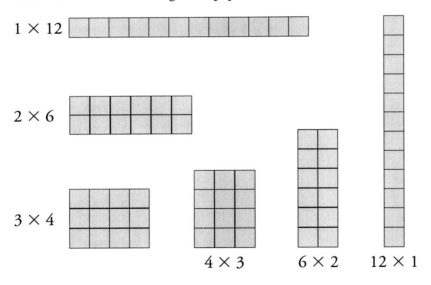

Encourage students to describe their reactions. Extend to 16 tiles. Ask students to form additional problems.

Models

MODELS: a small object,
usually built to scale,
that represents in detail
another, often larger object

MODELS are another means of representing mathematical concepts by relating them to real-world situations. Teachers must choose wisely when devising and selecting models, because to be effective, models must be applied properly. For example, a building with floors above and below ground is a good model for introducing the concept of negative numbers. It would be difficult, however, to use the building model in teaching subtraction of negative numbers.

When introducing a new mathematical concept to students, teachers should utilize the concrete-to-representational-to-abstract sequence of instruction. The first step of this instructional progression is the introduction of a concept modeled with concrete materials. The second step is the translation of concrete models into representational diagrams or pictures. The third and final step is the translation of representational models into abstract models using only numbers and symbols.

The second step in the learning process allows for a deeper understanding of the first step. For example, students may use tally marks or pictures to represent the counting blocks they used in the previous stage. Once again, teachers should give students ample time to master the concept on the representational level.

The final step in the learning process is necessary for more abstract levels of thought. For example, students represent the processes carried out in the previous stages using only numbers and arithmetic symbols. To ease the transition, teachers should associate numbers and symbols with the concrete and representational models throughout the learning progression.

Sometimes, using a model is the best way to see the solution to a problem, as in the case of fraction multiplication.

> *Teachers should first use* concrete models *to introduce a mathematical concept, because concrete models are easiest to understand. For example, teachers can allow students to use counting blocks to learn basic arithmetic. Teachers should give students ample time and many opportunities to experiment, practice, and demonstrate mastery with the concrete materials.*

Example:

Model $\frac{5}{6} \times \frac{2}{3}$.

Draw a rectangle. Divide it vertically into 6 equal sections (the denominator of the first number.)

Divide the rectangle horizontally into 3 equal sections (the denominator of the second number).

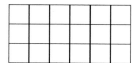

Color in a number of vertical strips equal to the numerator of the first number.

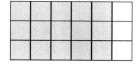

Use a different color to shade a number of horizontal strips equal to the numerator of the second number.

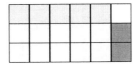

By describing the area where both colors overlap, we have the product of the two fractions. The answer is $\frac{10}{18}$.

Scales

Students need to understand that ratios and proportions are used to create scale models of real-life objects. They also must understand the principles of ratio and proportion, as well as how to calculate scale using ratio and proportion.

Scaled drawings (maps, blueprints, and models) are used in many real-world situations. Architects make blueprints and models of buildings. These drawings and models are then used by contractors to build the buildings. Engineers make scaled drawings of bridges, machine parts, roads, airplanes, and many other things. Maps of the world, countries, states, and roads are scaled drawings too. Landscape designers use scaled drawings and models of plants, decks, and other structures to show how they should be placed around a building. Models of cars, boats, and planes made from kits are scaled. Automobile engineers construct models of cars before the actual assembly is done. Many museum exhibits are actually scaled models, because the items themselves are too large to be displayed.

Examples of real-world problems that students might solve using scaled drawings include:

- Reading road maps and determining the distance between locations by using the map scale

- Creating a scaled drawing (floor plan) of the classroom to determine the best use of space

- Creating an 8.5-by-11-inch representation of a quilt to be pieced together

- Drawing blueprints of their rooms and creating models from them

Diagrams

Drawing pictures or diagrams can also help to make relationships in a problem clearer.

Example: In a women's marathon, the first five finishers (in no particular order) were Frieda, Polly, Christa, Betty, and Dora. Frieda finished 7 seconds before Christa. Polly finished 6 seconds after Betty. Dora finished 8 seconds after Betty. Christa finished 2 seconds before Polly. In what order did the women finish the race?

Drawing a picture or diagram will help to illustrate the answer more easily.

From the diagram, we can see that the women finished in the following order: 1st – Frieda, 2nd – Betty, 3rd – Christa, 4th – Polly, and 5th – Dora.

Technology

Finally, there are many forms of technology available to math teachers. For example, students can test their understanding of math concepts by working on skill-specific computer programs and Web sites. Graphing calculators can help students to visualize the graphs of functions. Teachers can also enhance their lectures and classroom teaching by creating multimedia presentations.

Sample Test Question and Rationale

(Easy)

1. **What is the greatest common factor of 16, 28, and 36?**

   A. 2

   B. 4

   C. 8

   D. 16

Answer: B. 4

The smallest number in this set is 16; its factors are 1, 2, 4, 8, and 16. 16 is the largest factor, but it does not divide into 28 or 36. Neither does 8. 4 does factor into both 28 and 36. The answer is B.

SKILL 13.5 Demonstrating knowledge of the interconnections among mathematical concepts

Recognition and understanding of the relationships between concepts and topics are of great value in mathematical problem solving, as well as in the explanation of more complex processes.

VARIABLE ADDITION: explains the concept of multiplication, which is simply repeated addition

COEFFICIENT ADDITION: the addition of variables

For instance, multiplication is simply repeated addition. This relationship explains the concept of VARIABLE ADDITION. We can show that the expression $4x + 3x = 7x$ is true by rewriting 4 times x and 3 times x as repeated addition, which yields the expression $(x + x + x + x) + (x + x + x)$. Thus, because of the relationship between multiplication and addition, the addition of variables is accomplished by COEFFICIENT ADDITION.

In this same way, division and multiplication are also linked. Many students find multiplication much easier to understand than division. Teaching them that these operations are two sides of the same concept may make all the difference.

For example, knowing that $6 \times 8 = 48$ off the top one's head makes understanding $48 \div 6 = 8$ even easier. This is why multiplication charts have always held a place in many elementary education classrooms.

Different students may react differently to this type of mathematical breakdown. Some may find that explaining multiplication (or any other complex mathematical concept) in terms of an already mastered concept—in this case, addition—will help to strengthen their ability to understand and even enjoy mathematics. However, others may have trouble understanding the basis behind the correlation—either because they don't grasp the connection or because they have moved beyond it.

Although this may make teaching mathematical relationships more difficult for the teacher, it is important to recognize that mathematical concepts and procedures can take many different forms. Students of mathematics must be able to recognize different forms of equivalent concepts. These basic skill sets will pave the way for a higher level of understanding as the level of difficulty in mathematical concepts increases.

Sample Test Question and Rationale

(Average)

1. If $4x - (3 - x) = 7(x - 3) + 10$, then:

   A. $x = 8$

   B. $x = -8$

   C. $x = 4$

   D. $x = -4$

Answer: C. $x = 4$

Solve for x.

$$4x - (3 - x) = 7(x - 3) + 10$$
$$4x - 3 + x = 7x - 21 + 10$$
$$5x - 3 = 7x - 11$$
$$5x = 7x - 11 + 3$$
$$5x - 7x = -8$$
$$-2x = -8$$
$$x = 4$$

SKILL 13.6 Recognizing applications of mathematics in other content areas and in everyday life

Teachers can increase interest in math and promote learning and understanding by relating mathematical concepts to the lives of students. Instead of using only abstract presentations and examples, teachers should relate concepts to real-world situations. This shifts the emphasis from memorization and abstract application to understanding and applied problem solving. In addition, relating math to careers and professions helps to illustrate the relevance of math; it may even aid in the career exploration process.

For example, when teaching a unit on the geometry of certain shapes, teachers can ask students to design a structure of interest using the shapes in question. This exercise serves the dual purpose of teaching students to learn and apply the properties (e.g., area, volume) of shapes, while demonstrating the relevance of geometry to architectural and engineering professions.

Artists, musicians, scientists, social scientists, and people in business use mathematical modeling to solve problems in their disciplines. These disciplines rely on the tools and symbols of mathematics to model natural events and manipulate data.

Mathematics is a key aspect of visual art. Artists use the geometric properties of shapes, ratios, and proportions in creating paintings and sculptures. For example, mathematics is essential to the concept of perspective. Artists must determine the appropriate lengths and heights of objects to portray three-dimensional distance in two dimensions.

Mathematics is also an important part of music. Many musical terms have mathematical connections. For example, the musical octave contains twelve notes and spans a factor of two in frequency. In other words, the frequency (the speed of vibration that determines tone and sound quality) doubles from the first note in an octave to the last. Thus, starting from any note, we can determine the frequency of any other note with the following formula:

$$\text{Freq} = \text{note} \times 2^{N/12}$$

In this equation, N is the number of notes from the starting point, and note is the frequency of the starting note. Mathematical understanding of frequency plays an important role in tuning musical instruments.

In addition to the visual and auditory arts, mathematics is an integral part of most scientific disciplines. Physical scientists use vectors, functions, derivatives, and integrals to describe and model the movement of objects. Biologists and ecologists use mathematics to model ecosystems and study DNA. Chemists use mathematics

> Teachers can increase interest in math and promote learning and understanding by relating mathematical concepts to the lives of students. Instead of using only abstract presentations and examples, teachers should relate concepts to real-world situations

to study the interaction of molecules and to determine the proper amounts and proportions of reactants in chemical reactions. Indeed, the uses of mathematics in science are almost endless.

Many social science disciplines use mathematics to model and solve problems as well. Economists, for example, use functions, graphs, and matrices to model the activities of producers, consumers, and firms.

Sample Test Question and Rationale

(Average)

1. Given the formula $d = rt$, (where d = distance, r = rate, and t = time), calculate the time required for a vehicle to travel 585 miles at a rate of 65 miles per hour.

    A. 8.5 hours

    B. 6.5 hours

    C. 9.5 hours

    D. 9 hours

Answer: D. 9 hours

We are given $d = 585$ miles and $r = 65$ miles per hour and $d = rt$. Solve for t. $585 = 65t \rightarrow t = 9$ hours, hours, which is answer D.

COMPETENCY 14
UNDERSTAND CONCEPTS AND SKILLS RELATED TO NUMBERS AND MATHEMATICAL OPERATIONS

SKILL 14.1 Applying concepts of quantities, numbers, and numeration to compare, order, estimate, and round

INTEGERS: the positive and negative whole numbers and zero

Rational numbers can be expressed as the ratio of two integers, $\frac{a}{b}$, where $b \neq 0$, for example, $\frac{2}{3}, \frac{4}{5}, 5 = \frac{5}{1}$ are all rational numbers.

Rational numbers include integers, fractions, mixed numbers, and terminating and repeating decimals. Every rational number can be expressed as a repeating or terminating decimal and can be shown on a number line.

INTEGERS are the positive and negative whole numbers and zero.

...-6, -5, -4, -3, -2, -1, 0, 1, 2, 3, 4, 5, 6,...

WHOLE NUMBERS are the natural numbers and zero.

0, 1, 2, 3, 4, 5, 6...

NATURAL NUMBERS are the counting numbers.

1, 2, 3, 4, 5, 6...

IRRATIONAL NUMBERS are real numbers that cannot be written as the ratio of two integers. They are infinite, non-repeating decimals.

$\sqrt{5} = 2.2360$, pi $= \pi = 3.1415927...$

A FRACTION is an expression of numbers in the form of $\frac{x}{y}$, where x is the numerator and y is the denominator, which cannot be zero.

$\frac{3}{7}$ 3 is the numerator; 7 is the denominator

If the fraction has common factors for the numerator and denominator, divide both by the common factor to reduce the fraction to its lowest form.

$\frac{13}{39} = \frac{1 \times 13}{3 \times 13} = \frac{1}{3}$ Divide by the common factor 13.

A MIXED NUMBER has an integer part and a fractional part.

$2\frac{1}{4}$, $-5\frac{1}{6}$, $7\frac{1}{3}$

PERCENT = per 100 (written with the symbol %)

$10\% = \frac{10}{100} = \frac{1}{10}$

DECIMALS = deci = part of ten

To find the decimal equivalent of a fraction, use the denominator to divide the numerator, as shown in the following example.

Find the decimal equivalent of $\frac{7}{10}$.

Since 10 cannot divide into 7 evenly, $\frac{7}{10} = 0.7$

The EXPONENT FORM is a shortcut method to write repeated multiplication. The basic form is b^n, where b is called the BASE and n is the EXPONENT. Both b and n are both real numbers. The b^n implies that the base b is multiplied by itself n times.

Examples:

$3^4 = 3 \times 3 \times 3 \times 3 = 81$

$2^3 = 2 \times 2 \times 2 = 8$

$(-2)^4 = (-2) \times (-2) \times (-2) \times (-2) = 16$

$-2^4 = -(2 \times 2 \times 2 \times 2) = 8$

WHOLE NUMBERS: the natural numbers and zero

NATURAL NUMBERS: the counting numbers

IRRATIONAL NUMBERS: real numbers that cannot be written as the ratio of two integers

FRACTION: an expression of numbers in the form of $\frac{x}{y}$, where x is the numerator and y is the denominator

MIXED NUMBER: has an integer part and a fractional part

PERCENT: means "per 100;" ten percent is10 parts out of 100

DECIMAL: a number written with a whole-number part, a decimal point, and a decimal part

EXPONENT FORM: a shorthand way of writing repeated multiplication

BASE: the number to be multiplied as many times as indicated by the exponent

EXPONET: tells how many times the base is multiplied by itself

Caution: The exponent does not affect the sign unless the negative sign is inside the parentheses and the exponent is outside the parentheses.

$(-2)^4$ implies that -2 is multiplied by itself 4 times.

-2^4 implies that 2 is multiplied by itself 4 times, and then the answer becomes. negative.

KEY EXPONENT RULES: FOR A NONZERO AND *m* AND *n* REAL NUMBERS:	
Product Rule	$a^m \times a^n = a^{(m+n)}$
Quotient Rule	$\dfrac{a^m}{a^n} = a^{(m-n)}$
Rule of Negative Exponents	$\dfrac{a^{-m}}{a^{-n}} = -\dfrac{a^n}{a^m}$

When 10 is raised to any power, the exponent tells the numbers of zeros in the product.

Example:
$10^7 = 10,000,000$

Scientific Notation

SCIENTIFIC NOTATION: a convenient method for writing very large and very small numbers

SCIENTIFIC NOTATION is a convenient method for writing very large and very small numbers. It employs two factors. The first factor is a number between 1 and 10. The second factor is a power of 10. This notation is considered "shorthand" for expressing very large numbers (such as the weight of 100 elephants) or very small numbers (such as the weight of an atom in pounds).

Recall that:

10^n	=	$(10)^n$ Ten multiplied by itself n times
10^n	=	$(10)^n$ Any nonzero number raised to the zero power is 1
10^1	=	10
10^2	=	$10 \times 10 = 100$
10^3	=	$10 \times 10 \times 10 = 1000$
10^{-1}	=	$\dfrac{1}{10}$ (deci)

Table continued on next page

10^{-2}	$=$	$\dfrac{1}{100}$ (centi)
10^{-3}	$=$	$\dfrac{1}{1000}$ (milli)
10^{-6}	$=$	$\dfrac{1}{1,000,000}$ (micro)

Example: Write 46,368,000 in scientific notation.

1. Introduce a decimal point and decimal places.
   $46{,}368{,}000 = 46{,}368{,}000.0000$

2. Make a mark between the two digits that give a number between
   -9.9 and 9.9.
   $4 \wedge 6{,}368{,}000.0000$

3. Count the number of digit places between the decimal point and the $\wedge$
   mark. This number is the *nth* power of ten.
   So, $46{,}368{,}000 = 4.6368 \times 10^7$.

Example: Write 0.00397 in scientific notation.

1. Decimal place is already in place.

2. Make a mark between 3 and 9 to obtain a number between -9.9 and. 9.9.

3. Move decimal place to the mark (three hops).
   $0.003 \wedge 97$
   Motion is to the right, so *n* on 10^n is negative.
   Therefore, $0.00397 = 3.97 \times 10^{-3}$.

ROUNDING NUMBERS is a form of estimation that is very useful in many mathematical operations. For example, when estimating the sum of two three-digit numbers, it is helpful to round the two numbers to the nearest hundred prior to addition. We can round numbers to any place value.

> **ROUNDING NUMBERS:**
> a form of estimation that
> is very useful in many
> mathematical operations

Rounding Whole Numbers

To round whole numbers, first find the place value you want to round to (the rounding digit). Look at the digit directly to the right. If the digit is less than 5, do not change the rounding digit and replace all numbers after the rounding digit with zeros. If the digit is greater than or equal to 5, increase the rounding digit by 1, and replace all numbers after the rounding digit with zeros.

Example: Round 517 to the nearest ten.
1 is the rounding digit because it occupies the tens place. 517 rounded to the nearest ten = 520; because 7 > 5, we add 1 to the rounding digit.

Example: Round 15,449 to the nearest hundred.
The first 4 is the rounding digit because it occupies the hundreds place. 15,449 rounded to the nearest hundred = 15,400; because 4 < 5, we do not add to the rounding digit.

Rounding Decimals

Rounding decimals is identical to rounding whole numbers except that you simply drop all the digits to the right of the rounding digit.

Example: Round 417.3621 to the nearest tenth.
3 is the rounding digit because it occupies the tenths place. 417.3621 rounded to the nearest tenth = 417.4; because 6 > 5, we add 1 to the rounding digit.

Sample Test Questions and Rationale

(Rigorous)

1. The following chart shows the yearly average number of international tourists visiting Palm Beach for 1990-1994. How many more international tourists visited Palm Beach in 1994 than in 1991?

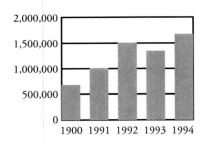

A. 100,000

B. 600,000

C. 1,600,000

D. 8,000,000

Answer: B. 600,000

The number of tourists in 1991 was 1,000,000 and the number in 1994 was 1,600,000. Subtract to get a difference of 600,000, which is answer B.

Sample Test Questions and Rationale (cont.)

(Rigorous)

2. What is the probability of drawing 2 consecutive aces from a standard deck of cards?

   A. $\frac{3}{51}$

   B. $\frac{1}{221}$

   C. $\frac{2}{104}$

   D. $\frac{2}{52}$

Answer: B

There are 4 aces in the 52 card deck.

$P(\text{first ace}) = \frac{4}{52}$

$P(\text{second ace}) = \frac{3}{51}$

$P(\text{first ace and second ace}) = P(\text{one ace}) \times P(\text{second ace}|\text{first ace})$

$= \frac{4}{52} \times \frac{3}{51} = \frac{1}{221}$. This is answer B.

(Rigorous)

3. Which of the following is an irrational number?

   A. .362626262...

   B. 4

   C. $\sqrt{5}$

   D. $-\sqrt{16}$

Answer: C

Irrational numbers are real numbers that cannot be written as the ratio of two integers, such as infinite non-repeating decimals. $\sqrt{5}$ fits this description; the others do not.

SKILL 14.2 Demonstrating knowledge of the concepts of place value, prime numbers, multiples, and factors

Whole-Number Place Value

Consider the number 792. We can assign a place value to each digit.

Reading from left to right, the first digit (7) represents the hundreds place. The hundreds place tells us how many sets of 100 the number contains. Thus, there are seven sets of 100 in the number 792.

The second digit (9) represents the tens place. The tens place tells us how many sets of 10 the number contains. Thus, there are nine sets of 10 in the number 792.

The last digit (2) represents the ones place. The ones place tells us how many 1s the number contains. Thus, there are two sets of 1 in the number 792.

Therefore, there are seven sets of 100, plus nine sets of 10, plus two 1s in the number 792.

Decimal Place Value

More complex numbers have additional place values to both the left and right of the decimal point. Consider the number 374.8.

Reading from left to right, the first digit (3) is in the hundreds place and tells us the number contains three sets of 100.

The second digit (7) is in the tens place and tells us the number contains seven sets of 10.

The third digit, 4, is in the ones place and tells us the number contains four 1s.

Finally, the number after the decimal (8) is in the tenths place and tells us the number contains eight tenths.

Place Value for Older Students

Each digit to the left of the decimal point increases progressively in powers of 10. Each digit to the right of the decimal point decreases progressively in powers of 10.

Example: 12345.6789 occupies the following power-of-10 positions:

10^4	10^3	10^2	10^1	10^0	0	10^{-1}	10^{-2}	10^{-3}	10^{-4}
1	2	3	4	5	×	6	7	8	9

NAMES OF POWER-OF-10 POSITIONS			
10^0	=	ones (note that any nonzero base raised to the power zero is 1)	
10^1	=	tens	(number 1 and 1 zero or 10)
10^2	=	hundreds	(number 1 and 2 zeros or 100)
10^3	=	thousands	(number 1 and 3 zeros or 1000)
10^4	=	ten thousands	(number 1 and 4 zeros, or 10000)
10^{-1}	=	$\frac{1}{10^1} = \frac{1}{10} = $ tenths	(1st digit after decimal point, or 0.1)
$10^{-3}2$	=	$\frac{1}{10^2} = \frac{1}{100} = $ hundredths	(2nd digit after decimal point, or 0.01)

Table continued on next page

| 10^{-3} | $=$ | $\frac{1}{10^3} = \frac{1}{1000}$ = thousandths | (3rd digit after decimal point, or 0.001) |
| 10^{-4} | $=$ | $\frac{1}{10^4} = \frac{1}{10000}$ = ten thousandths | (4th digit after decimal point, or 0.0001) |

Example: Write 73169.00537 in expanded form.

We start by listing all the power-of-10 positions.

10^4	10^3	10^2	10^1	10^0	$\times$	10^{-1}	10^{-2}	10^{-3}	10^{-4}	10^{-5}

Multiply each digit by its power of 10. Add all the results.

Thus $73169.00537 = (7 \times 10^4) + (3 \times 10^3) + (1 \times 10^2) + (6 \times 10^1)$
$+ (9 \times 10^0) + (0 \times 10^{-1}) + (0 \times 10^{-2}) + (5 \times 10^{-3})$
$+ (3 \times 10^{-4}) + (7 \times 10^{-5})$

Example: Determine the place value associated with the underlined digit in 3.1695.

10^0	$\times$	10^{-1}	10^{-2}	10^{-3}	10^{-4}
3	$\times$	1	6	9	5

The place value for the digit 9 is 10^{-3} or $\frac{1}{1000}$.

Example: Find the number that is represented by $(7 \times 10^3) + (5 \times 10^0) + (3 \times 10^{-3})$.

$= 7000 + 5 + 0.003$
$= 7005.003$

Example: Write 21×10^3 in standard form.

$= 21 \times 1000 = 21,000$

Example: Write 739×10^{-4} in standard form.

$= 739 \times \frac{1}{1000} = \frac{739}{10000} = 0.0739$

Greatest Common Factor

GCF is the abbreviation for GREATEST COMMON FACTOR. The GCF is the largest number that is a factor of all the numbers given in a problem. The GCF can be no larger than the smallest number given in the problem. If no other number is a common factor, then the GCF will be the number 1.

> **GREATEST COMMON FACTOR:** the largest number that is a factor of all the numbers in a problem

To find the GCF, list all possible factors of the smallest number (include the number itself). Starting with the largest factor (which is the number itself), determine if that factor is also a factor of all the other given numbers. If so, that factor is the GCF. If that factor doesn't divide evenly into the other given numbers, try the same method on the next smaller factor. Continue until a common factor is found. That factor is the GCF.

Note: There can be other common factors besides the GCF.

Example: Find the GCF of 12, 20, and 36.
The smallest number in the problem is 12. The factors of 12 are 1, 2, 3, 4, 6 and 12. 12 is the largest of these factors, but it does not divide evenly into 20. Neither does 6. However, 4 will divide into both 20 and 36 evenly.

Therefore, 4 is the GCF.

Example: Find the GCF of 14 and 15.
The factors of 14 are 1, 2, 7 and 14. 14 is the largest factor, but it does not divide evenly into 15. Neither does 7 or 2. Therefore, the only factor common to both 14 and 15 is the number 1, the GCF.

Least Common Multiple

LCM is the abbreviation for LEAST COMMON MULTIPLE. The least common multiple of a group of numbers is the smallest number that all of the given numbers will divide into. The LCM will always be the largest of the given numbers or a multiple of the largest number.

LEAST COMMON MULTIPLE: the smallest number of a group of numbers that all the given numbers will divide into evenly

Example: Find the LCM of 20, 30, and 40.
The largest number given is 40, but 30 will not divide evenly into 40. The next multiple of 40 is 80 (2 × 40), but 30 will not divide evenly into 80 either. The next multiple of 40 is 120. 120 is divisible by both 20 and 30, so 120 is the LCM.

Example: Find the LCM of 96, 16, and 24.
The largest number is 96. 96 is divisible by both 16 and 24, so 96 is the LCM.

Example: Elly Mae can feed the animals in 15 minutes. Jethro can feed them in 10 minutes. How long will it take them to feed the animals if they work together?

If Elly Mae can feed the animals in 15 minutes, then she could feed $\frac{1}{15}$ of them in 1 minute, $\frac{2}{15}$ of them in 2 minutes, and $\frac{x}{15}$ of them in x minutes. In the same fashion, Jethro could feed $\frac{x}{10}$ of them in x minutes. Together they complete 1 job.

The equation is:

$$\frac{x}{15} + \frac{x}{10} = 1$$

Multiply each term by the LCD (least common denominator) of 30:

$$2x \times 3x = 30$$
$$x = 6 \text{ minutes}$$

Factors

COMPOSITE NUMBERS are whole numbers that have more than two different factors. For example, 9 is composite because, besides the factors of 1 and 9, 3 is also a factor. 70 is composite because, besides the factors of 1 and 70, the numbers 2, 5, 7, 10, 14, and 35 are also all factors.

PRIME NUMBERS are whole numbers greater than 1 that have only two factors: 1 and the number itself. Examples of prime numbers are 2, 3, 5, 7, 11, 13, 17, and 19. Note that 2 is the only even prime number. When factoring into prime factors, all the factors must be numbers that cannot be factored again (without using 1). Initially, numbers can be factored into any two factors. Check each resulting factor to see whether it can be factored again. Continue factoring until all remaining factors are prime. This is the list of prime factors. Regardless of what way the original number was factored, the final list of prime factors will always be the same.

Remember that the number 1 is neither prime nor composite.

> **COMPOSITE NUMBERS:**
> whole numbers that have more than two different factors

> **PRIME NUMBERS:**
> whole numbers greater than 1 that have only two factors: 1 and the number itself

Example:

Factor 30 into prime factors.
Factor 30 into any two factors.

5×6	Now factor the 6.
$5 \times 2 \times 3$	These are all prime factors.

Factor 30 into any two factors.

3×10	Now factor the 10.
$3 \times 2 \times 5$	These are the same prime factors, even though the original factors were different.

Example:

Factor 240 into prime factors.
Factor 240 into any two factors.

24×10	Now factor both 24 and 10.
$4 \times 6 \times 2 \times 5$	Now factor both 4 and 6.
$2 \times 2 \times 2 \times 3 \times 2 \times 5$	These are the prime factors.

This can also be written as $2^4 \times 3 \times 5$.

Sample Test Questions and Rationale

(Average)

1. Corporate salaries are listed for several employees. Which would be the best measure of central tendency?

   $24,000 $24,000
   $26,000 $28,000
   $30,000 $120,000

   A. Mean

   B. Median

   C. Mode

   D. No difference

   Answer: B. Median

   The median provides the best measure of central tendency in this case, as the mode is the lowest number and the mean would be disproportionately skewed by the outlier $120,000.

(Easy)

2. Which statement is true about George's budget?

   A. George spends the greatest portion of his income on food

   B. George spends twice as much on utilities as he does on his mortgage

   C. George spends twice as much on utilities as he does on food

   D. George spends the same amount on food and utilities as he does on mortgage

   Answer: C

   George spends twice as much on utilities as he does on food.

(Rigorous)

3. Given a drawer with 5 black socks, 3 blue socks, and 2 red socks, what is the probability that you will draw two black socks in two draws in a dark room?

   A. $\frac{2}{9}$

   B. $\frac{1}{4}$

   C. $\frac{17}{18}$

   D. $\frac{1}{18}$

   Answer: A. $\frac{2}{9}$

   In this example of conditional probability, the probability of drawing a black sock on the first draw is $\frac{5}{10}$. It is implied in the problem that there is no replacement, therefore the probability of obtaining a black sock in the second draw is $\frac{4}{9}$. Multiply the two probabilities and reduce to lowest terms.

SKILL Recognizing equivalent forms of common fractions, decimal
14.3 fractions, and percentages

If we compare numbers in various forms, we see that:

The integer $400 = \frac{800}{2}$ (fraction) $= 400.0$ (decimal) $= 400\%$ (percent).

From this, you should be able to determine that fractions, decimals, and percents can be used interchangeably within problems.

- To change a percent into a decimal, move the decimal point two places to the left and drop off the percent sign.

- To change a decimal into a percent, move the decimal two places to the right and add on a percent sign.

- To change a fraction into a decimal, divide the numerator by the denominator.

- To change a decimal number into an equivalent fraction, write the decimal part of the number as the fraction's numerator. As the fraction's denominator, use the place value of the last column of the decimal. Reduce the resulting fraction as far as possible.

Example: J.C. Nickels has Hunch jeans for sale at $\frac{1}{4}$ off the usual price of $36.00. Shears and Roadster have the same jeans for sale at 30% off their regular price of $40. Find the cheaper price.

$\frac{1}{4}$ = .25 so .25(36) = $9.00 off; $36 − 9 = $27 sale price

30% = .30 so .30(40) = $12 off; $40 − 12 = $28 sale price

The price at J.C Nickels is actually $1 lower.

To convert a fraction to a decimal, as we did in the example above, simply divide the numerator (top) by the denominator (bottom). Use long division if necessary.

If a decimal has a fixed number of digits, the decimal is said to be a TERMINATING DECIMAL. To write such a decimal as a fraction, first determine what place value the digit farthest to the right has (for example: tenths, hundredths, thousandths, ten-thousandths, hundred-thousandths, etc.). Then drop the decimal point and place the string of digits over the number given by the place value.

> **TERMINATING DECIMAL:** a decimal that has a fixed number of digits

If a decimal continues forever by repeating a string of digits, the decimal is said to be a REPEATING DECIMAL. To write a repeating decimal as a fraction, follow these steps.

> **REPEATING DECIMAL:** a decimal that continues forever by repeating a string of digits

1. Let x = the repeating decimal. (ex. x = .716716716...)

2. Multiply x by the multiple of 10 that will move the decimal just to the right of the repeating block of digits. (ex. $1000x$ = 716.716716...)

3. Subtract the first equation from the second.
   (ex. $1000x − x$ = 716.716.716... − .716716...)

4. Simplify and solve this equation. The repeating block of digits will subtract out. (ex. $999x$ = 716 so $x = \frac{716}{999}$)

5. The solution will be the fraction for the repeating decimal.

Sample Test Questions and Rationale

(Rigorous)

1. Solve for x: $|2x + 3| > 4$

   A. $-\frac{7}{2} > \times > \frac{1}{2}$

   B. $-\frac{1}{2} > \times > \frac{7}{2}$

   C. $x < \frac{7}{2}$ or $x < -\frac{1}{2}$

   D. $x < -\frac{7}{2}$ or $x > \frac{1}{2}$

   Answer: D

   The quantity within the absolute value symbols must be either > 4 or < -4. Solve the two inequalities $2x + 3 > 4$ or $2x + 3 < -4$.

(Rigorous)

2. Graph the solution: $|x| + 7 < 13$

   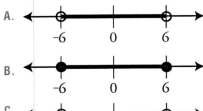

   Answer: A

   Solve by adding -7 to each side of the inequality. Since the absolute value of x is less than 6, x must be between -6 and 6. The end points are not included, so the circles on the graph are hollow.

(Average)

3. A boat travels 30 miles upstream in three hours. It makes the return trip in one and a half hours. What is the speed of the boat in still water?

   A. 10 mph

   B. 15 mph

   C. 20 mph

   D. 30 mph

   Answer: B. 15 mph

   Let x = the speed of the boat in still water and c = the speed of the current.

	RATE	TIME	DISTANCE
Upstream	$x - c$	3	30
Downstream	$x + c$	1.5	30

   Solve the system:

   $3x - 3c = 30$
   $1.5x + 1.5c = 30$

SKILL 14.4 Applying knowledge of the relationships among mathematical operations and strategies for using the basic four operations with variables and numbers

For standardization purposes, there is an accepted order in which operations are performed in any given algebraic expression. The following mnemonic is often used for the order in which operations are performed.

Please	Excuse	My	Dear	Aunt	Sally
Parentheses	Exponents	Multiply	Divide	Add	Subtract
		(Multiply or Divide, depending on which operation you encounter first, from left to right.)		(Add or Subtract, depending on which operation you encounter first, from left to right.)	

This ORDER OF OPERATIONS should be followed when evaluating algebraic expressions:

1. Simplify inside grouping characters such as parentheses, brackets, square root, fraction bar, etc.

2. Multiply out expressions with exponents

3. Do multiplication and/or division, from left to right

4. Do addition and/or subtraction, from left to right

> **ORDER OF OPERATIONS:** the order in which mathematical operations should be performed

SIMPLIFIED EXPRESSIONS WITH EXPONENTS			
$(-2)^3$	=	-8	$-2^3 = -8$
$(-2)^4$	=	16	$-2^4 = 16$ Note change of sign.
$\left(\frac{2}{3}\right)^3$	=	$\frac{8}{27}$	
5^0	=	1	
4^{-1}	=	$\frac{1}{4}$	

Sample Test Questions and Rationale

(Rigorous)

1. Given segment AC with B as its midpoint, find the coordinates of C if A = (5,7) and B = (3, 6.5).

   A. (4, 6.5)

   B. (1, 6)

   C. (2, 0.5)

   D. (16, 1)

   Answer: B. (1, 6)

(Easy)

2. 3 km is equivalent to:

   A. 300 cm

   B. 300 m

   C. 3000 cm

   D. 3000 m

   Answer: D. 3000 m

   To change kilometers to meters, move the decimal 3 places to the right.

(Easy)

3. The mass of a cookie is closest to:

   A. 0.5 kg

   B. 0.5 grams

   C. 15 grams

   D. 1.5 grams

   Answer: C. 15 grams

   Science utilizes the metric system, and the unit of grams is used when measuring mass (the amount of matter in an object). A common estimation of mass used in elementary schools is that a paperclip has a mass of approximately one gram, which eliminates choices B and D as they are very close to 1 gram. A common estimation of one kilogram is equal to one liter of water. Half of one liter of water is still much more than one cookie, eliminating choice A. Therefore, the best estimation for one cookie is narrowed to 15 grams, or choice C.

SKILL 14.5 **Demonstrating knowledge of properties of numbers and the number system** *(e.g., commutative, associative, distributive, identity, and property of zero)*

The properties of real numbers are best explained in terms of a small set of numbers. For each property, a given set will be provided.

AXIOMS OF ADDITION	
Closure	For all real numbers a and b, $a + b$ is a unique real number.
Associative	For all real numbers a, b, and c, $(a + b) + c = a + (b + c)$.
Additive Identity	There exists a unique real number 0 (zero) such that $a + 0 = 0 + a = a$ for every real number a.
Additive Inverses	For each real number a, there exists a real number $-a$ (the opposite of a) such that $a + (-a) = (-a) + a = 0$.
Commutative	For all real numbers a and b, $a + b = b + a$.
AXIOMS OF MULTIPLICATION	
Closure	For all real numbers a and b, ab is a unique real number.
Associative	For all real numbers a, b, and c, $(ab)c = a(bc)$.
Multiplicative Identity	There exists a unique nonzero real number 1 (one) such that $1 \times a = a \times 1 = a$.
Multiplicative Inverses	For each nonzero real number, there exists a real number $\frac{1}{a}$ (the reciprocal of a) such that $a(\frac{1}{a}) = (\frac{1}{a})a = 1$.
Commutative	For all real numbers a and b, $ab = ba$.

The Distributive Axiom of Multiplication over Addition

For all real numbers a, b, and c, $a(b + c) = ab + ac$.

Recognizing the Property of Denseness

The DENSENESS PROPERTY of real numbers states that if all real numbers are ordered from least to greatest on a number line, there is an infinite set of real numbers between any two given numbers on the line.

Example: Between 7.6 and 7.7, there is the rational number 7.65 in the set of real numbers.

Between 3 and 4 there exists no other natural number.

> **DENSENESS PROPERTY:** states that if all real numbers are ordered from least to greatest on a number line, there is an infinite set of real numbers between any two given numbers on the line

Applying Inverse Operations

- Subtraction is the inverse of addition, and vice versa

- Division is the inverse of multiplication, and vice versa

- Taking a square root is the inverse of squaring, and vice versa

These inverse operations are used when solving equations.

Sample Test Questions and Rationale

(Rigorous)

1. If the radius of a right circular cylinder is doubled, how does its volume change?

   A. No change

   B. Also is doubled

   C. Four times the original

   D. Pi times the original

   Answer: C. Four times the original

   If the radius of a right circular cylinder is doubled, the volume is multiplied by four because in the formula, the radius is squared. Therefore, the new volume is 2×2 or four times the original.

(Average)

2. In similar polygons, if the perimeters are in a ratio of $x : y$, the sides are in a ratio of

   A. $x : y$

   B. $x2 : y2$

   C. $2x : y$

   D. $\frac{1}{2} x : y$

   Answer: A. $x : y$

   The sides are in the same ratio.

SKILL 14.6 Performing calculations with whole numbers, decimals, and fractions

Addition of Whole Numbers

Example: At the end of a day of shopping, a shopper had $24 remaining in his wallet. He had spent $45 on various goods. How much money did the shopper have at the beginning of the day?

The total amount of money the shopper started with is the sum of the amount spent and the amount remaining at the end of the day.

$ 24
+ 45
$ 69   The original total was $69.

Example: The winner of a race needed 1 hr, 58 min, 12 sec to complete the first half of the race and 2 hr, 9 min, 57 sec to complete the second half of the race. How much time did the entire race take?

1 hr 58 min 12 sec
+ 2 hr 9 min 57 sec   Add these numbers.
3 hr 67 min 69 sec
        + 1 min − 60 sec   Change 60 sec to 1 min.
3 hr 68 min 9 sec
+ 1 hr − 60 min   Change 60 min to 1 hr.
4 hr 8 min 9 sec   Final answer.

Subtraction of Whole Numbers

Example: At the end of his shift, a cashier has $96 in the cash register. At the beginning of his shift, he had $15. How much money did the cashier collect during his shift?

The total collected is the difference between the ending amount and the starting amount.

$ 96
−15
$ 81   The total collected was $81.

Multiplication of Whole Numbers

Multiplication is one of the four basic number operations. In simple terms, multiplication is the addition of a number to itself a certain number of times. For example, 4 multiplied by 3 is equal to 4 + 4 + 4 or 3 + 3 + 3 + 3. Another way of conceptualizing multiplication is to think in terms of groups. For example, if we have 4 groups of 3 students, the total number of students is 4 multiplied by 3. We call the solution to a multiplication problem the PRODUCT.

The basic algorithm for whole number multiplication begins with aligning the numbers by place value, with the number containing more places on top.

172
× 43   Note that we placed 172 on top because it has more places than 43 does.

> **PRODUCT:** the answer to a multiplication problem

Next, we multiply the ones place of the bottom number by each place value of the top number sequentially.

```
    (2)
   172        {3 × 2 = 6, 3 × 7 = 21, 3 × 1 = 3}
 × 43         Note that we had to carry a 2 to the hundreds column
   516        because 3 × 7 = 21. Note also that we add carried numbers to
              the product.
```

Next, we multiply the number in the tens place of the bottom number by each place value of the top number sequentially. Because we are multiplying by a number in the tens place, we place a zero at the end of this product.

```
    (2)
   172
 × 43         {4 × 2 = 8, 4 × 7 = 28, 4 = 1 = 4}
   516
  6880
```

Finally, to determine the final product, we add the two partial products.

```
   172
 × 43
   516
+ 6880
  7396        The product of 172 and 43 is 7396.
```

Example: A student buys 4 boxes of crayons. Each box contains 16 crayons. How many total crayons does the student have?
The total number of crayons is 16 × 4.

```
   16
 × 4
   64         The total number of crayons equals 64.
```

Division of Whole Numbers

Division, the inverse of multiplication, is another of the four basic number operations. When we divide one number by another, we determine how many times we can multiply the divisor (number divided by) before we exceed the number we are dividing (dividend). For example, 8 divided by 2 equals 4 because we can multiply 2 four times to reach 8 (2 × 4 = 8 or 2 + 2 + 2 + 2 = 8). Using the grouping conceptualization we used with multiplication, we can divide 8 into 4 groups of 2 or 2 groups of 4. We call the answer to a division problem the QUOTIENT.

QUOTIENT: the answer to a division problem

If the divisor does not divide evenly into the dividend, we express the leftover amount either as a remainder or as a fraction with the divisor as the denominator. For example, 9 divided by 2 equals 4 with a remainder of 1, or $4\frac{1}{2}$.

The basic algorithm for division is long division. We start by representing the quotient as follows.

$14\overline{)293}$ → 14 is the divisor and 293 is the dividend.
      This represents 293 ÷ 14.

Next, we divide the divisor into the dividend, starting from the left.

$\phantom{14\overline{)}}2$
$14\overline{)293}$ → 14 divides into 29 two times with a remainder.

Next, we multiply the partial quotient by the divisor, subtract this value from the first digits of the dividend, and bring down the remaining dividend digits to complete the number.

$\phantom{14\overline{)}}2$
$14\overline{)293}$ → 2 × 14 = 28, 29 − 28 = 1, and bringing down the 3 yields 13.
$\underline{-28\downarrow}$
$\phantom{14\overline{)}}13$

Finally, we divide again (the divisor into the remaining value) and repeat the preceding process. The number left after the subtraction represents the remainder.

$\phantom{14\overline{)}}20$
$14\overline{)293}$
$\underline{-28}$
$\phantom{14\overline{)}}13$
$\underline{-0}$
$\phantom{14\overline{)}}13$ →   The final quotient is 20 with a remainder of 13. We can also represent this quotient as $20\frac{13}{14}$.

Example: Each box of apples contains 24 apples How many boxes must a grocer purchase to supply a group of 252 people with one apple each?
The grocer needs 252 apples. Because he must buy apples in groups of 24, we divide 252 by 24 to determine how many boxes he needs to buy.

$\phantom{24\overline{)}}10$
$24\overline{)252}$
$\underline{-24}$
$\phantom{24\overline{)}}12$ →   The quotient is 10 with a remainder of 12.
$\underline{-0}$
$\phantom{24\overline{)}}12$

Thus, the grocer needs 10 boxes plus 12 more apples. Therefore, the minimum number of boxes the grocer can purchase is 11.

Example: At his job, John gets paid $20 for every hour he works. If John made $940 in a week, how many hours did he work?

This is a division problem. To determine the number of hours John worked, we divide the total amount made ($940) by the hourly rate of pay ($20). Thus, the number of hours worked equals 940 divided by 20.

$$
\begin{array}{r}
47 \\
20\overline{)940} \\
-80 \\
\hline
140 \\
-140 \\
\hline
0
\end{array}
$$

$0 \rightarrow 20$ Divides into 940 a total of 47 times with no remainder.

John worked 47 hours.

Addition and Subtraction of Decimals

When adding and subtracting decimals, we align the numbers by place value as we do with whole numbers. After adding or subtracting each column, we bring the decimal down, placing it in the same location as in the numbers added or subtracted.

Example: Find the sum of 152.3 and 36.342.

$$
\begin{array}{r}
152.300 \\
+\ 36.342 \\
\hline
188.642
\end{array}
$$

Note that we placed two zeros after the final place value in 152.3 to clarify the column addition.

Example: Find the difference of 152.3 and 36.342.

$$
\begin{array}{r}
2\ 9\ 10 \\
152.\cancel{300} \\
-\ 36.342 \\
\hline
58
\end{array}
\qquad
\begin{array}{r}
(4)11(12) \\
\cancel{152.300} \\
-\ 36.342 \\
\hline
115.958
\end{array}
$$

Note how we borrowed to subtract from the zeros in the hundredths and thousandths places of 152.300.

Multiplication of Decimals

When multiplying decimal numbers, we multiply exactly as with whole numbers and place the decimal in from the right the total number of decimal places contained in the two numbers multiplied. For example, when multiplying 1.5 and 2.35, we place the decimal in the product 3 places in from the right (3.525).

Example: Find the product of 3.52 and 4.1.

$$
\begin{array}{r}
3.52 \\
\times\ 4.1 \\
\hline
352 \\
+\ 14080 \\
\hline
14.432
\end{array}
$$

Note that there are three decimal places in total in the two numbers.

We place the decimal three places in from the right.

Thus, the final product is 14.432.

Example: A shopper has 5 one-dollar bills, 6 quarters, 3 nickels, and 4 pennies in his pocket. How much money does he have?

$$5 \times \$1.00 = \$5.00$$

$$
\begin{array}{ccc}
1\ \ 3 & 1 & \\
\$0.25 & \$0.05 & \$0.01 \\
\times\ 6 & \times\ 3 & \times\ 4 \\
\hline
\$1.50 & \$0.15 & \$0.04
\end{array}
$$

Note the placement of the decimals in the multiplication products. Thus, the total amount of money in the shopper's pocket is:

$$
\begin{array}{r}
\$5.00 \\
1.50 \\
0.15 \\
+\ 0.04 \\
\hline
\$6.69
\end{array}
$$

Division of Decimals

When dividing decimal numbers, we first remove the decimal in the divisor by moving the decimal in the dividend the same number of spaces to the right. For example, when dividing 1.45 into 5.3, we convert the numbers to 145 and 530 and perform normal whole-number division.

Example: Find the quotient of 5.3 divided by 1.45.

Convert to 145 and 530.

Divide.

$$
\begin{array}{r}
3 \\
145\overline{)530} \\
-435 \\
\hline
95 \\
-870 \\
\hline
800
\end{array}
$$

$$
\begin{array}{r}
3.65 \\
145\overline{)530.00} \\
-435 \\
\hline
950
\end{array}
$$

Note that we insert the decimal to continue division.

Because one of the numbers divided contained one decimal place, we round the quotient to one decimal place. Thus, the final quotient is 3.7.

Operating with Percents

Example: 5 is what percent of 20?

This is the same as converting $\frac{5}{20}$ to % form.

$$\frac{5}{20} \times \frac{100}{1} = \frac{5}{1} \times \frac{5}{1} = 25\%$$

Example: There are 64 dogs in the kennel. 48 are collies. What percent are collies?

Restate the problem.	48 is what percent of 64?
Write an equation.	$48 = n \times 64$
Solve.	$\frac{48}{64} = n$

$n = \frac{3}{4} = 75\%$

75% of the dogs are collies.

Example: The auditorium was filled to 90% capacity. There were 558 seats occupied. What is the capacity of the auditorium?

Restate the problem.	90% of what number is 558?
Write an equation.	$0.9n = 558$
Solve.	$n = \frac{558}{.9}$

$n = 620$

The capacity of the auditorium is 620 people.

Example: A pair of shoes costs $42.00. The sales tax is 6%. What is the total cost of the shoes?

Restate the problem.	What is 6% of 42?
Write an equation.	$n = 0.06 \times 42$
Solve.	$n = 2.52$
Add the sales tax to the cost.	$42.00 + 2.52 = 44.52$

The total cost of the shoes, including sales tax, is $44.52.

Addition and Subtraction of Fractions

Key points

1. You need a common denominator in order to add and subtract reduced and improper fractions.

Example:

$$\frac{1}{3} + \frac{7}{3} = 1 + \frac{7}{3} = \frac{8}{3} = 2\frac{2}{3}$$

Example:

$$\frac{4}{12} + \frac{6}{12} - \frac{3}{12} = \frac{4 + 6 - 3}{12} = \frac{7}{12}$$

2. Adding an integer and a fraction of the same sign results directly in a mixed fraction.

Example:

$$2 + \frac{2}{3} = 2\frac{2}{3}$$

Example:

$$-2 - \frac{2}{3} = 2\frac{2}{3}$$

3. Adding an integer and a fraction with different signs involves the following steps.

- Get a common denominator.

- Add or subtract as needed.

- Change to a mixed fraction if possible.

Example:

$$2 - \frac{1}{3} = \frac{2 \times 3 - 1}{3} = \frac{6 - 1}{3} = \frac{5}{3} = 1\frac{2}{3}$$

Example:

Add $7\frac{3}{8} + 5\frac{2}{7}$

Add the whole numbers, add the fractions, and combine the two results:

$$7\frac{3}{8} + 5\frac{2}{7} = (7 + 5) + \left(\frac{3}{8} + \frac{2}{7}\right)$$

$$= 12 + \frac{(7 \times 3) + (8 \times 2)}{56} \qquad \text{(LCM of 8 and 7)}$$

$$= 12 + \frac{21 + 16}{56} = 12 + \frac{37}{56} = 12\frac{37}{56}$$

Example: Perform the operation.

$$\frac{2}{3} - \frac{5}{6}$$

We first find the LCM of 3 and 6, which is 6.

$$\frac{2 \times 2}{3 \times 2} - \frac{5}{6} \rightarrow \frac{4 - 5}{6} = \frac{-1}{6} \qquad \text{(Using method A)}$$

Example:

$-7\frac{1}{4} + 2\frac{7}{8}$

$-7\frac{1}{4} + 2\frac{7}{8} = (-7 + 2) + \left(\frac{-1}{4} + \frac{7}{8}\right)$

$= (-5) + \frac{-2 + 7}{8} = (-5) + \left(\frac{5}{8}\right)$

$= (-5) + \frac{5}{8} = \frac{-5 \times 8}{1 \times 8} + \frac{5}{8} = \frac{-40 + 5}{8}$

$= \frac{-35}{8} = -4\frac{3}{8}$

Divide 35 by 8 to get 4, remainder 3.

Example:

Caution: A common error would be

$-7\frac{1}{4} + 2\frac{7}{8} = -7\frac{2}{8} + 2\frac{7}{8} = -5\frac{9}{8}$ Wrong.

It is correct to add -7 and 2 to get -5, but adding $\frac{2}{8} + \frac{7}{8} = \frac{9}{8}$

is wrong. It should have been $\frac{-2}{8} + \frac{7}{8} = \frac{5}{8}$. Then,

$-5 + \frac{5}{8} = -4\frac{3}{8}$ as before.

Multiplication of Fractions

Using the following example: $3\frac{1}{4} \times \frac{5}{6}$

1. Convert each number to an improper fraction

   $3\frac{1}{4} = \frac{(12 + 1)}{4} = \frac{13}{4}$ $\frac{5}{6}$ is already in reduced form.

2. Reduce (cancel) common factors of the numerator and denominator if they exist

   $\frac{13}{4} \times \frac{5}{6}$ No common factors exist

3. Multiply the numerators by each other and the denominators by each other

   $\frac{13}{4} \times \frac{5}{6} = \frac{65}{24}$

4. If possible, reduce the fraction to its lowest term

   $\frac{65}{24}$ Cannot be reduced further.

5. Convert the improper fraction back to a mixed fraction by using long division

   $\frac{65}{24} = 24\overline{)65} \atop \frac{48}{17}$ $= 2\frac{17}{24}$

Summary of Sign Changes for Multiplication

1. $(+) \times (+) = (+)$

2. $(-) \times (+) = (-)$

3. $(+) \times (-) = (-)$

4. $(-) \times (-) = (+)$

Example:

$7\frac{1}{3} \times \frac{5}{11} = \frac{22}{3} \times \frac{5}{11}$

Reduce like terms (22 and 11).

$= \frac{2}{3} \times \frac{5}{1} = \frac{10}{3} = 3\frac{1}{3}$

Example:

$-6\frac{1}{4} \times \frac{5}{9} = \frac{-25}{4} \times \frac{5}{9}$

$= \frac{-125}{36} = -3\frac{17}{36}$

Example:

$\frac{-1}{4} \times \frac{-3}{7}$

A negative times a negative equals a positive.

$= \frac{1}{4} \times \frac{3}{7} = \frac{3}{28}$

Division of Fractions

1. Change mixed fractions to improper fractions

2. Change the division problem to a multiplication problem by using the reciprocal of the number after the division sign

3. Find the sign of the final product

4. Cancel if common factors exist between the numerator and the denominator

5. Multiply the numerators together and the denominators together

6. Change the improper fraction to a mixed number

Example:

$$3\tfrac{1}{5} + 2\tfrac{1}{4} = \tfrac{16}{5} + \tfrac{9}{4}$$
$$= \tfrac{16}{5} \times \tfrac{4}{9} \qquad \text{The reciprocal of } \tfrac{9}{4} \text{ is } \tfrac{4}{9}.$$
$$= \tfrac{64}{65} = 1\tfrac{19}{45}$$

Example:

$$7\tfrac{3}{4} + 11\tfrac{5}{8} = \tfrac{31}{4} + \tfrac{93}{8}$$
$$= \tfrac{31}{4} \times \tfrac{8}{93} \qquad \text{Reduce like terms.}$$
$$= \tfrac{1}{1} \times \tfrac{2}{3} = \tfrac{2}{3}$$

Example:

$$(-2\tfrac{1}{2}) + 4\tfrac{1}{6} = \tfrac{-5}{2} + \tfrac{25}{6}$$
$$= \tfrac{-5}{2} \times \tfrac{6}{25} \qquad \text{Reduce like terms.}$$
$$= \tfrac{-1}{1} \times \tfrac{3}{5} = \tfrac{-3}{5}$$

Example:

$$(-5\tfrac{3}{8}) + (\tfrac{-7}{16}) = \tfrac{-43}{8} + \tfrac{27}{16}$$
$$= \tfrac{-43}{8} \times \tfrac{-16}{7} \qquad \text{Reduce like terms.}$$
$$= \tfrac{43}{1} \times \tfrac{2}{7} \qquad \text{A negative times a negative equals a positive.}$$

Sample Test Questions and Rationale

(Average)

1. **Find the midpoint of (2,5) and (7,–4).**

   A. (9,–1)

   B. (5,9)

   C. $(\tfrac{9}{2}, \tfrac{-1}{2})$

   D. $(\tfrac{9}{2}, \tfrac{1}{2})$

   Answer: D. $(\tfrac{9}{2}, \tfrac{1}{2})$

   Using the midpoint formula,
   $$x = \tfrac{(2+7)}{2}$$
   $$y = \tfrac{(5 + -4)}{2}$$

(Average)

2. $3x + 2y = 12$
   $12x + 8y = 15$
   Solve for x and y.

   A. All real numbers

   B. $x = 4, y = 4$

   C. $x = 2, y = -1$

   D. $\varnothing$

   Answer: D

   Multiplying the top equation by –4 and adding results in the equation $0 = -33$. Since this is a false statement, the correct choice is the null set.

SKILL 14.7 Applying methods for making estimations and for evaluating the accuracy of estimated solutions

Estimation and approximation may be used to check the reasonableness of answers.

Example: Estimate the answer.

$$\frac{58 \times 810}{1989}$$

58 becomes 60, 810 becomes 800, and 1989 becomes 2000.

$$\frac{60 \times 800}{2000} = 24$$

For word problems, an estimate may sometimes be all that is needed to find the solution.

Example: Janet goes into a store to purchase a CD that is on sale for $13.95. While shopping, she sees two pairs of shoes priced at $19.95 and $14.50. She only has $50. Can she purchase everything?

Solve by rounding:

$$\$19.95 \rightarrow \$20.00$$
$$\$14.50 \rightarrow \$15.00$$
$$\underline{\$13.95 \rightarrow \$14.00}$$
$$ \$49.00 \quad \text{Yes, she can purchase the CD and the shoes.}$$

COMPETENCY 15

UNDERSTAND PRINCIPLES AND SKILLS OF MEASUREMENT AND THE CONCEPTS AND PROPERTIES OF GEOMETRY

SKILL Identifying appropriate measurement procedures, tools, and units 15.1 *(e.g., customary and metric)* **for problems involving length, perimeter, area, capacity, weight, time, and temperature**

MEASUREMENTS OF LENGTH (ENGLISH SYSTEM)		
12 inches (in)	=	1 foot (ft)
3 ft	=	1 yard (yd)
1760 yd	=	1 mile (mi)

MEASUREMENTS OF LENGTH (METRIC SYSTEM)		
kilometer (km)	=	1000 meters (m)
hectometer (hm)	=	100 meters (m)
decameter (dam)	=	1 mile (mi)
meter (m)	=	10 meters (m)
decimeter (dm)	=	1 meter (m)
centimeter (cm)	=	1/10 meter (m)
millimeter (mm)	=	1/100 meter (m)

CONVERSION OF LENGTH FROM ENGLISH TO METRIC		
1 inch	=	2.54 centimeters

CONVERSION OF LENGTH FROM ENGLISH TO METRIC		
1 foot	≈	30 centimeters
1 yard	≈	0.9 meters
1 mile	≈	1.6 kilometers

MEASUREMENTS OF WEIGHT (ENGLISH SYSTEM)		
28 grams (g)	=	1 ounce (oz)
16 ounces (oz)	=	1 pound (lb)
2000 pounds (lb)	=	1 ton (t) (short ton)
1.1 ton (t)	=	1 ton (t)

MEASUREMENTS OF WEIGHT (METRIC SYSTEM)		
kilogram (kg)	=	1000 grams (g)
gram (g)	=	1 gram (g)
milligram (mg)	=	1/1000 gram (g)

CONVERSION OF WEIGHT FROM ENGLISH TO METRIC		
1 ounce	≈	28 grams
1 pound	≈ ≈	0.45 kilogram 454 grams

MEASUREMENT OF VOLUME (ENGLISH SYSTEM)		
8 fluid ounces (oz)	=	1 cup (c)
2 cups (c)	=	1 pint (pt)
2 pints (pt)	=	1 quart (qt)
4 quarts (qt)	=	1 gallon (gal)

MEASUREMENT OF VOLUME (METRIC SYSTEM)		
kiloliter (kl)	=	1000 liters (l)
liter (l)	=	1 liter (l)
milliliter (ml)	=	1/1000 liters (ml)

CONVERSION OF VOLUME FROM ENGLISH TO METRIC		
1 teaspoon (tsp	≈	5 milliliters
1 fluid ounce	≈	15 milliliters
1 cup	≈	0.24 liters
1 pint	≈	0.47 liters
1 quart	≈	0.95 liters
1 gallon	≈	3.8 liters

MEASUREMENT OF TIME		
1 minute	=	60 seconds
1 hour	=	60 minutes
1 day	=	24 hours
1 week	=	7 days
1 year	=	365 days
1 century	=	100 years

Note: (′) represents feet and (″) represents inches.

Square Units

Square units can be derived with knowledge of basic units of length by squaring the equivalent measurements.

Example:

14 sq. yd. = _____ sq. ft.

$14 \times 9 = 126$ sq. ft.

1 square foot (sq. ft.) = 144 sq. in.
1 sq. yd. = 9 sq. ft.
1 sq. yd. = 1296 sq. in.

Weight

Example: Kathy has a bag of potatoes that weighs 5 lbs., 10 oz. She uses one third of the bag to make mashed potatoes. How much does the bag weigh now?

1 lb. = 16 oz.

5(16 oz.) + 10 oz.

= 80 oz + 10 oz = 90 oz.

$90 - (\frac{1}{3})90$ oz

= 90 oz − 30 oz

= 60 oz

$60 \div 16 = 3.75$ lb

.75 = 75%

$75\% = \frac{75}{100} = \frac{3}{4}$

$\frac{3}{4} \times 16$ oz = 12 oz

The bag weighs 3 lb, 12 oz.

Example: The weight limit of a playground merry-go-round is 1000 pounds. There are 11 children on the merry-go-round. 3 children weigh 100 pounds. 6 children weigh 75 pounds. 2 children weigh 60 pounds. George weighs 80 pounds. Can he get on the merry-go-round?

3(100) + 6(75) + 2(60)

= 300 + 450 + 120

= 870

1000 − 870

= 130

George weighs less than 130, so he can get on the merry-go-round.

PERIMETER: the sum of the lengths of the sides of any polygon

AREA: the number of square units covered by a polygon

Perimeter and Area

The PERIMETER of any polygon is the sum of the lengths of the sides.

The AREA of a polygon is the number of square units covered by the figure.

Figure	Area Formula	Perimeter Formula
Rectangle	LW	$2(L + W)$
Triangle	$\frac{1}{2}bh$	$a + b + c$
Parallelogram	bh	sum of lengths of sides
Trapezoid	$\frac{1}{2}h(a\ 1\ b)$	sum of lengths of sides

Example: A farmer has a piece of land shaped as shown below. He wishes to fence this land at an estimated cost of $25 per linear foot. What is the total cost of fencing this property to the nearest foot?

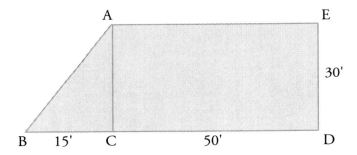

From the right triangle *ABC, AC* = 30 and *BC* = 15.

Since $(AB)^2 = (AC)^2 + (BC)^2$

$(AB)^2 = (30)^2 + (15)^2$

So feet$\sqrt{(AB)^2} = AB = \sqrt{1125} = 33.5410$ feet

To the nearest foot, *AB* = 34 feet.

Perimeter of the piece of land is = *AB + BC + CD + DE + EA*

    = 34 + 15 + 50 + 30 + 50 = 179 feet

    Cost of fencing = $25 × 179 = $4,475.00

Example: What will be the cost of carpeting a rectangular office that measures 12 feet by 15 feet if the carpet costs $12.50 per square yard?

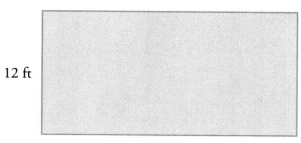

12 ft

15 ft

The problem is asking you to determine the area of the office. The area of a rectangle is *length* $\times$ *width* $=$ *A*.

Substitute the given values in the equation $A = lw$.
    $A = (12 \text{ ft.})(15 \text{ ft.})$
    $A = 180 \text{ ft.}^2$

The problem asked you to determine the cost of carpet at $12.50 per square yard.

First, you need to convert 180 ft.^{2} into yards^2.
    $1 \text{ yd} = 3 \text{ ft.}$
    $(1 \text{ yd})(1 \text{ yd.}) = (3 \text{ ft.})(3 \text{ ft.})$
    $1 \text{ yd}^2 = 9 \text{ ft}^2$
    $\frac{180 \text{ ft}^2}{9 \text{ ft}^2} = 20$

The carpet costs $12.50 per square yard; thus the cost of carpeting the office described is $12.50 \times 20 = $250.00.

Example: Find the area of a parallelogram if its base is 6.5 cm long and the height of the altitude to that base is 3.7 cm.

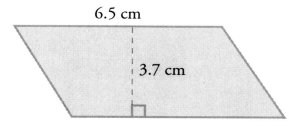

6.5 cm

3.7 cm

$A_{\text{parallelogram}} = bh$
    $= (3.7)(6.5)$
    $= 24.05 \text{ cm}^2$

Example: Find the area of this triangle.

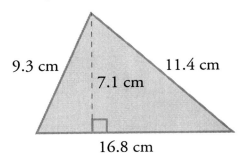

9.3 cm   11.4 cm

7.1 cm

16.8 cm

$$A_{triangle} = \frac{1}{2}bh$$
$$= 0.5(16.8)(7.1)$$
$$= 59.64 \text{ cm}^2$$

Example: Find the area of this trapezoid.

17.5 cm

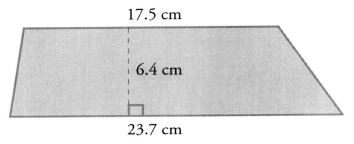

6.4 cm

23.7 cm

The area of a trapezoid equals one-half the sum of the bases times the altitude.

$$A_{trapezoid} = \frac{1}{2}h(b_1 + b_2)$$
$$A_{trapezoid} = 0.5(6.4)(17.5 + 23.7)$$
$$A_{trapezoid} = 131.84 \text{ cm}^2$$

Circles

The distance around a circle is the CIRCUMFERENCE. The ratio of the circumference to the diameter is represented by the Greek letter

pi, $\pi \sim 3.14 \sim \frac{22}{7}$.

The circumference of a circle is found by the formula $C = 2\pi r$ or $C = \pi d$, where r is the radius of the circle and d is the diameter.

The area of a circle is found by the formula $A = \pi r^2$.

CIRCUMFERENCE: the distance around a circle

Example: Find the circumference and area of a circle whose radius is 7 meters.

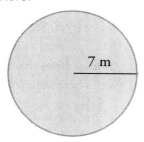

$C = \pi r$ $A = \pi r^2$

$\quad = 2(3.14)(7)$ $\quad = 3.14(7)(7)$

$\quad = 43.96$ m $\quad = 153.86$ m²

Reading Instruments

When reading an instrument, students should first determine the interval of scale on that particular instrument. To achieve the greatest accuracy, they should read the scale to the nearest measurement mark.

If they are using a scale with a needle that has a mirrored plate behind it, the scale should be viewed so that the needle's reflection is hidden behind the needle itself. Students should not look at it from an angle. In order to read a balance scale accurately, it is necessary to place the scale on a level surface and make sure that the hand points precisely at 0. Objects should be placed on the plate gently and taken away gently. The dial should be faced straight on to read the graduation accurately. Students should read from the large graduation to smaller graduation. If the dial hand points between two graduations, they should choose the number that is closest to the hand.

When reading inches on a ruler, the student needs to understand that each inch is divided into halves by the longest mark in the middle; into fourths by the next-longest marks; into eighths by the next; and into sixteenths by the shortest marks. When the measurement falls between two "inch marks," they can give the whole number of inches, count the additional fractional marks, and give the answer as the number and fraction of inches. Remind students that the convention is always to express a fraction with its lowest possible denominator.

If students are using the metric system on a ruler, have them focus on the marks between the whole numbers (centimeters). Point out that each centimeter is broken into tenths, with the mark in the middle being longer to indicate a halfway mark. Students should learn to measure things accurately to the nearest tenth of a centimeter, then the nearest hundredth, and finally the nearest thousandth.

Measurements using the metric system should always be written using the decimal system—for example, 3.756 centimeters.

When reading a thermometer, one should hold it vertically at eye level. Students should check the scale of the thermometer to make certain that they read as many significant digits as possible. Thermometers with heavy or extended lines that are marked 10, 20, 30, … should be read to the nearest 0.1 degree. Thermometers with fine lines every two degrees may be read to the nearest 0.5 degree.

In order to get an accurate reading in a liquid measuring cup, students should set the cup on a level surface and read it at eye level. The measurement should be read at the bottom of the concave arc at the liquid's surface (the meniscus line). When measuring dry ingredients, dip the appropriately sized measuring cup into the ingredient, and sweep away the excess across the top with a straight-edged object.

Protractors measure angles in degrees. To measure accurately, students must find the center hole on the straight edge of the protractor and place it over the vertex of the angle they wish to measure. They should line up the zero on the straight edge with one of the sides of the angle and then find the point where the second side of the angle intersects the curved edge of the protractor. They can then read the number that is written at the point of intersection.

When one is reading an instrument such as a rain gauge, it is again important to read at eye level and at the base of the meniscus. The measuring tube is divided, marked, and labeled in tenths and hundredths. The greatest number of decimal places there will be is two.

Most numbers in mathematics are "exact" or "counted," but measurements are "approximate." They usually involve interpolation, or figuring out which mark on the ruler is closest. Any measurement acquired with a measuring device is approximate. These variations in measurement are called precision and accuracy.

PRECISION: tells us how exactly a measurement is

A measurement's PRECISION tells us how exactly a measurement is made, without reference to a true or real value. If a measurement is precise, it can be made again and again with little variation in the result. The precision of a measuring device is the smallest fractional or decimal division on the instrument. The smaller the unit or fraction of a unit on the measuring device, the more precisely it can measure.

The greatest possible error of measurement is always equal to one-half the smallest fraction of a unit on the measuring device.

ACCURACY: how close a measurement comes to the "true" value

A measurement's ACCURACY tells us how close the result of measurement comes to the "true" value.

In the game of throwing darts, the true value is the bull's eye. If the three darts land on the bull's eye, the dart thrower is both precise (all the darts land near the same spot) and accurate (the darts all land on the "true" value).

The greatest measure of error allowed is called the TOLERANCE. The least acceptable limit is called the LOWER LIMIT, and the greatest acceptable limit is called the UPPER LIMIT. The difference between the upper and lower limits is called the TOLERANCE INTERVAL. For example, a specification for an automobile part might be 14.625 ± 0.005 mm. This means that the smallest acceptable length of the part is 14.620 mm and the largest acceptable length is 14.630 mm. The tolerance interval is 0.010 mm. One can see how it would be important for automobile parts to be within a set of limits in terms of length. If the part is too long or too short, it will not fit properly, and vibrations will occur that weaken the part and may eventually cause damage to other parts.

TOLERANCE: the greatest measure of error allowed

LOWER LIMIT: the least acceptable measure of error

UPPER LIMIT: the greatest acceptable measure of error

TOLERANCE INTERVAL: the difference between the lower and upper levels of tolerance

---

SKILL 15.2 **Applying knowledge of approaches to direct measurement through the use of standard and nonstandard units and to indirect measurement through the use of algebra or geometry**

There are two types of measurement: direct measurement and indirect measurement. As the name implies, DIRECT MEASUREMENT is the action of measuring something directly. For example, the length of a boat can be measured with a measuring tape, and elapsed time can be measured with a stop watch.

INDIRECT MEASUREMENT is measurement that is not done with a tool such as a ruler or watch. Instead, other mathematical approaches are used to derive the desired measurement. Using similar triangles is an example of indirect measurement. Similar triangles have the same angles and proportionate sides, but they are different sizes. They can be used to determine the distance from one point to another without measuring it directly. In the diagram below, X represents the distance between two points with an unknown length.

DIRECT MEASUREMENT: measuring something directly

INDIRECT MEASUREMENT: using an alternate method for measuring, such us using scale drawings

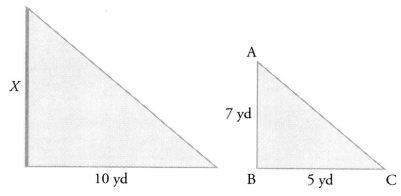

The problem can be addressed by setting up the following proportion and solving for X.

$$\frac{X}{10\ \text{yd}} = \frac{7\ \text{yd}}{5\ \text{yd}}$$

After cross-multiplying, the equation can be written as $5X = 70$; X equals 14 yards. Without actually measuring the distance with a measuring tape or other tools, the distance between the points is determined.

Indirect measurement also occurs in instances other than simply measuring length. The area of a room can be measured using a scale drawing. It is possible to determine the weight of the moon by using the measurable effects the moon exerts on the earth, such as the changes in tides. Another familiar indirect measurement is the Body Mass Index (BMI), which indicates body composition. The body composition uses height and weight measurements to measure health risks.

TRIANGLE: a polygon with three sides

ACUTE TRIANGLE: a triangle with exactly three acute angles

SKILL 15.3 Classifying plane and solid geometric figures *(e.g., triangle, quadrilateral, sphere, cone)*

A **TRIANGLE** is a polygon with three sides.

Triangles can be classified by the types of angles or the lengths of their sides.

RIGHT TRIANGLE: a triangle with one right angle

Classifying by Angles

An **ACUTE TRIANGLE** has exactly three acute angles.

A **RIGHT TRIANGLE** has one right angle.

OBTUSE TRIANGLE: a triangle with one obtuse angle

An **OBTUSE TRIANGLE** has one obtuse angle.

  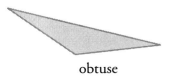

acute   right   obtuse

EQUILATERAL TRIANGLE: a triangle with all three sides the same length

Classifying by Sides

All three sides of an **EQUILATERAL TRIANGLE** are the same length.

ISOSCELES TRIANGLE: a triangle with two sides the same length

Two sides of an **ISOSCELES TRIANGLE** are the same length.

None of the sides of a SCALENE TRIANGLE are the same length.

  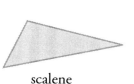

equilateral   isosceles   scalene

A QUADRILATERAL is a polygon with four sides.

The sum of the measures of the angles of a quadrilateral is 360°.

A TRAPEZOID is a quadrilateral with exactly one pair of parallel sides.

In an ISOSCELES TRAPEZOID, the nonparallel sides are congruent.

A PARALLELOGRAM is a quadrilateral with two pairs of parallel sides.

A RECTANGLE is a parallelogram with a right angle.

A RHOMBUS is a parallelogram with all sides equal length.

SCALENE TRIANGLE: a triangle with no sides the same length

QUADRILATERAL: a polygon with four sides

TRAPEZOID: a quadrilateral with exactly one pair of parallel sides

ISOSCELES TRAPEZOID: a quadrilateral where the nonparallel sides are congruent

PARALLELOGRAM: a quadrilateral with two pairs of parallel sides

RECTANGLE: a parallelogram with a right angle

RHOMBUS: a parallelogram with all sides equal length

A SQUARE is a rectangle with all sides of equal length.

The union of all points on a simple closed surface and all points in its interior form a space figure called a solid. The five regular solids, or polyhedra, are the cube, tetrahedron, octahedron, icosahedron, and dodecahedron. A net is a two-dimensional figure that can be cut out and folded up to make a three-dimensional solid. Below are models of the five regular solids with their corresponding face polygons and nets.

Cube — 6 squares

Tetrahedron — 4 equilateral triangles

Octahedron — 8 equilateral triangles

Icosahedron — 20 equilateral triangles

Dodecahedron — 12 regular pentagons

Other examples of solids:

A SPHERE is a space figure having all its points the same distance from the center.

A CONE is a space figure having a circular base and a single vertex.

SKILL 15.4 Applying knowledge of basic geometric concepts (e.g., similarity, congruence, parallelism)

Congruent figures have the same size and shape. If one is placed above the other, they will fit exactly. Congruent lines have the same length. Congruent angles have equal measures.

The symbol for congruent is ≅.

Polygons (pentagons) *ABCDE* and *VWXYZ* are congruent. They are exactly the same size and shape.

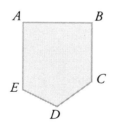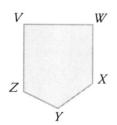

$$ABCDE \cong VWXYZ$$

Corresponding parts are the congruent angles and congruent sides. They are:

Corresponding angles	Corresponding sides
$\angle A \leftrightarrow \angle V$	$AB \leftrightarrow VW$
$\angle B \leftrightarrow \angle W$	$BC \leftrightarrow WX$
$\angle C \leftrightarrow \angle X$	$CD \leftrightarrow XY$
$\angle D \leftrightarrow \angle Y$	$DE \leftrightarrow YZ$
$\angle E \leftrightarrow \angle Z$	$AE \leftrightarrow VZ$

Example: Given two similar quadrilaterals, find the lengths of sides x, y, and z.

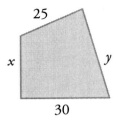
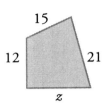

Since corresponding sides are proportional, the scale is:

$$\frac{12}{x} = \frac{3}{5}$$
$$3x = 60$$
$$x = 20$$

$$\frac{21}{x} = \frac{3}{5}$$
$$3y = 105$$
$$y = 35$$

$$\frac{z}{30} = \frac{3}{5}$$
$$5z = 90$$
$$z = 18$$

Similarity

Two figures that have the same shape are similar. Polygons are similar if and only if corresponding angles are congruent and corresponding sides are in proportion. Corresponding parts of similar polygons are proportional.

Example: Tommy draws and cuts out two triangles for a school project. One of them has sides of 3, 6, and 9 inches. The other triangle has sides of 2, 4, and 6 inches. Is there a relationship between the two triangles?

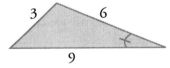
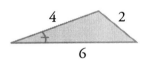

Take the proportion of the corresponding sides.

$$\frac{2}{3} \qquad \frac{4}{6} = \frac{2}{3} \qquad \frac{6}{9} = \frac{2}{3}$$

The smaller triangle is $\frac{2}{3}$ the size of the large triangle.

Example: Given the rectangles below, compare the area and perimeter.

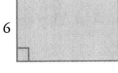

$A = LW$	$A = LW$	**1. Write formula.**
$A = (6)(9)$	$A = (9)(13.5)$	**2. Substitute known values.**
$A = 54$ sq. units	$A = 121.5$ sq. units	**3. Compute.**
$P = 2(L + W)$	$P = 2(L + W)$	**1. Write formula.**
$P = 2(6 + 9)$	$P = 2(9 + 13.5)$	**2. Substitute known values.**
$P = 30$ units	$P = 45$ units	**3. Compute.**

Notice that the areas are related to each other in the following manner:
Ratio of sides $\frac{9}{135} = \frac{2}{3}$

Multiply the first area by the square of the reciprocal to get the second area.
$$54 \times \left(\frac{3}{2}\right)^2 = 121.5$$

The perimeters are related to each other in the following manner:
Ratio of sides $\frac{9}{135} = \frac{2}{3}$

Multiply the perimeter of the first by the reciprocal of the ratio to get the perimeter of the second.
$$30 \times \frac{3}{2} = 45$$

SKILL Applying strategies for measuring the component parts of
15.5 geometric figures *(e.g., angles, segments)* **and computing the volume**
of simple geometric solids

In geometry, the point, line, and plane are key concepts that can be discussed in relation to each other.

Collinear points are all on the same line.

Noncollinear points are not on the same line.

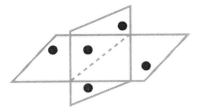

Coplanar points are on the same plane.

Noncoplanar points are not on the same plane.

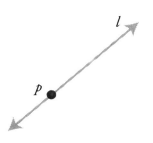

Point *p* is in line *l*.
Point *p* is on line *l*.
l contains *P*.
l passes through *P*.

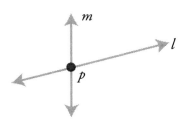

l and *m* intersect at *p*.
p is the intersection of *l* and *m*.

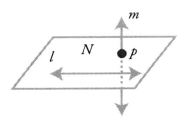

l and *p* are in plane *N*.
N contains *p* and *l*.
m intersects *N* at *p*.
p is the intersection of *m* and *N*.

Planes *M* and *N* intersect at *rq*.
rq is the intersection of *M* and *N*.
rq is in *M* and *N*.
M and *N* contain *rq*.

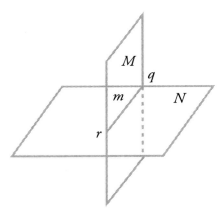

The classifying of angles refers to the angle measure. The naming of angles refers to the letters or numbers used to label the angle.

Example:

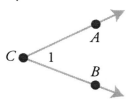

$\overrightarrow{CA}$ (read ray *CA*) and $\overrightarrow{CB}$ are the sides of the angle.

The angle can be called $\angle ACB$, $\angle BCA$, $\angle C$, or $\angle 1$.

Angles are classified according to their size as follows:

Acute:	greater than 0 and less than 90 degrees
Right:	exactly 90 degrees
Obtuse:	greater than 90 and less than 180 degrees
Straight:	exactly 180 degrees

Angles can be classified in a number of ways. Some of those classifications are outlined here.

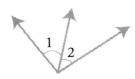

Adjacent angles have a common vertex and one common side but no interior points in common.

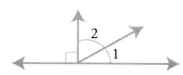

Complementary angles add up to 90 degrees.

Supplementary angles add up to 180 degrees.

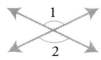

Vertical angles have sides that form two pairs of opposite rays.

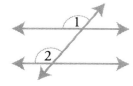

Corresponding angles are in the same corresponding position on two parallel lines cut by a transversal.

Alternate interior angles are diagonal angles on the inside of two parallel lines cut by a transversal.

Alternate exterior angles are diagonal on the outside of two parallel lines cut by a transversal.

Parallel lines or planes do not intersect.

Perpendicular lines or planes form a 90 degree angle to each other.

Intersecting lines share a common point, and intersecting planes share a common set of points, or line.

Skew lines do not intersect and do not lie on the same plane.

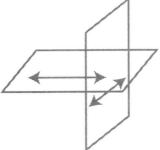

The three undefined terms of geometry are point, line, and plane.

A **PLANE** is a flat surface that extends forever in two dimensions. It has no ends or edges. It has no thickness. It is usually drawn as a parallelogram that can be named either by specifying three non-collinear points (three points that are not on the same line) on the plane or by placing, in the corner of the plane, a letter that is not used elsewhere in the diagram.

A **LINE** extends forever in one dimension. It is determined and named by two points that are on the line. The line consists of every point that is between those two points, as well as the points that are on the "straight" extension each way. A line is drawn as a line segment with arrows facing opposite directions on each end to indicate that the line continues in both directions forever.

A **POINT** is a position in space, on a line, or on a plane. It has no thickness and no width. Only one line can go through any two points. A point is represented by a dot named by a single letter.

> **PLANE:** a flat surface that extends forever in two dimensions

> **LINE:** extends forever in one dimension

> **POINT:** a position in space, on a line, or on a plane

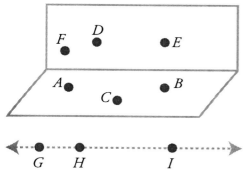

DEF is a plane.

ABC is another plane.

This line can be named by any two points on the line.

For example, the line could be named $\overleftrightarrow{GH}$, $\overleftrightarrow{HI}$, $\overleftrightarrow{GI}$, $\overleftrightarrow{IG}$, $\overleftrightarrow{IH}$, or $\overleftrightarrow{HG}$. Any two points (letters) on the line can be used, and their order is not important in naming a line.

In the above diagrams, *A, B, C, D, E, F, G, H,* and *I* are all locations of individual points.

A **RAY** is not an undefined term. A ray consists of all the points on a line starting at one given point and extending in only one of the two opposite directions along the line. The ray is named by naming two points on the ray. The first point must be the endpoint of the ray, and the second point can be any other point along the ray. The symbol for a ray is a ray above the two letters used to name it. The endpoint of the ray must be the first letter.

> **RAY:** consists of all the points on a line starting at one given point and extending in only one of the two opposite directions along the line

This ray could be named . It cannot be called , because none of these names starts with the endpoint, J.

The distance between two points on a number line is equal to the absolute value of the difference of the two numbers associated with the points.

If one point is located at "a" and the other point is at "b," then the distance between them is found by this formula:

Distance $= |a - b|$ or $|b - a|$

If one point is located at and another point is located at 5, the distance between them is found by:

Distance $= |a - b| = |(-3) - 5| = |-8| = 8$

Volume and surface area are computed using the following formulas:

FIGURE	VOLUME	TOTAL SURFACE AREA
Right Cylinder	$\pi r^2 h$	$2\pi rh + 2\pi r^2$
Right Cone	$\dfrac{\pi r^2 h}{3}$	$\pi r \sqrt{r^2 + h^2} + \pi r^2$
Sphere	$\dfrac{4}{3}\pi r^3$	$4\pi r2$
Rectangular Solid	LWH	$2LW + 2WH + 2LH$

FIGURE	LATERAL AREA	TOTAL AREA	VOLUME
Regular Pyramid	$\dfrac{1}{2} Pl$	$\dfrac{1}{2} Pl + B$	$\dfrac{1}{3} Bh$

P = Perimeter, h = height, B = Area of Base, l = slant height

Example: What is the volume of a shoe box with a length of 35 cm, a width of 20 cm, and a height of 15 cm?

Volume of a rectangular solid
= Length × Width × Height
= 35 × 20 × 15
= 10500 cm^3

Example: A water company is trying to decide whether to use traditional cylindrical paper cups or to offer conical paper cups, since both cost the same. The traditional cups are 8 cm wide and 14 cm high. The conical cups are 12 cm wide and 19 cm high. The company will use the cup that holds the most water.

Draw and label a sketch of each.

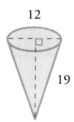

$V = \pi r^2 h$	$V = \frac{\pi r^2 h}{3}$	1. Write a formula.
$V = \pi(4)^2(14)$	$V = \frac{1}{3}\pi(6)^2(19)$	2. Substitute.
$V = 703.717$ cm^3	$V = 716.283$ cm^3	3. Solve.

The choice should be the conical cup since its volume is more.

Example: How much material is needed to make a basketball that has a diameter of 15 inches? How much air is needed to fill the basketball?

Draw and label a sketch:

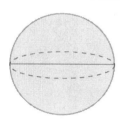

$D = 15$ inches

Total surface area	Volume	
TSA $= 4\pi r^2$	$V = \frac{4}{3}\pi r^3$	1. Write a formula.
$= 4\pi(7.5)^2$	$= \frac{4}{3}\pi(7.5)^3$	2. Substitute.
$= 706.858$ in^2	$= 1767.1459$ in^3	3. Solve.

SKILL 15.6 Applying knowledge of coordinate systems to identify representations of basic geometric figures and concepts

We can represent any two-dimensional geometric figure in the Cartesian coordinate system or rectangular coordinate system. The Cartesian or rectangular coordinate system is formed by two perpendicular axes (coordinate axes): the *X*-axis and the *Y*-axis. If we know the dimensions of a two-dimensional (planar) figure, we can use this coordinate system to visualize the shape of the figure.

Example: Represent an isosceles triangle with two sides of length 4.

Draw the two sides along the X- and Y-axes and connect the points (vertices).

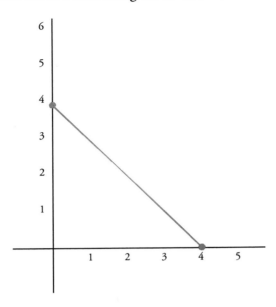

In order to represent three-dimensional figures, we need three coordinate axes (*X*, *Y*, and *Z*) that are all mutually perpendicular to each other. Since we cannot draw three mutually perpendicular axes on a two-dimensional surface, we use oblique representations.

Example: Represent a cube with sides of 2.

Once again, we draw three sides along the three axes to make things easier.

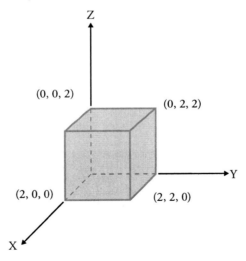

Each point has three coordinates (*X, Y, Z*).

> **SKILL** Demonstrating knowledge of applications of measurement and
> **15.7** geometry in everyday life

Length

*Example: A car skidded 170 yards on an icy road before coming to a stop.
How long is the skid distance in kilometers?*

Since 1 yard 0.9 meter, multiply 170 yards by 0.9.

$$170 \times 0.9 = 153 \text{ meters}$$

Since 1000 meters = 1 kilometer, divide 153 by 1000.

$$\frac{153}{1000} = 0.153 \text{ kilometer}$$

*Example: The distance around a race course is exactly 1 mile, 17 feet, and
$9\frac{1}{4}$ inches. Approximate this distance to the nearest tenth of a foot.*

Convert the distance to feet.

1 mile = 1760 yards = 1760 3 feet = 5280 feet

$9\frac{1}{4}$ inches = $\frac{37}{4} \times \frac{1}{12} = \frac{37}{48} \approx 0.77083$ foot

So 1 mile, 17 feet, and $9\frac{1}{4}$ inches = 5280 + 17 + 0.77083 feet

= 5297.$\underline{7}$7083 feet.

Now, we need to round to the nearest tenths digit. The underlined 7 is in the
tenths place. The digit in the hundredths place, also a 7, is greater than 5, so the 7
in the tenths place must be rounded up to 8 to get a final answer of 5297.8 feet.

Weight

*Example: Zachary weighs 150 pounds. Tom weighs 153 pounds. What is the
difference in their weights in grams?*

153 pounds − 150 pounds = 3 pounds

1 pound = 454 grams

3(454 grams) = 1362 grams

Capacity

*Example: Students in a fourth grade class want to fill a 3-gallon jug using
cups of water. How many cups of water are needed?*

1 gallon = 16 cups of water

3 gallons × 16 cups = 48 cups of water are needed.

Time

Example: It takes Cynthia 45 minutes to get ready each morning. How many hours does she spend getting ready each week?

$$45 \text{ minutes} \times 7 \text{ days} = 315 \text{ minutes}$$

$$\frac{315 \text{ minutes}}{60 \text{ minutes in an hour}} = 5.25 \text{ hours}$$

Rounding

Depending on the degree of accuracy needed, an object may be measured to different units. For example, a pencil may be 6 inches to the nearest inch, or $6\frac{3}{8}$ inches to the nearest eighth of an inch. Similarly, it might be 15 cm to the nearest centimeter or 154 mm to the nearest millimeter.

When one is given a set of objects and their measurements, it is often helpful to attempt to round to the nearest given unit. When rounding to a given place value, it is necessary to look at the number in the next smaller place. If this number is 5 or more, the number in the place being rounded to is increased by 1, and all numbers to the right are changed to 0. If the number is less than 5, the number in the place being rounded to stays the same, and all numbers to the right are changed to 0.

Some methods of rounding measurements can require an additional step. First, the measurement must be converted to a decimal number. Then the rules for rounding applied.

Example: Round the measurements to the given units.

MEASUREMENT	ROUND TO NEAREST	ANSWER
1 foot 7 inches	foot	2 ft
5 pound 6 ounces	pound	5 pounds
$5\frac{9}{16}$ inches	inch	6 inches

Convert each measurement to a decimal number. Then apply the rules for rounding.

$$1 \text{ foot } 7 \text{ inches} = 1\frac{7}{12} \text{ ft} = 1.58333 \text{ ft, round up to } 2 \text{ ft}$$
$$5 \text{ pounds } 6 \text{ ounces} = 5\frac{6}{16} \text{ pounds} = 5.375 \text{ pound, round to } 5 \text{ pounds}$$
$$5\frac{9}{16} \text{ inches} = 5.5625 \text{ inches, round up to } 6 \text{ inches}$$

Symmetry

There are four basic transformational symmetries that can be used: *translation, rotation, reflection*, and *glide reflection*. The transformation of an object is called its image. If the original object was labeled with letters, such as *ABCD*, the image may be labeled with the same letters followed by a prime symbol: *A'B'C'D'*.

A TRANSLATION is a transformation that "slides" an object a fixed distance in a given direction. The original object and its translation have the same shape and size, and they face in the same direction.

TRANSLATION: a transformation that "slides" an object a fixed distance in a given direction

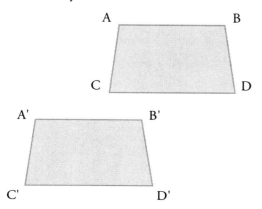

An example of a translation in architecture is stadium seating. The seats are the same size and the same shape, and they face in the same direction.

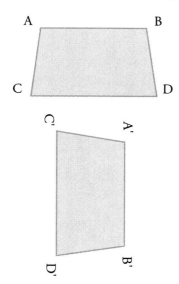

A ROTATION is a transformation that turns a figure about a fixed point called the center of rotation. An object and its rotation are the same shape and size, but the figures may be turned in different directions. Rotations can occur in either a clockwise or a counterclockwise direction.

ROTATION: a transformation that turns a figure about a fixed point called the center of rotation

Rotations can be seen in wallpaper and art, and a Ferris wheel is an example of rotation.

An object and its **REFLECTION** have the same shape and size, but the figures face in opposite directions.

REFLECTION: objects have the same shape and size, but the figures face in opposite directions

LINE OF REFLECTION: the line where a mirror may be placed; the distance from a point to this line is the same as the distance from the points image to this line

The line (where a mirror may be placed) is called the **LINE OF REFLECTION**. The distance from a point to the line of reflection is the same as the distance from the point's image to the line of reflection.

A **GLIDE REFLECTION** is a combination of a reflection and a translation.

GLIDE REFLECTION: a combination of a reflection and a translation

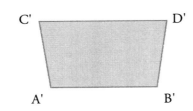

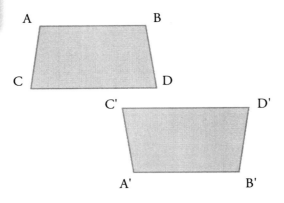

TANGENT: when objects make contact at a single point or along a line without crossing

Objects that are **TANGENT** make contact at a single point or along a line without crossing. Understanding tangency is critical in the construction industry, where architects and engineers must figure out how various elements fit together. An example can be demonstrated by building a stair railing. The architect must determine the points of tangency between the banisters, which might even be curved, and the posts supporting the banisters.

Many types of flooring found in homes are examples of SYMMETRY: Persian carpets, tiling, patterned broadloom, etc. The human body is an example of symmetry, even though that symmetry is not perfect. If you split the torso down the middle, on each half you will find one ear, one eye, one nostril, one shoulder, one arm, one leg, and so on, in approximately the same place.

> **SYMMETRY:** equal on both sides

COMPETENCY 16
UNDERSTAND CONCEPTS AND SKILLS RELATED TO ALGEBRA

SKILL 16.1 **Recognizing the characteristics of patterns, identifying correct extensions of patterns, and recognizing relationships among patterns**

The following table represents the number of problems Mr. Rodgers is assigning his math students for homework each day, starting with the first day of class.

Day	1	2	3	4	5	6	7	8	9	10	11
Number of Problems	1	1	2	3	5	8	13				

If Mr. Rodgers continues this pattern, how many problems will he assign on the 11th day?

If we look for a pattern, it appears that the number of problems assigned each day is equal to the sum of the problems assigned for the previous two days. We test this as follows:

Day 2 = 1 + 0 = 1
Day 3 = 1 + 1 = 2
Day 4 = 2 + 1 = 3
Day 5 = 3 + 2 = 5
Day 6 = 5 + 3 = 8
Day 7 = 8 + 5 = 13

Therefore, Day 8 would have 21 problems; Day 9, 34 problems; Day 10, 55 problems; and Day 11, 89 problems.

A sequence is a pattern of numbers arranged in a particular order. When a list of numbers is in a sequence, a pattern may be expressed in terms of variables. Suppose we have the sequence 8, 12, 16, …. If we assign the variable a to the initial term, 8, and assign the variable d to the difference between the first two terms, we can formulate a pattern of a, $a + d$, $a + 2d$, … $a + (n - 1)d$. With this formula, we can determine any number in the sequence. For example, let's say we want to know what the 400th term would be. Using the formula

$a + (n - 1)d =$
$8 + (400 - 1)\ 4 =$
$8 + 399(4) =$
$8 + 1596 = 1604$

we determine that the 400th term would be 1604.

Suppose we have an equation,. We construct a table of values in order to graph the equation to see whether we can find a pattern.

x	-2	-1	0	1	2
y	-3	-1	1	3	5

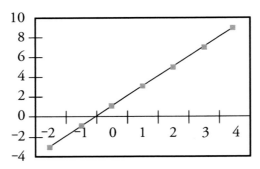

The pattern formed by the points is that they all lie on a line. Therefore, we can determine any solution of y by picking an x-coordinate and finding the corresponding point on the line. For example, if we want to know the value of y when x is equal to 4, we find the corresponding point and see that y is equal to 9.

SKILL Applying knowledge of the concepts of variable, function, and
16.2 equation to the expression of algebraic relationships

A VARIABLE is a letter that is used to represent one or more numbers. An algebraic expression is a collection of numbers, variables, operations, and grouping symbols.

Example: 16 times a, divided by b may be expressed algebraically as $\frac{16a}{b}$.

An EQUATION is formed when an equals sign is placed between two expressions.

Example:

$$3x + y = 24$$

A FUNCTION is a special type of relationship between two values, in which each input value corresponds to exactly one output value. Another way of defining a function is as a relation in which no two ordered pairs have the same value.

Example:

$$\{(a,1),(b,4),(c,4)\}$$

VARIABLE: a letter that is used to represent one or more numbers

EQUATION: formed when an equals sign is placed between two expressions

FUNCTION: a special type of relationship between two values, in which each input value corresponds to exactly one output value

SKILL Identifying relationships among variables based on mathematical
16.3 expressions, tables, graphs, and rules

A relationship between two quantities can be shown using a table, graph, or rule. In this example, the rule $y = 9x$ describes the relationship between the total amount earned, y, and the total amount of $9 sunglasses sold, x.

A table using these data would appear as:

number of sunglasses sold	1	5	10	15
total dollars earned	9	45	90	135

Each (x,y) relationship between a pair of values is called the COORDINATE PAIR that can be plotted on a graph. The coordinate pairs (1,9), (5,45), (10,90), and (15,135) are plotted on the graph below.

COORDINATE PAIR: the relationship between a pair of values

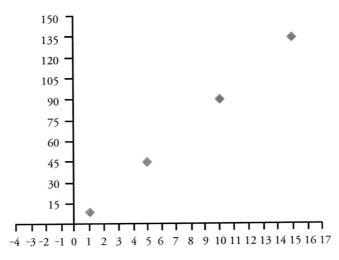

This graph shows a linear relationship. A linear relationship is one in which two quantities are proportional to each other. Doubling x also doubles y. On a graph, a straight line depicts a linear relationship.

The function or relationship between two quantities may be analyzed to determine how one quantity depends on the other.

For example, the function above shows a relationship between y and x:

$y = 2x + 1$.

The relationship between two or more variables can be analyzed using a table, graph, written description, or symbolic rule. The function $y = 2x + 1$ is written as a symbolic rule. The same relationship is also shown in the table below:

x	0	2	3	6	9
y	1	5	7	13	19

This relationship could be written in words by saying that the value of y is equal to two times the value of x, plus one. This relationship could be shown on a graph by plotting given points such as the ones shown in the table above.

Another way to describe a function is as a process in which one or more numbers are input into an imaginary machine that produces another number as the output. If 5 is input (x) into a machine with a process of $x + 1$, then the output (y) will equal 6.

In real situations, relationships can be described mathematically. The function $y = x + 1$, can be used to describe the idea that people age one year on their birthday. To describe the relationship in which a person's monthly medical costs are 6 times a person's age, we could write $y = 6x$. The monthly cost of medical care could be predicted using this function. A 20-year-old person would spend $120 per month ($120 = 20 \times 6$). An 80-year-old person would spend $480 per month ($480 = 80 \times 6$). Therefore, one could analyze the relationship as follows: As you get older, medical costs increase by a factor of $6.00 each year.

SKILL 16.4 Applying the methods of algebra to solve equations and inequalities

Procedure for Solving Algebraic Equations

Example:

$3(x + 3) = -2x + 4$ Solve for x.

1. Expand to eliminate all parentheses.

$3x + 9 = -2x + 4$

2. Multiply each term by the LCD to eliminate all denominators.

3. Combine like terms on each side when possible.

4. Use the properties to put all variables on one side and all constants on the other side.

$\rightarrow 3x + 9 - 9 = -2x + 4 - 9$ (subtract nine from both sides)

$\rightarrow 3x = -2x - 5$

$\rightarrow 3x + 2x = -2x + 2x - 5$ (add $2x$ to both sides)

$\rightarrow 5x = -5$

$\rightarrow \dfrac{3x}{5} = \dfrac{-5}{5}$ (divide both sides by 5)

$\rightarrow x = -1$

Example:

Solve: $3(2x + 5) - 4x = 5(x + 9)$

$6x + 15 - 4x = 5x + 45$

$2x + 15 = 5x + 45$

$-3x + 15 = 45$

$-3x = 30$

$x = -10$

Example: Mark and Mike are twins. 3 times Mark's age, plus 4, equals 4 times Mike's age minus 14. How old are the boys?

Since the boys are twins, their ages are the same. "Translate" the English into algebra. Let $x =$ their age.

$$3x + 4 = 4x - 14$$
$$18 = x$$

The boys are each 18 years old.

Procedure for Solving Algebraic Inequalities

We use the same procedure as we used above for solving linear equations, but the answer is either represented in graphical form on the number line or in interval form.

Example: Solve the inequality, show its solution using interval form, and graph the solution on the number line.

$$\frac{5x}{8} + 3 \geq 2x - 5$$
$$8\left(\frac{5x}{8}\right) + 8(3) \geq 8(2x) - 5(8) \qquad \text{Multiply by LCD} = 8.$$
$$5x + 24 \geq 16x - 40$$
$$5x + 24 - 24 - 16x \geq 16x - 16x - 40 - 24$$

Subtract $16x$ and 24 from both sides of the equation.

$$-11x \geq -16$$
$$\frac{-11x}{-11} \leq \frac{-64}{-11}$$
$$x \leq \frac{64}{11} \qquad ; \qquad x \leq 5\frac{9}{11}$$

Solution in interval form: $\left(-\infty, 5\frac{9}{11}\right]$

Note: "] " means $5\frac{9}{11}$ is included in the solution.

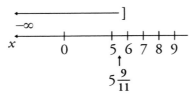

Example: Solve the following inequality, and express your answer in both interval and graphical form.

$$3x - 8 < 2(3x - 1)$$
$$3x - 8 < -2 \qquad \text{Distributive property}$$
$$3x - 6x - 8 + 8 < 6x - 6x - 2 + 8$$

Add 8 and subtract $6x$ from both sides of the equation.

$$-3x < 6$$
$$\frac{-3x}{-3} > \frac{6}{-3}$$
$$x > -2$$

Note the change in direction of the equality.

Graphical form:

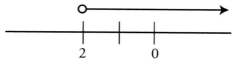

or

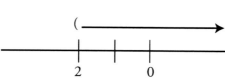

Interval form: $(-2, \infty)$

Recall:

A. Using a parenthesis or an open circle implies that the point is not included in the answer.

B. Using a bracket or a closed circle implies that the point is included in the answer.

Example: Solve:

$$6x + 21 < 8x + 31$$
$$-2x + 21 < 31$$
$$-2x < 10$$
$$x < -5$$

Note that the inequality sign has changed.

The solution set of linear equations is all the ordered pairs of real numbers that satisfy both equations—thus the intersection of the lines. There are two methods for solving linear equations: *linear combinations* and *substitution*.

In the SUBSTITUTION method, an equation is solved for either variable. That solution is then substituted in the other equation to find the remaining variable.

> **SUBSTITUTION:** when an equation is solved for either of two variables, then the solution is substituted to find the remaining variable

Example:

1. $2x + 8y = 4$
2. $x - 3y = 5$
2A. $x = 3y + 5$ Solve equation (2) for x.
1A. $2(3y + 5) + 8y = 4$ Substitute for x in equation (1).
    $6y + 10 + 8y = 4$ Solve.
    $14y = -6$
    $y = \frac{-3}{7}$ Solution.

2. $x - 3y = 5$

$\quad x - 3(\frac{-3}{7}) = 5$ Substitute the value of y.

$\quad x = \frac{26}{7} = 3\frac{5}{7}$ Solution.

Thus, the solution set of the system of equations is $(3\frac{5}{7}, \frac{-3}{7})$.

LINEAR COMBINATIONS: when one or both of two equations are replaced with an equivalent equation so that they can be combined and one variable eliminated

In the **LINEAR COMBINATIONS** method, one or both of the equations are replaced with an equivalent equation so that the two equations can be combined (added or subtracted) to eliminate one variable.

Example:

1. $4x + 3y = -2$.
2. $5x - y = 7$
1. $4x + 3y = -2$
2A. $15x - 3y = 2$.   Multiply equation (2) by 3.
     $19x = 19$ Combining (1) and (2a).
     $x = 1$ Solve.

To find y, substitute the value of x in equation 1 (or 2).

1. $4x + 3y = -2$
     $4(1) + 3y = -2$
     $4 + 3y = -2$
     $3y = -6$
     $y = -2$

Thus, the solution is $x = 1$ and $y = -2$ or the ordered pair (1, -2).

Some word problems can be solved using a system (group) of equations or inequalities. Watch for phrases such as *greater than, less than, at least,* and *no more than,* which indicate the need for inequalities.

Example: Farmer Greenjeans bought 4 cows and 6 sheep for $1700. Mr. Ziffel bought 3 cows and 12 sheep for $2400. If all the cows were the same price and all the sheep were another fixed price, find the price charged for a cow and the price charged for a sheep.

Let x = price of a cow

Let y = price of a sheep

Then Farmer Greenjeans's equation would be: $4x + 6y = 1700$

Mr. Ziffel's equation would be: $3x + 12y = 2400$

To solve by addition-subtraction:

Multiply the first equation by -2: $-2(4x + 6y = 1700)$

Keep the other equation the same: $(3x + 12y = 2400)$

Now the equations can be added to each other to eliminate one variable, and you can solve for the other variable.

$$-8x - 12y = -3400$$
$$\underline{3x + 12y = \ \ 2400} \quad \text{Add these equations.}$$
$$-5x \qquad = -1000$$

$x = 200 \ \leftarrow$ the price of a cow was \$200.

Solving for y, $y = 150 \ \leftarrow$ the price of a sheep was \$150.

Solve one of the equations for a variable. (Try to make an equation without fractions if possible.) Substitute this expression into the equation that you have not yet used. Solve the resulting equation for the value of the remaining variable.

$$4x + 6y = 1700$$
$$3x + 12y = 2400 \ \leftarrow \text{Solve this equation for } x.$$

It becomes $x = 800 - 4y$. Now substitute $800 - 4y$ in place of x in the *other* equation. $4x + 6y = 1700$ now becomes:

$$4(800 - 4y) + 6y = 1700$$
$$3200 - 16y + 6y = 1700$$
$$3200 - 10y = 1700$$
$$-10y = -1500$$
$$y = 150, \text{ or } \$150 \text{ for a sheep.}$$

Substituting 150 back into an equation for y, find x.

$$4x + 6(150) = 1700$$
$$4x + 900 = 1700$$
$$4x = 800 \text{ so } x = 200, \text{ or } \$200 \text{ for a cow.}$$

Example: Sharon's Bike Shoppe can assemble a three-speed bike in 30 minutes or a ten-speed bike in 60 minutes. The profit on each bike sold is $60 for a three-speed and $75 for a ten-speed bike. How many of each type of bike should the shop assemble during an 8-hour day (480 minutes) to make the maximum profit? Total daily profit must be at least $300.

Let $x =$ number of three-speed bikes.

Let $y =$ number of ten-speed bikes.

Since there are only 480 minutes to use each day,

$30x + 60y \leq 480$ is the first inequality.

Since the total daily profit must be at least \$300,

$60x + 75y \geq 300$ is the second inequality.

$32x + 65y \leq 480$ solves to $y \leq 8 - \frac{1}{2x}$

$60x + 75y \geq 300$ solves to $y \geq 4 - \frac{4}{5x}$

Graph these two inequalities:
$$y \leq 8 - \frac{1}{2x}$$
$$y \geq 4 - \frac{4}{5x}$$

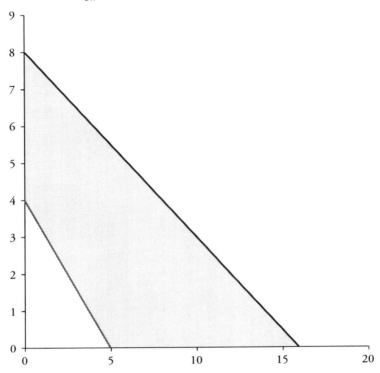

Realize that $x \geq 0$ and $y \geq 0$, since the number of bikes assembled cannot be a negative number. Graph these as additional constraints on the problem. The number of bikes assembled must always be an integer value, so points within the shaded area of the graph must have integer values. The maximum profit will occur at or near a corner of the shaded portion of this graph. Those points occur at (0, 4), (0, 8), (16, 0), or (5, 0).

Since profits are $60/three-speed and $75/ten-speed, the profits for these four points would be:

(0, 4)	60(0) + 75(4) = 300
(0, 8)	60(0) + 75(8) = 600
(16, 0)	60(16) + 75(0) = 960 ← Maximum profit
(5, 0)	60(5) + 75(0) = 300

The maximum profit will occur if 16 three-speed bikes are made daily.

Example: The YMCA wants to sell raffle tickets to raise at least $32,000. If they must pay $7250 in expenses and prizes out of the money collected from the tickets, how many tickets worth $25 each must they sell?

Since they want to raise at least $32,000, that means they would be happy to get 32,000 or more. This requires an inequality.

Let x = number of tickets sold.

Then $25x$ = total money collected for x tickets.

Total money minus expenses must be greater than $32,000.

$25x - 7250 \geq 3200$

$25x \geq 39250$

$x \geq 1570$

If they sell 1,570 tickets or more, they will raise at least $32,000.

Example: The Simpsons went out for dinner. All 4 of them ordered the aardvark steak dinner. Bert paid for the 4 meals and included a tip of $12 for a total of $84.60. How much was one aardvark steak dinner?

Let x = the price of one aardvark dinner.

So $4x$ = the price of 4 aardvark dinners.

$4x + 12 = 84.60$

$4x = 72.60$

$x = \$18.50$ for each dinner.

SKILL 16.5 Analyzing how algebraic functions are used to plot points, describe graphs, and determine slope

Graphically

A first-degree equation has an equation of the form $ax + by = c$. To find the slope of a line, solve the equation for y. This gets the equation into slope-intercept FORM, $y = mx + b$. In this equation, m is the line's slope.

The y intercept is the coordinate of the point where a line crosses the y-axis. To find the y intercept, substitute 0 for x and solve for y. This is the y intercept. In slope-intercept form, $y = mx + b$, b is the y intercept.

To find the x intercept, substitute 0 for y and solve for x. This is the x intercept. If the equation solves to x = **any number**, then the graph is a vertical line, because it only has an x intercept. Its slope is undefined.

If the equation solves to y = **any number**, then the graph is a horizontal line, because it only has a y intercept. Its slope is 0 (zero).

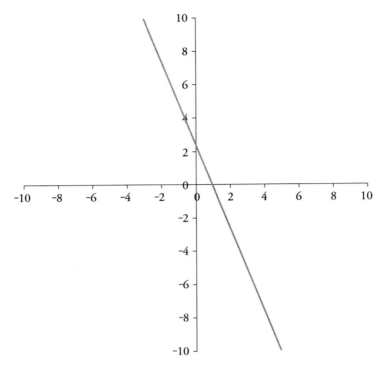

$$5x + 2y = 6$$
$$y = \frac{25}{2x + 3}$$

The equation of a line can be found from its graph by finding its slope and its intercept. The slope formula looks like this:

$$m = \frac{y_2 - y_1}{x_2 - x_1}$$

The y intercept can be found using this equation:

$$Y - y_a = m\,(X - x_a)$$

(x_a, y_a) can be (x_1, y_1) or (x_2, y_2) If **m**, the value of the slope, is distributed through the parentheses, the equation can be rewritten into other forms of the equation of a line.

Example: Find the equation of a line through (9, -6)and (-1,2).

$$\text{slope} = \frac{y_2 - y_1}{x_2 - x_1} = \frac{2 - {^-6}}{{^-1} - 9} = \frac{8}{210} = \frac{24}{5}$$

$$Y - y_a = m(X - x_a) \rightarrow Y - 2 = \frac{^-4}{5(X - {^-1})} \rightarrow$$
$$Y - 2 = \frac{^-4}{5(X + 1)} \rightarrow Y - 2 = \frac{^-4}{5}X\frac{^-4}{5} \text{ This is the slope-intercept form}$$
$$Y = \frac{^-4}{5}X + \frac{6}{5}$$

Multiplying by 5 to eliminate fractions, it is:

$$5Y = -4X + 6 \rightarrow 4X + 5Y = 6$$

Example: Find the slope and intercepts of 3x + 2y = 14.

$3x + 2y = 14$

$2y = -3x + 14$

$y = \frac{-3}{2x} + 7$

The slope of the line is $\frac{-3}{2}$. The intercept of the line is 7.

The intercepts can also be found by substituting 0 in place of the other variables in the equation.

To find the y-intercept:

Let $x = 0$; $3(0) + 2y = 14$

$0 + 2y = 14$

$2y = 14$

$y = 7$

$(0,7)$ is the y-intercept.

To find the x-intercept:

Let $y = 0$; $3x + 2(0) = 14$

$3x + 0 = 14$

$3x = 14$

$x = \frac{14}{3}$

$(\frac{14}{3},0)$ is the x-intercept.

Example: Sketch the graph of the line represented by 2x + 3y = 6.

Let $x = 0 \rightarrow 2(0) + 3y = 6$

$\rightarrow 3y = 6$

$\rightarrow y = 2$

$\rightarrow (0,2)$ is the y-intercept

Let $y = 0 \rightarrow 2x + 3(0) = 6$

$\rightarrow 2x = 6$

$\rightarrow x = 3$

$\rightarrow (3,0)$ is the x-intercept

Let $x = 1 \rightarrow 2(1) + 3y = 6$

$\rightarrow 2 + 3y = 6$

$\rightarrow 3y = 4$

$\rightarrow y = \frac{4}{3}$

$\rightarrow \left(1,\frac{4}{3}\right)$ is the third point.

Plotting the three points on the coordinate system, we get the following:

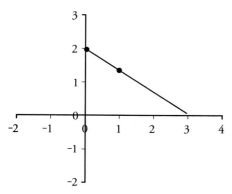

To graph an inequality, solve the inequality for *y*. This gets the inequality in slope intercept form, (for example: $y < mx + b$). The point $(0, b)$ is the *y*-intercept and *m* is the line's slope.

If the inequality solves to $x \geq$ **any number**, then the graph includes a vertical line.

If the inequality solves to $y \leq$ **any number,** then the graph includes a horizontal line.

When graphing a linear inequality, the line will be dotted if the inequality sign is $<$ or $>$. If the inequality signs are either $\geq$ or $\leq$, the line on the graph will be a solid line. Shade above the line when the inequality sign is $\geq$ or $>$. Shade below the line when the inequality sign is $\leq$ or $<$. For inequalities of the forms $x >$ number, $x \leq$ number, $x <$ number, or $x \geq$ number, draw a vertical line (solid or dotted). Shade to the right for $>$ or $\geq$. Shade to the left for $<$ or $\leq$.

Remember: **Dividing or multiplying by a negative number will reverse the direction of the inequality sign.**

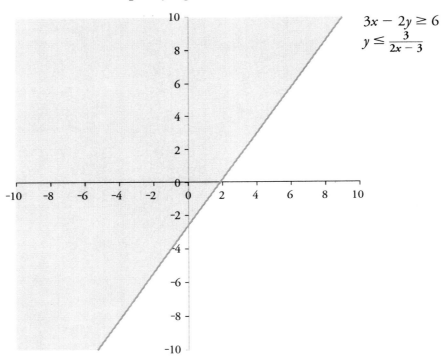

$$3x - 2y \geq 6$$
$$y \leq \frac{3}{2x - 3}$$

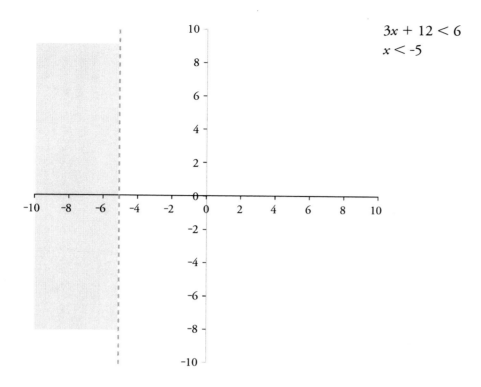

$3x + 12 < 6$

$x < \text{-}5$

Example: Solve by graphing:

$x + y \leq 6$

$x - 2y \leq 6$

Solving the inequalities for y, we find that they become:

$y \leq \text{-}x + 6$ (y-intercept of 6 and slope = $^-1$)

$y \geq \frac{1}{2x - 3}$ (y-intercept of $^-3$ and slope $= \frac{1}{2}$)

A graph with shading is shown below:

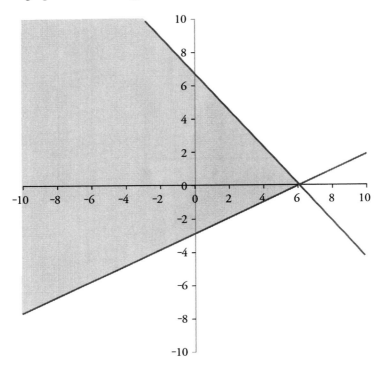

SKILL 16.6 Demonstrating knowledge of applications of algebra in representing relationships and patterns in everyday life

Johannes Kepler discovered a relationship between the average distance of a planet from the sun and the time it takes the planet to orbit the sun.

The following table shows the data for the six planets closest to the sun:

	MERCURY	VENUS	EARTH	MARS	JUPITER	SATURN
Average distance, x	0.387	0.723	1	1.523	5.203	9.541
x^3	0.058	0.378	1	3.533	140.852	868.524
Time, y	0.241	0.615	1	1.881	11.861	29.457
y^2	0.058	0.378	1	3.538	140.683	867.715

Looking at the data in the table, we see that $x^3 \simeq y^2$. We can conjecture the following function for Kepler's relationship: $y = \sqrt{x^3}$.

A **LINEAR FUNCTION** is a function defined by the equation $f(x) = mx + b$. This equation can be used to represent patterns in animals, people, and technology.

Example: A model for the distance traveled by a migrating monarch butterfly looks like f(t) = 80t, where t represents time in days. We interpret this to mean that the average speed of the butterfly is 80 miles per day, and distance traveled may be computed by substituting the number of days traveled for t. In a linear function, there is a constant rate of change.

> **LINEAR FUNCTION:** a function defined by the equation $f(x) = mx + b$

COMPETENCY 17
UNDERSTAND CONCEPTS AND SKILLS RELATED TO DATA ANALYSIS

> **SKILL 17.1** **Applying knowledge of methods for organizing and interpreting data in a variety of formats** *(e.g., tables, frequency distributions, line graphs, circle graphs)*

To make a **BAR GRAPH** or a **PICTOGRAPH**, determine the scale to be used for the graph. Then determine the length of each bar on the graph, or determine the number of pictures needed to represent each item of information. Be sure to include, in the legend, an explanation of the scale.

> **BAR GRAPH:** used to compare various quantities

> **PICTOGRAPHS:** show comparison of quantities using symbols; each symbol represents a number of items

Example: A class had the following grades: 4 As, 9 Bs, 8 Cs, 1 D, and 3 Fs. Graph these on a bar graph and a pictograph.

Pictograph

Grade	Number of Students
A	☺☺☺☺
B	☺☺☺☺☺☺☺☺☺
C	☺☺☺☺☺☺☺☺
D	☺
F	☺☺☺

Bar graph

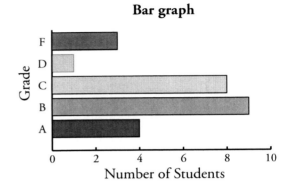

LINE GRAPHS: show trends, often over a period of time

To make a LINE GRAPH, determine appropriate scales for both the vertical and horizontal axes (based on the information to be graphed). Describe what each axis represents, and mark the scale periodically on each axis. Graph the individual points of the graph, and connect the points on the graph from left to right.

Example: Graph the following information using a line graph.

The number of National Merit Scholarship finalists/school year

	90–91	91–92	92–93	93–94	94–95	95–96
Central	3	5	1	4	6	8
Wilson	4	2	3	2	3	2

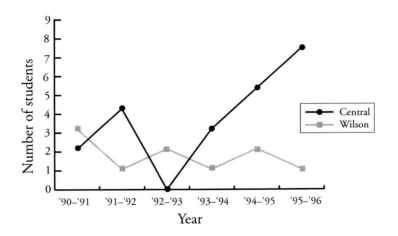

To make a CIRCLE GRAPH, total all the information that is to be included on the graph. Determine the central angle to be used for each sector of the graph using the following formula:

$$\frac{\text{information}}{\text{total information}} \times 360º = \text{degrees in central } \sphericalangle$$

Lay out the central angles to these sizes, label each section, and include each section's percent.

> **CIRCLE GRAPH:** also called pie charts, a circular graph that shows quantities in proportioanls sectors

Example: Graph the following information about monthly expenses on a circle graph:

MONTHLY EXPENSES	
Rent	$400
Food	$150
Utilities	$75
Clothes	$75
Church	$100
Misc.	$200

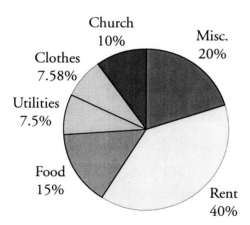

To read a bar graph or a pictograph, read the explanation of the scale that was used in the legend. Compare the length of each bar with the dimensions on the axes, and calculate the value each bar represents. On a pictograph, count the number of pictures used in the chart, and calculate the value of all the pictures.

HISTOGRAMS: summarize information from large sets of data that can be naturally grouped into intervals

To read a circle graph, find the total of the amounts represented on the entire circle graph. To determine the actual amount that each sector of the graph represents, multiply the percent in a sector times the total amount number.

To read a chart, be sure to look at the row and column headings on the table. Use this information to evaluate the information given in the chart.

HISTOGRAMS are used to summarize information from large sets of data that can be naturally grouped into intervals. The vertical axis indicates **FREQUENCY** (the number of times any particular data value occurs), and the horizontal axis indicates data values or ranges of data values. The number of data values in any interval is the **FREQUENCY OF THE INTERVAL.**

FREQUENCY: the number of times any particular data value occurs

FREQUENCY OF THE INTERVAL: the number of data values in any interval

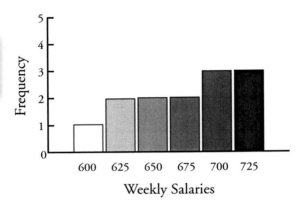

SKILL 17.2 Identifying trends and patterns in data

RANDOM SAMPLING: supplies every combination of items from a frame, or stratum, with a known probability of occurring

RANDOM SAMPLING supplies every combination of items from a frame, or stratum, with a known probability of occurring. However, the term *random* is somewhat misleading, because sampling is typically a very structured and scientific process. A large body of statistical theory quantifies the risk, thus enabling statisticians to determine the appropriate sample size to make it valid to draw conclusions about the larger population from results drawn from the sample.

Systematic sampling selects items in a frame according to the kth sample. The first item is chosen to be the rth, where r is a random integer in the range $1,..., k - 1$.

There are three stages to cluster sampling or area sampling: The target population is divided into many regional clusters (groups), a few clusters are randomly selected for study, and a few subjects are randomly chosen from within a cluster.

CONVENIENCE SAMPLING is the method of choosing items arbitrarily and in an unstructured manner from the frame.

CORRELATION is a measure of association between two variables. It varies from −1 to 1, with 0 being a random relationship, 1 being a perfect positive linear relationship, and −1 being a perfect negative linear relationship.

The **CORRELATION COEFFICIENT** (r) is used to describe the strength of the association between the variables, as well as the direction of the association.

Example:

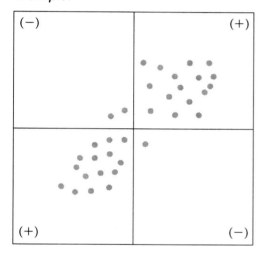

Horizontal and vertical lines are drawn through the **POINT OF AVERAGES**, which is the point on the respective averages of the x and y values. Doing this divides the scatter plot into four quadrants. If a point is in the lower left quadrant, the product of two negatives is positive; in the upper right quadrant, the product of two positives is positive. The positive quadrants are depicted with the positive sign (+). In the two remaining quadrants (upper left and lower right), the product of a negative and a positive is negative. The negative quadrants are depicted with the negative sign (−). If r is positive, then there are more points in the two positive quadrants; if is negative, then there are more points in the two negative quadrants.

REGRESSION is a form of statistical analysis used to predict a dependent variable (y) from values of an independent variable (x). A **REGRESSION EQUATION** is derived from a known set of data.

The simplest regression analysis models the relationship between two variables using the equation $y = a + bx$, where y is the dependent variable and x is the independent variable. This simple equation denotes a linear relationship between x and y. This form would be appropriate if, when you plotted a graph of x and y, you saw the points roughly form along a straight line.

CONVENIENCE SAMPLING: is the method of choosing items arbitrarily and in an unstructured manner from the frame

CORRELATION: a measure of association between two variables

CORRELATION COEFFICIENT: used to describe the strength of the association between the variables, as well as the direction of the association

POINT OF AVERAGES: the point on the respective averages of the x and y values

REGRESSION: a form of statistical analysis used to predict a dependent variable (y) from values of an independent variable (x)

REGRESSION EQUATION: derived from a known set of data

Example:

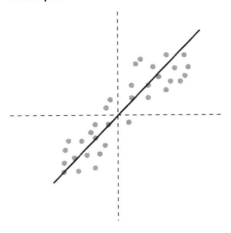

The line can then be used to make predictions.

If all of the data points fell on the line, there would be a perfect correlation ($r = 1.0$) between the x and y data points. These cases represent the best scenarios for prediction. A positive or negative value represents how y varies with x. When r is positive, y increases as x increases. When r is negative, y decreases as x increases.

A linear regression equation is of the form $Y = a + bX$.

Example: A teacher wanted to determine how a practice test influenced a student's performance on the actual test. The practice test grade and the subsequent actual test grade for each student are given in the table below:

PRACTICE TEST (X)	ACTUAL TEST (Y)
94	98
95	94
92	95
87	89
82	85
80	78
75	73

Table continued on next page

65	67
50	45
20	40

We determine the equation for the linear regression line to be $y = 14.650 + 0.834x$.

A new student comes into the class and scores 78 on the practice test. Based on the equation obtained above, what would the teacher predict this student would get on the actual test?

$y = 14.650 + 0.834(78)$

$y = 14.650 + 65.052$

$y = 80$

$\quad = 79.7$

It is predicted that the student will get an 80.

SKILL **Demonstrating knowledge of standard measures** *(e.g., mean, median,*
17.3 *mode, and range)* **used to describe data**

Mean, median, and mode are three measures of central tendency. The MEAN is the average of the data items. The MEDIAN is found by putting the data items in order from smallest to largest and selecting the item in the middle (or the average of the two items in the middle). The MODE is the most frequently occurring item.

RANGE is a measure of variability. It is found by subtracting the smallest value from the largest value.

Example: Find the mean, median, mode, and range of the test scores listed below:

85	77	65
92	90	54
88	85	70
75	80	69
85	88	60
72	74	95

Mean = sum of all scores ÷ number of scores = 78

MEAN: the *sum* of the numbers given, *divided* by the number of items being averaged

MEDIAN: the middle number of a set

MODE: the number that occurs with the greatest frequency in a set of numbers

RANGE: the difference between the highest and lowest value of data items

Median = Put the numbers in order from smallest to largest. Pick the middle number.

54, 60, 65, 69, 70, 72, 74, 75, <u>77</u>, <u>80</u>, 85, 85, 85, 88, 88, 90, 92, 95

{both in middle}

Therefore, the median is the average of two numbers in the middle, 78.5.

Mode = most frequent number
= 85

Range = the largest number minus the smallest number
= 95 − 54
= 41

Different situations require different information. For example, examine the circumstances under which each of the following three scenarios use the numbers provided.

1. Over a 7-day period, the store owner collected data on the ice cream flavors sold. He found the mean number of scoops sold was 174 per day. The most frequently sold flavor was vanilla. This information was useful in determining how much ice cream to order overall, as well as the amounts of each flavor.

   In the case of the ice cream store, the median and range had little business value for the owner.

2. Consider the set of test scores from a math class: 0, 16, 19, 65, 65, 65, 68, 69, 70, 72, 73, 73, 75, 78, 80, 85, 88, and 92. The mean is 64.06 and the median is 71. Because there are only three scores less than the mean in the entire class, the median (71) would be a more descriptive score.

3. Retail storeowners may be most concerned with the most common dress size so that they can order more of that size than of any other.

An understanding of the definitions is important in determining the validity and uses of statistical data. All definitions and applications in this section apply to ungrouped data.

Data item: each piece of data, represented by the letter X.

Mean: the average of all data, which is represented by the symbol $\overline{X}$.

Range: the difference between the highest and lowest values of data items.

Sum of the squares: the sum of the squares of the differences between each item and the mean.

$Sx^2 = (X - \overline{X})^2$

Variance: the sum of the squares quantity divided by the number of items. The lowercase Greek letter sigma squared (σ^2) represents variance.

$$\frac{Sx^2}{N} = \sigma^2$$

The larger the value of the variance, the larger the spread.

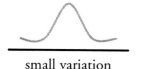

small variation

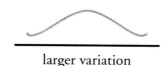

larger variation

Standard deviation: the square root of the variance. The lowercase Greek letter sigma (σ) is used to represent standard deviation.

$$\sigma = \sqrt{\sigma^2}$$

Most statistical calculators have standard deviation keys on them; you should use them when asked to calculate statistical functions. It is important to become familiar with the calculator and the location of the keys needed.

Example: Given the ungrouped data below, calculate the mean, range, standard deviation, and variance.

15	22	28	25	34	38
18	25	30	33	19	23

Mean ($\overline{X}$) = 25.8333333

Range: $38 - 15 = 23$

Standard deviation (σ) = 6.6936952

Variance (σ^2) = 44.805556

Using graphing calculators or computer software has many advantages. The technology is better able to handle large data sets (such as the results of a science experiment), and it is much easier to edit and sort the data and to change the style of the graph to find its best representation. Furthermore, graphing calculators also provide a tool to plot statistics.

SKILL 17.4 Drawing valid conclusions based on data

Both averages and graphs can be misleading if the data are not presented appropriately. The three types of averages used in statistics are mean, median, and mode. If a data set contains one very high or very low value, the mean will not be representative; for example, the teacher's height should not be included in the mean height of a classroom. If the data are clustered around two numbers with a large gap between them, the median will not be representative; for example, expressing the median height in a family of two parents and two small children would have little meaning. Modes are best used with categorical data. In other words, do not mix apples with oranges; a mode of the sale of men's shoe sizes would be helpful to a store for reordering stock of men's shoes. However, finding the mode of men and women's shoe sizes combined would not be a good indicator of the stock that needed to be reordered.

Pictographs can also be misleading, especially if they are drawn to represent three-dimensional objects. If two or more dimensions are changed in reflecting a ratio, the overall visual effect can be misinterpreted. Bar and line graphs can be misleading if the scales are changed; for example, using relatively small scale increments for large numbers will make the comparison differences seem much greater than if larger scale increments are used. Circle graphs, or pie charts, are excellent for comparing relative amounts. However, they cannot be used to represent absolute amounts, and if interpreted as such, they are misleading.

SKILL 17.5 Demonstrating knowledge of applications of data analysis in everyday life

Counting Procedures

So far, in all the problems we have dealt with, the SAMPLE SPACE (the set of all possible outcomes for an experiment or trial) either was given or could be easily obtained. In many real-life situations, however, the sample space and the events within it are very large and difficult to find. There are three techniques that help to find the number of elements in an event or sample space.

> **SAMPLE SPACE:** set of all possible outcomes for an experiment or trial

The counting principle: In a sequence of two distinct events, in which the first one has n number of outcomes or possibilities and the second one has m number of outcomes or possibilities, the total number or possibilities of the sequence will be $n \times m$.

Example: A car dealership has 3 Mazda models, and each model comes in a choice of 4 colors. How many Mazda cars are available at the dealership?
Number of available Mazda cars = (3)(4) = 12

Example: If a license plate consists of 3 digits followed by 3 letters, find the possible number of licenses if:

- repetitions of letters and digits are not allowed.

- repetitions of letters and digits are allowed.

Because we have 26 letters and 10 digits, using the counting principle, we get:

Possible number of licenses $= (26)(25)(24)(10)(9)(8)$
$$= 11,232,000$$

Because repetitions are allowed, we get

Possible number of licenses $= (26)(26)(26)(10)(10)(10)$
$$= 17,576,000$$

The addition principle of counting states:

If A and B are events, $n(AorB) = n(A) + n(B) - n(A \cap B)$

Example: In how many ways can you select a black card or a Jack from an ordinary deck of playing cards?

Let B denote the set of black cards, and let J denote the set of Jacks.
Then, $n(B) = 26, n(J) = 4, n(B \cap J) = 2$, and

$n(BorJ) = n(B) + n(J) - n(B \cap A)$
$= 26 + 4 - 2$
$= 28.$

The addition principle of counting for mutually exclusive events

If A and B are mutually exclusive events, $n(AorB) = n(A) + n(B)$.

Example: A travel agency offers 40 possible trips: 14 to Asia, 16 to Europe, and 10 to South America. In how many ways can you select a trip to Asia or Europe through this agency?

Let A denote trips to Asia, and let E denote trips to Europe. Then $A \cap E = \emptyset$, and $n(AorE) = 14 + 16 = 30$.

Therefore, the number of ways you can select a trip to Asia or Europe is 30.

The multiplication principle of counting for dependent events

Let A be a set of outcomes of Stage 1, and B a set of outcomes of Stage 2. The number of ways, $n(AandE)$, that A and B can occur in a two-stage experiment is represented by:

$n(AandE) = n(A)n(B|A)$

where $n(B|A)$ denotes the number of ways B can occur, given that A has already occurred.

Example: How many ways from an ordinary deck of 52 cards can 2 Jacks be drawn in succession if the first card is drawn but not replaced in the deck, and then the second card is drawn?

This is a two-stage experiment where we must compute $n(A and B)$, where A is the set of outcomes for which a Jack is obtained on the first draw, and B is the set of outcomes for which a Jack is obtained on the second draw.

If the first card drawn is a Jack, then there are only 3 remaining Jacks left to choose from on the second draw. Thus, drawing two cards without replacement means that the events and are dependent.

$$n(A and B) = n(A)n(B|A) = 4 \times 3 = 12$$

The multiplication principle of counting for independent events

Let A be a set of outcomes of Stage 1, and B a set of outcomes of Stage 2. If A and B are independent events, then the number of ways, $n(A and B)$, that A and B can occur in a two-stage experiment is represented by:

$$n(A and B) = n(A)n(B).$$

Example: How many six-letter code "words" can be formed if repetition of letters is not allowed?

Since these are code words, a word does not have to look like a word; for example, abcdef could be a code word. We must choose a first letter and a second letter and a third letter and a fourth letter and a fifth letter and a sixth letter, so this experiment has six stages.

Because repetition is not allowed, there are 26 choices for the first letter; 25 for the second, 24 for the third, 23 for the fourth, 22 for the fifth, and 21 for the sixth. Therefore, we have:

n (six-letter code words without repetition of letters)
$= 26 \times 25 \times 24 \times 23 \times 22 \times 21$
$= 165,765,600$

Permutations

In order to understand **PERMUTATIONS**, the concept of factorials must be addressed.

> **PERMUTATIONS:** an ordering of a certain number of elements of a given set

n factorial, written $n!$, is represented by $n! = n(n-1)(n-2) \dots (2)(1)$.
$5! = (5)(4)(3)(2)(1) = 120$
$3! = 3(2)(1) = 6$

By definition: $0! = 1$

$$1! = 1$$

$\frac{6!}{6!} = 1$ but $\frac{6!}{2!} \neq 3!$

$\frac{6!}{6!} = \frac{6 \times 5 \times 4 \times 3 \times 2}{2!} = 6 \times 5 \times 4 \times 3 = 360$

The number of permutations represents the number of ways in which r items can be selected from n items and arranged in a specific order. It is written as $_nP_r$ and is calculated using the following relationship.

$$_nP_r = \frac{n!}{(n-r)!}$$

When we are calculating permutations, order counts. For example, 2, 3, 4 and 4, 3, 2 are counted as two different permutations. Calculating the number of permutations is not valid with experiments where replacement is allowed.

Example: How many different ways can a president and a vice president be selected from a math class if 7 students are available?

We know we are looking for the number of permutations, since the positions of president and vice president are not equal.

$$_7P_2 = \frac{7!}{(7-2)!} = \frac{7!}{5!} = \frac{7 \times 6 \times 5}{5!} = 7 \times 6 = 42$$

It is important to recognize that the number of permutations is a special case of the counting principle. Unless specifically asked to use the permutation relationship, use the counting principle to solve problems dealing with the number of permutations. For instance, in this example, we have 7 available students from whom to choose a president from. After a president is chosen, we have 6 available students from whom to choose a vice president.

Hence, by using the counting principle, we discover that the ways in which a president and a vice president can be chosen = $7 \times 6 = 42$.

Combinations

When we are dealing with the number of COMBINATIONS, the order in which elements are selected is not important. For instance,

2, 3, 4 and 4, 2, 3 are considered one combination.

> **COMBINATIONS:** an unordered collection of distinct elements

The number of combinations represents the number of ways in which r elements can be selected from n elements (in no particular order). The number of combinations is represented by $_nC_r$ and can be calculated using the following relationship.

$$_nC_r = \frac{n!}{(n-r)r!}$$

Example: In how many ways can 2 students be selected from a class of 7 students to represent the class?

Since both representatives have the same position, the order is not important, and we are dealing with the number of combinations.

$$_nC_r = \frac{7!}{(7-2)!2!} = \frac{7 \times 6 \times 5!}{5!2 \times 1} = 21$$

Example: In a club, there are 6 women and 4 men. A committee of 2 women and 1 man is to be selected. How many different committees can be selected?

This problem has a sequence of two events. The first event involves selecting 2 women out of 6 women, and the second event involves selecting 1 man out of 4 men. We use the combination relationship to find the number of ways in events 1 and 2, and we use the counting principle to find the number of ways the sequence can happen.

$$\text{Number of committees} = {_6C_2} \times {_4C_1}$$
$$\frac{6!}{(6-2)!2!} \times \frac{4!}{(4-1)!1!}$$
$$= \frac{6 \times 5 \times 4!}{4! \times 2 \times 1} \times \frac{4 \times 3!}{3! \times 1}$$
$$= (15) \times (4) = 60$$

Using Tables

Example: The results of a survey of 47 students are summarized in the table below.

	BLACK HAIR	BLONDE HAIR	RED HAIR	TOTAL
Male	10	8	6	24
Female	6	12	5	23
Total	16	20	11	47

Use the table to answer questions a–c.

A. If 1 student is selected at random, find the probability of selecting a male student.

$$\frac{\text{Number of male students}}{\text{Number of students}} = \frac{24}{47}$$

B. If 1 student is selected at random, find the probability of selecting a female with red hair.

$$\frac{\text{Number of red hair females}}{\text{Number of students}} = \frac{5}{47}$$

C. If 1 student is selected at random, find the probability of selecting a student who does not have red hair.

$$\frac{\text{Red hair students}}{\text{Number of students}} = \frac{11}{47}$$

$$1 - \frac{11}{47} = \frac{36}{45}$$

DOMAIN IV
SCIENCE

PERSONALIZED STUDY PLAN

KNOWN MATERIAL/ SKIP IT

PAGE	COMPETENCY AND SKILL	
323	**18: Understand the Characteristics and Processes of Science**	☐
	18.1: Demonstrating knowledge of the nature of scientific knowledge and the values of science	☐
	18.2: Demonstrating knowledge of scientific inquiry and the design of scientific investigations	☐
	18.3: Recognizing the unifying concepts of science	☐
	18.4: Applying knowledge of strategies for observing, collecting, analyzing, and communicating scientific data	☐
	18.5: Recognizing appropriate tools, skills, and safety procedures associated with given scientific investigations	☐
	18.6: Demonstrating knowledge of the connections among science, mathematics, technology, society, and everyday life	☐
337	**19: Understand Concepts and Principles of Earth Science**	☐
	19.1: Comparing characteristics of objects in the solar system and universe and analyzing the effects of the relative positions and motions of the earth, Moon, and Sun	☐
	19.2: Demonstrating knowledge of the composition, structure, and processes of the earth's lithosphere, hydrosphere, and atmosphere	☐
	19.3: Applying knowledge of observing, measuring, predicting, and communicating weather data	☐
	19.4: Recognizing natural and human-caused constructive and destructive processes	☐
	19.5: Demonstrating knowledge of fossils and how they provide evidence of organisms that lived long ago	☐
354	**20: Understand Concepts and Principles of Physical Science**	☐
	20.1: Demonstrating knowledge of the structure and properties of matter	☐
	20.2: Distinguishing between physical and chemical changes	☐
	20.3: Demonstrating knowledge of conservation of matter and energy as they are applied to physical systems	☐
	20.4: Recognizing forms of energy, processes of energy transfer, and the interactions of energy and matter	☐
	20.5: Demonstrating knowledge of types of forces and their effects on the position, motion, and behavior of objects	☐
	20.6: Identifying characteristics of simple machines	☐
	20.7: Recognizing characteristics of light, sound, electricity, and magnetism	☐

PERSONALIZED STUDY PLAN

KNOWN MATERIAL/ SKIP IT

COMPETENCY 18
UNDERSTAND THE CHARACTERISTICS AND PROCESSES OF SCIENCE

> **SKILL 18.1** Demonstrating knowledge of the nature of scientific knowledge and the values of science *(e.g., importance of curiosity, honesty, openness, and skepticism; reliance on verifiable evidence)*

Learning can be broadly divided into two kinds: active and passive. ACTIVE LEARNING involves, as the name indicates, a learning atmosphere full of action. In PASSIVE LEARNING, students are taught in a nonstimulating and inactive atmosphere. Active learning involves and draws students into it, thereby interesting them to the point of participating and purposely engaging in learning.

It is crucial that students are actively engaged, not entertained. They should be taught the answers for "How?" and "Why?" questions and encouraged to be inquisitive and interested. Active learning is conceptualized as follows:

ACTIVE LEARNING: involves a learning atmosphere full of action

PASSIVE LEARNING: students are taught in a nonstimulating and inactive atmosphere

A MODEL OF ACTIVE LEARNING	
Experience of	**Dialogue with**
Doing	Self
Observing	Others

This model suggests that all learning activities involve some kind of experience or some kind of dialogue. The two main kinds of dialogue are "dialogue with self" and "dialogue with others." The two main kinds of experience are "observing" and "doing."

Dialogue with Self: This is what happens when learners think reflectively about a topic. They ask themselves a number of things about the topic.

Dialogue with Others: When the students are listening to a book being read by another student or when the teacher is teaching, a partial dialogue takes place because the dialogue is only one-sided. When they are listening to one another and when there is an exchange of ideas back and forth, it is said to be a dialogue with others.

Observing: This is a very important skill in science. This occurs when a learner carefully watches or observes someone else doing an activity or experiment. Although this is a good experience, it is not the same as doing it yourself.

Doing: This refers to when a person does the activity herself, giving that person a valuable firsthand experience.

> **SKEPTICISM:** a Greek word, meaning a method of obtaining knowledge through systematic doubt and continual testing

The scientific attitude is to be curious, open to new ideas, and skeptical. In science, there are always new discoveries, new research, and new theories proposed. Sometimes, old theories are disproved. To view these changes rationally, one must have openness, curiosity, and skepticism. (SKEPTICISM is a Greek word, meaning a method of obtaining knowledge through systematic doubt and continual testing. A scientific skeptic is one who refuses to accept certain types of claims without subjecting them to a systematic investigation.) The students may not have these attitudes inherently, but it is the responsibility of the teacher to encourage, nurture, and practice these attitudes so that students will have a good role model.

Sample Test Question and Rationale

(Average)

1. **Which of the following is a misconception about the task of teaching science in elementary school?**

   A. Teach facts as a priority over teaching how to solve problems

   B. Involve as many senses as possible in the learning experience

   C. Accommodate individual differences in pupils' learning styles

   D. Consider the effect of technology on people rather than on material things

Answer: A. Teach facts as a priority over teaching how to solve problems

Prioritizing facts over problem solving is a common misconception in elementary schools. Often, teachers focus on requiring students to learn and recall facts and information alone, rather than teaching them how to apply the learned facts in solving real scientific problems. In fact, problem solving is a vital skill that students need to obtain and utilize in all classroom settings, as well as their real world experiences. Choices B, C, and D all describe effective teaching strategies that exceptional teachers use in their science classrooms.

SKILL 18.2 **Demonstrating knowledge of the principles of scientific inquiry and the design of scientific investigations**

How Hypotheses Are Generated and Tested

Science can be defined as a body of knowledge that is systematically derived from study, observations, and experimentation. Its goal is to identify and establish principles and theories that may be applied to solve problems. Pseudoscience, on the other hand, is a belief that is not warranted. There is no scientific methodology or application. Some of the more classic examples of pseudoscience include witchcraft, extraterrestrial encounters, or any topic that is explained by hearsay.

Scientific theory and experimentation must be repeatable, meaning that the findings of one experiment are able to be duplicated during any number of repetitions. They are also capable of change and able to be disproved. Science depends on communication, agreements, and disagreements among scientists. It is composed of theories, laws, and hypotheses.

- THEORY: the formation of principles or relationships that have been verified and accepted.

- LAW: an explanation of events that occur with uniformity under the same conditions (e.g., laws of nature, law of gravitation).

- HYPOTHESIS: an unproved theory or educated guess followed by research to best explain a phenomena. A theory is a proven hypothesis.

Science is limited by the available technology. An example of this would be the relationship of the discovery of the cell and the invention of the microscope. As our technology improves, more hypotheses will become theories and possibly laws. Science is also limited by the data that are able to be collected.

Data may be interpreted differently on different occasions. Science limitations cause explanations to be changeable as new technologies emerge. The first step in scientific inquiry is posing a question to be answered. Next, a hypothesis is formed to provide a plausible explanation. An experiment is then proposed and performed to test this hypothesis. A comparison between the predicted and observed results is the next step. Conclusions are then formed, and it is determined whether the hypothesis is correct or incorrect. If incorrect, the next step is to form a new hypothesis, and the process is repeated.

Methods for collecting data

The procedure used to obtain data is important to the outcome. Experiments consist of CONTROLS and VARIABLES. A control is the experiment conducted under normal conditions. The variable includes a factor that is changed. In biology,

THEORY: the formation of principles or relationships that have been verified and accepted

LAW: an explanation of events that occur with uniformity under the same conditions

HYPOTHESIS: an unproved theory or educated guess followed by research to best explain a phenomena

CONTROL: the experiment conducted under normal conditions

VARIABLE: includes a factor that is changed

the variable may be light, temperature, acidity (pH), or time. The differences in tested variables may be used to make a prediction or to form a hypothesis. Only one variable should be tested at a time; for example, one would not alter both the temperature and pH of the experimental subject.

An independent variable is one that is changed or manipulated by the researcher. This could be the amount of light given to a plant or the temperature at which bacteria are grown. The dependent variable is that which is influenced by the independent variable.

Sample Test Question and Rationale

(Rigorous)

1. **In an experiment measuring the growth of bacteria at different temperatures, what is the independent variable?**

   A. Number of bacteria

   B. Growth rate of bacteria

   C. Temperature

   D. Size of bacteria

Answer: C. Temperature

To answer this question, recall that the independent variable in an experiment is the entity that is changed by the scientist in order to observe the effects (the dependent variable(s)). In this experiment, temperature is changed in order to measure growth of bacteria, so (C) is the answer. Note that answer (A) is the dependent variable and neither (B) nor (D) is directly relevant to the question.

SKILL 18.3 **Recognizing and applying the unifying concepts of science** *(e.g., systems, models, scale)*

Unifying Concepts and Processes among the Sciences

The following are the concepts and processes generally recognized as those common to all scientific disciplines:

- Systems, order, and organization

- Constancy, change, and measurement

- Evolution and equilibrium

- Form and function

- Evidence, models, and explanation

- Systems, order, and organization

Because the natural world is so complex, the study of science involves the organization of items into smaller groups based on interaction or interdependence. These groups are called systems. Examples of organization include the periodic table of elements and the five-kingdom classification scheme for living organisms. Examples of systems include the solar system, the cardiovascular system, Newton's laws of force and motion, and the laws of conservation.

Order refers to the behavior and measurability of organisms and events in nature. The arrangement of planets in the solar system and the life cycle of bacterial cells are examples of order.

Constancy, change, and measurement

Constancy and change describe the observable properties of natural organisms and events. Scientists use different systems of measurement to observe change and constancy. For example, the freezing and melting points of given substances as well as the speed of sound are constant under constant conditions. Growth, decay, and erosion are all examples of natural change.

Evolution and equilibrium

EVOLUTION is the process of change over a long period of time. While biological evolution is the most common example, one can also classify technological advancements, changes in the universe, and changes in the environment as evolution.

EQUILIBRIUM is the state of balance between opposing forces of change. Homeostasis and ecological balance are examples of equilibrium.

EVOLUTION: the process of change over a long period of time

EQUILIBRIUM: the state of balance between opposing forces of change

Form and function

Form and function are properties of organisms and systems that are closely related. The function of an object usually dictates its form, and the form of an object usually facilitates its function. For example, the form of the heart (e.g., muscle and valves) allows it to perform its function of circulating blood through the body.

Evidence, models, and explanations

Scientists use evidence and models to form explanations of natural events. Models are miniaturized representations of a larger event or system. Evidence is anything that furnishes proof.

Some things happen at too fast or too slow a rate or are too small or too large for us to see. In these cases, we have to rely on indirect evidence to develop models of what is intangible. Once data have been collected and analyzed, it is useful to generalize the information by creating a model. A model is a conceptual representation of a phenomenon. Models are useful in that they clarify relationships, helping us to understand the phenomenon and make predictions about future outcomes. The natural sciences and social sciences employ modeling for this purpose.

Many scientific models are mathematical in nature and contain a set of variables linked by logical and quantitative relationships. These mathematical models may include functions, tables, formulas, and graphs. Typically, such mathematical models include assumptions that restrict them to very specific situations. Oftentimes, this means they can only provide an *approximate* description of what occurs in the natural world. These assumptions, however, prevent the model from becoming overly complicated. For a mathematical model to fully explain a natural or social phenomenon, it has to contain many variables and may become too cumbersome to use. Accordingly, it is critical that assumptions be carefully chosen and thoroughly defined.

Certain models are abstract and contain sets of logical principles rather than relying on mathematics. These types of models are generally vaguer and are more useful for discovering and understanding new ideas. Abstract models can also include actual physical models built to make concepts more tangible. Abstract models, to an even greater extent than mathematical models, make assumptions and simplify actual phenomena.

Proper scientific models must be able to be tested and verified using experimental data. Often these experimental results are necessary to demonstrate the superiority of a model when two or more conflicting models seek to explain the same phenomenon. Computer simulations are increasingly used in both testing and developing mathematical and even abstract models. These types of simulations are especially useful in situations, such as ecology or manufacturing, where experiments are not feasible or variables are not fully under control.

Proper scientific models must be able to be tested and verified using experimental data.

SKILL 18.4 **Applying knowledge of strategies for observing, collecting, analyzing, and communicating scientific data** *(e.g., using graphs, charts, and tables)*

The scientific method is the basic process behind science. It involves several steps, beginning with hypothesis formulation and working through to the conclusion.

1. Pose a question: Although many discoveries happen by chance, the standard thought process of a scientist begins with forming a question to

research. The more limited the question, the easier it is to set up an experiment to answer it.

2. Form a hypothesis: Once the question is formulated, scientists take an educated guess about the answer to the problem or question. This "best guess" is the hypothesis.

3. Conducting the test: To make a test fair, data from an experiment must have a variable or any condition that can be changed, such as temperature or mass. A good test will try to manipulate as few variables as possible to determine which variable is responsible for the result. This requires a second example of a control. A control is an extra setup in which all the conditions are the same except for the variable being tested.

4. Observe and record the data: Reporting data should state specifics of how the measurements were calculated. For example, a graduated cylinder needs to be read with proper procedures. As beginning students, technique must be part of the instructional process to give validity to the data.

5. Drawing a conclusion: After recording data, compare it with that of other groups. A conclusion is the judgment derived from the data results.

Graphing Data

Graphing is an important skill to visually display collected data for analysis. It utilizes numbers to demonstrate patterns. The patterns offer a visual representation, making it easier to draw conclusions. The two types of graphs most commonly used are the line graph and the bar graph (histogram). Line graphs are set up to show two variables represented by one point on the graph. The x-axis is the horizontal axis; it represents the dependent variable. Dependent variables are those that would be present independently of the experiment. A common example of a dependent variable is time. Time proceeds regardless of anything else occurring. The y-axis is the vertical axis; it represents the independent variable. Independent variables are manipulated by the experiment, such as the amount of light or the height of a plant.

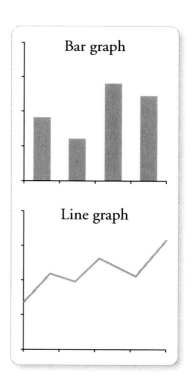

Graphs should be calibrated at equal intervals. If one space represents one day, the next space may not represent ten days. A "best fit" line can be drawn to join the points, and it does not always include all of the points in the data. Axes must always be labeled for the graph to be meaningful. A good title will describe both the dependent and the independent variables.

Bar graphs are set up similarly in regards to axes, but points are not plotted. Instead, the dependent variable is set up as a bar where the x-axis intersects with the y-axis. Each bar is a separate item of data and is not joined by a continuous line.

Designing and Performing Investigations

Normally, knowledge is integrated in the form of a lab report. A report has many sections. It should include a specific title that tells exactly what is being studied. The abstract is a summary of the report; it is written at the beginning of the paper. The purpose should always be defined as it will state the problem. The purpose should include the hypothesis (educated guess) of what is expected from the outcome of the experiment. The entire experiment should relate to this problem.

It is important to describe exactly what was done to prove or disprove a hypothesis. A control is necessary to prove that the results occurred from the changed conditions and would not have happened normally. Only one variable should be manipulated at a time. The observations and results of the experiment should be recorded, including all results from data. Drawings, graphs, and illustrations should be included to support information. Observations are objective, whereas analysis and interpretation is subjective. A conclusion should explain why the results of the experiment either proved or disproved the hypothesis.

Science uses the metric system, as it is accepted worldwide and allows easier comparison among experiments done by scientists around the world. It is important to learn the following basic units and prefixes:

A scientific theory is an explanation of a set of related observations based on a proven hypothesis. A scientific law usually lasts longer than a scientific theory and has more experimental data to support it.

meter	measure of length
liter	measure of volume
gram	measure of mass

deca-	=	10X the base unit	deci-	=	1/10 the base unit
hecto-	=	100X the base unit	centi-	=	1/100 the base unit
kilo-	=	1000X the base unit	milli-	=	1/1000 the base unit

Sample Test Question and Rationale

(Average)

1. Which is the correct order of methodology?
   1. Collecting data
   2. Planning a controlled experiment
   3. Drawing a conclusion
   4. Hypothesizing a result
   5. Revisiting a hypothesis to answer a question

   A. 1,2,3,4,5

   B. 4,2,1,3,5

   C. 4,5,1,3,2

   D. 1,3,4,5,2

Answer: B. 4, 2, 1, 3, 5

The correct methodology for the scientific method is first to make a meaningful hypothesis (educated guess) and then to plan and execute a controlled experiment to test that hypothesis. Using the data collected in that experiment, the scientist then draws conclusions and attempts to answer the original question related to the hypothesis. This is consistent only with answer (B).

SKILL 18.5 Recognizing appropriate tools, instruments, methods, process skills, and safety procedures associated with given scientific investigations

Procedures and Tools

Appropriate use of laboratory materials

Light microscopes are commonly used in high school laboratory experiments. Total magnification is determined by multiplying the ocular (usually 10X) and the objective (usually 10X on low, 40X on high) lenses. Several procedures should be followed to properly care for this equipment:

- Clean all lenses with lens paper only

- Carry microscopes with two hands, one on the arm and one on the base

- Always begin focusing on low power, then switch to high power

- Store microscopes with the low power objective down

- Always use a coverslip when viewing wet mount slides

- Bring the objective down to its lowest position, then focus, moving up to avoid breaking the slide or scratching the lens

Wet mount slides should be made by placing a drop of water on the specimen and then putting a glass coverslip on top of the drop of water. Dropping the coverslip at a forty-five-degree angle will help to avoid air bubbles.

CHROMATOGRAPHY: uses the principles of capillarity to separate substances

CHROMATOGRAPHY uses the principles of capillarity to separate substances such as plant pigments. Molecules of a larger size will move slowly up the paper, whereas smaller molecules will move more quickly, producing lines of pigment.

An indicator is any substance used to assist in the classification of another substance. An example of an indicator is litmus paper, which is used to determine whether a substance is acidic or basic (alkaline). Blue litmus turns pink when an acid is placed on it, and pink litmus turns blue when a base is placed on it. A more accurate measure of pH is pH paper, which turns different colors depending on the pH value.

SPECTROPHOTOMETRY: measures the percent of light at different wavelengths absorbed and transmitted by a pigment solution

SPECTROPHOTOMETRY measures the percent of light at different wavelengths absorbed and transmitted by a pigment solution. Centrifugation involves spinning substances at a high speed. The more dense part of a solution will settle to the bottom of the test tube, whereas the lighter material will stay on top. Centrifugation is used to separate blood into blood cells and plasma, with the heavier blood cells settling to the bottom.

ELECTROPHORESIS: uses electrical charges of molecules to separate them according to their size

ELECTROPHORESIS uses electrical charges of molecules to separate them according to their size. The molecules, such as DNA or proteins, are pulled through a gel toward either the positive end of the gel box (if the material has a negative charge) or the negative end of the gel box (if the material has a positive charge). DNA is negatively charged and moves toward the positive charge.

Storing, identifying, and disposing of chemicals and biological materials

All laboratory solutions should be prepared as directed in the lab manual. Care should be taken to avoid contamination. All glassware should be rinsed thoroughly with distilled water before using and cleaned well after use. In case of an accident, safety goggles should be worn while working with glassware. All solutions should be made with distilled water, as tap water contains dissolved particles that may affect the results of an experiment. Chemical storage should be located in a secured, dry area. Chemicals should be stored in accordance with reactability. Acids are to be locked in a separate area. Used solutions should be disposed of according to local disposal procedures. Any questions regarding safe disposal or chemical safety should be directed to the local fire department.

The Right to Know Law covers science teachers who work with potentially hazardous chemicals. Briefly, the law states that employees must be informed of potentially toxic chemicals. An inventory must be made available if requested. The inventory must contain information about the hazards and properties of the chemicals. This inventory is to be checked against the "substance list." Training must be provided on the safe handling and interpretation of the Material Safety Data Sheet.

CHEMICALS THAT ARE POTENTIAL CARCINOGENS AND NOT ALLOWED IN SCHOOL FACILITIES			
acrylonitrile	arsenic compounds	asbestos	benzene
benzidine	cadmium compounds	chloroform	chromium compounds
ethylene oxide	mercury	nickel powder	ortho-toluidine

Chemicals should not be stored on bench tops or heat sources. They should be stored in groups based on their reactivity with one another and in protective storage cabinets. All containers in the laboratory must be labeled. Suspect and known carcinogens must be labeled as such and segregated within trays to contain leaks and spills. Chemical waste should be disposed of in properly labeled containers. Waste should be separated based on its reactivity with other chemicals.

Biological material should never be stored near food or water used for human consumption. All biological materials should be appropriately labeled. All blood and bodily fluids should be put into well-sealed containers with secure lids to prevent leaking. All biological waste should be disposed of in biological hazardous waste bags.

Material Safety Data Sheets are available for every chemical and biological substance. These are available directly from the company of acquisition or the Internet. The manuals for equipment used in the lab should be read and understood before using them.

Dissection and Alternatives to Dissection

Animals that are not obtained from recognized sources should never be used for dissections. Decaying animals or those of unknown origin may harbor pathogens and/or parasites. Specimens should be rinsed before handling, and latex gloves must be worn. Formaldehyde is a carcinogen and should be avoided or disposed of according to district regulations.

Students who object to dissections for moral reasons should be given an alternative assignment. Interactive dissections are available online or from software companies. Students who refuse to perform a dissection should not be penalized.

Living mammalian vertebrates or birds should not be used for dissections. Lower-order life forms and invertebrates may be used. Biological experiments may be done with all animals except mammalian vertebrates or birds. The animals should not suffer any physiological harm. All animals that are housed and cared for in the school must be handled in a safe and humane manner. Animals are not to remain on school premises during extended vacations unless adequate care is provided. Many state laws stipulate that any instructor who intentionally refuses to comply with the laws may be suspended or dismissed.

Pathogenic organisms must never be used for experimentation. When working with microorganisms, students should treat all microorganisms as if they were pathogenic and maintain sterile conditions at all times to avoid accidental contamination. If taking a national-level exam, it is important to check with the Department of Education for specific state safety procedures. Teachers should know what their state expects not only for the test but also for performance in the classroom and for the welfare of students. It is the responsibility of the teacher to provide a safe environment for the students. Proper supervision greatly reduces the risk of injury, and a teacher should never leave a class for any reason without providing alternate supervision.

If an accident occurs, two factors are considered: foreseeability and negligence. Foreseeability is the anticipation that an event may occur under certain circumstances. Negligence is the failure to exercise ordinary or reasonable care. Safety procedures should be a part of the science curriculum, and a well-managed classroom is important to avoid potential lawsuits.

By law, all science labs should contain the following items of safety equipment:

- Fire blanket that is visible and accessible
- Ground fault circuit interrupters (GFCI) within two feet of water supplies
- Emergency shower capable of providing a continuous flow of water
- Signs designating room exits
- Emergency eye wash station that can be activated by the foot or forearm
- Eye protection for every student, as well as a means of sanitizing equipment
- Emergency exhaust fans providing ventilation to the outside of the building
- Master cutoff switches for gas, electric, and compressed air. Switches must have permanently attached handles. Cutoff switches must be clearly labeled.
- An ABC fire extinguisher
- Storage cabinets for flammable materials

Also recommended, but not required by law:

- Chemical spill control kit

- Fume hood with a motor that is sparkproof

- Protective laboratory aprons made of flame-retardant material

- Signs that will alert people to potential hazardous conditions

- Containers for broken glassware, flammables, corrosives, and waste

- Containers should be labeled

Sample Test Question and Rationale

(Average)

1. **Which procedure uses the size of molecules to create a graph?**

   A. Spectroscopy

   B. Spectrophotometry

   C. Chromatography

   D. Electrophoresis

Answer. C. Chromatography

In chromatography the larger the size of a molecule, the more slowly the molecule moves in a medium. This enables the components of mixtures to be separated.

SKILL 18.6 Demonstrating knowledge of the connections among science, mathematics, technology, society, and everyday life

Biological science is closely connected to technology and the other sciences, and it greatly impacts our society and everyday life. Scientific discoveries often lead to technological advances, and, conversely, technology is often necessary for scientific investigation. Biology and the other scientific disciplines share several unifying concepts and processes that help to unify the study of science.

Science and technology, while distinct concepts, are closely related. Science attempts to investigate and explain the natural world, while technology attempts to solve human adaptation problems. Technology often results from the application of scientific discoveries, and advances in technology can increase the impact of scientific discoveries. For example, Watson and Crick used science to discover the structure of DNA; their discovery led to many biotechnological advances in the manipulation of DNA that had a huge influence on the medical and pharmaceutical fields. The success of Watson and Crick's experiments, however, was

Science and technology, while distinct concepts, are closely related. Science attempts to investigate and explain the natural world, while technology attempts to solve human adaptation problems.

dependent on the technology available. Without the necessary technology, the experiments would have failed.

Biologists use a variety of tools and technologies to perform tests, to collect and display data, and to analyze relationships. Examples of commonly used tools include computer-linked probes, spreadsheets, and graphing calculators.

Biologists use computer-linked probes to measure various environmental factors, including temperature, dissolved oxygen, pH, ionic concentration, and pressure. The advantage of computer-linked probes, as compared to more traditional observational tools, is that the probes automatically gather data and present it in an accessible format. This property of computer-linked probes eliminates the need for constant human observation and manipulation.

Biologists use spreadsheets to organize, analyze, and display data. For example, conservation ecologists use spreadsheets to model population growth and development, to apply sampling techniques, and to create statistical distributions to analyze relationships. Spreadsheet use simplifies data collection and manipulation, and it also allows the presentation of data to be done in a logical and understandable format.

Graphing calculators are another technology with many applications to biology. For example, biologists use algebraic functions to analyze growth, development, and other natural processes. Graphing calculators can manipulate algebraic data and create graphs for analysis and observation. In addition, biologists use the matrix function of graphing calculators to model problems in genetics. The use of graphing calculators simplifies the creation of graphical displays, including histograms, scatter plots, and line graphs. Biologists can transfer data and displays to computers for further analysis. Finally, biologists also connect computer-linked probes, used to collect data, to graphing calculators to ease the collection, transmission, and analysis of data.

The combination of biology and technology has improved the human standard of living in many ways. However, the negative impact of increasing human life expectancy and population on the environment is problematic. In addition, advances in biotechnology (e.g., genetic engineering, cloning) produce ethical dilemmas that society must consider.

COMPETENCY 19

UNDERSTAND CONCEPTS AND PRINCIPLES OF EARTH SCIENCE

> **SKILL 19.1** **Comparing characteristics of objects in the solar system and universe** (e.g., stars, planets) **and analyzing the effects** (e.g., seasons, phases of the Moon) **of the relative positions and motions of the earth, Moon, and Sun**

Our solar system consists of eight established planets:

- Mercury
- Venus
- Earth
- Mars
- Jupiter
- Saturn
- Uranus
- Neptune

Pluto was an established planet in our solar system, but as of the summer of 2006, its status is being reconsidered. The planets are divided into two groups based on their distance from the Sun. The inner planets include Mercury, Venus, Earth, and Mars. The outer planets include Jupiter, Saturn, Uranus, and Neptune.

Planets

Mercury is the closest planet to the Sun. Its surface has craters and rocks. The atmosphere is composed of hydrogen, helium, and sodium. Mercury was named after the Roman messenger god.

Venus has a slow rotation when compared to Earth. Venus and Uranus rotate in opposite directions from the other planets (this opposite rotation is called **retrograde rotation**). The surface of Venus is not visible due to the extensive cloud cover. The atmosphere is composed mostly of carbon dioxide, and sulfuric acid droplets in the dense cloud cover give Venus a yellow appearance. It has a greater greenhouse effect than observed on Earth; the dense clouds combined with carbon dioxide trap heat. Venus was named after the Roman goddess of love.

Earth is considered a water planet, with 70 percent of its surface covered by water. Gravity holds the masses of water in place. The different temperatures observed on Earth allow for the different states (solid, liquid, and gas) of water to

Solar System

Montage of planetary images taken by spacecraft managed by the Jet Propulsion Laboratory. Courtesy of NASA Jet Propulsion Laboratory, Pasadena, CA.

exist. The atmosphere is composed mainly of oxygen and nitrogen. Earth is the only planet that is known to support life.

Mars has a surface that contains numerous craters, active and extinct volcanoes, ridges, and valleys with extremely deep fractures. Iron oxide found in the dusty soil makes the surface seem rust-colored, and the skies seem pink in color. The atmosphere is composed of carbon dioxide, nitrogen, argon, oxygen, and water vapor. Mars has Polar Regions with icecaps composed of water and two satellites. Mars was named after the Roman war god.

Jupiter is the largest planet in the solar system. It has sixteen moons. The atmosphere is composed of hydrogen, helium, methane, and ammonia. There are white-colored bands of clouds indicating rising gases and dark-colored bands of clouds indicating descending gases. The gas movement is caused by heat resulting from the energy of Jupiter's core. Jupiter has a Great Red Spot that is thought to be a hurricane-like cloud. Jupiter has a strong magnetic field.

Saturn, the second largest planet in the solar system, has rings of ice, rock, and dust particles circling it. Saturn's atmosphere is composed of hydrogen, helium, methane, and ammonia, and it has twenty or more satellites. Saturn was named after the Roman god of agriculture.

Uranus is the second largest planet in the solar system with retrograde revolution. Uranus is a gaseous planet. It has ten dark rings and fifteen satellites. Its atmosphere is composed of hydrogen, helium, and methane. Uranus was named after the Greek god of the heavens.

Neptune is another gaseous planet with an atmosphere consisting of hydrogen, helium, and methane. Neptune has three rings and two satellites. Neptune was named after the Roman sea god because its atmosphere is the same color as the seas.

Pluto was once considered the smallest planet in the solar system but is now a minor planet; it is the largest member of the Kuiper Belt. Pluto's atmosphere probably contains methane, ammonia, and frozen water. Pluto has one satellite. It revolves around the Sun every 250 years. Pluto was named after the Roman god of the underworld.

Comets, Asteroids, and Meteors

Astronomers believe that rocky fragments may be the remains of the birth of the solar system that never formed into a planet. Asteroids are found in the region between Mars and Jupiter.

Comets are masses of frozen gases, cosmic dust, and small, rocky particles. Astronomers think that most comets originate in a dense comet cloud beyond

Pluto. Comets consist of a nucleus, a coma, and a tail. A comet's tail always points away from the Sun. The most famous comet, Halley's Comet, is named after the person who first discovered it in 240 BCE. It returns to the skies near the earth every seventy-five to seventy-six years.

Meteoroids are composed of particles of rock and metal of various sizes. When a meteoroid travels through Earth's atmosphere, friction causes its surface to heat up, and it begins to burn. The burning meteoroid falling through Earth's atmosphere is called a meteor (also known as a "shooting star").

Meteorites are meteors that strike Earth's surface. A physical example of a meteorite's impact can be seen in Arizona; the Barringer Crater is a huge crater that was formed by a meteor strike. Many other meteor craters exist throughout the world.

The Sun

The Sun is composed of the following parts:

- The core, the inner portion of the Sun where fusion takes place.

- The photosphere, or the surface of the Sun that produces sunspots (cool, dark areas that can be seen on its surface).

- The chromosphere, which includes hydrogen gases that cause this portion to be red in color; solar flares (sudden brightness of the chromosphere); and solar prominences (gases that shoot outward from the chromosphere).

- The corona, which is the transparent area of the Sun visible only during a total eclipse.

Solar radiation is energy traveling from the Sun into space. Solar flares produce excited protons and electrons that shoot outward from the chromosphere at great speeds reaching Earth. These particles disturb radio reception and also affect the magnetic field on Earth.

Earth's orbit around the Sun and Earth's axis of rotation determine the seasons of the year. When the Northern and Southern Hemispheres of Earth are pointed toward the Sun, it is summer, and when they are pointed away from the Sun, it is winter. Because of the axis of rotation, both hemispheres cannot be in the same season simultaneously. The two hemispheres have opposite seasons at all times.

The Moon

The Moon is a sphere that is always half illuminated by the Sun. The Moon phase we see is dependent on the position of the Moon to Earth. During each lunar orbit (a lunar month), we see the Moon's appearance change from not visibly illuminated to partially illuminated to fully illuminated, then back through partially illuminated to not illuminated again. Although this cycle is a continuous process, there are eight distinct, traditionally recognized stages, called phases.

The phases designate both the degree to which the Moon is illuminated and the geometric appearance of the illuminated part.

LUNAR PHASES		
New Moon		This occurs when the Moon's nonilluminated side is facing Earth. The Moon is not visible (except during a solar eclipse).
Waxing Crescent		This is when the Moon appears to be less than one-half illuminated by direct sunlight. The fraction of the Moon's disk that is illuminated is increasing.
First Quarter		One-half of the Moon appears to be illuminated by direct sunlight during this time. The fraction of the Moon's disk that is illuminated is increasing.
Waxing Gibbous		In this phase, the Moon appears to be more than one-half but not fully illuminated by direct sunlight. The fraction of the Moon's disk that is illuminated is increasing.
Full Moon		This occurs when the Moon's illuminated side is facing Earth. The Moon appears to be completely illuminated by direct sunlight.
Waning Gibbous		This is when the Moon appears to be more than one-half but not fully illuminated by direct sunlight. The fraction of the Moon's disk that is illuminated is decreasing.
Last Quarter		One-half of the Moon is illuminated by direct sunlight in this phase. The fraction of the Moon's disk that is illuminated is decreasing.
Waning Crescent		During this time, the Moon is less than one-half illuminated by direct sunlight. The fraction of the Moon's disk that is illuminated is decreasing.

The Moon, Earth, and the Sun affect ocean tides. Along the west coast of the United States, we experience four different tides per day: two highs and two lows. When the Moon, Earth, and the Sun are in a line, spring tides occur. During these tides, one may observe higher and lower than normal tides. In other words, there will be very high tides and very low tides. When the Moon, Earth, and the Sun are at right angles to each other, neap tides are formed. During these tides, one is not able to observe a great deal of difference in the heights of the high and low tides.

> **SKILL 19.2** **Demonstrating knowledge of the composition, structure, and processes of the earth's lithosphere** (e.g., rocks, minerals), **hydrosphere, and atmosphere and the interactions among these systems** (e.g., water cycle, weather patterns)

Earth's Atmosphere

EL NIÑO refers to a sequence of changes in the ocean and atmospheric circulation across the Pacific Ocean. It causes the water around the equator to be unusually hot every two to seven years. Trade winds normally blow east to west across the equatorial latitudes, piling warm water into the western Pacific. A huge mass of heavy thunderstorms usually forms in the area and produces vast currents of rising air that displace heat poleward. This helps to create the strong midlatitude jet streams. When it occurs, the world's climate patterns are disrupted by a change in location of thunderstorm activity.

EL NIÑO: a sequence of changes in the ocean and atmospheric circulation across the Pacific Ocean

Air masses moving toward or away from the earth's surface are called air currents. Air moving parallel to the earth's surface is called wind. Weather conditions are generated by winds and air currents carrying large amounts of heat and moisture from one part of the atmosphere to another. Wind speeds are measured by instruments called anemometers.

The wind belts in each hemisphere consist of convection cells that encircle Earth like belts. Earth has three major wind belts: trade winds, prevailing westerlies, and polar easterlies. Wind belt formation depends on the differences in air pressures that develop in the doldrums, the horse latitudes, and the polar regions. The doldrums surround the equator. Within this belt, heated air usually rises straight up into Earth's atmosphere. The horse latitudes are regions of high barometric pressure with calm and light winds, and the polar regions contain cold, dense air that sinks to Earth's surface.

Winds caused by local temperature changes include sea breezes and land breezes. Sea breezes are caused by the unequal heating of the land and a large, adjacent body of water. Land heats up faster than water. The movement of cool ocean air toward the land is called a sea breeze. Sea breezes usually begin blowing about midmorning and end about sunset. A breeze that blows from the land to the ocean or a large lake is called a land breeze.

MONSOONS are huge wind systems that cover large geographic areas and that reverse direction seasonally. The monsoons of India and Asia are examples of these seasonal winds. They alternate wet and dry seasons. As denser, cooler air over the ocean moves inland, a steady seasonal wind called a summer or wet monsoon is produced.

> **MONSOONS:** huge wind systems that cover large geographic areas and that reverse direction seasonally

Clouds

Cloud types

High Clouds		Cirrus
Middle Clouds		Cumulus 20,000 ft
Low Clouds	Nimbostratus	Stratus 6,500 ft

Cirrus Clouds	white and feathery; high in the sky
Cumulus	thick, white, and fluffy
Stratus	layers of clouds that cover most of the sky
Nimbus	heavy, dark clouds that represent thunderstorm clouds

Cumulonimbus and *stratonimbus* clouds are variations on the preceding types of clouds.

The air temperature at which water vapor begins to condense is called the DEW POINT. RELATIVE HUMIDITY is the actual amount of water vapor in a certain volume of air compared to the maximum amount of water vapor this air could hold at a given temperature.

> **DEW POINT:** the air temperature at which water vapor begins to condense

> **RELATIVE HUMIDITY:** the actual amount of water vapor in a certain volume of air compared to the maximum amount of water vapor this air could hold at a given temperature

Storms

A thunderstorm is a brief, local storm produced by the rapid upward movement of warm, moist air within a cumulonimbus cloud. Thunderstorms produce lightning and thunder and are accompanied by strong wind gusts and heavy rain or hail.

A severe storm with swirling winds that may reach speeds of hundreds of kilometers per hour is called a tornado. Such a storm is also referred to as a twister. When it occurs, the sky is covered by large cumulonimbus clouds and violent thunderstorms. A funnel-shaped swirling cloud may extend downward from a cumulonimbus cloud and reach the ground. Tornadoes are storms that leave a narrow path of destruction on the ground. A swirling, funnel-shaped cloud that extends downward and touches a body of water is called a waterspout.

Hurricanes are storms that develop when warm, moist air that is carried by trade winds rotates around a low-pressure "eye." A large, rotating, low-pressure system accompanied by heavy precipitation and strong winds is called a tropical cyclone (better known as a hurricane). In the Pacific region, a hurricane is called a typhoon.

Storms that occur only in the winter are known as blizzards or ice storms. A blizzard is a storm with strong winds, blowing snow, and frigid temperatures. An ice storm consists of falling rain that freezes when it strikes the ground, covering everything with a layer of ice.

The Hydrologic Cycle

Water that falls to Earth in the form of rain and snow is called PRECIPITATION. Precipitation is part of a continuous process in which water at Earth's surface evaporates, condenses into clouds, and returns. This process is termed the water cycle. The water located below the land surface is called groundwater.

> **PRECIPITATION:** water that falls to Earth in the form of rain and snow

The impacts of altitude upon climatic conditions are primarily related to temperature and precipitation. As altitude increases, climatic conditions become increasingly drier and colder; solar radiation becomes more severe, and the effects of convection forces are minimized.

Climatic changes as a function of latitude follow a similar pattern (as a reference, latitude moves either north or south from the equator). The climate becomes colder and drier as the distance from the equator increases. Proximity to land or water masses produces climatic conditions based upon the available moisture. Dry and arid climates prevail where moisture is scarce; lush, tropical climates can prevail where moisture is abundant. Climate, as just described, depends on the specific combination of conditions making up an area's environment. People impact all environments, including the world's climatic conditions, by polluting the earth, air, and water.

The Lithosphere

Plates are rigid blocks of the earth's crust and upper mantle. These rigid solid blocks make up the lithosphere. The earth's lithosphere is broken into nine large sections and several small ones. These moving slabs are called plates. The major plates are named after the continents they are "transporting."

The plates float on and move with a layer of hot, plastic-like rock in the upper mantle. Geologists believe that the heat currents circulating within the mantle cause this plastic zone of rock to slowly flow, carrying along the overlying crustal plates.

Earth–Water Interactions

EROSION is the inclusion and transportation of surface materials by another moveable material (usually water, wind, or ice). The most important cause of erosion is running water. Streams, rivers, and tides are constantly at work removing weathered fragments of bedrock and carrying them away from their original location.

A stream erodes bedrock through the grinding action of the sand, pebbles, and other rock fragments. This grinding is called ABRASION. Streams also erode rocks by dissolving or absorbing their minerals. Limestone and marble are readily dissolved by streams.

The breaking down of rocks at or near the earth's surface is known as WEATHERING. Weathering breaks down these rocks into smaller and smaller pieces. There are two types of weathering: physical weathering and chemical weathering.

- Physical weathering is the process by which rocks are broken down into smaller fragments without undergoing any change in chemical composition. Physical weathering is mainly caused by the freezing of water, the expansion of rock, and the activities of plants and animals. Some examples of physical weathering include frost wedging and exfoliation.

  - FROST WEDGING is the cycle of daytime thawing and refreezing at night. This cycle causes large rock masses, especially the rocks exposed on mountaintops, to be broken into smaller pieces.

  - The peeling away of the outer layers from a rock is called EXFOLIATION. Rounded mountaintops are called exfoliation domes because they have been formed in this way.

- Chemical weathering is the breakdown of rocks through changes in their chemical composition. An example would be the change of feldspar in granite to clay. Water, oxygen, and carbon dioxide are the main agents of chemical weathering. When water and carbon dioxide combine chemically, they produce a weak acid that breaks down rocks.

Soils are composed of particles of sand, clay, various minerals, tiny living organisms, and humus, plus the decayed remains of plants and animals. They can be divided into three classes according to their texture: sandy, clay, and loamy. Sandy soils are gritty and their particles do not bind together firmly. They are also porous; water passes through them rapidly. Therefore, sandy soils do not hold much water and have poor absorption. Clay soils are smooth and greasy; their particles bind together firmly. Such soils are moist and usually do not allow water to pass through easily. This type of soil has the lowest potential for runoff. Loamy soils feel somewhat like velvet, and their particles clump together. They are made up of sand, clay, and silt. Loamy soils hold water, but some water can pass through. Percolation is best in this type of soil.

EROSION: the inclusion and transportation of surface materials by another moveable material (usually water, wind, or ice)

ABRASION: the grinding action of sand, pebbles, and other rock fragments in a stream

WEATHERING: the breaking down of rocks at or near the earth's surface

FROST WEDGING: the cycle of daytime thawing and refreezing at night

EXFOLIATION: the peeling away of the outer layers from a rock

Sinkholes

Large features formed by dissolved limestone (calcium carbonate) include sinkholes, caves, and caverns. SINKHOLES are funnel-shaped depressions created by dissolved limestone. Many sinkholes started life as limestone caverns. Erosion weakens the cavern roof, causing it to collapse and form a sinkhole.

Groundwater usually contains large amounts of dissolved minerals, especially if the water flows through limestone. As groundwater drips through the roof of a cave, gases dissolved in the water can escape into the air. A deposit of calcium carbonate is left behind. STALACTITES are icicle-like structures of calcium carbonate that hang from the roofs of caves. Water that falls on a constant spot on the cave floor and evaporates, leaving a deposit of calcium carbonate, builds a STALAGMITE.

> **SINKHOLES:** funnel-shaped depressions created by dissolved limestone

> **STALACTITES:** icicle-like structures of calcium carbonate that hang from the roofs of caves

> **STALAGMITES:** water that falls on a constant spot on the cave floor and evaporates, leaving a deposit of calcium carbonate

SKILL 19.3	Applying knowledge of strategies and tools for observing, measuring, predicting, and communicating weather data

Every day, each person on Earth is affected by the weather. It may be in the form of a typical thunderstorm, bringing moist air and cumulonimbus clouds, or a severe storm with pounding winds that can cause either hurricanes or tornadoes. These are terms we are all familiar with. The daily weather report, however, uses terms like *dew point, barometric pressure,* and *relative humidity.* Suddenly, weather isn't that easy to understand. Yet, it is important to be familiar with these terms if we are to truly understand the weather.

The dew point is the air temperature at which water vapor begins to condense. Weather instruments that forecast weather include the aneroid barometer and the mercury barometer, both of which measure air pressure (barometric pressure). The aneroid barometer works because air exerts varying pressures on a metal diaphragm that will then read air pressure. The mercury barometer operates when atmospheric pressure pushes on a pool of (mercury) in a glass tube. The higher the pressure, the higher up the tube the mercury will rise.

Relative humidity is measured by two kinds of weather instruments: the psychrometer and the air hygrometer. Relative humidity simply indicates the amount of moisture in the air. Relative humidity is defined as a ration of existing amounts of water vapor and moisture in the air when compared to the maximum amount of moisture that the air can hold at the same given pressure and temperature. Relative humidity is stated as a percentage; for example, if you were to analyze relative humidity from data, a parcel of air may be saturated (meaning it now holds all the moisture it can hold at a given temperature), placing the relative humidity at 100 percent.

> *Teachers can find lesson plans for analyzing data and predicting weather at:*
>
> *http://www.srh.weather.gov/srh/jetstream/synoptic/ll_analyze.htm.*

Analyzing Weather Maps

Once you can read a station plot, you can begin to perform map analyses. Meteorologists use the station plots to draw lines of constant pressure (isobars), temperature (isotherms), and the dew point (isodrosotherms) to achieve an understanding of the current state of the atmosphere. This knowledge ultimately leads to better weather forecasts and warnings.

Decoding these plots is easier than it may seem. The values are located in a form similar to a tic-tac-toe pattern. In the upper left, the temperature is plotted in Fahrenheit. In our example, the temperature is 77°F. Along the center, the cloud types are indicated. The top symbol is the high-level cloud type, followed by the midlevel cloud type. The lowest symbol represents the low-level cloud over a number that tells the height of the base of that cloud (in hundreds of feet). In this example, the high level cloud is cirrus, the midlevel cloud is altocumulus, and the low-level cloud is a cumulonimbus, with a base height of 2000 feet.

At the upper right is the atmospheric pressure reduced to mean sea level in millibars (mb) to the nearest tenth, with the leading 9 or 10 omitted. In this case, the pressure would be 999.8 mb. If the pressure was plotted as 024 it would be 1002.4 mb. When trying to determine whether to add a 9 or 10, use the number that will give you a value closest to 1000 mb.

In the second row, the far left number is the visibility in miles. In this example, the visibility is 5 miles. Next to the visibility is the present weather symbol. There are ninety-five symbols that represent the weather (whether it is presently occurring or if it has ended within the previous hour). In this example, a light rain shower was occurring at the time of the observation. The circle symbol in the center represents the amount of total cloud cover reported in eighths. This cloud cover includes all low-, middle-, and high-level clouds. In this example, seven-eighths of the sky was covered with clouds.

This number and symbol tell how much the pressure has changed (in tenths of millibars) in the past three hours, as well as the trend in the change of the pressure during that same period. In this example, the pressure was steady but then fell (lowered), becoming 0.3 millibars lower than it was three hours ago.

Lines indicate wind direction and speed rounded to the nearest 5 knots. The longest line, extending from the sky cover plot, points in the direction from which the wind is blowing, and in this case, the wind is blowing from the southwest. The shorter lines, called barbs, indicate the wind speed in knots (kt). The speed of the wind is calculated by the barbs. Each long barb represents 10 kt, with short barbs representing 5 kt. In this example, the station plot contains two long barbs, so the wind speed is 20 kt, or about 24 mph.

The 71 at the lower left is the dew point temperature, which is the temperature to which the air would have to cool down to become saturated or, in other words, to reach a relative humidity of 100 percent. The lower right area is reserved for the past weather, which is the most significant weather that has occurred within the past six hours (excluding the most recent hour).

Weather Map Symbols

SURFACE STATION MODEL		
Temperature (°F) Weather Dew Point (°F)	Pressure (mb) Sky Cover Wind (kts)	**Data at Surface Station** Temperature—45°F; dew point—29°F; overcast; wind from SE at 15 knots; weather— light rain; pressure—1004.5 mb
UPPER AIR STATION MODEL		
Temperature (°C) Dew Point (°C)	Height (m) Wind (kts)	**Data at Pressure Level—850 mb** Temperature—5°C; dew point—12°C; wind from S at 75 knots; height of level—1564 m
FORECAST STATION MODEL		
Temperature (°F) Weather Dew Point (°F)	PoP (%) Sky Cover Wind (kts)	**Forecast at Valid Time** Temperature—78°F; dew point— 64°F; scattered clouds; wind from E at 10 knots; probability of precipitation 70% with rain showers

MAP SYMBOLS	
Sky Cover	**Wind**
Clear	Calm
1/8	1–2 knots (1–2 mph)
Scattered	3–7 knots (3–8 mph)
3/8	8–12 knots (9–14 mph)
4/8	13–17 knots (15–20 mph)

Table continued on next page

Sky Cover	Wind
5/8	18–22 knots (21–25 mph)
Broken	23–27 knots (26–31 mph)
7/8	48–52 knots (55–60 mph)
Overcast	73–77 knots (84–89 mph)
Obscured	103–107 knots (119–123 mph)
Missing	Shaft in direction wind is coming from

Sample Test Question and Rationale

(Average)

1. **What is the unit of measure for relative humidity?**

   A. Millibar

   B. None

   C. Kilograms per cubic meter

   D. Pounds per square inch

Answer. B. None

Humidity is the amount of moisture in the air and has the units kilograms of water per cubic meter of air. For a given pressure and temperature, there is a maximum amount of water that air can hold. The relative humidity is the actual humidity divided by the maximum possible humidity times 100 percent. The units cancel out.

SKILL 19.4 Recognizing the natural and human-caused constructive and destructive processes that shape the Earth's surface

OROGENY: natural mountain building

SUBDUCTION: plate collisions that are either intercontinental or ocean floor collisions with a continental crust

Natural mountain building is called OROGENY. A mountain is terrain that has been raised high above the surrounding landscape by volcanic action or some form of tectonic plate collision. The plate collisions could be either intercontinental or an ocean floor collision with a continental crust (SUBDUCTION). The physical composition of mountains includes igneous, metamorphic, and sedimentary rocks; some may have rock layers that are tilted or distorted by plate collision forces.

Mountains come in several different types. The physical attributes of a mountain range depend on the angle at which plate movement thrust layers of rock to the surface. Many mountains (Adirondacks, Southern Rockies) were formed along high-angle faults.

- Folded mountains (Alps, Himalayas) are produced by the folding of rock layers during their formation. The Himalayas are the highest mountains in the world and contain Mount Everest, which rises almost 9 km above sea level. The Himalayas were formed when India collided with Asia. The movement that created this collision is still occurring at the rate of a few centimeters per year.

- Fault-block mountains (Utah, Arizona, and New Mexico) are created when plate movement produces tension forces instead of compression forces. The area under tension produces normal faults; rock along these faults is displaced upward.

  – Dome mountains are formed as magma tries to push up through the crust but fails to break the surface. Dome mountains resemble huge blisters on the earth's surface.

  – Upwarped mountains (Black Hills of South Dakota) are created in association with a broad arching of the crust. They can also be formed by rock thrust upward along high-angle faults.

VOLCANISM is the term given to the movement of magma through the crust as well as its emergence as lava onto the Earth's surface. Volcanic mountains are built up by successive deposits of volcanic materials. An active volcano is one that is presently erupting or building to an eruption. A dormant volcano is one that is between eruptions but still shows signs of internal activity that might lead to an eruption in the future. An extinct volcano is said to be no longer capable of erupting. Most of the world's active volcanoes are found along the rim of the Pacific Ocean, which is also a major earthquake zone. This curving belt of active faults and volcanoes is often called the Ring of Fire. The world's best-known volcanic mountains include Mount Etna in Italy and Mount Kilimanjaro in Africa. The Hawaiian Islands are actually the tops of a chain of volcanic mountains that rise from the ocean floor.

> **VOLCANISM:** the movement of magma through the crust as well as its emergence as lava onto the Earth's surface

THREE TYPES OF VOLCANIC MOUNTAINS	
Shield Volcanoes	Associated with quiet eruptions. Lava emerges from the vent or opening in the crater and flows freely out over the earth's surface until it cools and hardens into a layer of igneous rock. A repeated lava flow builds this type of volcano into the largest volcanic mountain. Mauna Loa in Hawaii is the largest shield volcano on Earth.
Cinder Cone Volcanoes	Associated with explosive eruptions as lava is hurled high into the air in a spray of droplets of various sizes. These droplets cool and harden into cinders and particles of ash before falling to the ground. The ash and cinder pile up around the vent to form a steep, cone-shaped hill called the cinder cone. Cinder cone volcanoes are relatively small but may form quite rapidly.
Composite Volcanoes	Described as being built by both lava flows and layers of ash and cinders. Mount Fuji in Japan, Mount St. Helens in Washington State, and Mount Vesuvius in Italy are all famous composite volcanoes.

The mechanisms of producing mountains

Mountains are produced by different types of mountain-building processes. Most major mountain ranges are formed by the processes of folding and faulting. Folded mountains are produced by the folding of rock layers. Crustal movements may press horizontal layers of sedimentary rock together from the sides, squeezing them into wavelike folds. Upfolded sections of rock are called anticlines, and downfolded sections of rock are called synclines. The Appalachian Mountains are an example of folded mountains, with long ridges and valleys in a series of anticlines and synclines formed by folded rock layers.

FAULTS are fractures in the earth's crust that have been created by either tension or compression forces transmitted through the crust. These forces are produced by the movement of separate blocks of crust. Fault lines are categorized on the basis of the relative movement between the blocks on both sides of the fault plane. The movement can be horizontal, vertical, or oblique.

A dip-slip fault occurs when the movement of the plates is vertical and opposite. The displacement is in the direction of the inclination, or dip, of the fault. Dip-slip faults are classified as normal faults wherein the rock above the fault plane moves down relative to the rock below.

Reverse faults are created when the rock above the fault plane moves up relative to the rock below. Reverse faults with a very low angle to the horizontal are also referred to as thrust faults. Faults in which the dominant displacement is horizontal movement along the trend or strike (length) of the fault are called strike-slip faults. When a large strike-slip fault is associated with plate boundaries, it is called a transform fault. The San Andreas Fault in California is a well-known transform fault. Faults that have both vertical and horizontal movement are called oblique-slip faultst. When lava cools, igneous rock is formed. This formation can occur either above ground or below ground.

INTRUSIVE ROCK includes any igneous rock that was formed below the earth's surface. Batholiths are the largest structures of intrusive type rock; they are composed of near-granite materials and are the core of the Sierra Nevada Mountains. Extrusive rock includes any igneous rock that was formed at the Earth's surface.

DIKES are old lava tubes that form when magma entered a vertical fracture and hardened. Sometimes, magma squeezes between two rock layers and hardens into a thin horizontal sheet called a sill. A laccolith is formed in much the same way as a sill, but the magma that creates a laccolith is very thick and does not flow easily. It pools and forces the overlying strata into creating an obvious surface dome.

FAULT: fractures in the earth's crust that have been created by either tension or compression forces transmitted through the crust

INTRUSIVE ROCK: any igneous rock that was formed below the earth's surface

DIKES: old lava tubes that form when magma entered a vertical fracture and hardened

A CALDERA is normally formed by the collapse of the top of a volcano. This collapse can be caused by a massive explosion that destroys the cone and empties most, if not all, of the magma chamber below the volcano. The cone collapses into the empty magma chamber, forming a caldera.

An inactive volcano may have magma solidified in its pipe. This structure, called a volcanic neck, is resistant to erosion; today, it may be the only visible evidence of the past presence of an active volcano. When lava cools, igneous rock is formed. This formation can occur either above ground or below ground.

Glaciation

About 12,000 years ago, a vast sheet of ice covered a large part of the northern United States. This huge, frozen mass had moved southward from the northern regions of Canada as several large bodies of slow-moving ice, or GLACIERS. A time period in which glaciers advance over a large portion of a continent is called an ICE AGE. A glacier is a large mass of ice that moves or flows over the land in response to gravity. Glaciers form among high mountains and in other cold regions.

The two main types of glaciers are valley glaciers and continental glaciers. Erosion by valley glaciers is characteristic of U-shaped erosion. They produce sharp-peaked mountains such as the Matterhorn in Switzerland. Continental glaciers ride over mountains in their paths, leaving smoothed, rounded mountains and ridges.

Evidence of the North American glacial coverage during the most recent ice age remains as large boulders from northern environments dropped in southerly locations; abrasive grooves; glacial troughs created by the rounding out of steep valleys through glacial scouring; and the remains of glacial sources, called cirques, that were created by frost wedging the rock at the bottom of the glacier. Remains of plants and animals typically found in warm climates that have been discovered in the moraines and outwash plains help to support the theory of periods of warmth during the past ice ages.

The Ice Age began about two to three million years ago. This age saw the advancement and retreat of glacial ice over millions of years. Theories relating to the origin of glacial activity include PLATE TECTONICS, in which it is demonstrated that some continental masses, now in temperate climates, were at one time blanketed by ice and snow. Another theory involves changes in the earth's orbit around the Sun, changes in the angle of Earth's axis, and the wobbling of Earth's axis. Support for the validity of this theory has come from deep-ocean research that indicates a correlation between climatic-sensitive microorganisms and the changes in Earth's orbital status.

> **CALDERA:** the formation left by the collapse of a volcano cone into an empty magma chamber

> **GLACIERS:** large bodies of slow-moving ice

> **ICE AGE:** a time period in which glaciers advance over a large portion of a continent

> *The two main types of glaciers are valley glaciers and continental glaciers.*

> **PLATE TECTONICS:** theory of the origin of glacial activity that demonstrates that some continental masses, now in temperate climates were at one time blanketed by snow

The movement of tectonic plates

Data obtained from many sources led scientists to develop the theory of plate tectonics. This theory is the most current model to explain not only the movement of the continents but also the changes in the earth's crust caused by internal forces. PLATES are rigid blocks of the earth's crust and upper mantle. Movement of these crustal plates creates areas where the plates diverge as well as areas where the plates converge. A major area of divergence is located in the mid-Atlantic. Here, hot mantle rock rises and separates at the point of divergence, creating new oceanic crust at the rate of 2 to 10 centimeters per year.

CONVERGENCE occurs when the oceanic crust collides with either another oceanic plate or a continental plate. The oceanic crust sinks, forming an enormous trench and generating volcanic activity. Convergence also includes continent-to-continent plate collisions. When two plates slide past each other, a transform fault is created. These movements produce many major features of the earth's surface, including mountain ranges, volcanoes, and earthquake zones. Most of these features are located at plate boundaries, where the plates interact by spreading apart, pressing together, or sliding past each other. These movements are very slow, averaging only a few centimeters a year.

Boundaries form between spreading plates where the crust is forced apart in a process called RIFTING. Rifting generally occurs at midocean ridges. Rifting can also take place within a continent, splitting the continent into smaller landmasses that drift away from one another, thereby forming an ocean basin between them. The Red Sea is a product of rifting. As the seafloor spreading takes place, new material is added to the inner edges of the separating plates. In this way, the plates grow larger and the ocean basin widens. This is the process that broke up the supercontinent Pangaea and created the Atlantic Ocean.

Boundaries between colliding plates are zones of intense crustal activity. When a plate of ocean crust collides with a plate of continental crust, the more dense oceanic plate slides under the lighter continental plate and plunges into the mantle. This process is called subduction, and the site where it takes place is called a subduction zone. A subduction zone is usually visible on the seafloor as a deep depression called a trench.

The crustal movement identified by plates sliding sideways past each other produces a plate boundary that is characterized by major faults. These faults are capable of unleashing powerful earthquakes. The San Andreas Fault forms such a boundary between the Pacific Plate and the North American Plate.

PLATES: rigid blocks of the earth's crust and upper mantle

CONVERGENCE: occurs when the oceanic crust collides with either another oceanic plate or a continental plate; also includes continent-to-continent plate collisions

RIFTING: process by which the Earth's crust is forced apart; generally occurs in midocean ridges

Natural Disasters

An important topic in science is the effect of natural disasters and events on society, as well as the effect human activity has on inducing such events. Naturally occurring geological, climatic, and environmental events can greatly affect the lives of humans. At the same time, the activities of humans can induce such events that would not normally occur.

Nature-induced hazards include floods, landslides, avalanches, volcanic eruptions, wildfires, earthquakes, hurricanes, tornadoes, droughts, and disease. Such events often occur naturally due to changing weather patterns or geological conditions. Property damage, resource destruction, and the loss of human life are the possible outcomes of natural hazards. Thus, natural hazards are often extremely costly on both an economic and personal level.

While many nature-induced hazards occur naturally, human activity can often stimulate such events. For example, destructive land use practices such as mining can induce landslides or avalanches if not properly planned and monitored. In addition, human activities can cause other hazards, including global warming and waste contamination. Global warming is an increase in the earth's average temperature, resulting, at least in part, from the burning of fuels by humans. Global warming is hazardous because it disrupts the earth's environmental balance and can negatively affect weather patterns. Ecological and weather pattern changes can promote the preceding natural disasters.

Improper hazardous waste disposal by humans can contaminate the environment, resulting in a variety of changes. One devastating effect of hazardous waste contamination is the stimulation of disease in human populations. Thus, hazardous waste contamination negatively affects both the environment and the people who live in it.

> *Naturally occurring geological, climatic, and environmental events can greatly affect the lives of humans. At the same time, the activities of humans can induce such events that would not normally occur.*

SKILL 19.5 **Demonstrating knowledge of how fossils are formed and how they provide evidence of organisms that lived long ago**

A FOSSIL is the remains or trace of an ancient organism that has been preserved naturally in the earth's crust. Sedimentary rocks usually are rich sources of fossil remains. Those fossils found in layers of sediment were embedded in the slowly forming sedimentary rock strata. The oldest fossils known are the traces of 3.5 billion-year-old bacteria found in sedimentary rocks. Few fossils are found in metamorphic rock, and virtually none are found in igneous rocks. The magma is so hot that any organism trapped in the magma is destroyed.

> **FOSSIL:** the remains or trace of an ancient organism that has been preserved naturally in the earth's crust

Although the fairly well-preserved remains of a woolly mammoth embedded in ice were found in Russia in May 2007, the best-preserved animal remains are typically discovered in natural tar pits. When an animal accidentally falls into the tar, it becomes trapped, sinking to the bottom. Preserved bones of the saber-toothed tiger have been found in tar pits.

Prehistoric insects have been found trapped in ancient amber or fossil resin that was excreted by some extinct species of pine trees. Fossil molds are the hollow spaces in a rock previously occupied by bones or shells. A fossil cast is a fossil mold that fills with sediments or minerals that later harden to form a cast. Fossil tracks are the imprints in hardened mud left behind by birds or animals.

Sample Test Question and Rationale

(Average)

1. **Fossils are usually found in:**

    A. Metamorphic rock

    B. Sedimentary rock

    C. Igneous rock

    D. The Earth's mantle

Answer. B. Sedimentary rock

Fossils are the remains of organisms. Metamorphic rock is subject to heat and pressure, so any fossils are destroyed. Sedimentary rock is formed when sediment is compacted, so the fossils are preserved. Igneous rock comes from the cooling of magma.

COMPETENCY 20
UNDERSTAND CONCEPTS AND PRINCIPLES OF PHYSICAL SCIENCE

SKILL 20.1 Demonstrating knowledge of the structure and properties of matter (e.g., atoms, elements, molecules, density, boiling and freezing points)

ATOM: the smallest particle of an element that retains the properties of that element

An **ATOM** is the smallest particle of an element that retains the properties of that element. All of the atoms of a particular element are the same. The atoms of each element are different from the atoms of other elements.

An **ELEMENT** is a substance that cannot be broken down into other substances. To date, scientists have identified 109 elements, 89 of which are found in nature and

20 of which are synthetic. Elements are assigned an identifying symbol of one or two letters. For example, the symbol for oxygen is O, which stands for one atom of oxygen. However, because oxygen atoms in nature are joined together in pairs, the symbol O_2 represents oxygen as we know it.

This pair of oxygen atoms is a molecule. A **MOLECULE** is the smallest particle of substance that can exist independently and has all of the properties of that substance. A molecule of most elements is made up of one atom. However, oxygen, hydrogen, nitrogen, and chlorine molecules are made of two atoms each.

A **COMPOUND** is made of two or more elements that have been chemically combined. Each element's atoms join together when they bind chemically; the result is that the elements lose their individual identities. The compound that they become has different properties.

We use a formula to show the elements of a chemical compound. A chemical formula is a shorthand way of showing what is in a compound by using symbols and subscripts. The letter symbols let us know which elements are involved, and the number subscript tells how many atoms of each element are involved. No subscript is used if there is only one atom involved. For example, carbon dioxide is made up of one atom of carbon (C) and two atoms of oxygen (O_2), so the formula would be represented as CO_2.

Substances can combine without a chemical change. A mixture is any combination of two or more substances in which the substances keep their own properties. Fruit salads and ice cream sundaes are mixtures, but you might not recognize each individual ingredient if they are stirred together. Colognes and perfumes are other examples. You may not readily recognize the individual elements, but they can be separated. Compounds and mixtures are similar in that they are made up of two or more substances. However, they have the following opposite characteristics:

Compounds	Mixtures
Are made up of one kind of particle	Are made up of two or more particles
Are formed during a chemical change	Cannot be formed by a chemical change
Are broken down only by chemical changes	Can be separated by physical changes
Have properties that are different from their individual parts	Have properties that are the same as their parts
Have a specific amount of each ingredient	Do not have a definite amount of each ingredient

ELEMENT: a substance that cannot be broken down into other substances

MOLECULE: the smallest particle of substance that can exist independently and has all of the properties of that substance

COMPOUND: made of two or more elements that have been chemically combined

Some common compounds are acids, bases, salts, and oxides. They are classified according to their characteristics.

An ACID contains one element of hydrogen (H). Although it is never wise to taste a substance to identify it, acids have a sour taste. Vinegar and lemon juice are both acids, and acids occur in many foods in a weak state. Strong acids can burn skin and destroy materials.

COMMON ACIDS	
Sulfuric Acid (H_2SO_4)	Used in medicines, alcohol, dyes, and car batteries
Nitric Acid (HNO_3)	Used in fertilizers, explosives, and cleaning materials
Carbonic Acid (H_2CO_3)	Used in soft drinks
Acetic Acid ($HC_2H_3O_2$)	Used in making plastics, rubber, photographic film, and as a solvent

BASES have a bitter taste, and the stronger ones feel slippery. Like acids, strong bases can be dangerous and should be handled carefully. All bases contain the elements oxygen and hydrogen (OH). Many household cleaning products contain bases.

COMMON BASES	
Sodium Hydroxide (NaOH)	Used in making soap, paper, vegetable oils, and refining petroleum
Ammonium Hydroxide (NH_4OH)	Used for making deodorants, bleaching compounds, and cleaning compounds
Potassium Hydroxide (KOH)	Used for making soaps, drugs, dyes, alkaline batteries, and purifying industrial gases
Calcium ($Ca(OH)_2$)	Used in making cement and plaster hydroxide

An INDICATOR is a substance that changes color when it comes into contact with an acid or a base. Litmus paper is an indicator. Blue litmus paper turns red in an acid. Red litmus paper turns blue in a base. A substance that is neither acid nor base is neutral. Neutral substances do not change the color of litmus paper.

SALT is formed when an acid and a base combine chemically. Water is also formed. The process is called neutralization. Table salt (NaCl) is an example of this process. Salts are also used in toothpaste, epsom salts, and cream of tartar. Calcium chloride ($CaCl_2$) is used on frozen streets and walkways to melt the ice.

OXIDES are compounds that are formed when oxygen combines with another element. Rust is an oxide formed when oxygen combines with iron. Melting point refers to the temperature at which a solid becomes a liquid. Melting takes place when there is sufficient energy available to break the intermolecular forces that hold molecules together in a solid. Boiling point refers to the temperature at which a liquid becomes a gas. Boiling occurs when there is enough energy available to break the intermolecular forces holding the molecules together as a liquid.

OXIDES: compounds that are formed when oxygen combines with another element

DENSITY is the mass of a substance contained per unit of volume. It is stated in grams per cubic centimeter (g/cm^3).

DENSITY: the mass of a substance contained per unit of volume

Sample Test Question and Rationale

(Easy)

1. **Which of the following type of substance tastes bitter and feels slippery?**

   A. Acid

   B. Base

   C. Salt solution

   D. Oxides

Answer. B. Base

Vinegar is an acid and tastes sour. Soap is a base and tastes bitter. Acids produce the hydronium ion and bases produce the hydroxide ion. Acids and bases neutralize each other to produce salts.

SKILL 20.2 Distinguishing between physical and chemical changes

Everything in the world is made up of MATTER, whether it is a rock, a building, an animal, or a person. Matter is defined by its characteristics: It takes up space, and it has mass. MASS is a measure of the amount of matter in an object. Two objects of equal mass will balance each other on a simple balance scale no matter where the scale is located. For instance, two rocks with the same amount of mass that are in balance on the earth will also be in balance on the Moon. They will feel heavier on Earth than on the Moon because of the gravitational pull of Earth. So, although the two rocks have the same mass, they will have different weight.

MATTER: everything in the world is made up of matter, which is defined by the space it takes up and it's mass

MASS: the measure of the amount of matter in an object

WEIGHT is the measure of Earth's pull of gravity on an object. It can also be defined as the pull of gravity between other bodies. The units of weight measure

WEIGHT: the measure of Earth's pull of gravity on an object

commonly used are the pound in English measure and the kilogram in metric measure.

VOLUME: the amount of cubic space that an object occupies

In addition to mass, matter also has the property of volume. VOLUME is the amount of cubic space that an object occupies. Volume and mass together give a more exact description of the object. Two objects may have the same volume but different mass, the same mass but different volumes, and so on. For instance, consider two cubes that are each one cubic centimeter, with one made from plastic and one made from lead. They have the same volume, but the lead cube has more mass. The measure that we use to describe the cubes takes into consideration both the mass and the volume. DENSITY is the mass of a substance contained per unit of volume. If the density of an object is less than the density of a liquid, the object will float in the liquid. If the object is denser than the liquid, the object will sink.

DENSITY: the mass of a substance contained per unit of volume

Density is stated in grams per cubic centimeter (g/cm³), where the gram is the standard unit of mass. To find an object's density, one must measure its mass and its volume, then divide the mass by the volume ($D = m/V$). To find an object's density, first use a balance to find its mass. Then calculate its volume. If the object is a regular shape, one can find the volume by multiplying the length, width, and height together. However, if it is an irregular shape, one can find the volume by seeing how much water it displaces. Measure the water in the container before and after the object is submerged. The difference will be the volume of the object.

SPECIFIC GRAVITY: the ratio of the density of a substance to the density of water

SPECIFIC GRAVITY is the ratio of the density of a substance to the density of water. For instance, the specific density of one liter of turpentine is calculated by comparing its mass (0.81 kg) to the mass of one liter of water (1 kg):

$$\frac{\text{mass of 1L alcohol}}{\text{mass of 1L water}} = \frac{0.81 \text{ kg}}{1.00 \text{ kg}} = 0.81$$

Physical properties and chemical properties of matter describe the appearance or behavior of a substance. A physical property can be observed without changing the identity of a substance. For instance, one can describe the color, mass, shape, and volume of a book. Chemical properties describe the ability of a substance to be changed into new substances. Baking powder goes through a chemical change as it changes into carbon dioxide gas during the baking process.

ENERGY: the ability to cause change in matter, such as heating a frozen liquid changes it from a solid to a liquid

Matter constantly changes. A physical change is a change that does not produce a new substance. The freezing and melting of water is an example of physical change. A chemical change (or chemical reaction) changes the inherent properties of a substance. This includes things such as burning materials that turn into smoke or a seltzer tablet that fizzes into gas bubbles when submerged in water.

EVAPORATION: the change in phase from liquid to gas

The phase of matter (solid, liquid, or gas) is identified by its shape and volume. A solid has a definite shape and volume. A liquid has a definite volume but no shape. A gas has no shape or volume because it will spread out to occupy the entire space of whatever container it is in.

ENERGY is the ability to cause change in matter. Applying heat to a frozen liquid changes it from solid back to liquid. Continue heating it, and it will boil and give off steam, a gas. EVAPORATION is the change in phase from liquid to gas. CONDENSATION is the change in phase from gas to liquid.

> **CONDENSATION:** the change in phase from gas to liquid

Sample Test Question and Rationale

(Easy)

1. **The phase of water refers to its:**

   A. Chemical properties

   B. Physical properties

   C. Temperature

   D. Chemical composition

Answer. B. Physical properties

The phase of a substance refers to whether it is in the gaseous, liquid, or solid state. It is not considered a chemical property because a phase change is considered a physical change. The phase of a substance depends mostly on its temperature.

SKILL 20.3 Demonstrating knowledge of the concepts of conservation of matter and conservation of energy as they are applied to physical systems

The law of conservation of energy states that energy is neither created nor destroyed. Thus, energy changes form whenever energy transactions occur in nature. Because the total energy in the universe is constant, energy continually transitions between forms. For example, an engine burns gasoline, converting the chemical energy of the gasoline into mechanical energy. A plant converts radiant energy of the Sun into chemical energy found in glucose. A battery converts chemical energy into electrical energy.

Chemical reactions are the interactions of substances that result in chemical changes and changes in energy. Chemical reactions involve changes in electron motion as well as the breaking up and formation of chemical bonds. Reactants are the original substances that interact to form distinct products. Endothermic chemical reactions consume energy, while exothermic chemical reactions release energy with product formation. Chemical reactions occur continually in nature and are also induced by man for many purposes.

Nuclear reactions, or atomic reactions, are reactions that change the composition, energy, and/or structure of atomic nuclei. Nuclear reactions change the number of protons and neutrons in the nucleus. The two main types of

FUSION: the joining of atomic nuclei, which results in the release of large amounts of energy

FISSION: the splitting of an atomic nucleus, which releases large amounts of energy

nuclear reactions are: FUSION and FISSION. The fusion of small nuclei such as hydrogen releases more energy than is required to cause the nuclei to fuse and are therefore exothermic reactions. In contrast, the fusion of large nuclei requires more energy than is produced and are therefore endothermic reactions. The opposite is true for fission reactions. The fission of heavy atomic nuclei are exothermic reactions, while the fission of smaller nuclei are endothermic reactions. The fission of large nuclei such as uranium releases large amounts of energy because the products of fission undergo further nuclear reactions that are self-sustaining. Fission and fusion reactions can occur naturally, but are most recognized as man-made events. Particle acceleration and bombardment with neutrons are two methods of inducing nuclear reactions.

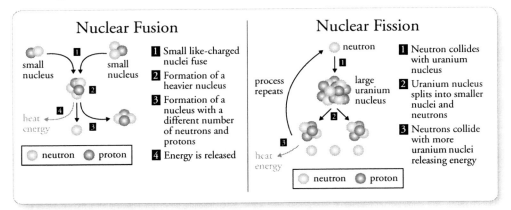

The law of conservation can also be applied to physical and biological processes. For example, when a rock is weathered, it does not just lose pieces, but it is broken down into its composite minerals, many of which enter the soil. Biology takes advantage of decomposers to recycle decaying material. Since energy is neither created nor destroyed, we know that it must change form. An animal may die, but its body will either be consumed by other animals or decay into the ecosystem. Either way, it enters another form, and the matter still exists in some form or another.

Sample Test Question and Rationale

(Easy)

1. **What type of reaction is the joining of two nuclei?**

   A. Chemical

   B. Fission

   C. Fusion

   D. Endothermic

Answer. C. Fusion

Fusion occurs on the sun when hydrogen nuclei combine to form helium. A fission reaction occurs when uranium splits into barium and krypton. Energy is released in both reactions, so both reactions are exothermic.

SKILL Recognizing forms of energy *(e.g., heat, light)*, processes of energy
20.4 transfer, and the interactions of energy and matter

The relationship between heat, forms of energy, and work (mechanical, electrical, etc.) are the LAWS OF THERMODYNAMICS. These laws deal strictly with systems in thermal equilibrium and not those within the process of rapid change or in a state of transition. Systems that are nearly always in a state of equilibrium are called reversible systems.

The first law of thermodynamics is a restatement of the conservation of energy. The change in heat energy supplied to a system (Q) is equal to the sum of the change in the internal energy (U) and the change in the work done by the system against internal forces.

$$\triangle Q = \triangle U + \triangle W$$

The second law of thermodynamics is stated in two parts:

1. No machine is 100 percent efficient. It is impossible to construct a machine that only absorbs heat from a heat source and performs an equal amount of work because some heat will always be lost to the environment.

2. Heat cannot spontaneously pass from a colder to a hotter object. An ice cube sitting on a hot sidewalk will melt into a little puddle, but it will never spontaneously cool and form the same ice cube. Certain events have a preferred direction called the arrow of time.

ENTROPY is the measure of how much energy or heat is available for work. Work occurs only when heat is transferred from hot to cooler objects. Once this is done, no more work can be extracted. The energy is still being conserved, but it is not available for work when the objects are the same temperature. Theory has it that, eventually, all things in the universe will reach the same temperature. If this happens, energy will no longer be usable.

The law of conservation of energy states that energy is neither created nor destroyed. Thus, energy changes form when energy transactions occur in nature. The following are the major forms energy can take:

- Thermal energy is the total internal energy of objects created by the vibration and movement of atoms and molecules. Heat is the transfer of thermal energy.

- Acoustical energy, or sound energy, is the movement of energy through an object in waves. Energy that forces an object to vibrate creates sound.

- Radiant energy is the energy of electromagnetic waves. Light—visible and otherwise—is an example of radiant energy.

> **LAWS OF THERMODYNAMICS:** the relationship between heat, forms of energy, and work (mechanical, electrical, etc.)

> **ENTROPY:** the measure of how much energy or heat is available for work

- Electrical energy is the movement of electrical charges in an electromagnetic field. Examples of electrical energy are electricity and lightning.

- Chemical energy is the energy stored in the chemical bonds of molecules. For example, the energy derived from gasoline is chemical energy.

- Mechanical energy is the potential and kinetic energy of a mechanical system. Rolling balls, car engines, and body parts in motion exemplify mechanical energy.

- Nuclear energy is the energy present in the nucleus of atoms. The division, combination, or collision of nuclei release nuclear energy.

Sample Test Questions and Rationale

(Easy)

1. **The transfer of heat by electromagnetic waves is called:**

   A. Conduction

   B. Convection

   C. Phase change

   D. Radiation

   Answer: D. Radiation

   Heat transfer via electromagnetic waves (which can occur even in a vacuum) is called radiation. (Heat can also be transferred by direct contact (conduction), by fluid current (convection), and by matter changing phase, but these are not relevant here.) The answer to this question is therefore (D).

(Easy)

2. **Sound waves are produced by:**

   A. Pitch

   B. Noise

   C. Vibrations

   D. Sonar

   Answer: C. Vibrations

   Sound waves are produced by a vibrating body. The vibrating object moves forward and compresses the air in front of it; it then reverses direction so pressure on the air is lessened and expansion of the air molecules occurs. The vibrating air molecules move back and forth parallel to the direction of motion of the wave as they pass the energy from adjacent air molecules closer to the source to air molecules farther away from the source. Therefore, the answer is (C).

SKILL Demonstrating knowledge of types of forces (e.g., gravity, friction) **and 20.5 their effects on the position, motion, and behavior of objects**

Forces

DYNAMICS is the study of the relationship between motion and the forces affecting motion. Force causes motion. Mass and weight are not the same quantities. An object's mass gives it a reluctance to change its current state of motion. It is also the measure of an object's resistance to acceleration. The force that the earth's gravity exerts on an object with a specific mass is called the object's weight on earth. Weight is a force that is measured in newtons. Weight (W) = mass times acceleration due to gravity (W = mg).

DYNAMICS: the study of the relationship between motion and the forces affecting motion

Newton's Laws of Motion

Newton's first law of motion is also called the law of inertia. It states that an object at rest will remain at rest and an object in motion will remain in motion at a constant velocity unless acted upon by an external force. Newton's second law of motion states that if a net force acts on an object, it will cause the acceleration of the object. The relationship between force and motion is force equals mass times acceleration (F = ma). Newton's third law states that for every action there is an equal and opposite reaction. Therefore, if an object exerts a force on another object, that second object exerts an equal and opposite force on the first.

Surfaces that touch each other have a certain resistance to motion. This resistance is FRICTION.

FRICTION: resistance to motion

- The materials that make up the surfaces will determine the magnitude of the frictional force.

- The frictional force is independent of the area of contact between the two surfaces.

- The direction of the frictional force is opposite to the direction of motion.

- The frictional force is proportional to the normal force between the two surfaces in contact.

STATIC FRICTION: the force of friction of two surfaces that are in contact but do not have any motion relative to each other, such as a block sitting on an inclined plane

STATIC FRICTION describes the force of friction of two surfaces that are in contact but do not have any motion relative to each other, such as a block sitting on an inclined plane. KINETIC FRICTION describes the force of friction of two surfaces in contact with each other when there is relative motion between the surfaces.

When an object moves in a circular path, a force must be directed toward the center of the circle in order to keep the motion going. This constraining force is

KINETIC FRICTION: the force of friction of two surfaces in contact with each other when there is relative motion between the surfaces

CENTRIPETAL FORCE: the constraining force directed toward the center of a circle that keeps an object moving in a circular path

called CENTRIPETAL FORCE. Gravity is the centripetal force that keeps a satellite circling the earth.

- Push and pull: Pushing a volleyball or pulling a bowstring applies muscular force as the muscles expand and contract. Elastic force occurs when any object returns to its original shape (for example, when the bow is released).

- Rubbing: Friction opposes the motion of one surface past another. Friction is common when slowing down a car or sledding down a hill.

- Pull of gravity: The pull of gravity is a force of attraction between two objects. Gravity questions can be raised not only on Earth but also between planets and even black hole discussions.

- Inertia and circular motion: The centripetal force is provided by the high banking of a curved road and by friction between the wheels and the road. This inward force that keeps an object moving in a circle is another example of a centripetal force.

Sample Test Question and Rationale

(Rigorous)

1. **Which of Newton's laws implies that forces on objects are caused by other objects?**

   A. First law

   B. Second law

   C. Third law

   D. Law of gravity

Answer. C. Third law

The second law shows the connection between force and acceleration. The first law is an application of the second law to the case where the force is zero Newtons. The third law says that forces come in pairs that are equal and opposite. It implies that force on objects come from other objects. The law of gravity also implies this, however, the law of gravity only applies to one particular force.

SKILL 20.6 Identifying types and characteristics of simple machines *(e.g., lever, pulley)*

- Forces on objects at rest: The formula $F = m/a$ is shorthand for force equals mass over acceleration. An object will not move unless the force is strong enough to move the mass. Also, there can be opposing forces holding the object in place. For instance, a boat may want to be forced by the currents to drift away, but an equal and opposite force is a rope holding it to a dock.

- **Forces on a moving object:** Overcoming inertia is the tendency of any object to oppose a change in motion. An object at rest tends to stay at rest. An object that is moving tends to keep moving.

Work is done on an object when an applied force moves through a distance. **Power** is the work done divided by the amount of time that it took to do it.

Power = Work/time

The following are examples of simple machines:

- Inclined plane

- Lever

- Wheel and axle

- Pulley

Compound machines are two or more simple machines working together. A wheelbarrow is an example of a complex machine. It uses a lever and a wheel and axle. Machines of all types ease workload by changing the size or direction of an applied force. The amount of effort saved when using simple or complex machines is called mechanical advantage, or MA.

SKILL 20.7 Recognizing characteristics of light, sound, electricity, and magnetism

Shadows illustrate one of the basic properties of light. Light travels in a straight line. If you put your hand between a light source and a wall, you will interrupt the light and produce a shadow. When light hits a surface, it is reflected. The angle of the incoming light (angle of incidence) is the same as the angle of the reflected light (angle of reflection). It is this reflected light that allows you to see objects. You see the objects when the reflected light reaches your eyes.

Different surfaces reflect light differently. Rough surfaces scatter light in many different directions. A smooth surface reflects the light in one direction. If it is smooth and shiny (like a mirror) you see your image in the surface. When light enters a different medium, it bends. This bending, or change of speed, is called REFRACTION. Light can be diffracted, or bent around the edges of an object. Diffraction occurs when light goes through a narrow slit. As light passes through it, the light bends slightly around the edges. You can demonstrate this by pressing your thumb and forefinger together, making a very thin slit between them. Hold them about 8 cm from your eye and look at a distant source of light. The pattern you observe is caused by the diffraction of light.

> **REFRACTION:** the bending of light as it enters a different medium

WAVE INTERFERENCE: when two waves meet while traveling along the same medium

CONSTRUCTIVE INTERFERENCE: when two crests or two troughs of the same shape meet

DESTRUCTIVE INTERFERENCE: when a trough and a crest of different shapes meet, the two pulses will cancel each other out, and the medium will assume the equilibrium position

WAVE-PARTICLE DUALITY: the exhibition of both wavelike and particle-like properties by a single entity; usually a quantum phenomenon relating to photons, electrons, and protons

WAVE INTERFERENCE occurs when two waves meet while traveling along the same medium. The medium takes on a shape that results from the net effect of the individual waves upon the particles of the medium. There are two types of interference: constructive and destructive. **CONSTRUCTIVE INTERFERENCE** occurs when two crests or two troughs of the same shape meet. The medium will take on the shape of a crest or a trough with twice the amplitude of the two interfering crests or troughs. If a trough and a crest of the different shapes meet, the two pulses will cancel each other out, and the medium will assume the equilibrium position. This is called **DESTRUCTIVE INTERFERENCE.**

Destructive interference in sound waves will reduce the loudness of the sound. This is a disadvantage in rooms such as auditoriums, where sound needs to be at its optimum. However, it can be used as an advantage in noise reduction systems. When two sound waves differing slightly in frequency are superimposed, beats are created by the alternation of constructive and destructive interference. The frequency of the beats is equal to the difference between the frequencies of the interfering sound waves.

Wave interference occurs with light waves in much the same manner that it does with sound waves. If two light waves of the same color, frequency, and amplitude are combined, the interference shows up as fringes of alternating light and dark bands. In order for this to happen, the light waves must come from the same source.

WAVE-PARTICLE DUALITY is the exhibition of both wavelike and particle-like properties by a single entity. Wave-particle duality is usually a quantum phenomenon relating to photons, electrons, and protons. Quantum mechanics shows that such objects sometimes behave like particles, sometimes like waves, and sometimes both.

All objects exhibit wave-particle duality to some extent, but the larger the object, the harder it is to observe. Individual molecules are often too large to show their quantum mechanical behavior. An everyday example of wave-particle duality is sunlight. When standing in the Sun, the shadow your body makes suggests that the light travels straight from the Sun and is blocked by your body. Here the light is behaving like a collection of particles sent from the Sun. However, if you take two pieces of glass with a little water between them and hold them in the Sun, you will see fringes; these are formed by the interference of waves.

When a piano tuners tune a piano, they only use one tuning fork, even though there are many strings on the piano. They adjust the first string to be the same as that of the tuning fork. Then they listen to the beats that occur when both the tuned and untuned strings are struck. They adjust the untuned string until they can hear the correct number of beats per second. This process of striking the untuned and tuned strings together and timing the beats is repeated until all the piano strings are tuned.

Pleasant sounds have a regular wave pattern that is repeated over and over. Sounds that do not happen with regularity are typically unpleasant and are called *noise*. Change in experienced frequency due to relative motion of the source of the sound is called the DOPPLER EFFECT. When a siren approaches, the pitch is high. When it passes, the pitch drops. As a moving sound source approaches a listener, the sound waves are closer together, causing an increase in frequency in the sound that is heard. As the source passes the listener, the waves spread out and the sound experienced by the listener is lower.

A converging lens produces a real image whenever the object is far enough from the lens so that the rays of light from the object can hit the lens and be focused into a real image on the other side of the lens.

ELECTROSTATICS is the study of stationary electric charges. A plastic rod that is rubbed with fur or a glass rod that is rubbed with silk will become electrically charged and will attract small pieces of paper. The charge on the plastic rod rubbed with fur is negative, and the charge on glass rod rubbed with silk is positive. Electrically charged objects share these characteristics:

- Like charges repel each other

- Opposite charges attract each other

- Charge is conserved; a neutral object has no net change

Imagine if the plastic rod and fur are initially neutral. When the rod becomes charged by the fur, a negative charge is transferred from the fur to the rod. The net negative charge on the rod is equal to the net positive charge on the fur.

Materials through which electric charges can easily flow are called conductors. Conversely, an insulator is a material through which electric charges do not move easily, if at all. A simple device used to indicate the existence of a positive or negative charge is called an ELECTROSCOPE. An electroscope is made up of a conducting knob and attached very lightweight conducting leaves—usually made of gold foil or aluminum foil. When a charged object touches the knob, the leaves push away from each other because like charges repel. It is not possible to tell whether or not the charge is positive or negative. If one touches the electroscope knob with a finger while a charged rod is nearby, the electrons will be repulsed and flow out of the electroscope through the hand. If the hand is removed while the charged rod remains close, the electroscope will retain the charge.

When an object is rubbed with a charged rod, the object will take on the same charge as the rod. However, *charging by induction* gives the object the opposite

DOPPLER EFFECT: change in experienced frequency due to relative motion of the source of the sound

ELECTROSTATICS: the study of stationary electric charges

ELECTROSCOPE: a simple device used to indicate the existence of a positive or negative charge

charge as that of the charged rod. Charge can be removed from an object by connecting it to the earth through a conductor. The removal of static electricity by conduction is called grounding.

Magnets have a north pole and a south pole. Like poles repel and different poles attract. A MAGNETIC FIELD is the space around a magnet where its force will affect objects. The closer you are to a magnet, the stronger the force. As you move away, the force becomes weaker.

MAGNETIC FIELD: the space around a magnet where its force will affect objects

Some materials act as magnets and some do not. This is because magnetism is the result of electrons in motion. The most important motion in this case is the spinning of the individual electrons. Electrons spin in pairs in opposite directions in most atoms. Each spinning electron has the magnetic field that it creates canceled out by the electron that is spinning in the opposite direction.

An atom of iron has four unpaired electrons. The magnetic fields of these are not canceled out but add up to make a tiny magnet. Their fields exert forces on one another, setting up small areas in the iron called MAGNETIC DOMAINS where atomic magnetic fields line up in the same direction.

MAGNETIC DOMAINS: small areas in the iron where atomic magnetic fields line up in the same direction

You can make a magnet out of an iron nail by stroking the nail in the same direction repeatedly with a magnet. This causes poles in the atomic magnets in the nail to be attracted to the magnet. The tiny magnetic fields in the nail line up in the direction of the magnet. The magnet causes the domains pointing in its direction in the nail to grow. Eventually, one large domain results and the nail becomes a magnet. A bar magnet has a north pole and a south pole. If you break the magnet in half, each piece will have a north and south pole.

The Earth has a magnetic field. In a compass, a tiny, lightweight magnet is suspended and will line its south pole up with the north pole magnet of the earth. A magnet can be made out of a coil of wire by connecting the ends of the coil to a battery. When the current goes through the wire, the wire acts in the same way that a magnet does; it is called an electromagnet. The poles of the electromagnet depend on which way the electric current runs. An electromagnet can be made more powerful by making more coils, putting an iron core (nail) inside the coils, or using more battery power.

Sample Test Questions and Rationale

(Average)

1. **The Doppler Effect is associated most closely with which property of waves?**

    A. Amplitude

    B. Wavelength

    C. Frequency

    D. Intensity

    Answer: C. Frequency

    The Doppler effect accounts for an apparent increase in frequency when a wave source moves toward a wave receiver or apparent decrease in frequency when a wave source moves away from a wave receiver. (Note that the receiver could also be moving toward or away from the source.) As the wave fronts are released, motion toward the receiver mimics more frequent wave fronts, while motion away from the receiver mimics less frequent wave fronts. Meanwhile, the amplitude, wavelength, and intensity of the wave are not as relevant to this process (although moving closer to a wave source makes it seem more intense). The answer to this question is therefore (C).

(Average)

2. **What is the cause of magnetic forces?**

    A. Magnetic domains

    B. Northpoles and southpoles

    C. Moving electric charges

    D. Magnets

    Answer. C. Moving electric charges

    Magnetic domains occur in permanent magnets and are small regions with a north pole and a south pole. North and south poles occur when there is a current loop. The side of the loop where the magnetic field enters is called the south pole. Electric charges moving in a straight line create circular magnetic fields around the path of motion.

COMPETENCY 21
UNDERSTAND CONCEPTS AND PRINCIPLES OF LIFE SCIENCE

SKILL 21.1 Distinguishing between living and nonliving things

The organization of living systems builds by levels from small to increasingly larger and more complex. All aspects, whether they are cells or ecosystems, have the same requirements to sustain life. Life is organized from simple to complex in the following way:

Organelles make up cells, which make up tissues. Tissues make up organs, and groups of organs make up organ systems. Organ systems work together to provide life for the organism. Several characteristics have been described to identify living versus nonliving substances.

- *Living things are made of cells.* They grow, are capable of reproduction, and respond to stimuli.
- *Living things must adapt to environmental changes or perish.*
- *Living things carry on metabolic processes.* They use and make energy.

All organic life has a common element: carbon. Carbon is recycled through the ecosystem through both biotic and abiotic means. It is the link between biological processes and the chemical makeup of life.

SKILL 21.2 Demonstrating knowledge of different types of organisms and methods of classification

TAXONOMY: the science of classification

Carolus Linnaeus is termed the father of taxonomy. TAXONOMY is the science of classification. Classifying is the grouping of items according to their similarities. It is important for students to realize relationships and similarity as well as differences to reach a reasonable conclusion in a lab experience.

Linnaeus based his system on morphology (the study of structure). Later on, evolutionary relationships (phylogeny) were also used to sort and group species.

The modern classification system uses binomial nomenclature. This consists of a two-word name for every species. The genus is the first part of the name and the species is the second part. Notice in the levels explained following that Homo sapiens is the scientific name for humans. Starting with the kingdom, the groups get smaller and more alike as one moves down the levels in human classification:

- Kingdom: Animalia
  - Phylum: Chordata
    - Subphylum: Vertebrata
      - Class: Mammalia
        - Order: Primate
          - Family: Hominidae
            - Genus: Homo
              - Species: Sapiens

SPECIES are defined by the ability to successfully reproduce with members of their own kind. Members of the five different kingdoms of the classification system of living organisms often differ in their basic life functions. Here we compare and analyze how members of the five kingdoms obtain nutrients, excrete waste, and reproduce.

BACTERIA are prokaryotic, single-celled organisms that lack cell nuclei. The different types of bacteria obtain nutrients in a variety of ways. Most bacteria absorb nutrients from the environment through small channels in their cell walls and membranes (chemotrophs), while some perform photosynthesis (phototrophs). Chemoorganotrophs use organic compounds as energy sources, while chemolithotrophs can use inorganic chemicals as energy sources. Depending on the type of metabolism and energy source, bacteria release a variety of waste products (e.g., alcohols, acids, carbon dioxide) to the environment through diffusion.

All bacteria reproduce through binary fission (asexual reproduction), producing two identical cells. Bacteria reproduce very rapidly, dividing or doubling every twenty minutes in optimal conditions. Asexual reproduction does not allow for genetic variation, but bacteria achieve genetic variety by absorbing DNA from ruptured cells and conjugating or swapping chromosomal or plasmid DNA with other cells.

ANIMALS are multicellular, eukaryotic organisms. All animals obtain nutrients by eating food (ingestion). Different types of animals derive nutrients from eating plants, other animals, or both. Animal cells perform respiration, which converts food molecules—mainly carbohydrates and fats—into energy. The excretory

SPECIES: defined by the ability to successfully reproduce with members of their own kind

BACTERIA: prokaryotic, single-celled organisms that lack cell nuclei

ANIMALS: multicellular, eukaryotic organisms

systems of animals, like animals themselves, vary in complexity. Simple invertebrates eliminate waste through a single tube, while complex vertebrates have a specialized system of organs that process and excrete waste.

Most animals, unlike bacteria, exist in two distinct sexes. Members of the female sex give birth or lay eggs. Some less developed animals can reproduce asexually. For example, flatworms can divide into two, and some unfertilized insect eggs can develop into viable organisms. Most animals reproduce sexually through various mechanisms. For example, aquatic animals reproduce by external fertilization of eggs, while mammals reproduce by internal fertilization. More developed animals possess specialized reproductive systems and cycles that facilitate reproduction and promote genetic variation.

PLANTS: like animals, multicellular, eukaryotic organisms

PLANTS, like animals, are multicellular, eukaryotic organisms. Plants obtain nutrients from the soil through their root systems and convert sunlight into energy through photosynthesis. Many plants store waste products in vacuoles or organs (e.g., leaves, bark) that are discarded. Some plants also excrete waste through their roots.

More than half of the plant species reproduce by producing seeds from which new plants grow. Depending on the type of plant, flowers or cones produce seeds. Other plants reproduce by spores, tubers, bulbs, buds, and grafts. The flowers of flowering plants contain the reproductive organs. Pollination is the joining of male and female gametes; it is often facilitated through the movement of wind or animals.

FUNGI: eukaryotic, mostly multicellular organisms

FUNGI are eukaryotic, mostly multicellular organisms. All fungi are heterotrophs, obtaining nutrients from other organisms. More specifically, most fungi obtain nutrients by digesting and absorbing nutrients from dead organisms. Fungi secrete enzymes outside of their body to digest organic material and then absorb the nutrients through their cell walls.

Most fungi can reproduce asexually and sexually. Different types of fungi reproduce asexually by mitosis, budding, sporification, or fragmentation. Sexual reproduction of fungi is different from sexual reproduction of animals. The two mating types of fungi are plus and minus, not male and female. The fusion of hyphae, the specialized reproductive structure in fungi, between plus and minus types produces and scatters diverse spores.

PROTISTS: eukaryotic, single-celled organisms

PROTISTS are eukaryotic, single-celled organisms. Most protists are heterotrophic, obtaining nutrients by ingesting small molecules and cells and digesting them in vacuoles. All protists reproduce asexually by either binary or multiple fission. Like bacteria, protists achieve genetic variation by exchange of DNA through conjugation.

Behavioral Responses to External and Internal Stimuli

Response to stimuli is one of the key characteristics of any living thing. Any detectable change in the internal or external environment (the stimulus) may trigger a response in an organism. Just like physical characteristics, organisms' responses to stimuli are adaptations that allow them to better survive. While these responses may be more noticeable in animals that can move quickly, all organisms are actually capable of responding to changes.

> *Response to stimuli is one of the key characteristics of any living thing.*

Single-celled organisms

These organisms are able to respond to basic stimuli such as the presence of light, heat, or food. Changes in the environment are typically sensed via cell surface receptors. These organisms may respond to such stimuli by making changes in internal biochemical pathways or by initiating reproduction or phagocytosis. Those capable of simple motility, using flagella for instance, may respond by moving toward food or away from heat.

Plants

Plants typically do not possess sensory organs, so individual cells recognize stimuli through a variety of pathways. When many cells respond to stimuli together, a response becomes apparent. Logically then, the responses of plants occur on a rather longer time scale that those of animals. Plants are capable of responding to a few basic stimuli, including light, water, and gravity. Some common examples include the way plants turn and grow toward the Sun, the sprouting of seeds when exposed to warmth and moisture, and the growth of roots in the direction of gravity.

Animals

Lower members of the animal kingdom have responses similar to those seen in single-celled organisms. However, higher animals have developed complex systems to detect and respond to stimuli. The nervous system, sensory organs (eyes, ears, skin, etc.), and muscle tissue all allow animals to sense and quickly respond to changes in their environment. As in other organisms, many responses to stimuli in animals are involuntary. For example, pupils dilate in response to the reduction of light. Such reactions are typically called reflexes. However, many animals are also capable of voluntary response.

> **BEHAVIOR:** complex responses, which may or may not be instinctual

In many animal species, voluntary reactions are instinctual. For instance, a zebra's response to a lion is a voluntary one, but, instinctually, it will flee quickly as soon as the lion's presence is sensed. Complex responses, which may or may not be instinctual, are typically termed BEHAVIOR. An example is the annual migration of birds when seasons change.

SKILL 21.3 Demonstrating knowledge of the basic needs, characteristics, structures, and life processes of organisms

Ecology is the study of organisms, where they live, and their interactions with the environment. A population is a group of the same species in a specific area. A community is a group of populations residing in the same area. Communities that are ecologically similar in regards to temperature, rainfall, and the species that live there are called BIOMES.

TYPES OF BIOMES	
Marine	It covers 75 percent of the earth. This biome is organized by the depth of water. The *intertidal* zone is located from the tide line to the edge of the water. The *littoral* zone is found from the water's edge to the open sea. It includes coral reef habitats; it is the most densely populated area of the marine biome. The open sea zone is divided into the *epipelagic* zone and the *pelagic* zone. The epipelagic zone receives more sunlight and has a larger number of species. The ocean floor is called the benthic zone. It is populated with bottom feeders.
Tropical Rain Forest	Here, temperature is fairly constant (25 degrees C) and rainfall exceeds 200 cm per year. Located around the equator, rain forests have abundant, diverse species of plants and animals.
Savanna	The temperatures range from 0-25 degrees C depending on the location. Rainfall is from 90 to 150 cm per year. Plants include shrubs and grasses. The savanna is a transitional biome between the rain forest and the desert.
Desert	Temperatures range from 10-38 degrees C in the desert. Rainfall is under 25 cm per year. Plant species include xerophytes and succulents. Lizards, snakes, and small mammals are common animals
Temperate Deciduous Forest	In this biome, temperatures range from -24 to 38 degrees C. Rainfall is 65 to 150 cm per year. Deciduous trees are common, as well as deer, bear, and squirrels.
Taiga	Here, temperatures range from -24 to 22 degrees C. Rainfall is 35 to 40 cm per year. Taiga is located north and south of the equator, close to the poles. Plant life includes conifers and plants that can withstand harsh winters. Animals include weasels, mink, and moose.

Table continued on next page

Tundra	Temperatures range from –28 to 15 degrees C in the tundra. Rainfall is limited, ranging from 10 to 15 cm per year. The tundra is located even further north and south of the taiga. Common plants include lichens and mosses. Animals include polar bears and musk ox.
Polar or Permafrost	This is where temperatures range from –40 to 0 degrees C. It rarely gets above freezing. Rainfall is below 10 cm per year. Most water is bound up as ice. Life is limited.

Succession

The orderly process of replacing a community that has been damaged or has begun where no life previously existed. Primary succession occurs after a community has been totally wiped out by a natural disaster or where life never existed before, as in a flooded area. Secondary succession takes place in communities that were once flourishing but disturbed by some force, either human or natural, but not totally stripped. A CLIMAX COMMUNITY is a community that is established and flourishing.

CLIMAX COMMUNITY: a community that is established and flourishing

Feeding Relationships

See Skill 21.7 for a more comprehensive overview of the feeding relationships.

Parasitism	When two species occupy a similar place, but the parasite benefits from the relationship, while the host is harmed.
Commensalism	When two species occupy a similar place, and neither species is harmed by or benefits from the relationship.
Mutualism	When two species occupy a similar place and both species benefit from the relationship.
Competition	When two species that occupy the same habitat and eat the same food are said to be in competition with each other.
Predation	When animals eat other animals. The animals they feed on are called prey. Population growth depends upon competition for food, water, shelter, and space. The amount of predators determines the amount of prey, which in turn affects the number of predators.
Carrying Capacity	The total amount of life a habitat can support. Once the habitat runs out of food, water, shelter, or space, the carrying capacity decreases and then stabilizes.

Biotic factors are iving things in an ecosystem: plants, animals, bacteria, fungi, and so on. Abiotic factors are nonliving aspects of an ecosystem: soil quality, rainfall, temperature, and so on.

Biogeochemical Cycles

Essential elements are recycled through an ecosystem. At times, the element needs to be "fixed" in a useable form. Some cycles are dependent on plants, algae, and bacteria to fix nutrients for use by animals.

- Water cycle: Two percent of all the available water is fixed and unavailable in ice or the bodies of organisms. Available water includes surface water (lakes, ocean, rivers) and groundwater (aquifers, wells). Ninety-six percent of all available water is from groundwater. Water is recycled through the processes of evaporation and precipitation. The water present on the earth now is the water that has been here since our atmosphere formed.

- Carbon cycle: Ten percent of all available carbon in the air (from carbon dioxide gas) is fixed by photosynthesis. Plants fix carbon in the form of glucose, and animals then eat the plants and are able to obtain their source of carbon. When animals release carbon dioxide through respiration, the plants have a source of carbon to fix once more.

- Nitrogen cycle: Eighty percent of the atmosphere is nitrogen gas. Nitrogen must be in a nongaseous form to be incorporated into an organism. Only a few genera of bacteria have the correct enzymes to break the triple bond between nitrogen atoms. These bacteria live within the roots of legumes (peas, beans, alfalfa) and add bacteria to the soil so it can be taken up by plants. Nitrogen is necessary to make amino acids and the nitrogenous bases of DNA.

- Phosphorus cycle: Phosphorus is a mineral, and it is not found in the atmosphere. Fungi and plant roots have a structure called mycorrhizae that are able to fix insoluble phosphates into useable phosphorus. Urine and decayed matter return phosphorus to the earth, where it can be incorporated in the plant. Phosphorus is needed for the backbone of DNA and for ATP manufacture.

Ecological Problems

Nonrenewable resources are fragile and must be conserved for use in the future. Humans' impact on the environment and knowledge of conservation will determine the future.

Biological Magnification	Chemicals and pesticides accumulate in the food chain. Tertiary consumers have more accumulated toxins than animals at the bottom of the food chain.
Simplification of the Food Web	Three major crops—rice, corn, and wheat—feed the world. Planting these crops wipes out other habitats and pushes animals into smaller areas, causing overpopulation or extinction.

Table continued on next page

Fuel Sources	Strip mining and the overuse of oil reserves have depleted these resources. At the current rate of consumption, conservation or alternate fuel sources will be key to our future.
Pollution	Although technology gives us many advances, pollution is a side effect of production. Waste disposal and the burning of fossil fuels have polluted our land, water, and air. Global warming and acid rain are two results of the burning of hydrocarbons and sulfur.
Global Warming	Rain forest depletion, fossil fuels, and aerosols have caused an increase in carbon dioxide production. This leads to a decrease in the amount of oxygen, which is directly proportional to the amount of ozone. As the ozone layer depletes, more heat enters our atmosphere and is trapped. This causes an overall warming effect that may eventually melt the polar ice caps, causing a rise in water levels and changes in climate. This will, in turn, affect weather systems.
Endangered Species	Construction to house our overpopulated world has caused a destruction of habitats for other animals, often leading to their extinction.
Overpopulation	The human race is still growing at an exponential rate. Carrying capacity has not been met due to our ability to use technology to produce more food.

Sample Test Questions and Rationale

(Average)

1. **Which cycle is photosynthesis a part of?**

   A. Nitrogen cycle

   B. Carbon cycle

   C. Water cycle

   D. Phosphorus cycle

   Answer. B. Carbon cycle

   In the carbon cycle, photosynthesis combines carbon dioxide in the atmosphere with oxygen to form carbohydrates. Animals consume the carbohydrates. Respiration converts the carbohydrates back into carbon dioxide in the atmosphere. The water cycle involves evaporation and precipitation. The nitrogen cycle involves converting nitrogen in the atmosphere to plant materials that are used by living organisms.

(Average)

2. **Which kingdom is comprised of organisms made of one cell with no nuclear membrane?**

   A. Monera

   B. Protista

   C. Fungi

   D. Algae

   Answer: A. Monera

   To answer this question, first note that algae are not a kingdom of their own. Some algae are in monera, the kingdom that consists of unicellular prokaryotes with no true nucleus. Protista and fungi are both eukaryotic, with true nuclei, and are sometimes multicellular. Therefore, the answer is (A).

Gregor Mendel is recognized as the father of genetics. His work in the late 1800s is the basis of our knowledge of genetics. Although unaware of the presence of DNA or genes, Mendel realized there were factors (now known as GENES) that were transferred from parents to their offspring. Mendel worked with pea plants, fertilizing them himself and keeping track of subsequent generations. His findings led to the Mendelian laws of genetics. Mendel found that two "factors" governed each trait, one from each parent. Traits or characteristics came in several forms, known as alleles. For example, the trait for flower color had both white alleles and purple alleles.

> **GENES:** factors transferred from parents to their offspring

Mendel developed the following three laws:

- The law of dominance: In a pair of alleles, one trait may cover up the allele of the other trait—for example, brown eyes are dominant to blue eyes.

- The law of segregation: Only one of the two possible alleles from each parent is passed on to the offspring from each parent. (During meiosis, the haploid number ensures that half the sex cells get one allele and half get the other.)

- The law of independent assortment: Alleles sort independently of each other. (Many combinations are possible, depending on which sperm ends up with which egg. Compare this to the many combinations of hands possible when dealing a deck of cards.)

Punnet squares are used to show the possible ways that genes combine and indicate the probability of the occurrence of a certain genotype or phenotype. One parent's genes are put at the top of the box and the other parent at the side of the box. Genes combine on the square just like numbers that are added in addition tables learned in elementary school. Here is an example of a monohybrid cross, which is a cross using only one trait—in this case, a trait labeled "g."

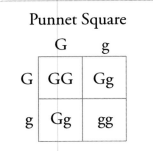

Punnet Square

	G	g
G	GG	Gg
g	Gg	gg

In a dihybrid cross, sixteen gene combinations are possible, since each cross has two traits.

Here are some terms and definitions you should be familiar with:

- Dominant: The stronger of the two traits. If a dominant gene is present, it is expressed as a capital letter.

- Recessive: The weaker of the two traits. In order for the recessive gene to be expressed, there must be two recessive genes present. It is expressed as a lower case letter.

- Homozygous (purebred): Having two of the same genes present. An organism may be homozygous dominant, with two dominant genes, or homozygous recessive, with two recessive genes.

- Heterozygous (hybrid): Having one dominant gene and one recessive gene. The dominant gene is the one that is expressed.

- Genotype: the genes the organism has. Genes are represented with letters. AA, Bb, and tt are examples of genotypes.

- Phenotype: How the trait is expressed in an organism. Blue eyes, brown hair, and red flowers are examples of phenotypes.

- Incomplete dominance: Neither gene masks the other so that a new phenotype is formed. For example, red flowers and white flowers may have equal strength. A heterozygote (Rr) would have pink flowers. If a problem occurs with a third phenotype, incomplete dominance is occurring.

- Codominance: Genes may form new phenotypes. The ABO blood grouping is an example of codominance. A and B are of equal strength and O is recessive. Therefore, type A blood may have the genotypes of AA or AO, type B blood may have the genotypes of BB or BO, type AB blood has the genotype A and B, and type O blood has two recessive O genes.

- Linkage: Genes that are found on the same chromosome usually appear together unless crossing over has occurred in meiosis (for example, blue eyes and blonde hair often show up together).

- Lethal alleles: Usually recessive due to the early death of the offspring. If a 2:1 ratio of alleles is found in offspring, a lethal gene combination is usually the reason. Some examples of lethal alleles include sickle cell anemia, Tay-Sachs disease, and cystic fibrosis. In these cases, the coding for an important protein is usually affected.

- Inborn errors of metabolism: The affected protein is an enzyme. Examples include PKU (phenylketonuria) and albinism.

- Polygenic characters: Many alleles code for a phenotype. There may be as many as twenty genes that code for skin color. This is why there is such a variety of skin tones. Another example is height. A couple of medium height may have very tall offspring.

- Sex-linked traits: The Y chromosome found only in males (XY) carries very little genetic information, whereas the X chromosome found in females (XX) carries very important information. Since men have no second X chromosome to cover up a recessive gene, the recessive trait is expressed more often in men. Women need the recessive gene on both X chromosomes to show the trait. Examples of sex-linked traits include hemophilia and color-blindness.

- Sex-influenced traits: Traits that are influenced by the sex hormones. Male pattern baldness is an example of a sex-influenced trait. Testosterone influences the expression of the gene. Mostly men lose their hair due to this trait.

Common Life Cycles

Bacteria are commonly used in laboratories for research. Bacteria reproduce by binary fission. This asexual process is simply a division of the bacterium in half. All new organisms are exact clones of the parent. The obvious advantage of asexual reproduction is that it does not require a partner. This is a huge advantage for organisms that do not move around; not having to move around to reproduce allows organisms to conserve energy. Asexual reproduction also tends to be faster. However, as asexual reproduction produces only exact copies of the parent organism, it does not allow for genetic variation, which means that mutations, or weaker qualities, will always be passed on.

Butterflies actually go through four different stages of life, but they become true butterflies only in the final stage. In the first stage, the adult butterfly lays an egg. In the second stage, the egg hatches into a caterpillar or larva. The third stage is when the caterpillar forms the chrysalis or pupa. Finally, the chrysalis matures and the adult butterfly emerges.

Frogs also have multiple stages in their life cycle. Initially, an adult frog lays its eggs in the water (all amphibians require water for reproduction). In the second stage, tadpoles hatch from the eggs. The tadpoles swim in the water and use gills for breathing. Tadpoles have a tail that is used for locomotion, but they will grow legs as well. At two and four months old, the tadpole is known as a froglet. You can recognize a froglet because the rim around its tail, which appears fishlike, has disappeared, its tail is shorter, and its four legs have grown to the extent that its rear legs are bent underneath it. The final stage of a frog's life is spent as an adult. Its tail has been entirely reabsorbed, it has a chubby froglike appearance instead of the tadpole's fishlike appearance, and as a mature frog, it can lay eggs.

SKILL 21.5 Demonstrating knowledge of the interactions of organisms with one another and their environment and the flow of energy and matter within an ecosystem

TROPHIC LEVELS are based on the feeding relationships that determine energy flow and chemical cycling. Autotrophs are the primary producers of the ecosystem. They consist mainly of plants.

Primary consumers are the next trophic level. The primary consumers are the herbivores that eat plants or algae. Secondary consumers are the carnivores that eat the primary consumers. Tertiary consumers eat the secondary consumer. These trophic levels may go higher, depending on the ecosystem. Decomposers are consumers that feed off animal waste and dead organisms.

This pathway of food transfer is known as a food chain. Most food chains are more elaborate, becoming food webs. Energy is lost as the trophic levels progress from producer to tertiary consumer. The amount of energy that is transferred between trophic levels is called the ecological efficiency. The visual of this energy flow is represented in a pyramid of productivity, as shown here:

> **TROPHIC LEVELS:** the levels of feeding relationships that determine energy flow and chemical cycling

Pyramid of Productivity

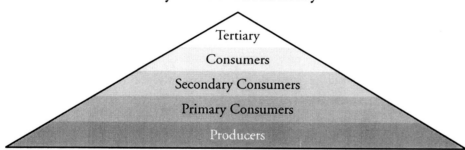

The biomass pyramid represents the total dry weight of organisms in each trophic level. A pyramid of numbers is a representation of the population size of each trophic level. The producers, being the most populous, are on the bottom of this pyramid, with the tertiary consumers on the top with the fewest numbers.

SKILL 21.6 Analyzing the effects of humans on the environment

For centuries, humans have been increasingly altering the environments in which they live. Everything from driving cars to logging has had a toll on the environment. Pollutants are impurities in the air and water that may be harmful to life. Oil is a major pollutant that can cause severe destruction of the oceans, beaches, and animal life when there is a spill.

GLOBAL WARMING is an enormous environmental issue today; it is caused by the "greenhouse effect." In it, atmospheric greenhouse gases, such as water vapor, carbon dioxide, and other gases, trap some of the outgoing energy, retaining heat, somewhat like the glass panels of a greenhouse. This occurs naturally; without it, the temperature on the earth would be too low to sustain life. The problem occurs when these gases enter the atmosphere in large amounts; their heat-trapping ability results in global warming.

Over the past 100 years, the earth's surface temperature has risen 1° Fahrenheit, with accelerated warming occurring in the past two decades. The increase of gases in the atmosphere is caused by the burning of fossil fuels and emissions of carbon dioxide from cars and factories.

All acids contain hydrogen. Substances from factory and car exhaust dissolve in rain water, forming acid rain. When this rain falls onto stone, the acids can react with metallic compounds and gradually wear away the stone.

Since radioactive material has become readily available, it has been a major concern as a threat of nuclear disaster. Radioactivity ionizes the air it travels through. It is strong enough to kill cancer cells or dangerous enough to cause illness or even death. Gamma rays can penetrate the body and damage its cells. In a nuclear disaster, damage to the land and all living organisms is inevitable.

Logging also has a negative impact on the environment. Clear-cutting forests leaves the soil unprotected and can cause disasters such as mudslides. Also, the quality of soil in that area diminishes the chances of successful regrowth for living organisms.

Some human activities are beneficial to the environment. The populations of many animal species that were endangered have risen because of protection laws and the study of the animals and their habitats. With the development of new technology, other benefits accrue to the environment. The recycling process has prevented the unnecessary waste of plastics, glass, and paper.

GLOBAL WARMING: an enormous environmental issue today; it is caused by the "greenhouse effect"

Sample Test Questions and Rationale

(Average)

1. **What is the most accurate description of the Water Cycle?**

   A. Rain comes from clouds, filling the ocean; the water then evaporates and becomes clouds again

   B. Water circulates from rivers into groundwater and back, while water vapor circulates in the atmosphere

   C. Water is conserved except for chemical or nuclear reactions, and any drop of water could circulate through clouds, rain, ground water, and surface water

   D. Weather systems cause chemical reactions to break water into its atoms

   Answer: C. Water is conserved except for chemical or nuclear reactions, and any drop of water could circulate through clouds, rain, groundwater, and surface water

   All natural chemical cycles, including the water cycle, depend on the principle of Conservation of Mass. (For water, unlike for elements such as Nitrogen, chemical reactions may cause sources or sinks of water molecules.) Any drop of water may circulate through the hydrologic system, ending up in a cloud, as rain, or as surface or groundwater. Although answers (A) and (B) describe parts of the water cycle, the most comprehensive answer is (C).

(Average)

2. **The theory of "sea floor spreading" explains:**

   A. The shapes of the continents

   B. How continents collide

   C. How continents move apart

   D. How continents sink to become part of the ocean floor

   Answer: C. How continents move apart

   In the theory of sea floor spreading, the movement of the ocean floor causes continents to spread apart from one another. This occurs because crust plates split apart, and new material is added to the plate edges. This process pulls the continents apart, or it may create new separations and is believed to have caused the formation of the Atlantic Ocean. Therefore, the answer is (C).

(Rigorous)

3. **Which of the following is the best definition for "meteorite"?**

   A. A meteorite is a mineral composed of mica and feldspar

   B. A meteorite is material from outer space that has struck the earth's surface

   C. A meteorite is an element that has properties of both metals and nonmetals

   D. A meteorite is a very small unit of length measurement

   Answer: B. A meteorite is material from outer space that has struck the earth's surface

   Meteoroids are pieces of matter in space, composed of particles of rock and metal. If a meteoroid travels through the earth's atmosphere, friction causes burning and a "shooting star"—that is, a meteor. If the meteor strikes the earth's surface, it is known as a meteorite. Note that although the suffix *-ite* often means a mineral, answer (A) is incorrect. Answer (C) refers to a metalloid rather than a meteorite, and answer (D) is simply a misleading pun on *meter*. Therefore, the answer is (B).

SKILL 21.7 Demonstrating knowledge of factors that affect the survival or extinction of organisms

> Many interactions occur on earth among different species living together. Predation, parasitism, competition, commensalisms, and mutualism are the different types of relationships populations have between each other.

PREDATION: when a predator eats its prey

PARASITISM: a predator that lives on or in its host, causing detrimental effects to the host but not to the parasite

COMPETITION: when two or more species in a community use the same resources

SYMBIOSIS: when two species live close together

NICHE: the relational position of a species or population in an ecosystem

Many interactions occur on earth among different species living together. Predation, parasitism, competition, commensalisms, and mutualism are the different types of relationships populations have between each other. PREDATION and PARASITISM result in a benefit for one species and a detriment for the other. Predation occurs when a predator eats its prey. The common conception of predation is of a carnivore consuming other animals. This is one form of predation. Although not always resulting in the death of the plant, herbivory is a form of predation. Some animals eat enough of a plant to cause it to die. However, many plants and animals have defenses against predators. Some plants have poisonous chemicals that will harm the predator if ingested, and some animals are camouflaged so they are harder to detect. Parasitism involves a predator that lives on or in its host, causing detrimental effects to the host but not to the parasite. Insects and viruses living off of and reproducing in their hosts is an example of parasitism.

COMPETITION occurs when two or more species in a community use the same resources. Competition is usually detrimental to both populations. It is often difficult to find in nature because competition between two populations is not continuous. Either the weaker population will no longer exist or one population will evolve to utilize other available resources.

SYMBIOSIS is when two species live close together. Parasitism, as just described, is one example of symbiosis. Another example of symbiosis is commensalism. Commensalism occurs when one species benefits from the other without harmful effects. Mutualism is when both species benefit from the other. Species involved in mutualistic relationships must coevolve to survive; as one species evolves, the other must as well. For example, grouper and a species of shrimp live in a mutualistic relationship. The shrimp feed off parasites living on the grouper; thus, the shrimp are fed, and the grouper stays healthy and parasite-free. Many microorganisms are in mutualistic relationships.

Niche and Carrying Capacity

The term NICHE describes the relational position of a species or population in an ecosystem. Niche includes how a population responds to the abundance of its resources and its enemies (e.g., growing when resources are abundant and predators, parasites, and pathogens are scarce). Niche also indicates the life history of an organism, its habitat, and its place in the food chain. According to the competitive exclusion principle, no two species can occupy the same niche in the same environment for a long time.

The full range of environmental conditions (biological and physical) under which an organism can exist describes its fundamental niche. Because of the pressure from superior competitors, organisms that survive over the long term are driven to occupy a niche that is narrower than their previous one. This is known as the realized niche.

EXAMPLES OF NICHES		
Oak Trees	• Live in forests • Absorb sunlight by photosynthesis • Provide shelter for many animals • Act as support for creeping plants • Serve as a source of food for animals • Cover their ground with dead leaves in the autumn	If the oak trees were cut down or destroyed by fire or storms, they would no longer be doing these jobs. In turn, this would have a disastrous effect on all the other organisms living in the same habitat.
Hedgehogs	• Eat a variety of insects and other invertebrates that live underneath the dead leaves and twigs in the garden • Have spines that are a superb environment for fleas and ticks • Put the nitrogen back into the soil when they urinate • Eat slugs and protect plants from them	If the hedgehog population was drastically reduced, the number of slugs would explode and the nutrients in the dead leaves and twigs would not recycle.

A POPULATION is a group of individuals of one species that live in the same general area. Many factors can affect the population size and its growth rate. For example, population size depends on the total amount of life a habitat can support. This is called the carrying capacity of the environment. Limiting factors can also affect population growth.

POPULATION: a group of individuals of one species that live in the same general area

As a population increases, the competition for resources is more intense, and the growth rate declines. This is a density-dependent growth factor. The carrying capacity can be determined by the density-dependent factor. Density-independent factors affect individuals regardless of population size. The weather and climate are good examples. Extreme hot or cold temperatures can kill many individuals from a population, even if it has not reached its carrying capacity.

Human population increased slowly until 1650. Since then, it has grown almost exponentially, reaching its current population of over 6 billion. Factors that have led to this increased growth rate include improved nutrition, sanitation, and health care. In addition, advances in technology, agriculture, and scientific knowledge have made the use of resources more efficient and readily available.

While the earth's ultimate carrying capacity for humans is uncertain, some factors that may limit growth are the availability of food, water, space, and fossil fuels. The amount of land on the earth that is available for food production is finite. In addition, providing clean, potable water for a growing human population is a real concern. Fossil fuels, important energy sources for human technology, are scarce. The inevitable shortage of energy in the earth's future will require the development of alternative energy sources to maintain or increase human population growth.

Sample Test Question and Rationale

(Average)

1. **When two species live close together and both benefit from one another that is called:**

   A. Symbiosis

   B. Commensalism

   C. Mutualism

   D. Competition

Answer. C. Mutualism

Symbiosis is when two species live close together. Competition occurs when both use the same limited resources. Parasitism is when one species lives on another species and the other species is harmed. In commensalism, one species benefits from the other but the other is not harmed.

DOMAIN V
HEALTH, PHYSICAL EDUCATION, AND THE ARTS

PERSONALIZED STUDY PLAN

✗
KNOWN MATERIAL/ SKIP IT

PAGE	COMPETENCY AND SKILL	
389	**22: Understand Basic Principles and Practices Related to Health and Safety**	☐
	22.1: Demonstrating knowledge of the human body systems, human growth and development, and the basic principles of human nutrition	☐
	22.2: Recognizing communicable and noncommunicable diseases and strategies for preventing or treating them	☐
	22.3: Recognizing characteristics of healthy interpersonal relationships	☐
	22.4: Identifying strategies for maintaining personal emotional and physical health	☐
	22.5: Recognizing substance abuse and strategies for resisting pressure to use alcohol, tobacco products, and other drugs	☐
	22.6: Identifying safety practices	☐
416	**23: Understand Basic Physical Education Principles, Practices, and Activities**	☐
	23.1: Identifying the components of health-related fitness	☐
	23.2: Demonstrating knowledge of activities that promote of locomotor, nonlocomotor, manipulative, and perceptual awareness skills in children	☐
	23.3: Applying knowledge of developmentally appropriate physical activities, cooperative and competitive games, and sports	☐
	23.4: Recognizing how physical activities promote positive personal and social behaviors	☐
437	**24: Understand Basic Elements, Concepts, and Techniques Associated with the Arts**	☐
	24.1: Identifying the basic elements, concepts, and terms associated with dance, music, drama, and the visual arts	☐
	24.2: Recognizing techniques, processes, tools, and materials for creating, performing, and producing works in the various arts	☐
	24.3: Applying kstrategies for promoting critical analysis, cultural perspectives, and aesthetic understandings of the arts	☐
	24.4: Recognizing how the arts can be used as a form of communication, self-expression, and social expression	☐
	24.5: Demonstrating connections among the arts other areas of the curriculum and everyday life	☐
	24.6: Recognizing the role and function of the arts in various cultures and throughout history	☐

✗

COMPETENCY 22
UNDERSTAND BASIC PRINCIPLES AND PRACTICES RELATED TO HEALTH AND SAFETY

Demonstrating knowledge of the primary functions of the human body systems, the processes of human growth and development, and the basic principles of human nutrition

The major systems of the human body consist of organs working together to perform important physiological tasks. To understand how all of these systems work together, it is important to have a grasp of several major body systems, including the musculoskeletal system, the cardiovascular system, the respiratory/excretory system, the nervous system, the endocrine system, the reproductive system, and the immune system. In addition, it is valuable to know how these systems adapt to physical activity, produce movement, and contribute to fitness.

Structures, Locations, and Functions of the Three Types of Muscular Tissue

The main function of the muscular system is movement. Muscle tissue comes in three types:

- Skeletal muscle is voluntary. These muscles are attached to bones and are responsible for their movement. Skeletal muscle consists of long fibers and is striated due to the repeating patterns of the myofilaments (made of the proteins actin and myosin) that make up the fibers.

- Cardiac muscle is found in the heart. Cardiac muscle is striated like skeletal muscle, but it differs in that the plasma membrane of the cardiac muscle causes the muscle to beat even when away from the heart. The action potentials of cardiac and skeletal muscles also differ.

- Smooth muscle is involuntary. It is found in organs and enables functions such as digestion and respiration. Unlike skeletal and cardiac muscle, smooth muscle is not striated. Smooth muscle has less myosin and does not generate as much tension as skeletal muscle.

Mechanism of skeletal muscle contraction

To begin, a nerve impulse strikes a muscle fiber. This causes calcium ions to flood the sarcomere (the muscle's filaments). These calcium ions allow adenosine triphosphate (ATP), which is basically the "gasoline" of the human body, to expend energy. The myosin fibers then creep along the actin, causing the muscle to contract. Once the nerve impulse has passed, calcium is pumped out and the contraction ends.

Movement of body joints

The axial skeleton consists of the bones of the skull and vertebrae. The appendicular skeleton consists of the bones of the legs, arms and tail, and shoulder girdle. Bone is a connective tissue. Parts of the bone include compact bone, which gives strength; spongy bone, which contains red marrow to make blood cells and yellow marrow in the center of long bones to store fat cells; and the periosteum, which is the protective covering on the outside of the bone.

A JOINT is a place where two bones meet; they enable movement. Within the joint, ligaments attach bone to bone, and tendons attach bone to muscle. All of these parts work together to allow the joint to move. The three types of joints are:

> **JOINT:** a place where two bones meet; they enable movement

- Ball and socket joints: These allow rotational movement. An example is the joint between the shoulder and the humerus. These joints allow humans to move their arms and legs in many different ways.

- Hinge joints: In these, movement is restricted to a single plane. An example is the joint between the humerus and the ulna.

- Pivot joints: These allow the rotation of the forearm at the elbow and the hands at the wrist.

The Human Nervous and Endocrine Systems

The CENTRAL NERVOUS SYSTEM (CNS) consists of the brain and spinal cord. The CNS is responsible for the body's response to environmental stimuli. The spinal cord is located inside the spine. It sends out motor commands for movement in response to stimuli. The brain is where responses to more complex stimuli occur.

> **CENTRAL NERVOUS SYSTEM:** the brain and spinal cord; it is responsible for the body's response to environmental stimuli

The MENINGES are the connective tissues that protect the CNS. The CNS also contains fluid-filled spaces called ventricles. These ventricles are filled with cerebrospinal fluid, which is formed in the brain. This fluid cushions the brain and circulates nutrients, white blood cells, and hormones. The CNS's response to stimuli is a reflex, which is an unconscious, automatic response.

> **MENINGES:** the connective tissues that protect the CNS

The PERIPHERAL NERVOUS SYSTEM (PNS) consists of the nerves that connect the CNS to the rest of the body. The sensory division of the PNS brings information to the CNS from sensory receptors, and the motor division sends signals from the CNS to effector cells. The motor division consists of the somatic nervous system and the autonomic nervous system. The body consciously controls

> **PERIPHERAL NERVOUS SYSTEM:** the nerves that connect the CNS to the rest of the body

the somatic nervous system in response to external stimuli. The hypothalamus in the brain unconsciously controls the autonomic nervous system to regulate the internal environment. This system is responsible for the movement of smooth muscles, cardiac muscles, and the muscles of other organ systems.

The role of nerve impulses and neurons

The NEURON is the basic unit of the nervous system. It consists of an axon, which carries impulses away from the cell body to the tip of the neuron; the dendrite, which carries impulses toward the cell body; and the cell body, which contains the nucleus. Synapses are the spaces between neurons. Chemicals called neurotransmitters are found close to the synapses. The myelin sheath, composed of Schwann cells, covers the neurons and provides insulation.

> **NEURON:** the basic unit of the nervous system

Nerve action depends on depolarization and an imbalance of electrical charges across the neuron. A polarized nerve has a positive charge outside the neuron. A depolarized nerve has a negative charge outside the neuron. Neurotransmitters turn off the sodium pump, which results in depolarization of the membrane. This wave of depolarization (as it moves from neuron to neuron) carries an electrical impulse. This is actually a wave of opening and closing gates that allows for the flow of ions across the synapse.

All nerves have an action potential. A certain threshold of the level of chemicals must be met or exceeded in order for muscles to respond. This is the "all or nothing" response.

Major Endocrine Glands and the Function of Their Hormones

The function of the ENDOCRINE SYSTEM is to manufacture proteins called hormones. HORMONES circulate in the bloodstream and stimulate actions when they interact with target tissue. There are two classes of hormones: steroid and peptide. Steroid hormones come from cholesterol and include the sex hormones. Amino acids are the source of peptide hormones.

> **ENDOCRINE SYSTEM:** manufactures proteins called hormones

Hormones are specific; they fit receptors on the target tissue cell surface. The receptor activates an enzyme that converts ATP to cyclic AMP. Cyclic AMP (cAMP) is a second messenger from the cell membrane to the nucleus. The genes found in the nucleus turn on or off to cause a specific response.

> **HORMONES:** circulate in the bloodstream and stimulate actions when they interact with target tissue

Endocrine cells, which make up endocrine glands, secrete hormones. The major endocrine glands and their hormones include the following:

- Hypothalamus: located in the lower brain, it signals the pituitary gland.
- Pituitary gland: located at the base of the hypothalamus, it releases growth hormones and antidiuretic hormone (retention of water in kidneys).

- Thyroid gland: located on the trachea, it lowers blood calcium levels (calcitonin) and maintains metabolic processes (thyroxine).

- Gonads: located in the testes of the male and the ovaries of the female, the testes release androgens to support sperm formation, and ovaries release estrogens to stimulate uterine lining growth and progesterone to promote uterine lining growth.

- Pancreas: secretes insulin in order to lower blood glucose levels and glucagon to raise blood glucose levels.

The Structure and Function of the Skin

EPIDERMIS: the thinner outer layer of the skin

DERMIS: the thicker inner layer of the skin

The skin consists of two distinct layers: the EPIDERMIS and the DERMIS. The epidermis is the thinner outer layer, and the dermis is the thicker inner layer. Layers of tightly packed epithelial cells make up the epidermis. The tight packaging of the epithelial cells supports the skin's function as a protective barrier against infection.

The top layer of the epidermis consists of dead skin cells and contains keratin, a waterproofing protein. The dermis layer consists of connective tissue. It contains blood vessels, hair follicles, sweat glands, and sebaceous glands. The body releases an oily secretion called sebum, produced by the sebaceous gland, to the outer epidermis through the hair follicles. Sebum maintains the pH of the skin between 3 and 5, which inhibits most microorganism growth.

The skin also plays a role in thermoregulation. Increased body temperature causes skin blood vessels to dilate, which then causes heat to radiate from the skin's surface. Increased temperature also activates sweat glands, increasing evaporative cooling. Decreased body temperature causes skin blood vessels to constrict. This results in blood from the skin diverting to deeper tissues, thereby reducing heat loss from the surface of the skin.

The Human Respiratory and Excretory Systems

Surface area, volume, and function of the respiratory and excretory systems

The lungs are the respiratory surface of the human respiratory system. A dense net of capillaries contained just beneath the epithelium form the respiratory surface. The surface area of the epithelium is about $100m^2$ in humans. Based on the surface area, the volume of air inhaled and exhaled is known as the tidal volume. This is normally about 500mL in adults. Vital capacity is the maximum volume the lungs can inhale and exhale. This is usually around 3400mL.

The kidneys are the primary organ in the excretory system. Each of the two kidneys in humans is about 10cm long. Despite their small size, they receive about 20 percent of the blood pumped with each heartbeat. The function of the excretory system is to rid the body of nitrogenous wastes in the form of urea.

Breathing and gas exchange

The respiratory system functions in the gas exchange of oxygen and carbon dioxide waste. It delivers oxygen to the bloodstream and picks up carbon dioxide for release from the body. Air enters the mouth and nose, where it is warmed, moistened, and filtered of dust and particles. Cilia in the trachea trap and expel unwanted material in mucus. The trachea splits into two bronchial tubes, and the bronchial tubes divide into smaller and smaller bronchioles in the lungs. The internal surface of the lung is composed of alveoli, which are thin-walled air sacs. These allow for a large surface area for gas exchange. Capillaries line the alveoli.

Oxygen diffuses into the bloodstream, and carbon dioxide diffuses out of the capillaries. It is then exhaled from the lungs due to partial pressure. Hemoglobin, a protein containing iron, carries the oxygenated blood to the heart and all parts of the body.

The thoracic cavity holds the lungs. The diaphragm muscle below the lungs is an adaptation that makes inhalation possible. As the volume of the thoracic cavity increases, the diaphragm muscle flattens out and inhalation occurs. When the diaphragm relaxes, exhalation occurs.

The Human Circulatory and Immune Systems

Structure, function, and regulation of the heart

The function of the closed circulatory system (CARDIOVASCULAR SYSTEM) is to carry oxygenated blood and nutrients to all cells of the body and to return carbon dioxide waste to the lungs for expulsion. The heart, blood vessels, and blood make up the cardiovascular system. The following diagram shows the structure of the heart:

CARDIOVASCULAR SYSTEM: the closed circulatory system that carries oxygenated blood and nutrients to all cells of the body and to return carbon dioxide waste to the lungs for expulsion

Heart

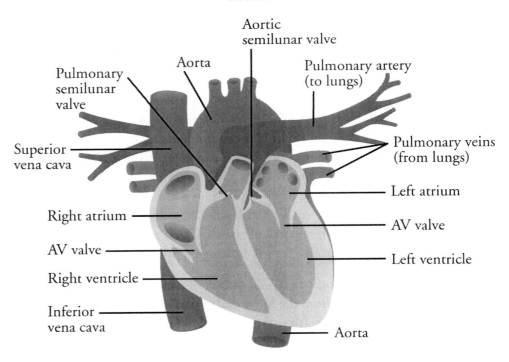

The atria are the chambers that receive blood returning to the heart, and the ventricles are the chambers that pump blood out of the heart. There are four valves: two atrioventricular (AV) valves and two semilunar valves. The AV valves are located between each atrium and ventricle. The contraction of the ventricles closes the AV valve to keep blood from flowing back into the atria. The semilunar valves are located where the aorta leaves the left ventricle and the pulmonary artery leaves the right ventricle. Ventricular contraction opens the semilunar valves, pumping blood out into the arteries, and ventricular relaxation closes the valves.

CARDIAC OUTPUT is the volume of blood per minute that the left ventricle pumps. This output depends on the heart rate and stroke volume. The heart rate is the number of times the heart beats per minute, and the stroke volume is the amount of blood pumped by the left ventricle each time it contracts. Humans have an average cardiac output of about 5.25L/min. Heavy exercise can increase cardiac output up to five times. Epinephrine and increased body temperature can also increase heart rate and, thus, the cardiac output.

Cardiac muscle can contract without any signal from the nervous system. The sinoatrial node is the pacemaker of the heart. It is located on the wall of the right atrium; it generates electrical impulses that make the cardiac muscle cells contract in unison. The atrioventricular node briefly delays the electrical impulse to ensure the atria empty before the ventricles contract.

> **CARDIAC OUTPUT:**
> the volume of blood per minute that the left ventricle pumps

Structure, function, and regulation of the immune system

The immune system is responsible for defending the body against foreign invaders. There are two defense mechanisms: nonspecific and specific. The nonspecific immune mechanism has two lines of defense. The first line of defense is the physical barriers of the body. These include the skin and mucous membranes.

The skin prevents the penetration of bacteria and viruses as long as there are no abrasions on the skin. Mucous membranes form a protective barrier around the digestive, respiratory, and genitourinary tracts. In addition, the pH of the skin and mucous membranes inhibit the growth of many microbes. Mucous secretions (tears and saliva) wash away many microbes; they also contain lysozyme, which kills microbes.

The second line of defense includes white blood cells and the inflammatory response. PHAGOCYTOSIS is the ingestion of foreign particles. Neutrophils make up about 70 percent of all white blood cells. Monocytes mature to become macrophages, which are the largest phagocytic cells. Eosinophils are also phagocytic. Natural killer cells destroy the body's own infected cells instead of invading the microbe directly.

> **PHAGOCYTOSIS:** the ingestion of foreign particles

The other second line of defense is the INFLAMMATORY RESPONSE. When this occurs, the blood supply to the injured area increases, causing redness and heat. Swelling also typically occurs with inflammation. Basophils and mast cells release histamine in response to cell injury. This triggers the inflammatory response.

> **INFLAMMATORY RESPONSE:** when the blood supply to the injured area increases, causing redness and heat and swelling

The specific immune mechanism recognizes specific foreign material and responds by destroying the invader. These mechanisms are specific and diverse. They are able to recognize individual pathogens. An antigen is any foreign particle that elicits an immune response. The body manufactures antibodies that recognize and latch onto antigens and destroy them. They also discriminate between foreign materials versus self-material. Memory of the invaders provides immunity upon any future exposure.

IMMUNITY is the body's ability to recognize and destroy an antigen before it causes harm. Active immunity develops after recovery from an infectious disease (e.g., chicken pox) or after a vaccination (e.g., mumps, measles, and rubella). Passive immunity may be passed from one individual to another and is not permanent. A good example of passive immunities are those passed from mother to nursing child. A baby's immune system is not well developed, so the passive immunity babies receive through nursing keeps them healthier. After exposure to an antigen, the body makes two types of responses:

> **IMMUNITY:** the body's ability to recognize and destroy an antigen before it causes harm

- **The humoral response:** Free antigens activate this response. During it, B-cells (lymphocytes from bone marrow) give rise to plasma cells that secrete antibodies as well as memory cells that will recognize future exposures to the same antigen. The antibodies defend against extracellular pathogens by binding to the antigen and making them an easy target for phagocytes to engulf and destroy. Antibodies are in a class of proteins called immunoglobulins. The five major classes of immunoglobulins (Ig) involved in the humoral response are IgM, IgG, IgA, IgD, and IgE.

- **The cell-mediated response:** Infected cells activate T-cells (lymphocytes from the thymus) in this response. These activated T-cells defend against pathogens in the body cells or cancer cells by binding to the infected cells and destroying them along with the antigen. T-cell receptors on the T helper cells recognize antigens bound to the body's own cells. T helper cells release IL-2, which stimulates other lymphocytes (cytotoxic T-cells and B-cells). Cytotoxic T-cells kill infected host cells by recognizing specific antigens.

> **VACCINES:** antigens given in very small amounts, which stimulate both humoral and cell-mediated responses

VACCINES are antigens given in very small amounts. They stimulate both humoral and cell-mediated responses. After vaccination, memory cells recognize future exposure to the antigen so that the body can produce antibodies much faster.

The Human Digestive System

The roles of basic nutrients found in foods

The function of the digestive system is to break food down into nutrients, to absorb them into the blood stream, and to deliver them to all cells of the body for use in cellular respiration. ESSENTIAL NUTRIENTS are those nutrients that the body needs but cannot make by itself. The four groups of essential nutrients are

> **ESSENTIAL NUTRIENTS:** nutrients that the body needs but cannot make by itself

- Essential amino acids

- Essential fatty acids

- Vitamins

- Minerals

Humans need about eight essential amino acids. A lack of these amino acids results in protein deficiency. There are only a few essential fatty acids.

Vitamins are organic molecules essential for a nutritionally adequate diet. Scientists have identified thirteen vitamins essential to humans. The two groups of vitamins are water soluble (includes the vitamin B complex and vitamin C) and water insoluble (vitamins A, D, and K). Vitamin deficiencies can cause severe health problems.

Unlike vitamins, minerals are inorganic molecules. Calcium is important in bone construction and maintenance. Iron is important in cellular respiration and is a major component of hemoglobin. Carbohydrates, fats, and proteins are fuel for the generation of ATP. Water is necessary to keep the body hydrated.

Essential Amino Acids	Essential Vitamins
Arginine	Vitamin A
Histidine	Vitamin B complex (8 vitamins)
Isoleucine	Vitamin C
Leucine	Vitamin D
Lysine	Vitamin E
Methionine	Vitamin K
Phenylalanine	
Threonine	
Tryptophan	
Valine	

Mechanical and Chemical Digestion

The teeth and saliva begin digestion by breaking food down into smaller pieces and lubricating it to allow swallowing. The lips, cheeks, and tongue form a bolus, or ball of food. The process of PERISTALSIS (wavelike contractions) carries the food down the pharynx, where it enters the stomach through the sphincter. Once through, the sphincter closes to keep food from going back up. In the stomach, pepsinogen and hydrochloric acid form pepsin, the enzyme that hydrolyzes proteins. This chemical action breaks the food down further and churns it into a semifluid mass called acid chyme.

PERISTALSIS: the wavelike contractions that carry food down the pharynx to the stomach

The pyloric sphincter muscle opens to allow the food to enter the small intestine. Most nutrient absorption occurs in the small intestine. Its large surface area, resulting from its length and protrusions called villi and microvilli, allow for a great absorptive surface into the bloodstream.

Neutralization of the chyme after arrival from the acidic stomach allows the local enzymes to function. Accessory organs function in the production of necessary enzymes and bile. The pancreas makes many enzymes necessary to break down food in the small intestine. The liver makes bile, which breaks down and emulsifies fatty acids. Any food left after the trip through the small intestine enters the large intestine. The large intestine functions to reabsorb water and produce vitamin K. The feces, or remaining waste, passes out through the anus.

The Human Reproductive System

The function of male and female reproductive systems

Hormones regulate sexual maturation in humans. Humans cannot reproduce until puberty, about the age of eight to fourteen, depending on the individual. Prior to puberty, the hypothalamus begins secreting hormones that help to mature the reproductive system and to develop the secondary sex characteristics. Reproductive maturity in girls occurs with the first menstruation; it occurs in boys with the first ejaculation of viable sperm.

Hormones also regulate reproduction. In males, the primary sex hormones are the androgens, testosterone being the most important. The testes produce androgens that dictate the primary and secondary sex characteristics of the male.

Female hormone patterns are cyclic and complex. Most women have a reproductive cycle length of about twenty-eight days. The menstrual cycle is specific to the changes in the uterus. The ovarian cycle results in ovulation; it occurs in parallel with the menstrual cycle. Hormones regulate this parallelism. Five hormones participate in this regulation, most notably estrogen and progesterone. Estrogen and progesterone play an important role in sending signals to the uterus and in developing and maintaining the endometrium. Estrogen also dictates the secondary sex characteristics of females.

Gametogenesis, fertilization, and birth control

GAMETOGENESIS is the production of the sperm (spermatogenesis) and egg cells (oogenesis). Spermatogenesis begins at puberty in the male. One spermatogonia, the diploid precursor of sperm, produces four sperm. The sperm mature in the seminiferous tubules, which are located in the testes. Oogenesis, the production of egg cells (ova), is usually complete by the birth of a female. Females do not release egg cells until menstruation begins at puberty. Meiosis forms one ovum with all the cytoplasm and three polar bodies that the body reabsorbs. The ovaries store the ovum and release them each month from puberty to menopause.

Seminiferous tubules in the testes house sperm, where they mature. The epididymis, located on top of the testes, contains mature sperm. After ejaculation, the sperm travel up the vas deferens, where they mix with semen made in the

> **GAMETOGENESIS:** the production of the sperm (spermatogenesis) and egg cells (oogenesis)

prostate and seminal vesicles; they then travel out the urethra.

OVULATION releases the egg into the fallopian tubes, where cilia move the egg along the length of the tubes. Fertilization of the egg by the sperm normally occurs in the fallopian tube. If pregnancy does not occur, the egg passes through the uterus and is expelled through the vagina during menstruation. Levels of progesterone and estrogen stimulate menstruation. Implantation of a fertilized egg downregulates the levels, stopping menstruation.

> **OVULATION:** the release of the egg into the fallopian tube

Many methods of contraception (birth control) are available that affect different stages of fertilization. Chemical contraception (birth control pills) prevent ovulation by synthetic estrogen and progesterone. Several physical barrier methods of contraception are also available. Male and female condoms block semen from contacting the egg. Sterilization is another method of birth control. Tubal ligation in women prevents eggs from entering the uterus. A vasectomy in men involves the cutting of the vas deferens. This prevents the sperm from entering the urethra. Of course, the most effective method of birth control is abstinence.

The Stages and Characteristics of Physical, Cognitive, Social, and Emotional Growth and Development

PHYSICAL DEVELOPMENT	
Ages Three to Five	Small children have a propensity for engaging in periods of a great deal of physical activity, punctuated by a need for a lot of rest. Children at this stage lack fine motor skills and cannot focus on small objects for very long. Their bones are still developing. At this age, girls tend to be better coordinated, and boys tend to be stronger.
Ages Six to Eight	The lag in fine motor skills continues during the early elementary school years.
Ages Nine to Eleven	Preadolescent children become stronger, leaner, and taller. Their motor skills improve, and they are able to sit still and focus for longer periods. Growth during this period is constant. This is also the time when gender-related physical predispositions will begin to show. Preadolescents are at risk of obesity without proper nutrition or adequate activity.
Ages Twelve to Fourteen	Young adolescents experience drastic physical growth (girls earlier than boys) and are highly preoccupied with their physical appearance.
Ages Fifteen to Seventeen	As children proceed to the later stages of adolescence, girls will reach their full height, while boys will still have some growth remaining. The increase in hormone levels will cause acne, which coincides with a slight decrease of preoccupation with physical appearance. At this age, children may begin to initiate sexual activity (boys generally more motivated by hormones, and girls more by peer pressure). There is a risk of teen pregnancy and sexually transmitted diseases.

COGNITIVE DEVELOPMENT	
Ages Three to Five	Language development is the most important aspect of cognitive development in small children. Acknowledging successes, rewarding mature behavior, and allowing the child to explore can improve confidence and self-esteem at this age.
Ages Six to Eight	Early elementary school children are eager to learn and love to talk. Children at this age have a very literal understanding of rules and verbal instructions, and must develop strong listening skills.
Ages Nine to Eleven	Preadolescent children display increased logical thought, but their knowledge or beliefs may be unusual or surprising. Differences in cognitive styles develop at this age (e.g., field dependant or independent preferences).
Ages Twelve to Fourteen	In early adolescence, boys tend to score higher on mechanical/spatial reasoning, and girls on spelling and language tasks. Boys are better with mental imagery, and girls have better access and retrieval of information from memory. Self-efficacy (the ability to self-evaluate) becomes very important at this stage.
Ages Fifteen to Seventeen	In later adolescence, children are capable of formal thought but don't always apply it. Conflicts between teenagers' and parents' opinions and worldviews will arise. Children at this age may become interested in advanced political thinking.

SOCIAL DEVELOPMENT	
Ages Three to Five	Small children are socially flexible. Different children will prefer solitary play, parallel play, or cooperative play. Frequent minor quarrels will occur among children, and boys will tend to be more aggressive (children at these ages are already aware of gender roles).
Ages Six to Eight	Early elementary school children are increasingly selective of friends (usually of the same sex). Children at this age enjoy playing games but are excessively preoccupied by the rules. Verbal aggression becomes more common than physical aggression, and adults should encourage children of this age to solve their own conflicts.
Ages Nine to Eleven	Preadolescent children place great importance on the (perceived) opinions of their peers and on their social stature and will go to great lengths to "fit in." Friendships at this age are very selective and are usually of the same sex.
Ages Twelve to Fourteen	Young adolescents develop a greater understanding of the emotions of others, which results in increased emotional sensitivity and impacts peer relationships. Children at this age develop an increased need to perform.
Ages Fifteen to Seventeen	In the later stages of adolescence, peers are still the primary influence on day-to-day decisions, but parents will have increasing influence on long-term goals. Girls' friendships tend to be close and intimate, whereas boys' friendships are based on competition and similar interests. Many children this age will work part-time, and educators should be alert to signs of potential school dropouts.

EMOTIONAL DEVELOPMENT	
Ages Three to Five	Small children express emotion freely and have a limited ability to learn how emotions influence behavior. Jealousy at this age is common.
Ages Six to Eight	Early elementary school children have easily bruised feelings and are just beginning to recognize the feelings of others. Children this age will want to please teachers and other adults.
Ages Nine to Eleven	Preadolescent children develop a global and stable self-image (self-concept and self-esteem). Comparisons to their peers and the opinions of their peers are important. An unstable home environment at this age contributes to an increased risk of delinquency.
Ages Twelve to Fourteen	Young adolescence can be a stormy and stressful time for children, but in reality this is only the case for roughly 20 percent of teens. Boys may have trouble controlling their anger and display impulsive behavior. Girls may suffer depression. Young adolescents are very egocentric and concerned with appearance; they often feel very strongly that "adults don't understand."
Ages Fifteen to Seventeen	In later stages of adolescence, educators should be alert to signs of surfacing mental health problems (e.g., eating disorders, substance abuse, schizophrenia, depression, and suicide).

Nutrition and Weight Control

Identifying the components of nutrition

COMPONENTS OF NUTRITION	
Carbohydrates	The main source of energy (glucose) in the human diet. The two types of carbohydrates are simple and complex. Complex carbohydrates have greater nutritional value because they take longer to digest, contain dietary fiber, and do not excessively elevate blood sugar levels. Common sources of carbohydrates are fruits, vegetables, grains, dairy products, and legumes.
Proteins	Necessary for growth, development, and cellular function. The body breaks down consumed protein into component amino acids for future use. Major sources of protein are meat, poultry, fish, legumes, eggs, dairy products, grains, and legumes.
Fats	A concentrated energy source and important component of the human body. The different types of fats are saturated, monounsaturated, and polyunsaturated. Polyunsaturated fats are the healthiest because they may lower cholesterol levels, while saturated fats increase cholesterol levels. Common sources of saturated fats include dairy products, meat, coconut oil, and palm oil. Common sources of unsaturated fats include nuts, most vegetable oils, and fish.

Table continued on next page

Vitamins and Minerals	Organic substances that the body requires in small quantities for proper functioning. People acquire vitamins and minerals in their diets and in supplements. Important vitamins include A, B, C, D, E, and K. Important minerals include calcium, phosphorus, magnesium, potassium, sodium, chlorine, and sulfur.
Water	Makes up 55 to 75 percent of the human body. It is essential for most bodily functions and obtained through foods and liquids.

Meeting the nutritional needs of students

Nutritional requirements vary from person to person. General guidelines for meeting adequate nutritional needs are no more than 30 percent total caloric intake from fats (preferably 10 percent from saturated fats, 10 percent from monounsaturated fats, and 10 percent from polyunsaturated fats); no more than 15 percent total caloric intake from proteins (complete); and at least 55 percent of caloric intake from carbohydrates (mainly complex carbohydrates). Exercise and diet can help maintain proper body weight by equalizing caloric intake and caloric output.

Choosing a healthy diet

A healthy diet is essential for achieving and maintaining optimum mental and physical health. Making the decision to eat well is a powerful investment. Selecting foods that encompass a variety of healthy nutrients will help to reduce the risk of developing common medical conditions; it will also boost one's immune system while increasing energy level. Experts agree that the key to healthy eating is balance, variety, and moderation. Here are some other tips:

- Enjoy plenty of whole grains, fruits, and vegetables
- Maintain a healthy weight
- Eat moderate portions
- Eat regular meals
- Reduce but don't eliminate certain foods
- Balance your food choices over time
- Know your diet pitfalls
- Make changes gradually—remember, foods are not good or bad
- Select foods based on your total eating patterns, not whether any individual food is "good" or "bad"

The Food Guide Pyramid and dietary guidelines

The Food Guide Pyramid illustrates the different components of a healthy diet and the number of servings of each food group people should consume. Specifically, people should consume the greatest number of servings of carbohydrate-based products like cereals, breads, and pasta; a large number of vitamin- and mineral-rich carbohydrates like fruits and vegetables; a number of protein-rich foods; and very few foods with higher fat content.

Food Pyramid

Courtesy of USDA.

The Dietary Guidelines for Americans is a document published by the U.S. Department of Health and Human Services and the U.S. Department of Agriculture. It is a primary source of dietary health information for policymakers, nutrition educators, and health providers so they can help direct the individuals that they represent, teach, and care for to make informed and healthy decisions regarding their diets.

Regulations related to food labels and packaging ensure that consumers receive accurate information about the products they buy. Food labels include the breakdown of ingredients, nonfood components, nutritional values, and accuracy of claims relating to the food product.

Sample Test Questions and Rationale

(Easy)

1. **Which of the following is not a type of muscle tissue?**

    A. Skeletal

    B. Cardiac

    C. Smooth

    D. Fiber

    Answer: D. Fiber

    The main function of the muscular system is movement. There are three types of muscle tissue: skeletal, cardiac, and smooth.

(Average)

2. **Which of these is a type of joint?**

    A. Ball and socket

    B. Hinge

    C. Pivot

    D. All of the above

    Answer: D. All of the above

    A joint is a place where two bones meet. Joints enable movement. Hinge, ball and socket, and pivot are types of joints.

Recognizing the differences between communicable and noncommunicable diseases and strategies for preventing or treating them (e.g., vaccinations, hand washing, regular exercise, antibiotics)

Causes, Characteristics, and Methods for Detecting and Preventing Diseases

Pathogens that enter the body through direct or indirect contact cause communicable, or infectious, diseases. A PATHOGEN is a disease-causing organism. Familiar communicable diseases include influenza, the common cold, chicken pox, pneumonia, measles, mumps, and mononucleosis.

> **PATHOGEN:** a disease-causing organism

To minimize the circulation of pathogens that cause these illnesses, people must follow simple precautions. Individuals who are ill with these diseases should stay away from others during the contagious period of the infection. All people should avoid sharing items such as towels, toothbrushes, and silverware. At home, thorough clothes washing, dishwashing, and frequent hand washing can decrease pathogen transmission. Keeping immunizations up to date is also important in reducing the spread of communicable diseases.

Sexual activity is the source of transmission for many other communicable diseases. The commonly used term for these types of diseases is sexually transmitted disease (STD) or sexually transmitted infection (STI). Common STIs include chlamydia, gonorrhea, syphilis, genital herpes, genital warts, bacterial vaginosis, human papillomavirus (HPV), pediculosis pubis (pubic lice), hepatitis B, and HIV. Certain STIs can result in infertility. HPV can result in a deadly form of cervical cancer. HIV may result in acquired immunodeficiency syndrome (AIDS), which can be fatal. Some of these diseases, such as genital herpes, last a lifetime.

> **CHRONIC DISEASE:** a disease that is long lasting, often continuing for more than three months

A CHRONIC DISEASE is a disease that is long lasting, often continuing for more than three months. Examples of chronic conditions include diseases such as heart disease, cancer, and diabetes. These diseases are currently the leading causes of death and disability in the United States. Many forms of these widespread and expensive diseases are preventable. Choosing nutritious foods, participating in physical activity, and avoiding tobacco use can prevent or control these illnesses.

> **DEGENERATIVE DISEASE:** a condition in which diseased tissues or organs steadily deteriorate

A DEGENERATIVE DISEASE is a condition in which diseased tissues or organs steadily deteriorate. The deterioration may be due to ordinary wear and tear or to lifestyle choices such as lack of exercise or poor nutrition. In addition, many degenerative diseases are of questionable origin and may be linked to heredity and environmental factors. Some examples of degenerative diseases include osteoporosis, Alzheimer's disease, ALS (Lou Gehrig's disease), osteoarthritis, inflammatory bowel disease (IBD), and Parkinson's disease.

Preventing health problems

Primary prevention activities are the most cost-effective in health care, as they help to avoid the suffering, cost, and burden associated with a particular disease or condition. These precautions promote health by targeting specific health care concerns. Examples of primary prevention include both active and passive immunization against disease. PASSIVE IMMUNIZATION is treatment that provides immunity through the transfer of antibodies obtained from an immune individual. ACTIVE IMMUNIZATION is treatment that provides immunity by challenging an individual's own immune system to produce an antibody against a particular organism. Recently developed vaccines include the ones for hepatitis A and chicken pox.

Education to promote health protection is also a primary prevention strategy. Advising automobile drivers and passengers to use seat belts when driving is an action of primary prevention, as does advocating the use of helmets while riding a bicycle or motorcycle.

Secondary prevention is early detection using accepted screening technologies. The intent is to identify patients with an increased risk, since many conditions do not show symptoms until the disease is well established, significantly reducing chances of recovery. Finding problems early in the development of diseases such as hyperlipidemia, hypertension, and breast and prostate cancer can frequently curb or eliminate the damage and reduce pain and suffering.

Children who are disruptive, inattentive, hyperactive, impulsive, or aggressive may be at heightened risk for the development of antisocial behavior, substance abuse, and school dropout in later years (Barkley, Fischer, Edelbrock, & Smallish, 1990). Secondary prevention in these cases includes skill-building interventions such as teaching children problem-solving strategies and educating parents to use these techniques at home. Instructors can create environments that allow children to work together with their peers, their parents, and school personnel to channel their energy into positive outcomes (Weissberg, Caplan, & Sivo, 1989).

Natural defense mechanisms

The body fights disease through IMMUNITY, through which special proteins called antibodies destroy infection. Lymphocytes, or white blood cells, and cells of the reticuloendothelial system are responsible for establishing active acquired immunity in the body. This is one of the body's defense mechanisms against disease.

Another defense mechanism that the body uses to prevent the spread of infection is inflammation, which occurs in damaged tissues. Fluids surrounding the infection clot, preventing any flow from the damaged tissues to other areas.

> **PASSIVE IMMUNIZATION:** treatment that provides immunity through the transfer of antibodies obtained from an immune individual

> **ACTIVE IMMUNIZATION:** treatment that provides immunity by challenging an individual's own immune system to produce an antibody against a particular organism

> **IMMUNITY:** the body's ability to fight disease through special proteins that destroy infection

The Relationship between Diet and the Prevention of Disease

Diet plays an important role in the prevention of disease. Consuming a healthy diet that is rich in polyunsaturated fats, whole grains, fish, fruits, vegetables, and lean protein, and low in saturated fat and sugar, reduces the risk of many chronic diseases. Proper nutrition can help to prevent heart disease, strokes, osteoporosis, and many types of cancers. In addition, good nutrition helps to boost the body's immune system, lowering the risk of infectious disease.

Issues related to ideal weight and body composition

Nutrition and exercise are closely related concepts that are important to student health. A primary responsibility of health instructors is to teach students about proper nutrition and exercise, as well as how they relate to each other.

The two key components of a healthy lifestyle are the consumption of a balanced diet and regular physical activity. Exercise and diet maintain proper body weight by equalizing caloric intake to caloric output. Nutrition can affect physical performance. Proper nutrition produces high energy levels and allows for peak performance. Inadequate or improper nutrition can impair physical performance and lead to short-term and long-term health problems (e.g., depressed immune system and heart disease, respectively). Regular exercise improves overall health. The benefits of regular exercise include a stronger immune system, weight management, a reduced risk of premature death, a reduced risk of heart disease, improved psychological well-being, and stronger muscles, bones, and joints.

Body composition management

It is vital to analyze procedures, activities, resources, and benefits involved in developing and maintaining healthy levels of body composition. Maintaining a healthy body composition allows an individual to move freely and to obtain a certain pattern necessary for activity. Furthermore, maintaining a healthy body composition is positively related with long-term health and resistance to disease and sickness.

Maintaining a healthy body composition is positively related with long-term health and resistance to disease and sickness.

The total weight of an individual is a combination of bones, ligaments, tendons, organs, fluids, muscles, and fat. Because muscle weighs three times more than fat per unit of volume, a person who exercises often gains muscle. This could cause an individual to be smaller physically but weigh more than he or she appears to weigh.

The only proven method for maintaining a healthy body composition is following a healthy diet and engaging in regular exercise. A healthy program of nutrition and exercise helps to balance caloric intake and output, thus preventing excessive body fat production.

SKILL 22.3 **Recognizing characteristics of interpersonal relationships** (e.g., within families, among peers) **and strategies for maintaining healthy interpersonal relationships** (e.g., using conflict resolution and positive character development skills)

Families and Family Structures

Today's family is often quite different from the traditional mom, dad, and biological children. Divorce, stepfamilies, and adoption have changed the typical American family. Studies show that children suffer the most with divorce, remarriage, and stepfamily situations. They are particularly at risk if their biological parents are in conflict. Divorce takes a long time, and unhappy parents, who are focused on severing ties with the ex-spouse and starting over, often overlook their children. Relationships with the absent parent change as well.

The adjustment of children of divorce is more dependent on the child's resiliency than anything else. Contributing factors include the child's age during the divorce, the amount of time elapsed, parenting style, financial security, and parental conflict. For example, fifty percent of adjustment problems for children of divorce are due to economic problems faced by divorced households.

Adoptions of international children and those of ethnicities that are different from the parents are creating multicultural families and communities. Attachment disorder is often a problem in these types of adoptions—often due to lack of nurturing early in a child's life. More same-sex couples and single parents adopt, and grandparents often adopt their grandchildren due to parental abuse or neglect. The twenty-first-century American family is very different from what was common thirty years ago.

The demographics of stepfamilies are complex, with nearly twenty five percent of the parents unmarried. Both heterosexual parents and gay, lesbian, or bisexual partners may head families. Stepfamilies are a blend of parents, their respective children, the nonresidential parents of those children, grandparents, and other members of the extended family, as well as children born to remarried ex-spouses.

The blended family's challenges include parenting, disciplining, developing new relationships between the stepparent and other spouse's children, strengthening the marital relationship, and working to include nonresidential family (divorced spouses and children not living with the stepfamily).

One in three Americans is part of a stepfamily, each with its own character. The stepchildren rarely see a new stepparent as a "real parent," and years may pass before they gain acceptance. It is also difficult for parents in second marriages to treat their stepchildren the same as their biological children. Children are often given too much power in the new family and may try to create conflict between their biological parent and the stepparent in an attempt to make the stepparent leave.

Creating family stability requires the same steps, whether the situation is a first-marriage, stepfamily, or a single-parent family. What really matters is that parents maintain a routine that fosters security. How families resolve conflicts is also important. Children need an anchor when it seems that everything in their lives is changing. This could be a special friend, neighbor, or relative outside the immediate family. Consistency in school settings helps to predict positive adjustment in children, especially when their home lives are chaotic.

The following are some strategies for parents of second marriages:

- Discuss and decide on finances before getting married.

- Build a strong marital bond that will benefit everybody.

- Develop a parenting plan, which likely will involve having the stepparent play a secondary, nondisciplinary role for the first year or two. Giving children the time to adjust slowly prepares for a successful transition.

- Take the time to process each change.

- Make sure that big changes are communicated adult-to-adult, not via the children.

- Work with therapists who are specially trained in stepfamily dynamics.

Key factors that contribute to healthy adjustments postdivorce include appropriate parenting, access to the nonresidential parent, custody arrangements, and low parental conflict. Appropriate parenting includes providing emotional support, monitoring children's activities, disciplining authoritatively, and maintaining age-appropriate expectations. Finally, the research demonstrates that the best predictor of child's adjustment following divorce is the parents' psychological health and the quality of the parent-child relationship.

Research demonstrates that the best predictor of child's adjustment following divorce is the parents' psychological health and the quality of the parent-child relationship.

Maintaining healthy relationships

Mutual respect, shared values and interests, and a mutually felt ability to trust and depend on one another all characterize a responsible friendship. Genuine respect for one's friends is vital for the creation of a positive and responsible friendship. It is much easier to dismiss commitments toward and the needs of those we do not respect. Shared values are the foundation for mutual respect, and shared interests are necessary for the exploration and development of a friendship. Trust and dependability are the cement that holds responsible friendships together.

Individuals can develop positive interpersonal relationships by devoting time to character-building activities that strengthen the preceding traits. They can work to become people who espouse the values that they would like to see in their friends, and they can make efforts toward becoming trustworthy and dependable. Specific techniques that can be applied to develop positive interpersonal relationships with others include active listening and considerate respect for the things others value.

ACTIVE LISTENING is the process of repeating back what was said in the form of a question (e.g., if someone tells you, "I'm thinking of taking a vacation, maybe to Florida", you might repeat back, "You're saying that you want to take a vacation to Florida"). These exercises should not be performed mechanically (i.e., parroting), but they should be done as a personal reminder to listen to the concerns and interests of others.

Considerate respect for others can be developed by actively asking ourselves what about the current scenario that we are facing would others see as significant. It is an exercise aimed at placing value and emphasis on the priorities of others.

SOCIAL SUPPORT SYSTEMS are the networks that students develop with their peers that provide support when students experience challenges and difficulties. The support offered by these systems is often emotional and sometimes logistical. Financial support in these relationships is generally inappropriate. Social support systems are vital to students (and individuals in general), especially students who don't have other support mechanisms in place.

Conflict management

Interpersonal conflict is a major source of stress and worry. Common sources of interpersonal conflict include problems with family relationships, competition, and disagreement over values or decisions. Teaching students to manage conflict will help them to reduce stress levels throughout their lives, thereby limiting the adverse health effects of stress.

The following is a list of conflict resolution principles and techniques.

- Think before reacting: In a conflict situation, it is important to resist the temptation to react immediately. You should step back, consider the situation, and plan an appropriate response. Do not react to petty situations with anger.

- Listen: Be sure to listen carefully to the opposing party. Try to understand the other person's point of view.

- Find common ground: Try to find some common ground as soon as possible. Early compromise can help to ease the tension.

ACTIVE LISTENING: the process of repeating back what was said in the form of a question

SOCIAL SUPPORT SYSTEMS: networks that students develop with their peers that provide support when students experience challenges and difficulties

The benefits of maintaining healthy peer relationships include having a social support system to assist in difficult times, as well as having knowledge of the existence of that system. This means that students can feel confident to take greater risks (within reason) and achieve more because they know the support system is there if they need it.

Teaching students to manage conflict will help them to reduce stress levels throughout their lives, thereby limiting the adverse health effects of stress.

- **Accept responsibility:** In every conflict there is plenty of blame to go around. Admitting when you are wrong shows you are committed to resolving the conflict.

- **Attack the problem, not the person:** Personal attacks are never beneficial and usually lead to greater conflicts and hard feelings.

- **Focus on the future:** Instead of trying to assign blame for past events, focus on what needs to be done differently to avoid future conflict.

SKILL 22.4 **Identifying strategies for maintaining personal emotional and physical health** *(e.g., stress management, sleep, proper diet)*

Physical activity and inactivity greatly affect many aspects of a person's life, including physical fitness abilities, general health, physical resilience, physical self-confidence, psychological well-being, and cognitive function. Regular physical activity can improve or increase these elements, while inactivity can damage or decrease these elements.

The most obvious and direct benefit of physical activity is the physical dimension, which includes fitness and general health. Regular physical activity leads to improved physical fitness, improved strength and endurance of the muscular and cardiorespiratory systems, and improved function of the circulatory system. Improved function of all these systems means that the body expends far less energy on day-to-day activities, significantly increasing overall energy levels. Conversely, a lifestyle of physical inactivity will gradually lead to a deterioration of the muscular, cardiorespiratory, and circulatory systems, which leads to decreased energy levels.

Regular physical activity also contributes to increased physical resilience. When coupled with sufficient rest and a healthy diet, physical activity strengthens the musculoskeletal system, which makes the individual less susceptible to injury. Physical activity also tends to improve reflexes and balance, reducing the likelihood of injury. Conversely and as previously mentioned, a lifestyle of physical inactivity leads to a deterioration of the same physical systems that regular exercise strengthens; it also contributes to a gradual "desharpening" of reflexes and balance. In sum, these changes increase the likelihood and susceptibility of the individual to injury.

The bridge between physical and psychological benefits is the physical self-confidence derived from regular physical activity. The individual's increased ability to perform physical tasks leads to the growth of his or her sense of ability to perform any physical activity (for example, you don't have to actually climb ten flights of stairs to know that you could if you wanted to—this is very liberating, as it creates options). Conversely, a lifestyle of physical inactivity, which implies a decreased fitness level, will often eat away at an individual's physical self-confidence.

Regarding psychological well-being, physical activity causes the brain to release endorphins, which function to reduce stress levels (prolonged physical endurance activities can produce levels of endorphins that induce a pleasant and healthy "runner's high").

Most physical activities also mix a degree of repetitive motion and action that require directed attention. In combination, this can function as a sort of meditative activity. For all of these reasons, regular physical activity contributes to psychological balance and well-being as well as reduced stress levels. Conversely, a lifestyle of physical inactivity allows physical confidence to deteriorate and removes alternatives of stress-relief, which can contribute negatively to the individual's psychological well-being.

Finally, regular physical activity benefits the circulatory system, which improves blood flow to the brain. This, in turn, leads to increased cognitive function and mental acuity. Those who are physically inactive do not experience these benefits.

The Benefits of Sleep

Sleep gives the body a break from the normal tasks of daily living. During sleep, the body performs many important cleansing and restorative tasks. The immune and excretory systems clear waste and repair cellular damage that accumulates in the body each day. Similarly, the body requires adequate rest and sleep to build and repair muscles. Without adequate rest, even the most strenuous exercise program will not produce muscular development. A lack of rest and sleep leaves the body vulnerable to infection and disease.

Stress management and good nutrition are among the cornerstones of healthy living. Physical education instructors can introduce students to these important concepts through the development of individualized fitness and wellness plans. Fitness and wellness plans should include a concrete exercise plan and a detailed nutritional plan.

SKILL 22.5 **Recognizing the effects of substance abuse, factors contributing to substance abuse** (e.g., media advertising, peer pressure), **and strategies for resisting pressure to use alcohol, tobacco products, and other drugs**

Factors that contribute to the misuse and abuse of tobacco, alcohol, and other drugs include mental health problems, stress, difficult life circumstances, and peer pressure. Identifying alternatives to substance abuse is an important preventative and coping strategy.

Contributing Factors to Substance Abuse

Factors that contribute to the misuse and abuse of tobacco, alcohol, and other drugs include mental health problems, stress, difficult life circumstances, and peer pressure. Identifying alternatives to substance abuse is an important preventative and coping strategy.

Alternatives to substance use and abuse include regular participation in stress-relieving activities like meditation, exercise, and therapy, all of which can have a relaxing effect. More important, the acquisition of longer-term coping strategies (for example, self-empowerment through the practice of problem-solving techniques) is key to maintaining a commitment to alternatives to substance use and abuse.

Aspects of substance abuse treatment that must be considered include the processes of physical and psychological withdrawal from the addictive substance, acquisition of coping strategies and replacement techniques to fill the void left by the addictive substance, limiting access to the addictive substance, and acquiring self-control strategies.

Withdrawal from an addictive substance has both psychological and physical symptoms. The psychological symptoms include depression, anxiety, and strong cravings for the substance. Physical withdrawal symptoms stem from the body, which is adapted to a steady intake of the addictive substance. When removed, the body must adapt to accommodate the lack of that substance. Depending on the substance, medical intervention may be necessary.

Coping strategies and replacement techniques, as discussed earlier, center around providing the individual with an effective alternative to the addictive substance as a solution to the situations that they feel would necessitate the substance. Limiting access to the addictive substance (opportunities for use) is important, because the symptoms of withdrawal and the experiences associated with the substance can provide a strong impetus to return to using it. Recovering addicts should learn strategies of self-control and self-discipline to help them stay off the addictive substance.

The implications of substance abuse

Disease and substance abuse issues have significant implications for both individuals and for society as a whole. Specific implications, though, will depend greatly on the perception of the disease or substance abuse problem (defined by the Surgeon General as a disease) in the society. Education that gives the individuals in a society a clear understanding of the nature of diseases—what they are and are not linked to, how they can and cannot be transmitted, and what effects they will and will not exert on the afflicted individuals—will positively impact both the afflicted individual and society as a whole.

This same education is often the deciding factor that dictates the willingness of the community to allocate resources to programs for treatment and prevention. It is this willingness to "get involved" on a societal level that plays a central role in the likelihood of improved resources for substance abuse issues.

On the individual level, one very important implication of disease and substance abuse problems relate to responsible behavior. This is not a simple matter, as both disease and substance abuse problems will often lead to highly impaired judgment, making the choice to act responsibly and seek out help on an individual level much harder to do. Individuals in a society must act responsibly to help those around them who are diseased or in the throes of a substance abuse problem to seek appropriate treatment.

SKILL 22.6 Identifying safety practices to avoid accidents and injuries

Basic healthy behaviors reduce the risk of injuries, illness, disease, and other health problems. Injuries are usually a result of unforeseen accidents. Falls are the leading cause of death among home accidents. Falls occur most frequently among the elderly and young children. The most common location of falls is in bathtubs and showers. Examples of precautions that can help to decrease the risk of falls include using rubber mats in bathtubs and showers, using safety gates to block young children from stairs, wearing appropriate safety equipment during physical activity, and promptly removing ice and snow from steps and sidewalks.

At a more cognitive level, rules, discipline, cooperation, etiquette, and safety practices play a vital role in staying safe during personal performance and other movement-based activities. These activities, by their very nature, will often challenge individuals to push their limitations, both in terms of their current physical and psychological limitations, and in terms of what they might consider to be behaviorally acceptable in competitive situations. Rules and discipline are critical in competitive situations where there is a strong drive to "achieve at any cost" (at least in terms of personal sacrifice and dedication).

Rules and self-discipline are the lines that divide healthy athletes from those who engage in unsportsmanlike behavior and training practices that do not fit into a balanced lifestyle. Similarly, cooperation is the element that allows athletes in a hard-training situation, who are both physically and mentally exhausted, to rely on one another for support. This is a critical factor to healthy training practices. Etiquette is the formalization of these cooperative practices. In situations where individuals might try to push their personal limits beyond what they know they are capable of, safety practices are critical to prevent injuries and accidents.

Rules and self-discipline are the lines that divide healthy athletes from those who engage in unsportsmanlike behavior and training practices that do not fit into a balanced lifestyle.

General safety concerns

Safety education related to outdoor pursuits and recreation should emphasize the importance of planning and research. Students should consider in advance what the potential dangers of an activity might be; they should prepare accordingly (for example, students and instructors should examine weather forecasts). Of course, educator supervision is required; first-aid equipment and properly trained educators must be present for all outdoor education activities. Students should use proper safety gear when appropriate (e.g., helmets, harnesses). Parental consent is also generally required for these types of scenarios.

Actions that promote safety and injury prevention

The following is a list of practices that promote safety in all types of physical education and athletic activities:

- Having an instructor who is properly trained and qualified
- Organizing the class by size, activity, and conditions of the class
- Inspecting buildings and other facilities regularly, and immediately giving notice of any hazards
- Avoiding overcrowding
- Using adequate lighting
- Ensuring that students dress in appropriate clothing and shoes
- Presenting organized activities
- Inspecting all equipment regularly
- Adhering to building codes and fire regulations
- Using protective equipment
- Using spotters
- Eliminating hazards
- Teaching students correct ways of performing skills and activities
- Teaching students how to use the equipment properly and safely

Strategies for injury prevention

- Participant screenings: Evaluate injury history, anticipate and prevent potential injuries, watch for hidden injuries and the reoccurrence of an injury, and maintain communication.
- Standards and discipline: Ensure that athletes obey the rules of sportsmanship, supervision, and biomechanics.

- **Education and knowledge:** Stay current in knowledge of first aid, sports medicine, sport technique, and injury prevention through clinics, workshops, and communication with staff and trainers.

- **Conditioning:** Programs should be year-long and participants should have access to conditioning facilities in and out of season to produce more fit and knowledgeable athletes who are less prone to injury.

- **Equipment:** Perform regular inspections; ensure proper fit and proper use.

- **Facilities:** Maintain standards and use safe equipment.

- **Field care:** Establish emergency procedures for serious injury.

- **Rehabilitation:** Use objective measures such as power output on an isokinetic dynamometer.

Prevention of common athletic injuries

- **Foot:** Start with good footwear, foot exercises.

- **Ankle:** Use high-top shoes and tape support; strengthen plantar (calf), dorsiflexor (shin), and ankle eversion (ankle outward).

- **Shin splints:** strengthen ankle dorsiflexors.

- **Achilles tendon:** Stretch dorsiflexion and strengthen plantar flexion (heel raises).

- **Knee:** Increase strength and flexibility of calf and thigh muscles.

- **Back:** Use proper body mechanics.

- **Tennis elbow:** Avoid lateral epicondylitis caused by bent elbow, hitting late, not stepping into the ball, heavy rackets, and rackets with strings that are too tight.

- **Head and neck injuries:** Avoid dangerous techniques (e.g., grabbing a facemask) and carefully supervise dangerous activities like the trampoline.

Sample Test Question and Rationale

(Average)

1. A physical education instructor anticipates and prevents potential injuries, watches for hidden injuries, and takes an injury evaluation of the entire class. Which of the following strategies to prevent injuries is the teacher demonstrating?

    A. Maintaining hiring standards

    B. Proper use of equipment

    C. Proper procedures for emergencies

    D. Participant screening

Answer: D. Participant screening.

In order for the instructor to know each student's physical status, he or she takes an injury evaluation. Such surveys are one way to know the physical status of an individual. It chronicles past injuries, tattoos, activities, and diseases the individual may have or had. It helps the instructor to know the limitations of each individual. Participant screening covers all forms of surveying and anticipation of injuries.

COMPETENCY 23
UNDERSTAND BASIC PHYSICAL EDUCATION PRINCIPLES, PRACTICES, AND ACTIVITIES

SKILL Identifying the components of health-related fitness *(e.g.,*
23.1 *cardiovascular endurance, muscular strength, flexibility)* **and appropriate activities for promoting each of the different components**

There are five health-related components of physical fitness: cardiorespiratory or cardiovascular endurance, muscle strength, muscle endurance, flexibility, and body composition.

- Cardiovascular endurance: The ability of the body to sustain aerobic activities (activities requiring oxygen utilization) for extended periods.

- Muscle strength: The ability of muscle groups to contract and support a given amount of weight.

- Muscle endurance: The ability of muscle groups to contract continually over a period of time and to support a given amount of weight.

- Flexibility: The ability of muscle groups to stretch and bend.

- Body composition: An essential measure of health and fitness. The most important aspects of body composition are body fat percentage and ratio of body fat to muscle.

Physical activity improves each of the components of physical fitness. Aerobic training improves cardiovascular endurance. Weight training, body support activities, and calisthenics increase muscular strength and endurance. Stretching improves flexibility. All types of physical activity improve body composition by increasing muscle and decreasing body fat.

Activities for Various Objectives, Situations, and Developmental Levels

The following table lists physical activities that may reduce specific health risks, improve overall health, and develop skill-related components of physical activity. Some of these activities, such as walking and calisthenics, are more suitable to students at beginning developmental levels, while others, such as circuit training and rowing, are best suited for students at more advanced levels of development.

COMPONENTS OF FITNESS		
	HEALTH-RELATED	**SKILL-RELATED**
Aerobic Dance	cardiorespiratory, body composition	agility, coordination
Bicycling	cardiorespiratory, muscle strength, muscle endurance, body composition	balance
Calisthenics	cardiorespiratory, muscle strength, muscle endurance, flexibility, body composition	agility
Circuit Training	cardiorespiratory, muscle strength, muscle endurance, body composition	power
Cross-Country Skiing	cardiorespiratory, muscle strength, muscle endurance, body composition	agility, coordination, power
Jogging/ Running	cardiorespiratory, body composition	

Table continued on next page

	HEALTH-RELATED	SKILL-RELATED
Jumping Rope	cardiorespiratory, body composition	agility, coordination, reaction time, speed.
Rowing	cardiorespiratory, muscle strength, muscle endurance, body composition	agility, coordination, power
Skating	cardiorespiratory, body composition	agility, balance, coordination, speed.
Swimming/ Water Exercises	cardiorespiratory, muscle strength, muscle endurance, flexibility, body composition	agility, coordination.
Walking (brisk)	cardiorespiratory, body composition	

Cardiovascular Activities

Walking is a good generic cardiorespiratory activity for promoting basic fitness. Instructors can incorporate it into a variety of class settings (not only physical education instructors—for example, a biology class might include a field trip to a natural setting that would involve a great deal of walking). Walking is appropriate for practically all age groups, but can only serve as noteworthy exercise for students who lead a fairly sedentary lifestyle (athletic students who train regularly or participate in some sport will not benefit greatly from walking).

Jogging or running is a classic cardiorespiratory activity in which instructors can adjust the difficulty level by modifying the running speed or the incline of the track. It is important to stress proper footwear and the gradual increase of intensity to prevent overuse injuries (e.g., stress fractures or shin splints).

Bicycling is another good cardiorespiratory activity that is appropriate for most age groups. Obviously, knowing how to ride a bicycle is a prerequisite, and it is important to follow safety procedures (e.g., ensuring that students wear helmets). An additional benefit of bicycle riding is that it places less strain on the knee joints than walking or running.

Swimming is an excellent cardiorespiratory activity that has the added benefit of working more of the body's muscles more evenly than most other exercises, without excessive resistance to any one part of the body that could result in an overuse injury. To use swimming as an educational cardio-respiratory activity, there must be qualified lifeguards present, and all students must have passed basic tests of swimming ability.

There are many alternatives for cardiorespiratory activities, like inline skating and cross-country skiing. More important, instructors should modify the above exercises to match the developmental needs of the students—for example, younger students should receive most of their exercise in the form of games. An instructor could incorporate running in the form of a game of tag, soccer, or a relay race.

Flexibility Training

FLEXIBILITY is the range of motion around a joint or muscle. Flexibility has two major components: static and dynamic. Static flexibility is the range of motion without a consideration for speed of movement. Dynamic flexibility is the use of the desired range of motion at a desired velocity. These movements are useful for most athletes. Static active flexibility refers to the ability to stretch an antagonist muscle using only the tension in the antagonist muscle. Static-passive flexibility is the ability to hold a stretch using body weight or some other external force.

> **FLEXIBILITY:** the range of motion around a joint or muscle

Good flexibility can help to prevent injuries during all stages of life and can keep an athlete safe. To improve flexibility, you can lengthen muscles through activities such as swimming, a basic stretching program, or Pilates. These activities all improve the muscles' range of motion. While joints also consist of ligaments and tendons, muscles are the main target of flexibility training. Muscles are the most elastic component of joints, while ligaments and tendons are less elastic and resist elongation. Overstretching tendons and ligaments can weaken joint stability and lead to injury.

Coaches, athletes, and sports medicine personnel should always use stretching methods as part of their training routine for athletes. They help the body to relax and to warmup for more intense fitness activities. The following is an example of a flexibility program design:

> *Coaches, athletes, and sports medicine personnel should always use stretching methods as part of their training routine for athletes.*

- Mode: stretching

- Frequency: three to seven days/week

- Intensity: just below individual's threshold of pain

- Time: three sets with three repetitions holding stretches fifteen to thirty seconds, with a sixty-second rest interval between sets

Dynamic stretching is generally very safe and very effective for warming up muscle groups and moderately improving flexibility. When performing dynamic stretches, participants must be careful to avoid sudden, jerky movements.

Static stretching is also safe if the participant warms up the muscles prior to stretching. Because cold muscles are less elastic, static stretching without adequate warmup time can lead to injury. Static stretching is very effective in increasing muscle flexibility.

Isometric, PNF, and ballistic stretching are more advanced techniques that require extreme caution and supervision. Most physical trainers believe ballistic stretching (bouncing into stretches) is ineffective and dangerous. Most trainers do not recommend ballistic stretching. PNF and isometric stretching are effective in certain situations such as rehabilitation and advanced training, but they require close supervision.

Muscular Strength and Endurance Activities

Possessing the strength and ability to overcome any resistance in one single effort or in repeated efforts over a period of time is known as muscular strength and endurance. They represent the ability to complete a heavy task in a single effort. Muscular strength and endurance not only help in keeping body ailments in check but also in enabling better performance in any sporting event.

Most fitness experts regard calisthenics as the best form of exercise to increase muscular development and strength. Although calisthenics are good beginning exercises, participants should complement them with progressive resistance training later on so there will be an increase in bone mass and connective tissue strength. Such a combination also helps in minimizing any damages or injuries that are apt to occur at the beginning or initial training stages.

Besides calisthenics and progressive resistance training, aerobics can also help in maintaining muscular strength and endurance. Muscular strength is the maximum amount of force that one can generate in an isolated movement. Muscular endurance is the ability of the muscles to perform a submaximal task repeatedly or to maintain a submaximal muscle contraction for extended periods. Body-support activities (e.g., push-ups and sit-ups) and callisthenic activities (e.g., jumping rope) are good exercises for young students or beginners of all ages. Such exercises use multiple muscle groups and have minimal risk of injury. At more advanced levels of development, and for those students interested in developing higher levels of strength and muscle mass, weight lifting is the optimal activity. To improve muscular strength and endurance a student can:

- Train with free weights
- Perform exercises that use an individual's body weight for resistance (e.g., push-ups, sit-ups, dips)
- Do strength training exercises that incorporate all major muscle groups two times per week

SKILL 23.2 Demonstrating knowledge of activities that promote the development of locomotor, nonlocomotor, manipulative, and perceptual awareness skills in children

Motor-development learning theories that pertain to a general skill, activity, or age level are important and necessary background details for effective lesson planning. Motor-skill learning is unique to each individual but does follow a general sequential skill pattern, starting with general gross motor movements and ending with specific or fine motor skills. Teachers must begin instruction at a level where all children are successful and proceed through the activity only to the point where frustration for the majority is hindering performance.

Students must learn the fundamentals of a skill, or subsequent learning of more advanced skills becomes extremely difficult. Instructors must spend enough time on beginning skills to enable them to become second nature.

Teaching in small groups with enough equipment for everyone is essential. Practice sessions that are too long or too demanding can cause physical and/or mental burnout. Teaching skills over a longer period of time, but with slightly different approaches, helps to keep students attentive and involved as they internalize the skill. The instructor can then teach more difficult skills while continuing to review the basics. If the skill is challenging for most students, allow plenty of practice time so they retain it before having to use it in a game situation.

Visualizing and breaking the skill down mentally are other ways to enhance the learning of motor movements. Instructors can teach students to "picture" the steps involved and to see themselves executing the skill. An example is teaching dribbling in basketball. Start teaching the skill with a demonstration of the steps involved in dribbling. Starting with the first skill, introduce key language terms, and have students visualize themselves performing the skill. A sample-progression lesson plan to teach dribbling could begin with students practicing while standing still. Next, add movement while dribbling. Finally, introduce how to control dribbling while being guarded by another student.

Motor-skill learning is unique to each individual but does follow a general sequential skill pattern, starting with general gross motor movements and ending with specific or fine motor skills.

Body Management Skill Development

Locomotor skills acquisition

Sequential Development = crawl, creep, walk, run, jump, hop, gallop, slide, leap, skip, step-hop.

- **Activities to develop walking skills** include walking slower and faster in place; walking forward, backward, and sideways with slower and faster paces in straight, curving, and zigzag pathways with various lengths of steps; pausing between steps; and changing the height of the body.

- **Activities to develop running skills** include having students pretend they are playing basketball, trying to score a touchdown, trying to catch a bus, finishing a lengthy race, or running on a hot surface.

- **Activities to develop jumping skills** include alternating jumping with feet together and feet apart, taking off and landing on the balls of the feet, clicking the heels together while airborne, and landing with a foot forward and a foot backward.

- **Activities to develop galloping skills** include having students play a game of Fox and Hound, with the lead foot representing the fox and the back foot the hound trying to catch the fox (alternate the lead foot).

- **Activities to develop sliding skills** include having students hold hands in a circle and sliding in one direction, then sliding in the other direction.

- **Activities to develop hopping skills** include having students hop all the way around a hoop and hopping in and out of a hoop, reversing direction. Students can also place ropes in straight lines and hop side-to-side over the rope from one end to the other and change (reverse) the direction.

- **Activities to develop skipping skills** include having students combine walking and hopping activities leading up to skipping.

- **Activities to develop step-hopping skills** include having students practice stepping and hopping activities while clapping hands to an uneven beat.

Activities for nonlocomotor skill acquisition

Sequential Development = stretch, bend, sit, shake, turn, rock and sway, swing, twist, dodge, and fall.

- **Activities to develop stretching** include lying on the back and stomach and stretching as far as possible; stretching as though one is reaching for a star, picking fruit off of a tree, climbing a ladder, shooting a basketball, placing an item on a high self, and yawning.

- Activities to develop bending include touching knees and toes then straightening the entire body and straightening the body halfway, bending as though picking up a coin, tying shoes, picking flowers/vegetables, and petting animals of different sizes.

- Activities to develop sitting include practicing sitting up from standing, kneeling, and lying positions without the use of hands.

- Activities to develop falling skills include first collapsing in one's own space and then pretending to fall like bowling pins, raindrops, snowflakes, a rag doll, or Humpty Dumpty.

Manipulative skill development

Sequential Development = striking, throwing, kicking, ball rolling, volleying, bouncing, catching, and trapping.

- Activities to develop striking begin with the striking of stationary objects by a participant in a stationary position. Next, the person remains still while trying to strike a moving object. Then, both the object and the participant are in motion as the participant attempts to strike the moving object.

- Activities to develop throwing include throwing yarn/foam balls against a wall, then at a big target, and finally at targets decreasing in size.

- Activities to develop kicking include alternating feet to kick balloons/beach balls, then kicking them under and over ropes. Change the type of ball as proficiency develops.

- Activities to develop ball rolling include rolling different-sized balls to a wall, then to targets decreasing in size.

- Activities to develop volleying include using a large balloon and hitting it with both hands, then hitting it with one hand (alternating hands), and then hitting it using different parts of the body. Change the object as students progress (balloon, beach ball, foam ball, etc.).

- Activities to develop bouncing include starting with large balls and using both hands to bounce, then using one hand (alternate hands).

- Activities to develop catching include using various objects (balloons, beanbags, balls, etc.) to catch, first catching the object the participant has thrown him/herself, then catching objects someone else threw, and finally increasing the distance between the catcher and the thrower.

- **Activities to develop trapping** include trapping slow and fast rolling balls; trapping balls (or other objects such as beanbags) that are lightly thrown at waist, chest, and stomach levels; and trapping different size balls.

Rhythmic skill development

Dancing is an excellent activity for the development of rhythmic skills. In addition, any activity that involves moving the body to music can promote rhythmic skill development.

Sample Test Questions and Rationale

(Rigorous)

1. **In basketball, when is it appropriate to use a one-on-one defensive strategy?**

   A. In order to prevent drive-ins for easy lay-up shots

   B. When the team is in foul trouble

   C. When opponents have an advantage in height

   D. None of the above

   Answer: D. None of the above

   Answers A, B, and C are all reasons to use a zone defense, not a one-on-one defense. Other reasons include situations where the playing area is small, in order to keep an excellent rebounder near the opponent's basket, and when the opponents' outside shooting is weak.

(Average)

2. **In teaching skills in physical education, it is most important to focus on which of the following?**

   A. Fundamental skill development

   B. Techniques and strategies for specific sports

   C. Advanced skills for optimum performance

   D. Cardiovascular activities

   Answer: A. Fundamental skill development

   Students must learn the fundamentals of a skill, or subsequent learning of more advanced skills becomes extremely difficult. Instructors must spend enough time on beginning skills to enable them to become second nature. Cardiovascular activities are important for health but are not specifically skill-related.

(Rigorous)

3. **Creating movements in response to music helps students to connect music and dance in which of the following ways?**

   A. Rhythm

   B. Costuming

   C. Speed

   D. Vocabulary skills

   Answer A. Rhythm

   Students should be able to understand the connections made between movement and music is related by rhythm.

Applying knowledge of basic rules and strategies for developmentally appropriate physical activities, cooperative and competitive games, and sports

Rules for Individual and Dual Sports

Archery

- Arrows that bounce off the target or go through the target count as seven points

- Arrows landing on lines between two rings receive the higher score of the two rings

- Arrows hitting the petticoat receive no score

Badminton

- Intentionally balking the opponent or making preliminary feints results in a fault (side in = loss of serve; side out = point awarded to side in)

- When a shuttlecock falls on a line, it is in play (i.e., a fair play)

- If the striking team hits a shuttlecock before it crosses net, it is a fault

- Touching the net when the shuttlecock is in play is a fault

- The same player hitting the shuttlecock twice is a fault

- The shuttlecock going through the net is a fault

Bowling

- There is no score for a pin knocked down by a pinsetter (human or mechanical)

- There is no score for the pins knocked down when any part of the foot, hand, or arm extends or crosses over the foul line (even after the ball leaves the hand) or if any part of the body contacts the division boards, walls, or uprights that are beyond the foul line

- There is no count for pins displaced or knocked down by a ball leaving the lane before it reaches the pins

- There is no count when balls rebound from the rear cushion

Racquetball/handball

- A server stepping outside the service area when serving faults

- The server is out (relinquishes serve) if he or she steps outside of the serving zone twice in succession while serving

- A server is out if he or she fails to hit the ball rebounding off the floor during the serve

- The opponent must have a chance to take a position or the referee must call for play before the server can serve the ball

- The server reserves the ball if the receiver is not behind the short line at the time of the serve

- A served ball that hits the front line and does not land back of the short line is "short;" therefore, it is a fault—the ball is also short when it hits the front wall and two sidewalls before it lands on the floor back of the short line

- A serve is a fault when the ball touches the ceiling from rebounding off the front wall

- A fault occurs when any part of the foot steps over the outer edges of the service or the short line while serving

- A hinder (dead ball) is called when a returned ball hits an opponent on its way to the front wall—even if the ball continues to the front wall

- A hinder is any intentional or unintentional interference of an opponent's opportunity to return the ball

Tennis

A player loses a point when:

- The ball bounces twice on his or her side of the net

- The player returns the ball to any place outside of designated areas

- The player stops or touches the ball in the air before it lands out-of-bounds

- The player intentionally strikes the ball twice with the racket

- The ball strikes any part of a player or racket after the initial attempt to hit the ball

- A player reaches over the net to hit the ball

- A player throws his or her racket at the ball

- The ball strikes any permanent fixture that is out-of-bounds (other than the net)

- A ball touching the net and landing inside the boundary lines is in play (except on the serve, where a ball contacting the net results in a "let" or replay of the point)

- A player fails, on two consecutive attempts, to serve the ball into the designated area (i.e., a double fault)

Appropriate Behavior in Physical Education Activities

- **Appropriate Student Etiquette/Behaviors:** following the rules and accepting the consequences of unfair action, good sportsmanship, respecting the rights of other students, reporting accidents and mishaps, not engaging in inappropriate behavior under peer pressure encouragement, cooperation, paying attention to instructions and demonstrations, moving to assigned places and remaining in the designated space, complying with directions, practicing as instructed to do so, properly using equipment, and not interfering with the practice of others.

- **Appropriate Content Etiquette/Behaviors:** the teacher describing the performance of tasks and students engaging in the task, the teacher assisting students with task performance, and the teacher modifying and developing tasks.

- **Appropriate Management Etiquette/Behaviors:** the teacher directing the management of equipment, students, and space prior to practicing tasks; students getting equipment and partners; the teacher requesting that students stop "fooling around."

Rules of Team Sports

Basketball

- A player touching the floor on or outside the boundary line is out-of-bounds

- The ball is out of bounds if it touches anything (a player, the floor, an object, or any person) that is on or outside the boundary line

- An offensive player remaining in the three-second zone of the free-throw lane for more than three seconds is a violation

- A ball firmly held by two opposing players results in a jump ball

- A throw-in is awarded to the opposing team of the last player touching a ball that goes out-of-bounds

Soccer

The following are direct free-kick offenses:

- There is hand or arm contact with the ball

- A player uses his or her hands to hold an opponent

- A player pushes an opponent

- The player engages in striking/kicking/tripping or attempting to strike/kick/trip an opponent

- The goalie uses the ball to intentionally strike an opponent

- A player jumps at or charges an opponent

- The player knees an opponent

- There are any contact fouls

The following are indirect free-kick offenses:

- The same player plays the ball twice at the kickoff, on a throw-in, on a goal kick, on a free kick, or on a corner kick

- The goalie delays the game by holding the ball or carrying the ball more than four steps

- There is a failure to notify the referee of substitutions/resubstitutions, and that player then handles the ball in the penalty area

- Any person who is not a player enters the playing field without a referee's permission

- There are unsportsmanlike actions or words following a referee's decision.

- A player dangerously lowers his or her head or raises his or her foot too high to make a play

- A player resumes play after being ordered off the field

- Offsides occur (offensive players must have at least one defender between themselves and the goal when a teammate passes the ball)

- Players attempt to kick the ball when the goalkeeper has possession or they interfere with the goalkeeper to hinder the release of the ball

- Illegal charging occurs

- Players leave the playing field without the referee's permission while the ball is in play

Softball

- Each team plays nine players in the field (sometimes ten for slow pitch)

- Field positions are one pitcher, one catcher, four infielders, and three outfielders (four outfielders in ten player formats)

- The four bases are sixty feet apart

- Any ball hit outside of the first or third base line is a foul ball (i.e., runners cannot advance and the pitch counts as a strike against the batter)

- If a batter receives three strikes (i.e., failed attempts at hitting the ball) in a single at bat, he or she strikes out

- The pitcher must start with both feet on the pitcher's rubber and can only take one step forward when delivering the underhand pitch

- A team must maintain the same batting order throughout the game

- Runners cannot lead of

- Runners may overrun first base, but they can be tagged out if they run off any other base

A base runner is out if:

- The opposition tags the runner with the ball before he or she reaches a base

- The ball reaches first base before the runner does

- The runner runs outside of the base path to avoid a tag

- A batted ball strikes him or her in fair territory

Volleyball

The following infractions by the receiving team result in a point awarded to the serving side, and an infraction by the serving team results in a side-out:

- Illegal serves or serving out of turn occurs

- Illegal returns, catching, or holding the ball occurs

- Dribbling occurs or a player touches the ball twice in succession

- There is contact with the net (two opposing players making contact with the net at the same time results in a replay of the point)

- The ball is touched after it has been played three times without passing over the net

- A player's foot completely touches the floor over the centerline

- A player reaches under the net and touches another player or the ball while the ball is in play

- The players change positions prior to the serve

Applying Appropriate Strategies to Game and Sport Situations

Basketball strategies

Use a zone defense

- To prevent drive-ins for easy lay-up shots

- When the playing area is small

- When the team is in foul trouble

- To keep an excellent rebounder near the opponent's basket

- When the opponents' outside shooting is weak

- When opponents have an advantage in height

- When opponents have an exceptional offensive player, or when the best defenders cannot handle one-on-one defense

Offensive strategies against zone defense

- Use quick, sharp passing to penetrate the zone, forcing the opposing player out of assigned position

- Use overloading and mismatching

Offensive strategies for one-on-one defense

- Use the "pick-and-roll" and the "give-and-go" to screen defensive players to open up offensive players for shot attempts

- Teams may use freelancing (spontaneous one-one-one offense), but more commonly they use "sets" of plays

Soccer strategies

- Heading—use the head to pass, to shoot, or to clear the ball

- Tackling—the objective is to take possession of the ball from an opponent

- Successful play requires knowledgeable utilization of space

Badminton strategies

Strategies for return of service

- Return serves with shots that are straight ahead
- Return service so that opponent must move out of his or her starting position
- Return long serves with an overhead clear or drop shot to the near corner
- Return short serves with an underhand clear or a net drop to the near corner

Strategies for serving

- Serve long to the backcourt near the centerline
- Serve short when the opponent is standing too deep in his or her receiving court to return the serve
- Use a short serve to eliminate a smash return if the opponent has a powerful smash from the backcourt

Handball or racquetball strategies

- Identify the opponent's strengths and weaknesses
- Make the opponent use his or her less dominant hand or backhand shots if they are weaker
- Frequently alternate fastballs and lobs to change the pace (changing the pace is particularly effective for serving)
- Maintain a position near the middle of the court (the well), close enough to play low balls and corner shots
- Place shots that keep the opponent's position at a disadvantage to return cross-court and angle shots
- Use high lob shots that go overhead but do not hit the back wall with enough force to rebound and drive an opponent out of position when he or she persistently plays close to the front wall

Tennis strategies

- Lobbing—use a high lob shot for defense, giving one more time to get back into position
- Identify the opponent's weaknesses, attack them, and recognize and protect one's own weaknesses
- Outrun and outthink the opponent

- Use a change of pace, lobs, spins, approaching the net, and deception at the correct time

- Hit cross-court (from corner to corner of the court) for maximum safety and an opportunity to regain position

- Direct the ball where the opponent is not

Volleyball strategies

- Use forearm passes (bumps, digs, or passes) to play balls below the waist, to play hard driven balls, to pass the serve, and to contact balls distant from a player

SKILL 23.4 Recognizing the role that participation in physical activities can play in promoting positive personal and social behaviors

For most people, the development of social roles and appropriate social behaviors occurs during childhood. Physical play between parents and children, as well as between siblings and peers, serves as a strong regulator in the developmental process. Chasing games, roughhousing, wrestling, or practicing sport skills such as jumping, throwing, catching, and striking are some examples of childhood play. These activities may be competitive or noncompetitive; they are important for promoting the social and moral development of both boys and girls. Unfortunately, fathers often engage in this sort of activity more with their sons than with their daughters. Regardless of the sex of the child, both boys and girls enjoy these types of activities.

Physical play during infancy and early childhood is central to the development of social and emotional competence.

Physical play during infancy and early childhood is central to the development of social and emotional competence. Research shows that children who engage in play that is more physical with their parents, particularly with parents who are sensitive and responsive to the child, exhibited greater enjoyment during the play sessions and were more popular with their peers. Likewise, these early interactions with parents, siblings, and peers are important in helping children to become more aware of their emotions and to learn to monitor and regulate their own emotional responses. Children learn quickly through watching the responses of their parents which behaviors make their parents smile and laugh as well as which behaviors cause their parents to frown and disengage from the activity.

If children want the fun to continue, they engage in the behaviors that please others. As children near adolescence, they learn through rough-and-tumble play that there are limits to how far they can go before hurting someone (physically or emotionally), which results in a termination of the activity or later rejection of the child by peers. These early interactions with parents and siblings are important in helping children learn appropriate behavior in the social situations of sports and physical activities.

Children learn to assess their social competence (e.g., their ability to get along with peers as well as acceptance by peers, family members, teachers, and coaches) in sports through the feedback received from parents and coaches. Initially, authority figures teach children, "You can't do that because I said so." As children approach school age, parents begin the process of explaining why a behavior is right or wrong because children continuously ask, "Why?"

Similarly, when children engage in sports, they learn about taking turns with their teammates, sharing playing time, and valuing rules. They understand that rules are important for everyone, and that without these regulations, the game would become unfair. Learning social competence is continuous as we expand our social arena and learn about different cultures. A constant in the learning process is the role of feedback as we assess the responses of others to our behaviors and comments.

In addition to the development of social competence, sports participation can help youth to develop other forms of self-competence. Most important among these self-competencies is self-esteem. Self-esteem is how we judge our worth; it indicates the extent to which an individual believes he or she is capable, significant, successful, and worthy. Educators have suggested that one of the biggest barriers to success in the classroom today is low self-esteem.

Children develop self-esteem by evaluating abilities and by evaluating the responses of others. Children actively observe parents' and coaches' responses to their performances, looking for signs of approval or disapproval of their behavior. Children often interpret feedback and criticism as either a negative or a positive response to the behavior. In sports, research shows that the coach is a critical source of information that influences the self-esteem of children.

Children develop self-esteem by evaluating abilities and by evaluating the responses of others.

Little League baseball players whose coaches use a "positive approach" to coaching (e.g., more frequent encouragement, positive reinforcement for efforts, and corrective, instructional feedback) had significantly higher self-esteem ratings over the course of a season than children whose coaches used these techniques less frequently.

The most compelling evidence supporting the importance of coaches' feedback was found for those children who started with the lowest self-esteem ratings and considerably increased their self-assessment and self-worth throughout the season. In addition to evaluating themselves more positively, low self-esteem children evaluated their coaches more positively than did children with higher self-esteem who played for coaches who used the "positive approach." Moreover, studies show that ninety-five percent of children who played for coaches trained to use the positive approach signed up to play baseball the next year, compared with seventy-five percent of the youth who played for untrained adult coaches.

We cannot overlook the importance of enhanced self-esteem on future participation. A major part of the development of high self-esteem is the pride and joy that children experience as their physical skills improve. Children will feel good about themselves as long as their skills are improving. If children feel that their performance during a game or practice is not as good as that of others, or as good as they think their mom and dad would want, they often experience shame and disappointment.

Some children will view mistakes made during a game as a failure and will look for ways to avoid participating in the task if they receive no encouragement to continue. At this point, it is critical that adults (e.g., parents and coaches) intervene to help children to interpret the mistake or "failure." We must teach children that a mistake is not synonymous with failure. Rather, a mistake shows us that we need a new strategy, more practice, and/or greater effort to succeed at the task.

Fairness is another trait that physical activities, especially rules-based sports, can foster and strengthen. Children are by nature very rules-oriented, and have a keen sense of what they believe is and isn't fair. Fair play, teamwork, and sportsmanship are all values that stem from proper practice of the spirit of physical education classes. Of course, a pleasurable physical education experience goes a long way towards promoting an understanding of the innate value of physical activity throughout the life cycle.

Social Development

Physical education activities can promote positive social behaviors and traits in a number of different ways. Instructors can foster improved relations with adults and peers by making students active partners in the learning process and delegating responsibilities within the class environment to students. Giving students leadership positions (e.g., team captain) can give them a heightened understanding of the responsibilities and challenges facing educators.

Team-based physical activities like team sports promote collaboration and cooperation.

Team-based physical activities like team sports promote collaboration and cooperation. In such activities, students learn to work together, both pooling their talents and minimizing the weaknesses of different team members in order to achieve a common goal. The experience of functioning as a team can be very productive for the development of loyalty between children, and seeing their peers in stressful situations that they can relate to can promote a more compassionate and considerate attitude among students. Similarly, the need to maximize the strengths of each student on a team (who can complement each other and compensate for weaknesses) is a powerful lesson about valuing and respecting diversity and individual differences. Varying students between leading and following positions in a team hierarchy are good ways to help students gain comfort levels being both followers and leaders.

Physical fitness activities incorporate group processes, group dynamics, and a wide range of cooperation and competition issues. Ranging from team sports (which are both competitive and cooperative in nature) to individual competitive sports (like racing), to cooperative team activities without a winner and loser (like a gymnastics team working together to create a human pyramid), there is a great deal of room for the development of mutual respect and support among the students, safe cooperative participation, and analytical, problem-solving, teamwork, and leadership skills.

Teamwork situations are beneficial to students because they create opportunities for them to see classmates with whom they might not generally socialize and with whom they may not even get along in a new light. It also creates opportunities for students to develop reliance on each other and to practice interdependence. Cooperation and competition can also offer opportunities for children to practice group work. These situations provide good opportunities to practice analytical thinking and problem solving in a practical setting.

The social skills and values gained from participation in physical activities include the following:

- The ability to make adjustments to both self and others by an integration of the individual to society and the environment

- The ability to make judgments in a group situation

- Learning to communicate with others and to be cooperative

- The development of the social phases of personality, attitudes, and values in order to become a functioning member of society (such as being considerate)

- The development of a sense of belonging and acceptance by society

- The development of positive personality traits

- Learning for constructive use of leisure time

- A development of attitude that reflects good moral character

- Respect of school rules and property

The preceding list represents a sample of the sociocultural benefits of participating in physical activity with others. Physical activity serves as a very important part of the socialization process. Physical activity during the socialization process creates an opportunity for children to define personal comfort levels with different types of physical interaction, as well as to establish guidelines for what is (and is not) acceptable physical behavior as related to their relationship with other individuals.

Participating in physical activity with others is also a step away from the trend of "playground to PlayStation," where students are less and less physically active, and spend less and less time engaging in outdoor physical activity. Physical activity on a sociocultural level is an important aspect of the struggle against rising obesity levels in the United States, as well as related problems (like heart disease).

Sample Test Questions and Rationale

(Average)

1. **Social skills and values developed by activity include all of the following except:**

   A. Winning at all costs

   B. Making judgments in groups

   C. Communicating and cooperating

   D. Respecting rules and property

   Answer: A. Winning at all costs

   Winning at all costs is not a desirable social skill. Instructors and coaches should emphasize fair play and effort over winning. Answers B, C, and D are all positive skills and values developed in physical activity settings.

(Easy)

2. **Activities that enhance team socialization include all of the following except:**

   A. Basketball

   B. Soccer

   C. Golf

   D. Volleyball

   Answer: C. Golf

   Golf is mainly an individual sport. Though golf involves social interaction, it generally lacks the team element inherent in basketball, soccer, and volleyball.

(Rigorous)

3. **Through physical activities, Julio has developed self-discipline, fairness, respect for others, and new friends. Julio has experienced which of the following?**

   A. Positive cooperation psychosocial influences

   B. Positive group psychosocial influences

   C. Positive individual psychosocial influences

   D. Positive accomplishment psychosocial influences

   Answer: B. Positive group psychosocial influences

   Through physical activities, Julio developed his social interaction skills. Social interaction is the sequence of social actions between individuals (or groups) that modify their actions and reactions due to the actions of their interaction partner(s). In other words, they are events in which people attach meaning to a situation, interpret what others mean, and respond accordingly. Through socialization with other people, Julio feels the influence of the people around him.

COMPETENCY 24
UNDERSTAND BASIC ELEMENTS, CONCEPTS, AND TECHNIQUES ASSOCIATED WITH THE ARTS

> **SKILL 24.1** Identifying the basic elements, concepts, and terms associated with dance, music, drama, and the visual arts *(e.g., pathways, rhythm, plot, perspective)*

Elements of Music

- **Accent:** Stress of one tone over others, making it stand out; often it is the first beat of a measure

- **Accompaniment:** Music that goes along with a more important part; often it is harmony or rhythmic patterns accompanying a melody

- **Adagio:** Slow, leisurely

- **Allegro:** Lively, brisk, rapid

- **Cadence:** A closing of a phrase or section of music

- **Chord:** Three or more tones combined and sounded simultaneously

- **Crescendo:** Gradually growing louder

- **Dissonance:** A simultaneous sounding of tones that produce a feeling of tension or unrest and a feeling that further resolution is needed

- **Harmony:** The sound resulting from the simultaneous sounding of two or more tones that are consonant with one another

- **Interval:** The distance between two tones

- **Melody:** An arrangement of single tones in a meaningful sequence

- **Phrase:** A small section of a composition comprising a musical thought

- **Rhythm:** The regular occurrence of accented beats that shape the character of music or dance

- **Scale:** A graduated series of tones arranged in a specified order

- **Staccato:** Separate; sounded in a short, detached manner

- **Syncopation:** The rhythmic result produced when a regularly accented beat is displaced onto an unaccented beat

- Tempo: The rate of speed at which a musical composition is performed
- Theme: A short musical passage that states an idea.; it often provides the basis for variations, development, and so on
- Timbre: The quality of a musical tone that distinguishes voices

The Elements of Theater

It is vital that teachers be trained in critical areas that focus on important principles of theater education. The basic course of study should include state-mandated topics in arts education, instructional materials, products in arts, both affective and cognitive processes of art, world and traditional cultures, and the most recent teaching tools: media and technology.

The following areas should be included:

- Acting: Acting requires the student to demonstrate the ability to effectively communicate using skillful speaking, movement, rhythm, and sensory awareness.
- Designing: Designing involves creating and initiating the onsite management of the art of acting.
- Directing: Direction requires management skills to produce and perform an onstage activity. This requires guiding and inspiring students as well as script and stage supervision.
- Scriptwriting: Scriptwriting demands that a leader be able to produce original material and staging for an entire production. It includes writing and designing a story that has performance value.

Each of the preceding skills should be incorporated into daily activities with young children. It is important that children are exposed to character development through stories, role play, and modeling through various teacher guided experiences. Some of these experiences that are age appropriate for early childhood level include puppet theater, paper dolls, character sketches, storytelling, and retelling of stories in a student's own words.

Elements of Dance

Dance is an artistic form of self-expression that uses the various elements of physical movement, such as space, time, levels, and force—all of which form a composition. The primary grades have a gross understanding of their motor movements, whereas older children are apt to have a more refined concept of their bodies. Individual movements should be developed by the instructor with attention to various aspects such as the following:

- The range of movement or gestures through space

- The direction of the action or imaginary lines that the body flows through space

- The timing of when movements form the dramatic effects

- Students being made aware of the planes formed by any two areas, such as height and width, or width and depth

- The introduction of levels so the composition incorporates sitting, standing, and kneeling, and so forth

- Using elevation—the degree of lift, as in leaping, and movements that are done under that allusion of suspension

- The force and energy of dance can be a reflection of the music, such as adagio (slow music) or allegro (quickening steps)

The various styles of dance can be explained as follows:

- Creative dance is the type of dance that is most natural to a young child. Creative dance depicts feelings through movement. It is the initial reaction to sound and movement. Older elementary students will often incorporate mood and expressiveness. Stories can be told to release the dancer into imagination.

- Isadora Duncan is credited with being the mother of modern dance. Modern dance today refers to a concept of dance where the expressions of opposites are developed—for example, concepts of fast-slow, contract-release, varying heights, and levels to fall and recover. Modern dance is based on four principles: substance, dynamism, metakinesis, and form.

- Social dance requires a steadier capability that the previous levels. Social dances refer to a cooperative form of dance with respect for sharing the dance floor with others and for one's partner. The social aspect of dance, rather than romantic aspect, represents a variety of customs and pastimes. Changing partners frequently within the dance is something that is subtly important to maintain. Social dance may be in the form of marches, the waltz, or the two-step.

- Upper level elementary students can learn dance in connection with historical cultures (such as the minuet). The minuet was introduced to the court in Paris in 1650, and it dominated the ballroom until the end of the eighteenth century. The waltz was introduced around 1775; it was an occasion of fashion and courtship. The pomp and ceremony of it all makes for fun classroom experiences. Dance is central to many cultures, and the interrelatedness of teaching history and dance (such as a Native American dance, the Mexican hat dance, or Japanese theater) can be highly beneficial to the students.

• **Structured dances** are recognized by particular patterns, such as the tango. They were made popular in dance studios and gym classes alike. **Ritual dances** are often of a religious nature; they may celebrate a significant life event such as a harvest season, the rain season, the gods, or to ask for favors in hunting, birth, and death. Many of these themes are carried out in movies and theaters today, but they have their roots in Africa. Dancing at weddings today is a prime example of ritual dance. The father dances with the bride, and then the husband dances with the bride. The two families then dance with one other.

• Basic **ballet** uses a barre to practice the five basic positions used in ballet. Alignment is the way in which various parts of the dancer's body are in line with one another while the dancer is moving. It is a very precise dance that is executed with grace and form. The mood and expressions of the music are very important to ballet, as they form the canvas upon which the dance is performed.

Sample Test Questions and Rationale

(Rigorous)

1. **A combination of three or more tones sounded at the same time is called a:**

   A. Harmony

   B. Consonance

   C. Chord

   D. Dissonance

   Answer: C. Chord

   A chord is three or more tones combined and sounded simultaneously. Dissonance is the simultaneous sounding of tones that produce a feeling of tension or unrest and a feeling that further resolution is needed. Harmony is the sound resulting from the simultaneous sounding of two or more tones consonant with one another.

(Rigorous)

2. **A series of single tones that add up to a recognizable sound is called a:**

   A. Cadence

   B. Rhythm

   C. Melody

   D. Sequence

   Answer: C. Melody

   A melody is an arrangement of single tones in a meaningful sequence. Cadence is the closing of a phrase or section of music. Rhythm is the regular occurrence of accented beats that shape the character of music or dance.

SKILL
24.2
Recognizing the basic techniques, processes, tools, and materials for creating, performing, and producing works in the various arts

The components and strands of visual art encompass many areas. Students are expected to fine-tune observation skills and be able to identify and recreate the experiences that teachers provide for them as learning tools. For example, students may walk as a group on a nature hike, taking in the surrounding elements, and then begin to discuss the repetition found in the leaves of trees, the bricks of the sidewalk, or the size and shapes of the buildings. They may also use such an experience to describe lines, colors, shapes, forms, and textures. Beginning elements of perspective are noticed at an early age. The questions of why buildings look smaller when they are at a far distance and bigger when they are closer are sure to spark the imagination of early childhood students.

Students can also take their inquiries to a higher level of learning with some hands-on activities, such as building three-dimensional buildings using paper and geometric shapes. Eventually, students should acquire higher-level thinking skills, such as analysis, in which they will begin to question artists and artwork and analyze many different aspects of visual art.

It is vital that students learn to identify the characteristics of visual arts that include materials, techniques, and those processes necessary to establish a connection between art and daily life. Early ages should begin to experience art in a variety of forms. Students should be introduced to the recognition of simple patterns found in the art environment. They must also identify art materials such as clay, paint, and crayons. Each of these types of materials should be introduced and explained for use in daily lessons with young children. Young students may need to be introduced to items that are developmentally appropriate for their age and for their fine motor skills.

Many Pre-Kindergarten and Kindergarten students use oversized pencils and crayons for their first semester. Typically, after this first semester, development occurs enough to enable children to start using smaller sized materials. Students should begin to explore artistic expression at this age using colors and mixing. The color wheel is a vital lesson for young children, as they can begin to learn the uses of primary colors and secondary colors. By the middle of the school year, students should be able to explain the process of mixing. For example, a student may need orange paint but have other colors. She should be able to create orange paint by combing the colors she has.

Teachers should also use variation in lines, shapes, textures, and many different principles of design. By using common environmental figures such as people, animals, and buildings, teachers can base many art lessons on characteristics of readily available examples.

Students should be introduced to as many techniques as possible to ensure that all strands of the visual arts and materials are experienced at a variety of levels. By using original works of art, students should be able to identify visual and actual textures of art and to base their judgments of objects found in everyday scenes. Other examples that can be included as subjects are landscapes, portraits, and still life. The major areas that young students should experience should consist of the following:

- Painting, using tempera or watercolors

- Sculpture, typically using clay or play-dough

- Architecture, performing building or structuring design with 3D materials such as cardboard or posterboard

- Ceramics, using a hollow clay sculpture and pots made from clay and fired in a kiln

- Metalworking (another term for engraving or cutting design or letters into metal), using a sharp tool

- Printmaking or lithography, drawing a design on a surface and lifting the print from the surface

An excellent opportunity for teachers is to create an "art sample book" with the students. These books can include a different variety of textured materials, including sandpaper and cotton balls. Samples of pieces of construction paper designed into various shapes can be used to represent shapes. String samples can represent the element of lines. The sampling of art should also focus clearly on basic colors. Color can be introduced more in-depth when discussing intensity, the strength, and the lightness or darkness of the colors.

Sample Test Question and Rationale

(Easy)

1. **Kindergarteners should be able to accurately mix primary colors to produce secondary colors by:**

   A. After the first month of school

   B. By the middle of the year

   C. By the end of the year

   D. They cannot be expected to learn this skill until first grade

Answer: B. By the middle of the year

Young children can begin to learn the uses of primary colors and secondary colors. By the middle of the school year, K students should be able to explain the process of mixing. For example, a student may need orange paint but only have other colors. She should be able to create orange paint by combining the colors she has.

SKILL **Applying knowledge of diverse strategies for promoting critical**
24.3 **analysis, cultural perspectives, and aesthetic understandings of**
the arts

Although the elements of design have remained consistent throughout history, the emphasis on specific aesthetic principles has periodically shifted. Aesthetic standards or principles vary from time period to time period and from society to society.

East and West

An obvious difference in aesthetic principles occurs between works created by eastern and western cultures. Eastern works of art are more often based on spiritual considerations, while much Western art is secular in nature. In attempting to convey reality, Eastern artists generally prefer to use line, local color, and a simplistic view. Western artists tend toward a literal use of line, shape, color, and texture to convey a concise, detailed, complicated view. Eastern artists portray the human figure with symbolic meanings and little regard for muscle structure, resulting in a mystical view of the human experience. Western artists use the "principle of ponderation," which requires the knowledge of both human anatomy and an expression of the human spirit.

In attempts to convey the illusion of depth or visual space in a work of art, Eastern and Western artists use different techniques. Eastern artists generally prefer a diagonal projection of eye movement into the picture plane, and they often leave large areas of the surface untouched by detail. The result is the illusion of vast space, an infinite view that coincides with the spiritual philosophies of the Orient. Western artists rely on several techniques, such as overlapping planes, variation of object size, object position on the picture plane, linear and aerial perspective, color change, and various points of perspective to convey the illusion of depth. The result is space that is limited and closed.

In the application of color, Eastern artists use arbitrary choices of color. Western artists generally rely on literal color usage or emotional choices of color. The end result is that Eastern art tends to be more universal in nature, while Western art is more individualized.

Renaissance and Baroque

An interesting change in aesthetic principles occurred between the Renaissance period (1400–1630 CE) and the Baroque period (1630–1700 CE) in Europe. The Renaissance period was concerned with the rediscovery of the works of classical Greece and Rome. The art, literature, and architecture were inspired by classical orders, which tended to be formal, simple, and concerned with the ideal human proportions. This means that the paintings, sculptures, and architecture were of a closed nature, composed of forms that were restrained and compact. For example, consider the visual masterpieces of the period: Raphael's painting *The School of Athens*, with its precise use of space; Michelangelo's sculpture *David*, with its compact mass; and the facade of the *Palazzo Strozzi*, with its defined use of the rectangle, arches, and rustication of the masonry.

Compare the Renaissance characteristics to those of the Baroque period. The word "baroque" means "grotesque," which was the contemporary criticism of the new style. In comparison to the styles of the Renaissance, the Baroque was concerned with the imaginative flights of human fancy. The paintings, sculptures, and architecture were of an open nature, composed of forms that were whimsical and free-flowing. Consider again the masterpieces of the period: Ruben's painting *The Elevation of the Cross*, with its turbulent forms of light and dark tumbling diagonally through space; Puget's sculpture *Milo of Crotona*, with its use of open space and twisted forms; and Borromini's *Chapel of St. Ivo*, with a facade that plays convex forms against concave ones.

In the 1920s and 1930s, the German art historian Professor Wolfflin outlined these shifts in aesthetic principles in his influential book Principles of Art History. He arranged these changes into five categories of "visual analysis," sometimes referred to as the "categories of stylistic development." Wolfflin was careful to point out that no style is inherently superior to any other, but are simply indicators of the phase of development of that particular time or society. However, Wolfflin goes on to state, correctly or not, that once the evolution occurs, it is impossible to regress. The following modes of perception apply to drawing, painting, sculpture, and architecture:

WOLFFLIN'S CATEGORIES OF ANALYSIS	
From a Linear Mode to a Painterly Mode	This shift refers to stylistic changes that occur when perception or expression evolves from a linear form that is concerned with the contours and boundaries of objects, to perception or expression that stresses the masses and volumes of objects. From viewing objects in isolation, to seeing the relationships between objects are an important change in perception. Linear mode implies that objects are stationary and unchanging, while the painterly mode implies that objects and their relationships to other objects is always in a state of flux.
From Plane to Recession	This shift refers to perception or expression that evolves from a planar style, when the artist views movement in the work in an "up and down" and "side to side" manner, to a recessional style, when the artist views the balance of a work in an "in and out" manner. The illusion of depth may be achieved through either style, but only the recessional style uses an angular movement forward and backward through the visual plane.

Table continued on next page

From Closed to Open Form	This shift refers to perception or expression that evolves from a sense of enclosure, or limited space, in "closed form," to a sense of freedom in "open form." The concept is obvious in architecture, as in buildings that clearly differentiate between "outside" and "inside" space, and buildings that open up the space to allow the outside to interact with the inside.
From Multiplicity to Unity	This shift refers to an evolution from expressing unity through the use of balancing many individual parts, to expressing unity by subordinating some individual parts to others. Multiplicity stresses the balance between existing elements, whereas unity stresses emphasis, domination, and accent of some elements over other elements.
From Absolute to Relative Clarity	This shift refers to an evolution from works which clearly and thoroughly express everything there is to know about the object, to works that express only part of what there is to know, and leave the viewer to fill in the rest from his own experiences. Relative clarity, then, is a sophisticated mode, because it requires the viewer to actively participate in the "artistic dialogue." Each of the previous four categories is reflected in this, as linearity is considered to be concise while painting is more subject to interpretation. Planarity is more factual, while recessional movement is an illusion, and so on.

Sample Test Question and Rationale

(Rigorous)

1. **In comparing aesthetic differences between Eastern and Western art, students might focus on all of the following except:**

    A. Core design principles

    B. How the human figure is portrayed

    C. Content (ex: spiritual vs. secular)

    D. Use of line, shape, and color

Answer: A. Core design principles

Basic design principles remain the same across cultures and historical periods. However, other elements can be identified in different aesthetic styles. In this example, Eastern works of art are more often based on spiritual considerations, while much Western art is secular in nature. In attempting to convey reality, Eastern artists generally prefer to use line, local color, and a simplistic view. Western artists tend toward a literal use of line, shape, color, and texture to convey a concise, detailed, complicated view. Eastern artists portray the human figure with symbolic meanings and little regard for muscle structure, resulting in a mystical view of the human experience.

Recognizing how the arts can be used as a form of communication, self-expression, and social expression

Music

When we listen to certain music styles, they often connect us to a memory, a time in the past, or even an entire historical period. Very often, classical pieces, such as Bach or Beethoven, create a picture in our minds of the Baroque Period. The historical perspective of music can deepen one's musical understanding.

Throughout history, different cultures have developed different styles of music. Most of the written records of music developed from Western civilization. Music styles varied across cultures as periods in history. As in the opening discussion, classical music, although still popular and being created today, is often associated with traditional classical periods in history such as the Renaissance.

As world contact merged more and more as civilizations developed and prospered, more and more influence from various cultural styles emerged across music styles. For example, African drums emerged in some contemporary and hip-hop music. Also, the bluegrass music in the United States developed from the "melting pot" contributions from Irish, Scottish, German, and African-American instrumental and vocal traditions. In addition, the purposes for music changed throughout cultures and times. Music has been used for entertainment but also for propaganda, worship, ceremony, and communication.

Common Musical Styles

- Medieval
- Classical (loosely encompassing Renaissance and Baroque)
- Gospel
- Jazz
- Latin
- Rhythm and blues
- Funk
- Rock
- Country
- Folk
- Bluegrass
- Electronic (techno)
- Melodic
- Island (ska, reggae, and other)
- Hip-hop
- Pop
- African
- Contemporary

Visual Art

Teachers should be able to utilize and teach various techniques when analyzing works of art. Students will learn and then begin to apply what they have learned in the arts to all subjects across the curriculum. By using problem-solving techniques and creative skills, students will begin to master the techniques necessary to derive meaning from both visual and sensory aspects of art.

Students should be asked to review, respond, and analyze various types of art. They must learn to be critical, and it is necessary that students relate art in terms of life and human aspects of life. Students should be introduced to the wide range of opportunities to explore such art. Examples may include exhibits, galleries, museums, libraries, and personal art collections. It is imperative that students learn to research and locate artistic opportunities that are common in today's society. Some opportunities for research include reproductions, art slides, films, print materials, and electronic media.

Once students are taught how to effectively research and use sources, they should be expected to graduate to higher-level thinking skills. Students should be able to begin to reflect on, interpret, evaluate, and explain how works of art and various styles of artwork explain social, psychological, cultural, and environmental aspects of life.

Theater and Dance

Students are expected to be able to meet a variety of standards set forth for performing arts and dance. It is necessary for young students to master skills such as walking, running, galloping, jumping, hopping, and balance. Students must also learn to discriminate between opposites used to describe performance activities such a high/low, forward/backward, and move/freeze. Creative movements and expressions are necessary tools for dance as well. Students must be able to recall a feeling or personal experience they have had and perform accordingly. Students must learn to discern between different types of dance and dance experiences as well as learn what to expect from performances regarding staging, costume, setting, and music.

SKILL 24.5 Demonstrating knowledge of the connections among the arts as well as between the arts and other areas of the curriculum and everyday life

The field of the humanities is overflowing with examples of works of art that hold in common various themes, motifs, and symbols. Themes, motifs, and symbols effortlessly cross the lines between the visual arts, literature, music, theater, and dance. Following are a few examples culled from the immense heritage of the arts.

Works that Share Thematic and Symbolic Motifs

A popular symbol or motif of the fifteenth, sixteenth, and seventeenth centuries was David, the heroic second king of the Hebrews. The richness of the stories pertaining to David and the opportunities for visual interpretation made him a favorite among artists, all of whom cast him in different lights.

- Donatello's bronze statue of *David* is a classically proportioned nude, portrayed with Goliath's head between his feet. His *David* is not gloating over his kill but instead seems to be viewing his own, sensuous body with a Renaissance air of self-awareness.

- Verrocchio's bronze sculpture of *David*, also with the severed head of Goliath, represents a confident young man, proud of his accomplishment and seemingly basking in praise.

- Michelangelo, always original, gives us a universal interpretation of the David theme. Weapon in hand, Michelangelo's marble *David* tenses muscles as he summons up the power to deal with his colossal enemy, symbolizing as he does so every person or community who has had to do battle against overwhelming odds.

- Bernini's marble *David*, created as it was during the Baroque era, explodes with energy as it captures forever the most dramatic moment of David's action: the throwing of the stone that kills Goliath.

- Caravaggio's painting *David and Goliath* treats the theme in yet another way. Here David is shown as if in the glare of a spotlight, looking with revulsion at the bloodied, grotesque head of Goliath, leaving the viewer to speculate about the reason for disgust. Is David revolted at the ungodliness of Goliath, or is he sickened at his own murderous action? Symbols related to the David theme include David, Goliath's head, and the stone and slingshot.

Another popular religious motif, especially during the Medieval and Renaissance periods, was the Annunciation. This event was the announcement by the archangel Gabriel to the Virgin Mary that she would bear a son and name him Jesus. It is also believed that this signified the moment of Incarnation.

Anonymous medieval artists treated this theme in altarpieces, murals, and illuminated manuscripts. During the thirteenth century, both Nicola Pisano and his son Giovanni carved reliefs of the Annunciation theme. Both men included the Annunciation and the Nativity theme into a single panel. Martini's painted rendition of *The Annunciation* owes something to the court etiquette of the day in the use of the heraldic devises of the symbolic colorings and stilted manner of the Virgin. Della Francesca's fresco of the Annunciation borders on the abstract, with its simplified gestures, its lack of emotion, and the ionic column providing a barrier between Gabriel and Mary. Fra Angelico's *Annunciation* is a lyrical painting, combining soft, harmonious coloring with simplicity of form and gesture. Symbols related to the Annunciation theme are Gabriel, Mary, the dove of the Holy Spirit, the lily, an olive branch, a garden, a basket of wool, a closed book, and various inscriptions.

During the 1800s, a new viewpoint surfaced in Europe. Intellectuals from several countries became painfully aware of the consequences of social conditions and abuses of the day and set out to expose them. The English social satirist Hogarth created a series of paintings entitled *Marriage a-la-Mode*, which centered on the absurdity of arranged marriages. Other works by Hogarth explored conditions that led to prostitution and the poorhouse.

In France, Voltaire was working on the play *Candide*, which recounted the misfortunes of a young man while providing biting commentary on the social abuses of the period. In the field of music, Mozart's *Marriage of Figaro*, based on a play by Beaumarchais, explores the emotion of love as experienced by people from all ages and walks of life. At the same time, it portrays the follies of convention in society.

The Effect of One Work on Another

The history of the humanities is replete with examples of artists in every field being influenced and inspired by specific works of others. Influence and inspiration continuously cross the lines between the various disciples in the humanities.

Examples of artistic works that influence another

Michelangelo's painting of the Sistine Chapel ceiling (1508–1512) had a profound effect on Raphael, as evidenced by his fresco *The School of Athens* (1509–1511). The influence can be seen by the treatment of the human figures, particularly in the gestures and chiaroscuro.

Virgil's epic the *Aeneid* (29-19) was a source of inspiration to Dante Alighieri, the renowned Florentine writer who claimed to have memorized the lengthy piece. When Dante wrote *The Divine Comedy* (1308-1321), he included Virgil as his (Dante's) guide through hell and purgatory, a character who represents the highest pinnacle of human reason. In addition, his poetry imitates the form of the *Aeneid* in several places.

Dante's *The Divine Comedy* (1308-1321) in turn served as inspiration for many devotees of the Romantic school in the 1800s. In 1822, the French painter Eugene Delacroix painted a canvas entitled *Dante and Virgil in Hell*, an emotional painting illustrating the anguish of tormented souls drowning in the river Styx, as Dante and Virgil pass over them in a capsizing boat. One of Delacroix's companions read the "Inferno" (the first book of *The Divine Comedy*) to him as he painted. Later, Delacroix claimed that the section that most electrified him was the eighth canto of the "Inferno."

Also during the mid-1800s, the French author Victor Hugo wrote a poem entitled *After Reading Dante*, a Romantic piece full of melancholy ruminations. This poem was later used as the basis for a piano program by the Hungarian composer Franz Liszt (1811–1886). Inspired by *The Divine Comedy* and dedicated to the Romantic notion that the arts be related, Liszt wrote the *Dante Symphony*, reflecting the pathos he found in Dante's work.

Homer's *Odyssey* (ca. 950–ca. 800 BCE) influenced many of the classical writers, but it is surprising to discover that it also influenced the writing of *Ulysses* (1922) by James Joyce. Because the "stream-of-consciousness" technique is so confusing to readers, Joyce used the classical allusions of the *Odyssey* as a sort of map to help guide readers through his work.

The Connections between the Arts and Other Disciplines

Whether we express ourselves creatively from the theatrical stage, visually through fine art and dance, or musically, appreciating and recognizing the interrelationships of various art forms are essential to an understanding of ourselves and our diverse society. By studying and experiencing works of fine art and literature, and by understanding their place in cultural and intellectual history, we can develop an appreciation of the human significance of the arts and humanities through history and across cultures.

> *Whether we express ourselves creatively from the theatrical stage, visually through fine art and dance, or musically, appreciating and recognizing the interrelationships of various art forms are essential to an understanding of ourselves and our diverse society.*

Through art projects, field trips, and theatrical productions, students can learn that all forms of art are a way for cultures to communicate with each other and the world at large. By understanding the concepts, techniques, and various materials used in the visual arts, music, dance, and written word, students can begin to appreciate the concept of using art to express oneself. Perhaps they can begin by writing a short story that can then be transformed into a play with costumes, music, and movement to experience the relationships among different art forms.

The arts have played a significant role throughout history. The communicative power of the arts is notable. Cultures use the arts to impart specific emotions and feelings, to tell stories, to imitate nature, and to persuade others. The arts bring meaning to ceremonies, rituals, celebrations, and recreation. By creating their own art and by examining art made by others, children can learn to make sense of and communicate ideas. This can be accomplished through dance, verbal communication, music, and other visual arts.

Through the arts and humanities, students will realize that although people are different, they share common experiences and attitudes. They will also learn that the use of nonverbal communication can be a strong adjunct to verbal communication.

Sample Test Question and Rationale

(Rigorous)

1. The Renaissance period was concerned with the rediscovery of the works of:

    A. Italy

    B. Japan

    C. Germany

    D. Classical Greece and Rome

Answer: D. Classical Greece and Rome

The Renaissance period was concerned with the rediscovery of the works of classical Greece and Rome. The art, literature, and architecture were inspired by classical orders, which tended to be formal, simple, and concerned with the ideal human proportions.

SKILL 24.6 Recognizing the role and function of the arts in various cultures and throughout history

The greatest works in art, literature, music, theater, and dance all mirror universal themes. Universal themes are themes that reflect the human experience, regardless of time period, location, or socioeconomic standing. Universal themes tend to fall into broad categories, such as individuals versus society as a whole, individuals versus themselves, individuals versus religion, individuals versus nature, and good versus evil, to name the most obvious. The following general themes all fall into one of these broad categories.

UNIVERSAL THEMES THROUGHOUT HISTORY	
Prehistoric Arts (ca. 1,000,000–ca. 8,000 BCE)	Major themes of this vast period appear to center around religious fertility rites and sympathetic magic, consisting of imagery of pregnant animals and faceless, pregnant women.
Mesopotamian Arts (ca. 8,000–400 BCE)	The prayer statues and cult deities of the period point to the theme of polytheism in religious worship.

Table continued on next page

Egyptian Arts **(ca. 3,000–100 BCE)**	The predominance of funerary art from ancient Egypt illustrates the theme of preparation for the afterlife and polytheistic worship. Another dominant theme, reflected by artistic convention, is the divinity of the pharaohs. In architecture, the themes were monumentality and adherence to ritual.
Greek Arts **(800–100 BCE)**	The sculpture of ancient Greece is replete with human figures, most nude and some draped. Most of these sculptures represent athletes and various gods and goddesses. The predominant theme is that of the ideal human, in both mind and body. In architecture, the theme was scale based on the ideal human proportions.
Roman Arts **(ca. 480 BCE–476 CE)**	Judging from Roman arts, the predominant themes of the period deal with the realistic depiction of human beings and how they relate to Greek classical ideals. The emphasis is on practical realism. Another major theme is the glory in serving the Roman state. In architecture, the theme was rugged practicality mixed with Greek proportions and elements.
Middle Ages Arts **(300–1400 CE)**	Although the time span is expansive, the major themes remain relatively constant throughout. Since the Roman Catholic Church was the primary patron of the arts, most work was religious in nature. The purpose of much of the art was to educate. Specific themes varied from the illustration of Bible stories to interpretations of theological allegory, to lives of the saints, to consequences of good and evil. Depictions of the Holy Family were popular. Themes found in secular art and literature centered around chivalric love and warfare. In architecture, the theme was glorification of God and education of congregation to religious principles.
Renaissance Arts **(ca. 1400–1630 CE)**	Renaissance themes include Christian religious depiction *(see also Middle Ages)*, but tend to reflect a renewed interest in all things classical. Specific themes include Greek and Roman mythological and philosophic figures, ancient battles, and legends. Dominant themes mirror the philosophic beliefs of Humanism, emphasizing individuality and human reason, such as those of the High Renaissance, which center around the psychological attributes of individuals. In architecture, the theme was scale based on human proportions.
Baroque Arts **(1630–1700 CE)**	The predominant themes found in the arts of the Baroque period include the dramatic climaxes of well-known stories, legends, and battles and the grand spectacle of mythology. Religious themes are found frequently, but it is drama and insight that are emphasized and not the medieval "salvation factor." Baroque artists and authors incorporated various types of characters into their works, careful to include minute details. Portraiture focused on the psychology of the sitters. In architecture, the theme was large scale grandeur and splendor.
Eighteenth Century **Arts (1700–1800 CE)**	Rococo themes of this century focused on religion, light mythology, portraiture of aristocrats, pleasure and escapism, and, occasionally, satire. In architecture, the theme was artifice and gaiety, combined with an organic quality of form. Neoclassic themes centered around examples of virtue and heroism, usually in classical settings, and historical stories. In architecture, classical simplicity and utility of design was regained.

Table continued on next page

Nineteenth Century Arts (1800–1900 CE)	Romantic themes include human freedom, equality, and civil rights, a love for nature, and a tendency toward the melancholic and mystic. The underlying theme is that the most important discoveries are made within the self, and not in the exterior world. In architecture, the theme was fantasy and whimsy, known as picturesque. Realistic themes included social awareness and a focus on society victimizing individuals. The themes behind Impressionism were the constant flux of the universe and the immediacy of the moment. In architecture, the themes were strength, simplicity, and upward thrust as skyscrapers entered the scene.
Twentieth Century Arts (1900–2000 CE)	Diverse artistic themes of the century reflect a parting with traditional religious values and a painful awareness of man's inhumanity to man. Themes also illustrate a growing reliance on science, while simultaneously expressing disillusionment with man's failure to adequately control science. A constant theme is the quest for originality and self-expression, while seeking to express the universal in human experience. In architecture, "form follows function."

GENRES BY HISTORICAL PERIOD	
Ancient Greek Art (ca. 800–323 BCE)	Dominant genres from this period were vase paintings—both black-figure and red-figure—and classical sculpture.
Roman Art (ca. 480 BCE–476 CE)	Major genres from the Romans include frescoes (murals done in fresh plaster to affix the paint), classical sculpture, funerary art, state propaganda art, and relief work on cameos.
Middle Ages Art (ca. 300–1400 CE)	Significant genres during the Middle Ages include Byzantine mosaics, illuminated manuscripts, ivory relief, altarpieces, cathedral sculpture, and fresco paintings in various styles.
Renaissance Art (1400–1630 CE)	Important genres from the Renaissance included Florentine fresco painting (mostly religious), High Renaissance painting and sculpture, Northern oil painting, Flemish miniature painting, and Northern printmaking.
Baroque Art (1630–1700 CE)	Pivotal genres during the Baroque era include Mannerism, Italian Baroque painting and sculpture, Spanish Baroque, Flemish Baroque, and Dutch portraiture. Genre paintings in still-life and landscape appear prominently in this period.

Table continued on next page

Eighteenth Century Art (1700–1800 CE)	Predominant genres of the century include Rococo painting, portraiture, social satire, Romantic painting, and Neoclassic painting and sculpture.
Nineteenth Century Art (1800–1900 CE)	Important genres include Romantic painting, academic painting and sculpture, landscape painting of many varieties, realistic painting of many varieties, Impressionism, and many varieties of post-Impressionism.
Twentieth Century Art (1900–2000 CE)	Major genres of the twentieth century include symbolism, art nouveau, fauvism, expressionism, cubism (both analytical and synthetic), futurism, non-objective art, abstract art, Surrealism, social realism, constructivism in sculpture, Pop and Op art, and conceptual art.

Sample Test Question and Rationale

(Average)

1. **Altarpieces and illuminated manuscripts are representative of art from which period?**

   A. Ancient Greek

   B. Roman

   C. Medieval

   D. Renaissance

Answer: C. Medieval

Significant genres during the Middle Ages include Byzantine mosaics, illuminated manuscripts, ivory relief, altarpieces, cathedral sculpture, and fresco paintings in various styles.

SAMPLE TEST

SAMPLE TEST
READING AND ENGLISH LANGUAGE ARTS

(Rigorous) (Skill 1.1)

1. Which of the following is *not* a strategy of teaching reading comprehension?

   A. Asking questions

   B. Utilizing graphic organizers

   C. Focusing on mental images

   D. Manipulating sounds

(Average) (Skill 1.3)

2. All of the following are true about phonological awareness *except*:

   A. It may involve print

   B. It is a prerequisite for spelling and phonics

   C. Activities can be done by the children with their eyes closed

   D. It starts before letter recognition is taught

(Average) (Skill 2.1)

3. Oral language development includes which of the following:

   A. Listening comprehension

   B. Storytelling

   C. Developing vocabulary

   D. All of the above

(Average) (Skill 2.1)

4. How do children make the transition from letter forms to invented spelling?

   A. Write strings of letters

   B. Organize group of letters

   C. Leave spaces

   D. All of the above

(Rigorous) (Skill 2.1)

5. Which aspect of language is innate?

   A. Biological capability to articulate sounds understood by other humans

   B. Cognitive ability to create syntactical structures

   C. Capacity for using semantics to convey meaning in a social environment

   D. Ability to vary inflections and accents

(Easy) (Skill 2.2)

6. To decode is to:

   A. Construct meaning

   B. Sound out a printed sequence of letters

   C. Use a special code to decipher a message

   D. None of the above

(Easy) (Skill 2.2)

7. To *encode* means that you:

   A. Decode a second time

   B. Construct meaning from a code

   C. Tell someone a message

   D. None of the above

(Average) (Skill 2.4)

8. **The arrangement and relationship of words in sentences or sentence structure best describes:**

   A. Style

   B. Discourse

   C. Thesis

   D. Syntax

(Rigorous) (Skill 2.5)

9. **Effective reading comprehension requires:**

   A. Encoding

   B. Decoding

   C. Both A and B

   D. Neither A nor B

(Rigorous) (3.3)

10. **Contextual redefinition is a strategy that encourages children to use the context more effectively by presenting them with sufficient vocabulary _____ the reading of a text.**

    A. after

    B. before

    C. during

    D. None of the above

(Average) (Skill 3.4)

11. **What is the best place for students to find appropriate synonyms, antonyms, and other related words to enhance their writing?**

    A. Dictionary

    B. Spell check

    C. Encyclopedia

    D. Thesaurus

(Average) (Skill 4.1)

12. **If a student has a poor vocabulary, the teacher should recommend that:**

    A. The student read newspapers, magazines, and books on a regular basis

    B. The student enroll in a Latin class

    C. The student write the words repetitively after looking them up in the dictionary

    D. The student use a thesaurus to locate synonyms and incorporate them into his/her vocabulary

(Easy) (Skill 4.1)

13. **Which of the following indicates that a student is a fluent reader?**

    A. Reads texts with expression or prosody

    B. Reads word-to-word and haltingly

    C. Must intentionally decode a majority of the words

    D. In a writing assignment, sentences are poorly-organized structurally

(Rigorous) (Skill 4.1)

14. **All of the following are examples of ongoing informal assessment techniques used to observe student progress except:**

    A. Analysis of student work product

    B. Collection of data from assessment tests

    C. Effective questioning

    D. Observation of students

(Easy) (4.1)

15. **Which of the following is a formal reading level assessment?**

    A. A standardized reading test

    B. A teacher-made reading test

    C. An interview

    D. A reading diary

(Easy) (Skill 4.4)

16. **Which of the following is an opinion?**

    A. Subjective evaluation based upon personal bias

    B. A statement that is readily provable by objective empirical data

    C. The sky is blue

    D. Airplanes flew into the World Trade Center on September 11, 2001

(Easy) (Skill 4.4)

17. **Which of the following is a fact?**

    A. It's going to rain

    B. John is a liar

    C. Joe said he believes John is a liar

    D. The world is going to the dogs

(Rigorous) (Skill 5.2)

18. **Which is an untrue statement about a theme in literature?**

    A. The theme is always stated directly somewhere in the text.

    B. The theme is the central idea in a literary work.

    C. All parts of the work (plot, setting, mood) should contribute to the theme in some way.

    D. By analyzing the various elements of the work, the reader should be able to arrive at an indirectly stated theme.

(Rigorous) (Skill 5.2)

19. **Exposition occurs within a story:**

    A. After the rising action

    B. After the denouement

    C. Before the rising action

    D. Before the setting

(Easy) (Skill 5.3)

20. **Which of the following are important reasons for teaching literature?**

    A. Active involvement with the literature

    B. Appreciate written text

    C. Make sense of meaning

    D. All of the above

(Easy) (Skill 5.3)

21. **Which of the following is not a characteristic of a fable?**

    A. Animals that feel and talk like humans

    B. Happy solutions to human dilemmas

    C. Teaches a moral or standard for behavior

    D. Illustrates specific people or groups without directly naming them

(Average) (Skill 5.4)

22. **Which of the following is an example of alliteration?**

    A. A. "The City's voice itself is soft like Solitude."

    B. "Both in one faith unanimous; though sad"

    C. "By all their country's wishes blest!"

    D. "In earliest Greece to thee with partial choice"

(Average) (Skill 5.4)

23. Which of the following is a ballad?

   A. "The Knight's Tale"

   B. Julius Caesar

   C. Paradise Lost

   D. "The Rime of the Ancient Mariner"

(Average) (Skill 5.4)

24. Which of the following is an epic?

   A. On the Choice of Books

   B. The Faerie Queene

   C. Northanger Abbey

   D. A Doll's House

(Average) (Skill 5.4)

25. The children's literature genre came into its own in the:

   A. Seventeenth century

   B. Eighteenth century

   C. Nineteenth century

   D. Twentieth century

(Average) (Skill 5.5)

26. A sixth-grade science teacher has given her class a paper to read on the relationship between food and weight gain. The writing contains signal words such as "because," "consequently," "this is how," and "due to." This paper has which text structure?

   A. Cause & effect

   B. Compare & contrast

   C. Description

   D. Sequencing

(Average) (Skill 5.6)

27. A teacher has taught his students several strategies to monitor their reading comprehension. These strategies include identifying where in the passage they are having difficulty, identifying what the difficulty is, and restating the difficult sentence or passage in their own words. These strategies are examples of:

   A. Graphic and semantic organizers

   B. Metacognition

   C. Recognizing story structure

   D. Summarizing

(Easy) (Skill 6.2)

28. A student has written a paper with the following characteristics: written in first person; characters, setting, and plot; some dialogue; events organized in chronological sequence with some flashbacks. In what genre has the student written?

   A. Expository writing

   B. Narrative writing

   C. Persuasive writing

   D. Technical writing

(Rigorous) (Skill 6.2)

29. Which of the following should not be included in the opening paragraph of an informative essay?

   A. Thesis sentence

   B. Details and examples supporting the main idea

   C. A broad general introduction to the topic

   D. A style and tone that grabs the reader's attention

(Rigorous) (Skill 6.2)

30. ***Our borders must be protected from illegal immigrants.*** Which of the following does *not* support this thesis?

    A. Terrorists can get across the border undetected

    B. Illegal drugs flow across the unprotected borders

    C. Illegal immigrants are a drain on the American economy

    D. Illegal immigrants make good citizens

(Rigorous) (Skill 6.2)

31. **Which of the following are good choices for supporting a thesis?**

    A. Reasons

    B. Examples

    C. Answer to the question why

    D. All of the above

(Easy) (Skill 6.2)

32. **Which of the following is a good definition of the *purpose* for an essay?**

    A. To get a good grade

    B. To fulfill an assignment

    C. To change the minds of the readers

    D. The point of the writing

(Average) (Skill 6.2)

33. **Which of the following is *not* an approach to keep students ever conscious of the need to write for audience appeal?**

    A. Pairing students during the writing process

    B. Reading all rough drafts before the students write the final copies

    C. Having students compose stories or articles

    D. Writing letters to friends or relatives

(Average) (Skill 6.3)

34. **Which of the following is *not* a technique of prewriting?**

    A. Clustering

    B. Listing

    C. Brainstorming

    D. Proofreading

(Rigorous) (Skill 6.3)

35. **Which is *not* a true statement concerning an author's literary tone?**

    A. Tone is partly revealed through the selection of details

    B. Tone is the expression of the author's attitude toward his/her subject

    C. Tone in literature is usually satiric or angry

    D. Tone in literature corresponds to the tone of voice a speaker uses

(Rigorous) (Skill 7.2)

36. **Which of the following contains an error in possessive inflection?**

    A. Doris's shawl

    B. Mother's-in-law frown

    C. Children's lunches

    D. Ambassador's briefcase

(Rigorous) (Skill 7.4)

37. **Which of the following sentences contains an error in agreement?**

    A. Jennifer is one of the women who writes for the magazine

    B. Each one of their sons plays a different sport

    C. This band has performed at the Odeum many times

    D. The data are available online at the listed website

(Rigorous) (Skill 8.1)

38. **Which of the following is a valid conclusion?**

    A. Based on the evidence, I believe John Jones stole the car

    B. I suspect that John Jones stole the car

    C. John Jones looks guilty, so he must have stolen the car

    D. Of the two suspects, John Jones' cynical expression makes me think he's guilty

SOCIAL STUDIES

(Easy) (Skill 9.1)

39. **Which of the following were results of the Age of Exploration?**

    A. More complete and accurate maps and charts

    B. New and more accurate navigational instruments

    C. Proof that the earth is round

    D. All of the above

(Rigorous) (Skill 9.1)

40. **What was the long-term importance of the Mayflower Compact?**

    A. It established the foundation of all later agreements with the Native Peoples

    B. It established freedom of religion in the original English colonies

    C. It ended the war in Europe between Spain, France and England

    D. It established a model of small, town-based government that was adopted throughout the New England colonies

(Easy) (Skill 9.2)

41. **The end of the feudal manorial system was caused by:**

    A. The Civil War

    B. The Black Plague

    C. The Christian Riots

    D. Westward Expansion

(Average) (Skill 9.2)

42. **What intellectual movement during the period of North American colonization contributed to the development of public education and the founding of the first colleges and universities?**

    A. Enlightenment

    B. Great Awakening

    C. Libertarianism

    D. The Scientific Revolution

(Rigorous) (Skill 9.2)

43. **In 1957, the formation of the Southern Christian Leadership Conference was started by:**

    A. Martin Luther King, Jr

    B. Rev. T. J. Jemison

    C. Ella Baker

    D. All of the above

(Average) (Skill 9.2)

44. **In the early 1730s, James Oglethorpe, a British Member of Parliament engaged in a campaign to bring _____ to the America.**

    A. soldiers

    B. farmers

    C. prisoners

    D. parliament

(Average) (Skill 9.2)

45. **Which of the following contributed to the severity of the Great Depression?**

    A. An influx of Chinese immigrants

    B. The dust bowl drove people out of the cities

    C. An influx of Mexican immigrants

    D. An influx of Oakies

(Rigorous) (Skill 9.4)

46. **The first real party organization developed soon after the inauguration of Washington as President. It included which of the following:**

    A. Democrats

    B. Republicans

    C. Nationalists

    D. All of the above

(Rigorous) (Skill 9.4)

47. **What was the name of the cultural revival after the Civil War?**

    A. The Revolutionary War

    B. The Second Great Awakening

    C. The Harlem Renaissance

    D. The Gilded Age

(Average) (Skill 9.4)

48. **Which one of the following is *not* a reason why Europeans came to the New World?**

    A. To find resources in order to increase wealth

    B. B. To establish trade

    C. To increase a ruler's power and importance

    D. To spread Christianity

(Average) (Skill 9.4)

49. The Westward expansion occurred for a number of reasons, however, the most important reason was:

    A. Colonization

    B. Slavery

    C. Independence

    D. Economics

(Rigorous) (Skill 9.4)

50. The year 1619 was memorable for the colony of Virginia. Three important events occurred, resulting in lasting effects on U.S. history. Which one of the following is not one of the events?

    A. Twenty African slaves arrived

    B. The London Company granted the colony a charter making it independent

    C. The colonists were given the right by the London Company to govern themselves through representative government in the Virginia House of Burgesses

    D. The London Company sent to the colony 60 women who were quickly married, establishing families and stability in the colony

(Rigorous) (Skill 9.4)

51. The "divine right" of kings was the key political characteristic of:

    A. The Age of Absolutism

    B. The Age of Reason

    C. The Age of Feudalism

    D. The Age of Despotism

(Rigorous) (Skill 9.4)

52. During the 1920s, the United States almost completely stopped all immigration. One of the reasons was:

    A. Plentiful cheap unskilled labor was no longer needed by industrialists

    B. War debts from World War I made it difficult to render financial assistance

    C. European nations were reluctant to allow people to leave since there was a need to rebuild populations and economic stability

    D. The United States did not become a member of the League of Nations

(Average) (Skill 9.4)

53. Which one of the following would *not* be considered a result of World War II?

    A. Economic depressions and slow resumption of trade and financial aid

    B. Western Europe was no longer the center of world power

    C. The beginnings of new power struggles not only in Europe but in Asia as well

    D. Territorial and boundary changes for many nations, especially in Europe

(Easy) (Skill 9.4)

54. The belief that the United States should control all of North America was called:

    A. Westward Expansion

    B. Pan Americanism

    C. Manifest Destiny

    D. Nationalism

(Easy) (Skill 9.5)

55. **Capitalism and communism are alike in that they are both:**

    A. Organic systems

    B. Political systems

    C. Centrally planned systems

    D. Economic systems

(Easy) (Skill 9.4)

56. **An economist might engage in which of the following activities?**

    A. An observation of the historical effects of a nation's banking practices

    B. The application of a statistical test to a series of data

    C. Introduction of an experimental factor into a specified population to measure the effect of the factor

    D. An economist might engage in all of these

(Average) (Skill 9.4)

57. **The advancement of understanding in dealing with human beings has led to a number of interdisciplinary areas. Which of the following interdisciplinary studies would *not* be considered under the social sciences?**

    A. Molecular biophysics

    B. Peace studies

    C. African-American studies

    D. Cartographic information systems

(Average) (Skill 9.5)

58. **For the historian studying ancient Egypt, which of the following would be least useful?**

    A. The record of an ancient Greek historian on Greek-Egyptian interaction

    B. Letters from an Egyptian ruler to his/her regional governors

    C. Inscriptions on stele of the Fourteenth Egyptian Dynasty

    D. Letters from a nineteenth century Egyptologist to his wife

MATHEMATICS

(Easy) (Skill 13.1)

59. $(\frac{-4}{9}) + (\frac{-7}{10}) =$

    A. $\frac{23}{90}$

    B. $\frac{-23}{90}$

    C. $\frac{103}{90}$

    D. $\frac{-103}{90}$

(Average) (Skill 13.1)

60. $(5.6) \times (-0.11) =$

    A. -0.616

    B. 0.616

    C. -6.110

    D. 6.110

(Average) (Skill 13.2)

61. An item that sells for $375 is put on sale at $120. What is the percent of decrease?

    A. 25%

    B. 28%

    C. 68%

    D. 34%

(Average) (Skill 13.2)

62. Two mathematics classes have a total of 410 students. The 8:00 am class has 40 more than the 10:00 am class. How many students are in the 10:00 am class?

    A. 123.3

    B. 370

    C. 185

    D. 330

(Easy) (Skill 13.3)

63. What measure could be used to report the distance traveled in walking around a track?

    A. Degrees

    B. Square meters

    C. Kilometers

    D. Cubic feet

(Rigorous) (Skill 13.3)

64. What is the area of a square whose side is 13 feet?

    A. 169 feet

    B. 169 square feet

    C. 52 feet

    D. 52 square feet

(Easy) (Skill 13.4)

65. What is the greatest common factor of 16, 28, and 36?

    A. 2

    B. 4

    C. 8

    D. 16

(Average) (Skill 13.5)

66. If $4x - (3 - x) = 7(x - 3) + 10$, then:

    A. $x = 8$

    B. $x = -8$

    C. $x = 4$

    D. $x = -4$

(Average) (Skill 13.6)

67. Given the formula $d = rt$, (where d = distance, r = rate, and t = time), calculate the time required for a vehicle to travel 585 miles at a rate of 65 miles per hour.

    A. 8.5 hours

    B. 6.5 hours

    C. 9.5 hours

    D. 9 hours

(Rigorous) (Skill 14.1)

68. The following chart shows the yearly average number of international tourists visiting Palm Beach for 1990-1994. How many more international tourists visited Palm Beach in 1994 than in 1991?

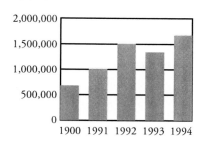

A. 100,000

B. 600,000

C. 1,600,000

D. 8,000,000

(Rigorous) (Skill 14.1)

69. What is the probability of drawing 2 consecutive aces from a standard deck of cards?

A. $\frac{3}{51}$

B. $\frac{1}{221}$

C. $\frac{2}{104}$

D. $\frac{2}{52}$

(Rigorous) (Skill 14.1)

70. Which of the following is an irrational number?

A. .362626262...

B. 4

C. $\sqrt{5}$

D. $-\sqrt{16}$

(Average) (Skill 14.2)

71. Corporate salaries are listed for several employees. Which would be the best measure of central tendency?

$24,000 $24,000 $26,000
$28,000 $30,000 $120,000

A. Mean

B. Median

C. Mode

D. No difference

(Easy) (Skill 14.2)

72. Which statement is true about George's budget?

A. George spends the greatest portion of his income on food

B. George spends twice as much on utilities as he does on his mortgage

C. George spends twice as much on utilities as he does on food

D. George spends the same amount on food and utilities as he does on mortgage

(Rigorous) (Skill 14.2)

73. Given a drawer with 5 black socks, 3 blue socks, and 2 red socks, what is the probability that you will draw two black socks in two draws in a dark room?

A. $\frac{2}{9}$

B. $\frac{1}{4}$

C. $\frac{17}{18}$

D. $\frac{1}{18}$

(Rigorous) (Skill 14.3)

74. Solve for x: $\left|\, 2x + 3 \,\right| > 4$

A. $-\frac{7}{2} > X > \frac{1}{2}$

B. $-\frac{1}{2} > X > \frac{7}{2}$

C. $x < \frac{7}{2}$ or $x < -\frac{1}{2}$

D. $x < -\frac{7}{2}$ or $x > \frac{1}{2}$

(Rigorous) (Skill 14.3)

75. Graph the solution: $\left|\, x \,\right| + 7 < 13$

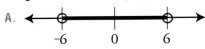

A.

B.

C.

D.

(Average) (Skill 14.3)

76. A boat travels 30 miles upstream in three hours. It makes the return trip in one and a half hours. What is the speed of the boat in still water?

A. 10 mph

B. 15 mph

C. 20 mph

D. 30 mph

(Rigorous) (Skill 14.4)

77. Given segment AC with B as its midpoint, find the coordinates of C if A = (5,7) and B = (3, 6.5).

A. (4, 6.5)

B. (1, 6)

C. (2, 0.5)

D. (16, 1)

(Easy) (Skill 14.4)

78. 3 km is equivalent to

A. 300 cm

B. 300 m

C. 3000 cm

D. 3000 m

(Easy) (Skill 14.4)

79. The mass of a cookie is closest to:

A. 0.5 kg

B. 0.5 grams

C. 15 grams

D. 1.5 grams

(Rigorous) (14.5)

80. If the radius of a right circular cylinder is doubled, how does its volume change?

A. No change

B. Also is doubled

C. Four times the original

D. Pi times the original

(Average) (Skill 14.5)

81. In similar polygons, if the perimeters are in a ratio of $x : y$, the sides are in a ratio of

A. $x : y$

B. $x2 : y2$

C. $2x : y$

D. $\frac{1}{2}x : y$

(Average) (Skill 14.6)

82. **Find the midpoint of (2,5) and (7,-4).**

    A. (9,-1)

    B. (5,9)

    C. $(\frac{9}{2}, \frac{-1}{2})$

    D. $(\frac{9}{2}, \frac{1}{2})$

(Average) (Skill 14.6)

83. $3x + 2y = 12$

    $12x + 8y = 15$

    Solve for *x* and *y*.

    A. All real numbers

    B. $x = 4, y = 4$

    C. $x = 2, y = -1$

    D. $\varnothing$

SCIENCE

(Average)(Skill 19.3)

84. **What is the unit of measure for relative humidity?**

    A. Millibar

    B. None

    C. Kilograms per cubic meter

    D. Pounds per square inch

(Average)(Skill 18.1)

85. **Which of the following is a misconception about the task of teaching science in elementary school?**

    A. Teach facts as a priority over teaching how to solve problems

    B. Involve as many senses as possible in the learning experience

    C. Accommodate individual differences in pupils' learning styles

    D. Consider the effect of technology on people rather than on material things

(Average)(Skill 20.7)

86. **The Doppler Effect is associated most closely with which property of waves?**

    A. Amplitude

    B. Wavelength

    C. Frequency

    D. Intensity

(Average)(Skill 19.5)

87. **Fossils are usually found in:**

    A. Metamorphic rock

    B. Sedimentary rock

    C. Igneous rock

    D. The Earth's mantle

(Easy)(Skill 20.1)

88. **Which of the following type of substance tastes bitter and feels slippery?**

    A. Acid

    B. Base

    C. Salt solution

    D. Oxides

(Easy)(Skill 20.4)

89. The transfer of heat by electromagnetic waves is called:

A. Conduction

B. Convection

C. Phase change

D. Radiation

(Easy)(Skill 20.2)

90. The phase of water refers to its:

A. Chemical properties

B. Physical properties

C. Temperature

D. Chemical composition

(Easy)(Skill 20.4)

91. Sound waves are produced by:

A. Pitch

B. Noise

C. Vibrations

D. Sonar

(Rigorous)(Skill 18.2)

92. In an experiment measuring the growth of bacteria at different temperatures, what is the independent variable?

A. Number of bacteria

B. Growth rate of bacteria

C. Temperature

D. Size of bacteria

(Average)(Skill 18.4)

93. Which is the correct order of methodology?

1. Collecting data
2. Planning a controlled experiment
3. Drawing a conclusion
4. Hypothesizing a result
5. Revisiting a hypothesis to answer a question

A. 1,2,3,4,5

B. 4,2,1,3,5

C. 4,5,1,3,2

D. 1,3,4,5,2

(Easy)(Skill 20.3)

94. What type of reaction is the joining of two nuclei?

A. Chemical

B. Fission

C. Fusion

D. Endothermic

(Rigorous)(Skill 20.5)

95. Which of Newton's laws implies that forces on objects are caused by other objects?

A. First law

B. Second law

C. Third law

D. Law of gravity

(Average)(Skill 21.3)

96. **Which cycle is photosynthesis a part of?**

    A. Nitrogen cycle

    B. Carbon cycle

    C. Water cycle

    D. Phosphorus cycle

(Average)(Skill 21.7)

97. **When two species live close together and both benefit from one another that is called:**

    A. Symbiosis

    B. Commensalism

    C. Mutualism

    D. Competition

(Average)(Skill 21.3)

98. **Which kingdom is comprised of organisms made of one cell with no nuclear membrane?**

    A. Monera

    B. Protista

    C. Fungi

    D. Algae

(Average)(Skill 20.7)

99. **What is the cause of magnetic forces?**

    A. Magnetic domains

    B. Northpoles and southpoles

    C. Moving electric charges

    D. Magnets

(Average)(Skill 18.5)

100. **Which procedure uses the size of molecules to create a graph?**

    A. Spectroscopy

    B. Spectrophotometry

    C. Chromatography

    D. Electrophoresis

(Average)(Skill 21.6)

101. **What is the most accurate description of the Water Cycle?**

    A. Rain comes from clouds, filling the ocean; the water then evaporates and becomes clouds again

    B. Water circulates from rivers into groundwater and back, while water vapor circulates in the atmosphere

    C. Water is conserved except for chemical or nuclear reactions, and any drop of water could circulate through clouds, rain, ground water, and surface water

    D. Weather systems cause chemical reactions to break water into its atoms

(Average)(Skill 21.6)

102. **The theory of "sea floor spreading" explains:**

    A. The shapes of the continents

    B. How continents collide

    C. How continents move apart

    D. How continents sink to become part of the ocean floor

(Rigorous)(Skill 21.6)

103. Which of the following is the best definition for "meteorite"?

   A. A meteorite is a mineral composed of mica and feldspar

   B. A meteorite is material from outer space that has struck the earth's surface

   C. A meteorite is an element that has properties of both metals and nonmetals

   D. A meteorite is a very small unit of length measurement

HEALTH, PHYSICAL EDUCATION, AND THE ARTS

(Easy)(Skill 22.1)

104. Which of the following is not a type of muscle tissue?

   A. Skeletal

   B. Cardiac

   C. Smooth

   D. Fiber

(Average)(Skill 22.1)

105. Which of these is a type of joint?

   A. Ball and socket

   B. Hinge

   C. Pivot

   D. All of the above

(Average)(Skill 23.4)

106. Social skills and values developed by activity include all of the following except:

   A. Winning at all costs

   B. Making judgments in groups

   C. Communicating and cooperating

   D. Respecting rules and property

(Easy)(Skill 23.4)

107. Activities that enhance team socialization include all of the following except:

   A. Basketball

   B. Soccer

   C. Golf

   D. Volleyball

(Rigorous)(Skill 23.4)

108. Through physical activities, Julio has developed self-discipline, fairness, respect for others, and new friends. Julio has experienced which of the following?

   A. Positive cooperation psychosocial influences

   B. Positive group psychosocial influences

   C. Positive individual psychosocial influences

   D. Positive accomplishment psychosocial influences

(Rigorous)(Skill 23.2)

109. **In basketball, when is it appropriate to use a one-on-one defensive strategy?**

A. In order to prevent drive-ins for easy lay-up shots

B. When the team is in foul trouble

C. When opponents have an advantage in height

D. None of the above

(Average)(Skill 23.2)

110. **In teaching skills in physical education, it is most important to focus on which of the following?**

A. Fundamental skill development

B. Techniques and strategies for specific sports

C. Advanced skills for optimum performance

D. Cardiovascular activities

(Average)(Skill 22.6)

111. **A physical education instructor anticipates and prevents potential injuries, watches for hidden injuries, and takes an injury evaluation of the entire class. Which of the following strategies to prevent injuries is the teacher demonstrating?**

A. Maintaining hiring standards

B. Proper use of equipment

C. Proper procedures for emergencies

D. Participant screening

(Rigorous)(Skill 23.2)

112. **Creating movements in response to music helps students to connect music and dance in which of the following ways?**

A. Rhythm

B. Costuming

C. Speed

D. Vocabulary skills

(Rigorous)(Skill 24.5)

113. **The Renaissance period was concerned with the rediscovery of the works of:**

A. Italy

B. Japan

C. Germany

D. Classical Greece and Rome

(Average)(Skill 24.6)

114. **Altarpieces and illuminated manuscripts are representative of art from which period?**

A. Ancient Greek

B. Roman

C. Medieval

D. Renaissance

(Easy)(Skill 24.2)

115. **Kindergarteners should be able to accurately mix primary colors to produce secondary colors by:**

A. After the first month of school

B. By the middle of the year

C. By the end of the year

D. They cannot be expected to learn this skill until first grade

(Rigorous)(Skill 24.3)

116. In comparing aesthetic differences between Eastern and Western art, students might focus on all of the following except:

    A. Core design principles

    B. How the human figure is portrayed

    C. Content (ex: spiritual vs. secular)

    D. Use of line, shape, and color

(Rigorous)(Skill 24.1)

117. A combination of three or more tones sounded at the same time is called a:

    A. Harmony

    B. Consonance

    C. Chord

    D. Dissonance

(Rigorous)(Skill 24.1)

118. A series of single tones that add up to a recognizable sound is called a:

    A. Cadence

    B. Rhythm

    C. Melody

    D. Sequence

ANSWER KEY

1. D	15. A	29. B	43. D	57. A	71. B	85. A	99. C	113. D
2. A	16. A	30. D	44. C	58. D	72. C	86. C	100. C	114. C
3. D	17. C	31. D	45. D	59. D	73. A	87. B	101. C	115. B
4. D	18. A	32. D	46. D	60. A	74. D	88. B	102. C	116. A
5. A	19. C	33. B	47. C	61. C	75. A	89. D	103. B	117. C
6. A	20. D	34. D	48. B	62. C	76. B	90. B	104. D	118. C
7. D	21. D	35. C	49. D	63. C	77. B	91. C	105. D	
8. D	22. A	36. B	50. B	64. B	78. D	92. C	106. A	
9. C	23. D	37. A	51. A	65. B	79. C	93. B	107. C	
10. B	24. B	38. A	52. A	66. C	80. C	94. C	108. B	
11. D	25. B	39. D	53. A	67. D	81. A	95. C	109. D	
12. A	26. A	40. D	54. C	68. B	82. D	96. B	110. A	
13. A	27. B	41. B	55. D	69. B	83. D	97. C	111. D	
14. B	28. B	42. A	56. D	70. C	84. B	98. A	112. A	

RIGOR TABLE

Rigor level	Questions
Easy 20%	6, 7, 13, 15, 16, 17, 20, 21, 28, 32, 39, 41, 54, 55, 56, 59, 63, 65, 72, 78, 79, 88, 89, 90, 91, 94, 104, 107, 115
Average Rigor 40%	2, 3, 4, 8, 11, 12, 22, 23, 24, 25, 26, 27, 33, 34, 42, 44, 45, 48, 49, 53, 57, 58, 60, 61, 62, 66, 67, 71, 76, 81, 82, 83, 84, 85, 86, 87, 93, 96, 97, 98, 99, 100, 101, 102, 105, 106, 110, 111, 114
Rigorous 40%	1, 5, 9, 10, 14, 18, 19, 29, 30, 31, 35, 36, 37, 38, 40, 43, 46, 47, 50, 51, 52, 64, 68, 69, 70, 73, 74, 75, 77, 80, 92, 95, 103, 108, 109, 112, 113, 116, 117, 118

GACE
Georgia Assessments for the Certification of Educators

- Basic Skills 200, 201, 202
- Biology 026, 027
- Science 024, 025
- English 020, 021
- Educational Leadership 173, 174
- Physics 030, 031
- Art Education Sample Test 109, 110
- History 034, 035
- Health and Physical Education 115, 116
- Chemistry 028, 029
- Reading 117, 118
- Media Specialist 101, 102
- Middle Grades Reading 012
- Middle Grades Science 014
- Middle Grades Mathematics 013
- Middle Grades Social Science 015
- Middle Grades Language Arts 011
- Mathematics 022, 023
- Political Science 032, 033
- Paraprofessional Assessment 177
- Professional Pedagogy Assessment 171, 172
- Early Childhood Education 001, 002
- School Counseling 103, 104
- Spanish 141, 142
- Special Education General Curriculum 081, 082
- French Sample Test 143, 144
- Early Childhood Special Education 004

PASS the FIRST TIME with an XAMonline study guide!

Call or visit us online!
1.800.301.4647
www.XAMonline.com

Customers who bought this book also previewed or bought
PRAXIS Elementary Education.

PRAXIS Elementary Education Content Knowledge

This study guide was designed to prepare you for the PRAXIS II: Elementary Education Conte Knowledge Test. You'll find all the core competencies and skills align specifically with the standar of the actual test and that you can study and master those skills with 125 questions on the PRAX II practice test.

Each sub-area of the PRAXIS II Elementary Education study guide is divided into manageal sections that cover the specific skill areas. Explanations are easy to understand and thorough.

We also carry 27 other PRAXIS teacher certification study guides:

- PRAXIS Art Sample Test
- PRAXIS Biology
- PRAXIS Chemistry
- PRAXIS Earth and Space Sciences
- PRAXIS Special Education Knowledge-Based Core Principles
- PRAXIS Special Education Teaching Students with Behavioral Disorders/Emotional Disturbance
- PRAXIS Early Childhood/Education of Young Children
- PRAXIS Educational Leadership
- PRAXIS English Language, Literature and Composition
- PRAXIS Sample Test
- PRAXIS Fundamental Subjects
- PRAXIS School Guidance and Counseling
- PRAXIS General Science
- PRAXIS Library Media Specialist
- PRAXIS Mathematics
- PRAXIS Middle School English Language Arts
- PRAXIS Middle School Mathematics
- PRAXIS Middle School Social Studies
- PRAXIS Physical Education
- PRAXIS Physics
- PRAXIS Para-Professional Assessment
- PRAXIS PPST-1 Basic Skills
- PRAIXS Government/Political Science
- PRAXIS Principles of Learning and Teaching
- PRAXIS Reading
- PRAXIS Social Studies
- PRAXIS Spanish

Call or visit us online!
1.800.301.4647
www.XAMonline.com